A. DICTIONARY OF
MODERN HISTORY
1789 – 1945

A. W. Palmer

PENGUIN BOOKS

Penguin Books Ltd, Harmondsworth, Middlesex
U.S.A.: Penguin Books Inc., 3300 Clipper Mill Road, Baltimore 11, Md
AUSTRALIA: Penguin Books Pty Ltd, 762 Whitehorse Road,
Mitcham, Victoria

—

First published by the Cresset Press 1962
Published in Penguin Books 1964

—

Copyright © A. W. Palmer, 1962

—

Made and printed in Great Britain
by Hazell Watson & Viney Ltd, Aylesbury, Bucks
Set in Linotype Times

PENGUIN REFERENCE BOOKS

R26

A DICTIONARY OF MODERN HISTORY

A. W. PALMER

Alan Palmer was born in 1926 and educated at Bancroft's School in Essex. Having served in the navy at the end of the war, he went to Oriel College, Oxford, as a scholar, and in 1950 gained a 'first' in modern history. He then spent a year working for a research degree on Anglo-Russian relations at the turn of the century, and since 1953 he has been senior history master at Highgate School, London. Mr Palmer's chief historical interests are in south-eastern Europe; he is co-author (with C. A. Macartney) of *Independent Eastern Europe*, a history of the region in the inter-war years. He has also written a short introductory book on Yugoslavia and has contributed a number of articles to *History Today* and other periodicals. He is married and lives in north London. His main recreational interest is travel.

TO VERONICA

PREFACE

THIS Dictionary is intended as a reference-companion for those who are interested in the history of the modern world, particularly between the years 1789 and 1945. Chronological divisions are notoriously arbitrary guides to the past and, in a country whose oldest university begins the study of 'Modern History' with the Roman occupation, this starting-point may perhaps appear unduly late. Yet if any one year is to be chosen then 1789 has much to commend it. It was on 30 April 1789 that Washington was inaugurated as the first President of the United States and it was on 5 May that the States-General gathered at Versailles. In that same summer, Manchester installed its first steam-engine in a cotton-mill and an obscure Home Secretary, Viscount Sydney, resigned from Pitt's Government, having perpetuated his memory through a newly founded township on the shores of Botany Bay that was destined to become the second largest city in the Commonwealth. These four events, although vastly different in importance, were each symbols of a new age. The emergence of a nation, the conflict between autocracy and the people, the mastery of machines, the desire to carve one's name in remote lands – all are recurrent themes in the history of the next century and a half. We may seek the origin of these movements in earlier decades, but we must go back several hundreds of years to discover a greater divide in human affairs than the 'Revolutionary Epoch'.

We are, of course, too near 1945 to decide whether it, also, forms a historical climacteric, although it may seem so to our generation. I chose this year, rather than an earlier or later date, for two reasons. The arrival at manhood of young people who know the Second World War only by hearsay seems to me to justify the inclusion of some of the events of those years of upheaval, and yet I shrink from going into the period of Cold War, partly because of limitations of space and partly because I do not think we can yet appraise the significance of its more dramatic moments. Will future historians make the Bandung Conference of 1955 a chapter-heading or a footnote? And which phantom prime minister of the Fourth Republic has left anything that will endure? These are questions that we may leave for others to decide. For the moment, students of the post-war decade will find guidance in the excellent Penguin *Dictionary of Politics* by Florence Elliott and Michael Summerskill. Naturally I have mentioned relevant happenings of these years in a broad context, but there are no specific entries on the people or problems of the post-war world.

The selection of topics for a book of this size is difficult; many incidents and individuals have been omitted only with the greatest reluctance. I have tried to compile a guide to the states of the modern world in action. Inevitably, British affairs predominate, but it has seemed to me important to avoid, so far as possible, that insular concentration which is the besetting sin of much of our historical teaching (and even more, a practising schoolmaster may add, of our historical examining). Accordingly, the Dictionary includes many entries on the U.S.A. and the Slavonic countries, and some on Latin America and the Far East, as well as on Western Europe. I have attempted to summarize the history of individual states only where there are not many topics or biographies from that country included elsewhere; thus the reader will find 'Denmark' in but 'Italy' out. There are paragraphs on some of the main political and historical thinkers but not, unfortunately, on the poets, artists, and musicians who have enriched these years of conflict. Where scientists or men of business have made major changes in our social habits, they are included. So, too, are some essentially domestic events of comparatively minor importance but which seem to capture the challenge of their decade. Finally, I have included some famous descriptive phrases, for example 'Manifest Destiny' and 'Splendid Isolation'. In the last resort, the selection has to be a personal one, and I only hope that it is representative.

In compiling this Dictionary I have used the best available modern books and have tried to summarize the interpretations of historical events that are accepted in the year 1960. I would, however, emphasize that this book is intended as an aid to study, not a substitute for it. If it explains a passing allusion or stimulates an interest in an unfamiliar facet of historical writing, I shall be well satisfied.

My greatest debt, in writing a book of this type, must be to the authors of the specialized studies or biographies which I have used. There are so many of them that I hope they will forgive me for not rendering individual acknowledgement. I have received advice and assistance from a number of friends. Mr Dieter Pevsner has made many valuable suggestions and has saved me from some factual errors. My colleagues, Mr T. N. Fox and Mr R. Beament, have read and commented on particular sections. Miss Mary Wallis of Halstead, Essex, typed my manuscript with speed and efficiency. I am grateful to them all, and to others who have suggested topics for inclusion. Of course, I alone am responsible for vagaries of interpretation and any inaccuracies that there may be. My wife has helped me in all stages of the compilation of the Dictionary; and it seems right to me that the book should be dedicated to her.

A. W. PALMER

Highgate School, London
May 1962

NOTE TO THE PENGUIN EDITION

I am most grateful to a number of friends who were kind enough to point out small errors in the first edition of this Dictionary. These have now been corrected. At the same time, I have taken the opportunity to revise a number of entries, bringing some up to date and clarifying others. Finally, I have added some half a dozen new entries.

A.W.P.

September 1963

AUTHOR'S NOTE

THROUGHOUT this book my practice has been as follows:

Cross-references: Too many cross-references become tedious and, in consequence, I have inserted the letters 'q.v.' after a word only where fuller reference would clarify the specific topic under consideration. It would be ridiculous to put 'q.v.' each time after Napoleon, or Bismarck, or Hitler, or the French Revolution.

Place-names: The names that are used for places are normally those used in the period under consideration. Thus, Russia's city on the Neva is called 'St Petersburg' until 1914, 'Petrograd' between 1914 and 1924, and thereafter 'Leningrad'. In less famous instances I have added the present name in brackets. In some cases I have accepted the place-name most commonly used in Britain rather than the local name. Thus, the town which the Poles call 'Cieszyn' and the Czechs 'Těšin' seemed to look happiest in its Germanic form 'Teschen'; and I have used the German 'Schleswig' for the part-Danish province of 'Sleswick'.

Political parties: When a specific political party is mentioned I have used a capital letter, irrespective of whether the word is a noun or an adjective. When an individual or a group shows tendencies towards the ideology of another party which does not exist, under that name, in the particular country under consideration, I have not used a capital letter. Thus, Clemenceau was a *Radical* but Joseph Chamberlain a *radical*; and, while Mussolini's Italy was *Fascist*, the Austria of Dollfuss had a *fascist* constitution. I should, perhaps, add that none of these political terms is intended as a pejorative.

Christian names: The names of European Emperors, Kings, etc. have been anglicized; thus, 'William II' rather than 'Wilhelm II', 'Francis Joseph succeeded by Charles' rather than 'Franz Josef succeeded by Karl'. I have, however, left the first-names of the subjects of biographical entries in their original form as, in many instances, there are no English equivalents.

I hope these practices will not appear to be inconsistent.

A.W.P.

Aaland Islands. An archipelago half-way between Sweden and Finland in an important strategic position, bound by history to Finland but populated by Swedes. The islands passed (with Finland) from Sweden to Russia in 1809 and remained Russian until the Revolution, being neutralized after the Crimean War. In February 1918, Swedish troops occupied the islands but were ejected by Germans supporting the Finnish independence movement. The future of the islands was referred to the League of Nations. In 1921 the League declared the islands should remain Finnish but should be granted self-government and demilitarized. Except for the period June 1941 to September 1944, when the archipelago was occupied by Germany, this condition of neutralization and autonomy under Finland has remained ever since. The islands' assembly tried unsuccessfully to secure union with Sweden in September 1945.

Abdication Crisis of 1936. Arose from the desire of King Edward VIII to marry Mrs Simpson. Precedent suggested that it was in the spirit of the British Constitution for the sovereign to seek the advice of his ministers before marriage. The Prime Minister, Baldwin, felt that such a marriage would be unacceptable to the country at large, not because Mrs Simpson was a commoner of American birth, but because her two previous marriages had ended in divorce and it would be difficult to reconcile the King's marriage with his position as 'Supreme Governor' of the Church of England. A morganatic marriage (a private Act denying the King's wife the status of queen) was considered, but rejected after consultation with the Dominion governments. The King, faced with the alternative of giving up Mrs Simpson or the throne, chose to abdicate (11 December 1936). He was succeeded by his brother the Duke of York (King George VI), and departed for France, being created Duke of Windsor.

Abdul Hamid II, Sultan of Turkey (born 1842, Sultan 1876–1909, died 1915). Succeeded his brother, Murad V, at a time of great crisis for Turkey and was faced at the outset by a war with Russia which cost him much of his European territory (Treaty of San Stefano, q.v., 1878). He early rescinded the Constitution enforced by the Great Powers on his country and thereafter ruled despotically from his Palace of the Yildiz Kiosk, Constantinople. Although carrying out administrative reforms in some of the provinces (notably Syria

13

and Palestine), he ruled through favourites selected from the reactionary clerical class. By encouraging the growth of Kurdish
irregular troops he bore heavy responsibility for the Armenian
massacres (q.v.) of 1895–6. These atrocities alienated most of the
Great Powers who had earlier protected Turkey from the encroach-
ment of Russia, although the Germans maintained friendly relations
with the Sultan. Abdul Hamid was forced to summon a parliament
in 1908 by the Young Turk movement (q.v.) but when he attempted
a counter-revolution in April 1909 he was deposed and exiled from
the capital.

Aberdeen, Earl of (George Hamilton Gordon, 1784–1860). A distinguished classical archaeologist and scholar, brought up by the Pitt
family. He was Ambassador in Vienna in 1813 where his impulsive
independence caused much embarrassment. After a spell as Foreign
Secretary, 1828–30, he became a warm supporter of Peel, and, returning to the Foreign Office in 1841, for five years pursued the difficult
policy of cooperation with France, despite friction over Tahiti (q.v.)
and the Spanish Marriages. On Peel's death in 1850, Aberdeen was
accepted as leader of the 'Peelites' (Free Trade Conservatives). In
December 1852 he became Prime Minister of a coalition government; his Cabinet contained six Whigs, six Peelites, and a Radical.
Aberdeen was unable to control the strong personalities of his
government; in foreign policy he vacillated between appeasement of
Russia and support of the French, and by his irresolution allowed
public opinion in the country to stampede him into the Crimean
War. He fell from office in January 1855, when the Cabinet refused
to accept a motion for a committee of inquiry into the management
of the war.

Aboukir Bay, Battle of (1798). See *Nile, Battle of*.

Abyssinia (Ethiopia). A kingdom that has flourished since Biblical
times, maintaining its independence despite the incursions of Portuguese (1528–1633) and Italians (1882–1941). Italian colonial expansion in Eritrea led in 1895 to a full-scale war, since the Abyssinians
considered Eritrea to be their natural littoral. The Abyssinians, under
Emperor Menelek (reigned 1889–1913), decisively defeated the
Italians at Adowa (1 March 1896) and were thus the one independent
people in Africa after the era of imperial partition. The country
remained backward until the accession of Emperor Haile Selassie in
1930, when a programme of reform was undertaken. Friction with
the Italians on the Eritrean and Somali frontiers increased with the

advent of Mussolini's forward policy and his obvious desire to 'avenge Adowa'. Although a treaty of friendship was signed between Italy and Abyssinia in 1928, frontier incidents continued, culminating in a serious clash at the oasis of Walwal (5 December 1934) in which 100 Ethiopians and 30 Italian colonial troops were killed. The dispute was referred to the League of Nations, but the Italians were determined to secure a military success and invaded Abyssinia, without a declaration of war, on 3 October 1935. Despite a declaration by the League branding Italy as an aggressor and imposing limited sanctions (q.v.), the Italians captured Addis Ababa on 5 May 1936, with the help of air power, mechanized equipment, and poison gas. King Victor Emmanuel of Italy was thereupon proclaimed Emperor while Haile Selassie went into exile. Five years later Ethiopian levies helped the British reconquer the country and expel the Italians, and Haile Selassie returned to his throne (5 May 1941). In August 1952 Abyssinia, with United Nations approval, was federated with Eritrea, thus acquiring a sea coast.

Action Française. Right-wing political movement in France, founded in 1899 by Charles Maurras (1868–1952). From 1908 it attracted much support through its newspaper (of the same name), which was edited by the brilliantly invective pamphleteer, Léon Daudet (1867–1942). Maurras, although a freethinker himself, regarded Catholicism as essential to France, and attacked the democratic institutions of the Third Republic as corrupt and decadent. The movement rallied the defeated opponents of Dreyfus (q.v.); it was royalist and nationalistic. It was a powerful influence in the period 1906–11 and in 1933–4. The Papacy distrusted the nationalistic aspects of the movement, which in the inter-war period made it hardly distinguishable from Fascism. In 1926 Pope Pius XI sought to check the cooperation of Roman Catholics in the movement, but he was opposed by some of the older members of the French hierarchy. Subsequently, the Action Française became a prominent influence in the Vichy Government (q.v.). The movement, as such, was broken up with the liberation of France in 1944 and the suppression of its newspaper; but its traditions have lingered on. Maurras himself, who earlier in the century had been a violent anti-German, was tried in 1945 on a charge of collaboration, and died in prison.

Acton, John Dalberg-, Baron (1834–1902). Acton was born at Naples and educated privately. He was unable to go to Cambridge, as he was a Roman Catholic, barred by Religious Tests. He spent much time studying historical methods in Munich, where he was influenced by the work of Döllinger. While remaining a sincere Catholic, Acton became convinced of the vital importance of political liberty in the modern state. He sat as Liberal M.P. for Carlow, 1859–65, and became a personal friend and adviser of Gladstone, who offered him a peerage in 1869. He found himself unable to accept the decrees of the Vatican Council of 1870 (q.v.) on papal infallibility. He incurred censure from the church authorities but did not go so far as many of his German friends who joined the 'Old Catholics' (q.v.). In 1895 Acton was appointed Regius Professor of History at Cambridge (Religious Tests had been repealed in 1871) where he planned the first of the great corporate works, the *Cambridge Modern History*. Acton himself wrote little – his ambitious *History of Liberty* was unfinished – but his liberal sympathies, and reverence for German scholarship, had a profound influence on his contemporaries and on the development of British historical studies.

Adams, John (1735–1826). President of U.S.A. Born at Braintree on the outskirts of Boston, educated at Harvard, and called to the Bar. He played a prominent part in the agitation of the American colonists against the Stamp Act of 1765, and helped to draft the Declaration of Independence. (He is not to be confused with his distant cousin, Samuel Adams, 1722–1803, who was also a signatory of the Declaration.) John Adams gave administrative backing to the creation of an American Navy, acting as president of the board of war. From 1777 to 1782 he served the new American Republic on various diplomatic missions and became the first American Minister in London in 1785. He served as Vice-President under Washington (q.v.) and in 1796 was elected as second President of the U.S.A. in a contest with Jefferson (q.v.). In his four-year term of office he had difficulty in cooperating with the younger politicians and he showed a marked distrust of popular control of government. He was defeated by Jefferson in the election of 1800 and spent the rest of his life in literary pursuits. He was married to Abigail Smith, a 'First Lady' of character and of culture as well as of considerable personal charm.

Adams, John Quincy (1767–1848), President of the U.S.A. The son of John Adams (q.v.). Born, like his father, in Braintree, Massachusetts. He studied at Leyden and at Harvard and was appointed Minister at The Hague when only 27 years old. He became a Senator in 1801 but resigned in 1808 because he resented the attempt of the people of Massachusetts to dictate the policy he was to pursue in Congress. After a further spell in the diplomatic service, he became Secretary of State under President Monroe in 1817 and helped to formulate the Monroe Doctrine (q.v.). He served as sixth President of the United States from 1824 to 1828, but his suspicions of 'Jacksonian democracy' (see *Jackson*) brought him into conflict with Congress. For the last eighteen years of his life he was a member of the House of Representatives, active in furthering societies which aimed at exposing the evils of slavery.

Addington, Henry (1757–1844, created Viscount Sidmouth in 1805). Entered the Commons in 1783 and was a close friend of Pitt (q.v.), who secured his election as Speaker in 1789, an office he held for eleven years. As a firm opponent of Catholic Emancipation (q.v.), he was invited by George III to form a government when Pitt resigned in 1801, and held office until May 1804. The Addington Ministry was, thus, responsible for the negotiations leading up to the peace of Amiens (q.v.). Addington was never popular and, when war was resumed, proved himself an incompetent leader. He held minor offices from 1805 to 1807 and from 1809 to 1812, when he became Home Secretary. Sidmouth became identified as Home Secretary with repressive measures against popular demonstrations and with the so-called 'Six Acts' of 1819 to limit meetings. Although he ceased to be Home Secretary in 1822, he remained in the Cabinet of Lord Liverpool (q.v.) until 1827. He was an unswerving old Tory, opposing Catholic Emancipation in 1829 and the Reform Act in 1832.

Adullamites. A nickname coined by John Bright (q.v.) in 1866 to describe the Whigs who, led by Robert Lowe, revolted against the Liberal Government's proposals for further parliamentary reform (q.v.) and thereby caused the fall of the Russell Ministry and its replacement by a Conservative Government under Lord Derby (q.v.). The name was taken from the Old Testament (I Samuel, chapter 22) in which it is recorded that David summoned to the cave of Adullam 'everyone that was in distress'.

Afghan Wars. There were three wars fought between Britain and Afghanistan to check alleged Russian infiltration: (i) 1838–42, a long-drawn-out campaign, badly mismanaged; (ii) 1878–9, caused by the tendency of the Amir to favour a Russian representative while refusing a British agent; (iii) 1879–80, punitive expeditions led by Sir Frederick (later Lord) Roberts to put down anti-British demonstrations. (It was in the course of this campaign that Roberts made his famous march from Kabul to Kandahar – 320 miles in 23 days with a force of 10,000 men.) There was also heavy fighting between Afghans and British in 1919 after internal disturbances in Afghanistan.

Agadir. A small port on the Atlantic coast of Morocco. Agadir became the centre of an international crisis when, on 1 July 1911, the German gunboat *Panther* was sent to the port, allegedly to protect German interests menaced by French expansion in Morocco. Kiderlen-Waechter, the German Foreign Secretary, believed that French intrigues had broken the agreement reached five years earlier at Algeciras (q.v.) and that a display of strength would gain compensation for Germany. Britain, however, was alarmed at this exercise of German naval power so close to Gibraltar and her vital traderoutes; she feared that the Germans wished to turn Agadir into a naval base. On 21 July the Chancellor of the Exchequer, Lloyd George, gave a strong warning to Germany in a speech at the Mansion House. The Germans, though irritated by what they considered to be a threat of war, promptly denied any intention of annexing Moroccan territory. The French were not so alarmed by the crisis as the British and for some months continued negotiations with the Germans to find them adequate 'compensation'. The talks nearly broke down in September and war again seemed probable, but the Germans gave way and, by agreements signed on 3–4 November, recognized French rights in Morocco in return for the cession of two strips of territory in the French Congo. The German Navy thereupon withdrew. In Britain, the crisis had the effect of stimulating closer cooperation between the Admiralty and the War Office. It is sometimes termed the Second Moroccan Crisis.

Aix-la-Chapelle (Aachen), Congress of (1818). The first of the meetings that formed the Congress System (q.v.). The four Great Powers – Russia, Prussia, Austria, and Britain – extended their alliance to include France and ended the occupation of French territory, originally fixed in 1815 for five years. The Congress also settled the problem of French reparations; approved measures for Napoleon's security on St Helena; and confirmed a decision of the Congress of Vienna assuring German Jews of their civil rights. Although more amicable than the later Congresses, the Aix meeting marked the first tendency of the British to act independently of their eastern allies; Castlereagh (q.v.) rejected a Russian proposal for an alliance which would have guaranteed perpetuation of the existing form of government in the various European states.

Alabama **Dispute.** In July 1862 the *Alabama*, a newly-built vessel ordered by the Confederate States of America, was allowed to slip out of Liverpool and join other Southern ships raiding the mercantile marine of the Northern states. After the Civil War, the U.S.A. claimed damages from the British Government for losses inflicted by the *Alabama* and other British-built commerce-raiders. In 1871 Gladstone accepted a request from the U.S. Secretary of State, Hamilton Fish, to refer the dispute to the arbitration of an international tribunal consisting of representatives from Italy, Brazil, and Switzerland as well as the interested parties. The tribunal awarded the U.S.A. £3¼ million compensation. Although this was only a third of the amount claimed by the U.S. Government, the decision increased the unpopularity of Gladstone's foreign policy with the British electorate. Nevertheless, the settlement marked an important victory for the general principle of resorting to pacific arbitration for international disputes.

Alamein, El, Battle of. Alamein is a small Egyptian township about 50 miles west of Alexandria. In 1942 it was the site of two battles between British and Commonwealth forces in the Eighth Army and the combined German and Italian armies of Marshal Erwin Rommel (1891–1944). In the course of the first battle General Sir Claude Auchinleck successfully halted Rommel's advance towards the Nile (30 June to 25 July). The second battle, which began with a great artillery barrage on 23 October and continued until 4 November, has received greater publicity, since it marked the opening of the Allied offensive which was to clear North Africa of Axis troops. The Eighth Army was commanded in the second battle of Alamein by General Sir Bernard (later Lord) Montgomery. In its subsequent advance across Libya the Eighth Army covered 1,400 miles in 18 weeks.

Alaska. Occupied by Russian merchant-adventurers, the Russian-American Company, at the end of the eighteenth century, but Tsar Alexander II considered the territory an economic liability and authorized its sale to the U.S.A. Seward (Secretary of State 1861–9) negotiated the purchase in October 1867, acquiring the territory for about a million and a half pounds. For many years 'Seward's Folly' remained uneconomical, but all this was changed by the Klondyke Gold Rush of 1896. In 1903 an Alaskan boundary dispute between Canada and the U.S.A. was settled amicably. The strategic value of Alaska was not appreciated until 1942, when the international 'Alaskan Highway', a route of 1,500 miles was constructed in thirty-eight weeks; this allowed men and material to be transported rapidly from the U.S.A. to vital northern bases. Alaska was admitted as the forty-ninth state of the U.S.A. in 1957.

Albania. Under Turkish rule from the late fifteenth century until 1931 although enjoying virtual independence under a native-born chieftain, Ali Pasha of Janina, from 1798 to 1820. After the Balkan Wars (q.v.) Albania was made an independent Moslem principality under a German ruler (Prince William of Wied) but remained in an anarchical state throughout the First World War. (By December 1914 there were six régimes, each claiming to be the legitimate government.) Albania's future was finally settled in November 1921 after a long dispute between Italy, Greece, and Yugoslavia. A Council of Regency ruled the country until 1924, but in 1925 a republic was proclaimed following a rebellion by one of the large landowners, Ahmed Bey Zogu, who became President. In 1928 Zogu was proclaimed King Zog I. Throughout his reign there was economic dependence on Italy (thus the 'National Bank of Albania' had its head offices in Rome) and on Good Friday 1939 Mussolini formally occupied Albania and chased out Zog as a first step towards Italian dominance in south-east Europe. The King of Italy acquired the Albanian crown. An Italian attack on Greece from Albania in 1940 failed disastrously, but after the German occupation of the Balkans in 1941 the Axis Powers kept a tenuous hold on the country until October 1944 in the face of vigorous guerilla resistance led, for the most part, by the Communist Enver Hoxha, whose republican régime was recognized by the Great Powers in November 1945. The Albanians remained within the Soviet bloc until 1961, when ideological differences with Moscow led to their expulsion from the Warsaw Pact.

Alexander, King of Yugoslavia (born 1888; King 1921–34). A member of the Karadjordjević family, which came to the throne of Serbia in 1903. In July 1914 the ill-health of his father, King Peter of Serbia, forced Alexander to become Prince Regent and, in that capacity, he accompanied the Serbian Army in its retreat through Albania in 1915 and subsequently supervised its reorganization as a fighting unit in Corfu. On 1 December 1918 he accepted the Regency of the united Kingdom of Serbs, Croats, and Slovenes, succeeding as King in August 1921. Bitter disputes between Serbs and Croats, culminating in a shooting affray in the Belgrade Parliament, led Alexander to proclaim a royal dictatorship (6 January 1929). In the following

October he officially changed the name of the Kingdom to 'Yugo-slavia', although following a policy that favoured the Serbs at the expense of other nationalities. In foreign affairs he cooperated with the Czechs and Roumanians in the Little Entente and, at the end of his life, was improving relations between the Balkan States. He was assassinated on 9 October 1934 at Marseilles while on a state visit to France, by a terrorist in the pay of the extreme Croatian nationalist movement, the Ustaše. He was succeeded by his eleven-year-old son, Peter II, for whom Alexander's cousin, Prince Paul, acted as chief Regent, 1934–41.

Alexander I, Tsar of Russia (born 1777; Tsar 1801–25). The son of the 'mad Tsar', Paul I, who was murdered with Alexander's con-nivance. Alexander himself was unstable and exhibited signs of schizophrenia; his policy was full of vacillation and apparent con-tradiction. He entered the War of the Third Coalition in 1805, but when his troops were routed at Friedland (13–14 June 1807) he sought peace with Napoleon, whom he met at Tilsit (q.v.) and whom, at first, he greatly admired. Subsequently, Napoleon's economic policy, treatment of the German and Polish questions, and marriage to a Habsburg princess alienated Alexander. When Napoleon in-vaded Russia in 1812 the Tsar remained in St Petersburg, but emerged to lead his troops into the War of the Fourth Coalition. With his allies he reached Paris on 31 March 1814, and became the first invading sovereign to enter the city since Henry V of England (1420). He attended the Congress of Vienna, where his insistence on creating a Polish Kingdom under his own protection alarmed his former allies. Back in Paris after Waterloo, he proclaimed his much misunderstood ideal of Christian fraternity, the 'Holy Alliance' (q.v.). Although obsessed by fear of 'the Revolution' he possessed some liberal sentiments implanted by his Swiss tutor, La Harpe, and the Polish aristocrat, Adam Czartoryski, who was his intimate friend. From 1807 to 1811 Speransky (q.v.) reformed the central administra-tion of the Empire, but in his later years Alexander was dominated by two reactionaries, General Arakcheyev (1769–1834), who founded a cruel system of 'military colonies', and the Archimandrite Photius (1792–1838) a bigoted xenophobe. Alexander himself was subject to periods of religious mania and died mysteriously at Taganrog on 1 December 1825. There were persistent rumours in Russia that the Tsar was not dead but had fled to Siberia and become a hermit, Feodor Kusmitch, who lived on until 1864. To allay these reports the authorities opened Alexander's coffin in 1865; it was found to be empty.

Alexander II, Tsar of Russia (born 1818; Tsar 1855–81). Succeeded his father, Nicholas I, in the midst of the Crimean War. He perceived that much of the war chaos resulted from archaic institutions and the system of cruel repression and therefore carried through a series of reforms modernizing every facet of Russian life. The greatest of these was the Emancipation of the Serfs (q.v.) of 1861. It was followed by changes in the legal code (1862); creation of a new unit of local government, the *zemstvo* (q.v.); the encouragement of secondary education and university reform; and changes in army administration and the substitution of conscription for an inequitable forced levy. At the same time, new railways greatly increased the export of Russian grain and there was a considerable growth of credit institutions. By 1866, however, unrest in Russian Poland and an attempted assassination plot made the Tsar give way to the reactionaries and lapse into despotism. In foreign affairs his Minister, Gorchakov (q.v.), achieved valuable agreements with Bismarck, but throughout the seventies Alexander was mainly concerned with a policy of expansion in the Balkans, allowing almost free rein to Panslavism (q.v.) and seeing his troops reach the outskirts of Constantinople in January 1878. The Russians also made territorial advances in Central Asia, capturing Bokhara and Samarkand in 1868 and causing concern in Britain by their activities on the borders of Afghanistan. At the same time revolutionary societies were developing in St Petersburg and Kiev; a secret terrorist group, 'The People's Will', condemned Alexander to death in 1879 for failing to summon a Constituent Assembly. After several narrow escapes from death, he was blown up by a bomb hurled by a Polish student on 13 March 1881. He had, unknown to the public, given his consent to limited constitutional reform only that morning; with his death these proposals were abandoned.

Alexander III, Tsar of Russia (born 1845; Tsar 1881–94). Succeeded his father, Alexander II. He was a firm autocrat and throughout his reign followed a policy of political repression, choosing as his chief adviser the Procurator of the Holy Synod, Konstantin Pobedonostsev (q.v.). Alexander refused to make any concessions to liberalism and insisted on strengthening the hold of Russians over all other nationalities within his empire. The Jewish people suffered especially. Savage restrictions, the so-called 'Temporary Rules' (lasting thirty years), were imposed on Jews in May 1882. Political discontent was driven underground, the first Russian Marxist group being formed in St Petersburg in 1883. Despite the autocratic principles that he shared with his fellow Emperors in Berlin and Vienna, Alexander found

himself unable to maintain the diplomatic links of the Dreikaiserbund (q.v.) after the crisis over Bulgaria in 1885–6. By 1891, Alexander was so alarmed by the trend of German policy that he welcomed, in person, a visit to Kronstadt by a French naval squadron.
This visit initiated exchanges that led to a military convention between Russia and France in August 1892. The Franco-Russian Alliance (q.v.) was formally but secretly confirmed in January 1894, ten
months before Alexander's death. In the last years of his reign,
Alexander encouraged the development of Russia's Far Eastern territories, backing the projects of Witte (q.v.) and authorizing construction of the Trans-Siberian Railway (q.v.).

Alexandria. The ancient capital of Ptolemaic Egypt, used as a base
by Napoleon for his invasion of Egypt and Syria 1798–9, and the
scene of a battle between the British and the rump of the French
Levant Army in 1801. In June 1882 Egyptian nationalist riots led to
the despatch of a joint Franco-British fleet to keep order. The
French Admiral subsequently withdrew, but the British bombarded
and silenced batteries erected by the Egyptian commander, Arabi
Pasha. The Gladstone Government thereupon sent in troops under
Sir Garnet Wolseley, who defeated Arabi's followers at the battle of
Tel-el-Kebir (13 September 1882). The British proceeded to occupy
Egypt, intending to stay only until order was restored, but in fact
remaining for more than sixty years. Alexandria was developed
as the main naval base in the Eastern Mediterranean and was
not evacuated until 1947, although from June to November
1942 the proximity of Rommel's armies made it unusable as a major
port.

Algeciras, Conference of. An international conference of the Great
Powers to settle the disputes between Germany and France that had
led to the First Moroccan Crisis (q.v.) was held at Algeciras in
Southern Spain from January to April 1906. The Germans had insisted on the Conference in the hope of inflicting a diplomatic
humiliation on France and destroying the growing friendship between Britain and France. Largely through the skill of the British
delegate, Sir Arthur Nicolson, the Germans were isolated and outvoted, reluctantly accepting the 'Act of Algeciras', which authorized
France and Spain to police Morocco under a Swiss Inspector
General and respected the Sultan of Morocco's authority. The close
collaboration of the French and British representatives is of greater
historical importance than the terms of the actual settlement; by
their cooperation they strengthened the Anglo-French Entente and

showed Russia the advantages to be gained from a similar understanding with Britain.

Algeria. Algiers, a base for 'Barbary Pirates' from the sixteenth century, was seized by French troops to avenge a national insult on 5 July 1830. The Algerians (under Abd-el-Kadar) resisted until 1845, many of France's victories being won by Orleanist princes. Colonization was begun by military leaders, who, as a class, have played a disproportionate part in Algerian politics ever since. Frequent resistance from the interior provided the opportunity for campaigns in which military glory could be won swiftly and cheaply. The most serious rebellion came in 1871, and was followed by introduction of the system of 'attachment' by which Algeria became part of metropolitan France. There remained, however, administrative anomalies: thus Algeria was still controlled by a Governor General who ruled by decree, and only a minority of the population was enfranchised. Moreover, while Jews received political rights in 1870, these rights were denied to Arabs throughout the Third Republic; in consequence, one of the few attitudes shared by settlers and Arabs was political anti-semitism. In November 1942 allied troops landed in Algiers and on 3 June 1943 a 'Committee of National Liberation' was set up by de Gaulle's Free French movement and other French organizations. The rise of Arab nationalism and the intransigently right-wing attitude of the military authorities made Algeria a running sore for the Fourth Republic, which in 1958 was destroyed largely through the threats of the paratroop leaders in Algiers. A state of undeclared war, existing between the French and the Algerian nationalists since 1954, was ended in March 1962. Four months later the French acknowledged the independence of Algeria.

Allenby, Edmund, Viscount (1861–1936). British General. After service in South Africa, Allenby was appointed Commander of the cavalry division in the B.E.F. of 1914, subsequently commanding the Third Army in France 1915–17, culminating in the battle of Arras. In June 1917 he was moved to Palestine and began a methodically prepared advance in October, through Gaza and Jaffa, capturing Jerusalem in December 1917. Withdrawal of troops to France weakened his position, but by skilful use of cavalry he was able to begin a major offensive on 18 September 1918, which rolled the Turks back through Syria before the signing of the Armistice of Mudros (30 October 1918). Allenby was raised to the peerage in 1919 and served as High Commissioner in Egypt, 1919–25.

Alsace-Lorraine. Provinces of north-eastern France, linked in name only after annexation by Bismarck in 1871. Most of Alsace was first occupied by the French in 1648 (Peace of Westphalia), ten 'free cities' being annexed in 1681. Lorraine was formally added to the French Kingdom in 1766. After the Franco-Prussian War (q.v.) and the Treaty of Frankfurt (1871), both provinces, except for part of Lorraine around Belfort, were ceded to Germany; on 3 June 1871 they were declared 'Imperial Territory' (*Reichsland*). Until Bismarck's fall in 1890, Alsace and Lorraine were administered with severity, but thereafter tension relaxed and the Germans made an effort to assimilate the territory, even granting (in 1911) a mild degree of autonomy. At the same time, the industrial yield of the iron-ore deposits of Alsace and Lorraine was considerably increased by perfection of the Gilchrist-Thomas process of steel-making, 1878. A number of incidents showed Alsatian dissatisfaction with German administration; the most famous of these occurred in November 1913 at Zabern (Saverne), where riots broke out following insults heaped on Alsatian recruits by a German lieutenant. In France there was continuous resentment against the Germans for having annexed Alsace-Lorraine; thus, in Paris, the statue representing the city of Strasbourg was permanently veiled from 1871 to 1918. The territories were restored to France by the Treaty of Versailles, 1919. Between the wars conflicts over religious policy led to occasional demands of autonomy. In 1940 Alsace-Lorraine was made an integral part of Hitler's Germany but was liberated once more in 1945.

American Civil War. The ultimate origins of the Civil War lie in the rivalry between the agricultural slave-owning South and the industrialized, non-slave North; the immediate cause was the attempt by Lincoln (q.v.) to maintain an isolated Federal Garrison at Fort Sumter in South Carolina despite the decision of South Carolina and six other states to secede from the American Union rather than accept a President nominated by an anti-slavery party. Troops representing the Confederacy (q.v.) fired on Fort Sumter (12 April 1861), and Lincoln called for volunteers to suppress the insurrection. Four more border states seceded. Military operations began in June. The Union had all the advantages – an organized government, over twice the manpower of the South, command of the seas, and industry – but not until the twin defeats of Vicksburg and Gettysburg (q.v.) in July 1863 did the Confederates begin to falter. Throughout 1861 and 1862 Jackson (at Bull Run, q.v.) and Lee (q.v.) proved themselves superior commanders, but the emergence of Grant (q.v.) and Sherman (q.v.) as Union Generals and the cumulative effect of

naval blockade wore down the Confederates. With the Southern
armies divided and weakened by mass desertions, Lee surrendered to
Grant at Appomattox on 9 April 1865, isolated resistance continuing for seven more weeks. There were some 620,000 deaths on the
two sides. Since Lincoln had emancipated the slaves on 1 January
1863, the defeat of the Confederacy meant a social revolution for the
South. After Lincoln's assassination (14 April 1865) the defeated
states were politically exploited by a group of 'radical Republicans'
who treated the South as conquered territory. By their unscrupulous
exercise of one-party rule, enforced by military authority, they perpetuated the bitterness between North and South. This period of
'Black Reconstruction' continued until the withdrawal of the last
Federal troops from Louisiana and South Carolina in April 1877.

Amiens, Peace of. The Treaty of Amiens, signed by Britain, France,
Spain, and Holland on 25 March 1802, began a fourteen-month
breathing-space in the British conflict with France. By the Treaty
Britain was to keep Trinidad and Ceylon but restore Malta to the
Knights of St John, the Cape to the Dutch, and Egypt, evacuated by
the French, to Turkey. The French agreed to leave Naples; the
independence of the Ionian Islands and Portugal were guaranteed;
the British monarchy dropped the style 'King of France' borne by
English sovereigns since Edward III's reign. The treaty was unpopular in London. Within a few months Napoleon intervened in
the German states and in Switzerland and secured election as President of the new Italian Republic; the British thereupon decided not
to evacuate Malta, confirming their intention to hold on to the island
when it was rumoured that the French were preparing a new
Egyptian expedition. A British ultimatum demanding Malta for ten
years, French evacuation of Holland and Switzerland, and the
cession of Lampedusa was rejected; the British refused Napoleon's
suggestion of Russian mediation, and war was resumed on 16 May
1803.

Amritsar Riots. In 1919 impatient supporters of the movement for
Indian self-government caused disturbances in many parts of India
and especially in the Punjab. When rioting was threatened in the
town of Amritsar, the local commander, General Dyer, called out
his troops (10 April) and, without adequate warning, ordered them
to fire on an angry but unarmed mob; 379 Indians were killed and
1,200 injured. A Commission of Inquiry investigated the shooting,
severely censured Dyer, and required his resignation. The shooting
left a bitter legacy in Anglo-Indian relations.

Andrássy, Gyula, Count (1823–1890). Member of a distinguished Magyar family, became a radical nationalist and fought in the unsuccessful struggle for Hungarian independence of 1848–9, subsequently going into exile for eight years. He became a much more moderate politican on his return, supporting Deák (q.v.) in the negotiations of the Ausgleich (q.v.) and serving as the first Hungarian Premier (1867–71). From 1871 to 1879 he was Austro-Hungarian Foreign Minister; he was responsible for recovering the Monarchy's lost influence in the western Balkans and for improving relations with Germany. He headed the Austro-Hungarian delegation at the Congress of Berlin. His son (bearing the same name) became, in October 1918, the last Foreign Minister of the Monarchy.

Anglo-American War of 1812–14. Sprang from the strained relations of the two countries during the British struggle with Napoleon. American resentment was aroused by the activities of the Royal Navy in impressing U.S. seamen, blockading American ports, and enforcing the Orders in Council that barred neutral shipping from trading with French ports, and also by alleged British backing for Indian raids on American settlements. War began on 18 June 1812. American land forces tried to invade Canada at three points in 1812 – from Detroit, around Niagara, and around Lake Champlain – but met severe setbacks. In April 1813 an American force raided and set fire to Toronto. In the following year a British force of 4,000 veterans was brought over from France and landed in Chesapeake Bay. It occupied and set fire to Washington (24–25 August 1814), but failed to capture Baltimore a fortnight later. There was a series of naval engagements which normally took the form of 'duels' between individual ships; the most famous was fought off Boston (January 1813) between two frigates, U.S.S. *Chesapeake* and H.M.S. *Shannon* which resulted in the capture of the American vessel. The peace-treaty (signed at Ghent, Belgium, in December 1814) restored relations between the two countries but avoided the issues that had given rise to the conflict. News of the signing of peace did not reach America until 11 February 1815; on 8 January General Andrew Jackson had gained the main American land victory in the war by defeating a British attempt to seize New Orleans from the sea.

Anglo-French Entente ('Entente Cordiale'), 1904. The understanding reached by the two countries in an agreement signed on 8 April 1904, settling outstanding disputes in West Africa, Siam, Madagascar, the New Hebrides, over Newfoundland fishing rights and, above all, allowing Britain a free hand to develop Egypt in return for giving France a free hand in Morocco, provided that no fortifications should be erected menacing Gibraltar and that Spanish historic claims should be recognized. The agreement ended a long period of friction between the two powers that had nearly led to war six years earlier over Fashoda (q.v.). Negotiations for an agreement began in August 1903 – the main participants being Lansdowne and, from Cairo, Cromer (q.v.) on the British side, and Delcassé and Paul Cambon for France. The popular belief that Edward VII 'made the Entente' has no foundation in fact, although his tactful behaviour during a Paris visit in 1903 broke down latent anti-British feelings. The Entente was in no sense an alliance nor was it anti-German in intention; subsequent German policy, especially during the Moroccan Crisis (q.v.), strengthened Anglo-French collaboration and led to Military Conversations (q.v.), but no treaty of alliance was signed until *after* the outbreak of war in 1914.

Anglo-Russian Entente. An understanding, similar to the Anglo-French Entente, based on an agreement signed on 31 August 1907, defining spheres of influence in Persia and the attitudes of the two countries towards Tibet and Afghanistan. It was the culmination of long negotiations, which had begun with abortive proposals from Salisbury in 1898 and had been resumed in earnest by Grey after the Algeciras Conference (q.v.) had shown Britain's close relationship with Russia's ally, France. The agreement was anti-German only in the sense that it sought to prevent German penetration of the Middle East and to end German attempts to exacerbate Anglo-Russian relations. There was no mention of European affairs, although the Russians understood that Britain would in future not oppose Russian ambitions to control the Bosphorus and the Dardanelles if other powers agreed. The Anglo-Russian Entente was never so close as the Anglo-French Entente, partly because of continued Russian intrigues in Persia and partly because of criticism in Britain of Russia's internal policy. Nevertheless, the Entente opened the London money market to Russia and thereby assisted her to recover from her military defeat at the hands of Japan and from the revolutionary chaos of 1905. (See also *Triple Entente*.)

Anschluss. A term applied to the union of Austria and Germany. With the disintegration of Austria-Hungary in 1918, the majority of its German-speaking remnant wished to unite with Germany. This, however, was forbidden by the Allies in the Treaties of Versailles and St Germain. Agitation in favour of Anschluss continued throughout the 1920s, especially in the Tyrol and Salzburg. In 1931 a projected Customs Union between Germany and Austria was abandoned because France and the 'Little Entente' complained that this would have been a first step to Anschluss. Demands for union increased after Hitler became German Chancellor (1933). A Nazi coup in Vienna in July 1934 failed, although the Austrian Chancellor, Dollfuss (q.v.) was murdered. Internal discord in France and the reconciliation of Fascist Italy and Nazi Germany in 1936 left the Austrian Government isolated in the face of Hitler's demands. In February 1938 Hitler asked Chancellor Schuschnigg to meet him at Berchtesgaden and demanded concessions for the Austrian Nazis, including cooperation in the Government. When Schuschnigg tried to forestall Hitler by a plebiscite on the question of Austrian independence, the Germans submitted an ultimatum demanding his resignation (11 March 1938). Schuschnigg was forced to resign in favour of the Austrian Nazi, Seyss-Inquart, who invited the German Army to occupy Austria (12 March) and proclaimed union with Germany on the next day. On 10 April a Nazi-controlled plebiscite recorded a vote of 99·75 per cent in favour of the Anschluss.

Anti-Clericalism. The name applied in modern times to any policy of destroying the political power of the Church and subordinating its non-spiritual functions to the State. Although there have been instances of anti-clericalism at the expense of the Orthodox Church, and even in Moslem countries, the term is normally restricted to hostility towards Roman Catholicism. The nature of the struggle has varied from country to country. It originated in revolutionary France with an attack first upon church property and secondly upon the identification of Church and Monarchy. Papal condemnation of nationalism and liberalism (especially by the *Syllabus Errorum* of 1864) made anti-clericalism one of the characteristics of the Radicals of the Third French Republic. A similar struggle took place in Spain (especially in 1873, 1909–13, and 1931–6) and Latin America. Italian anti-clericalism was particularly concerned with the national issue, because of the Pope's position as a temporal sovereign until 1870. In Bismarck's Germany (half-Protestant) anti-clericalism was elevated to a high-sounding 'conflict of beliefs', *Kulturkampf* (q.v.), although in reality the basic issues were similar to the French, with particular emphasis on education and civil marriage. In recent times, anti-clericalism has flourished in communist states and has been embittered by communist identification of the upper clergy with former quasi-fascist régimes.

Anti-Comintern Pact. An agreement between Germany and Japan signed on 25 November 1936 and recording the two countries' opposition to international communism ('the Comintern', q.v.). The Pact represented a personal triumph for Ribbentrop (q.v.), who, although not appointed Foreign Minister until February 1938, had for several years previously been working for recognition of the principles of a specifically Nazi and anti-communist foreign policy. Italy adhered to the Pact in November 1937. On each occasion, the Japanese price was recognition of their puppet régime in Manchuria (q.v.).

Anti-Corn Law League. A movement with headquarters in Manchester founded in 1839 to advocate Free Trade and more especially abolition of the duties upon imported corn ('the Corn Laws', q.v.). The League was led by Richard Cobden (q.v.) and John Bright (q.v.). It was the first great national reformist campaign and employed all the devices of a well-organized mass agitation – pressure on M.P.s, monster meetings throughout Britain, pamphlets (cheaply circulated to every elector in the country by the new penny postage), and primitive public-opinion polls. The movement succeeded because of the rhetorical powers of its leaders, the clarity and simplicity of its purpose, the extent of its organization, and the identification of its objective with the suffering of the 'Hungry Forties'. The propaganda of the League was more successful after the bad harvests of 1839–41 than after the good harvests of 1842–4. The wet summer of 1845 and the concurrent failure of the Irish potato crop enabled the League to intensify its campaign and so complete the conversion of Peel to Free Trade. The Corn Laws were repealed in June 1846.

Anti-Semitism. Most European countries have experienced periods of hostility to the Jews, often disguising economic resentment by an insistence on religious conformity. With the growth of religious toleration, opposition on these grounds was replaced by essentially racialist prejudice. This so-called anti-semitism dates from the early 1870s when a group of German writers, using the Frenchman Renan's concept of the linguistic distinctions 'Semitic' and 'Aryan' as racial terms, began to attack Jews as members of a distinct and inferior race. In Germany particular resentment was felt against Jewish businessmen who had profited from the wave of speculation of 1871–3. The movement developed rapidly in Austria-Hungary as well as in Germany, and in the nineties spread to France, where it was reflected in the Panama Canal scandal (q.v.) and the Dreyfus

Case (q.v.). The worst outbreak was in Russia, where in 1881 there were serious pogroms (a Russian word for 'devastation') resulting in many deaths. Anti-Jewish laws passed in May 1882 remained operative for thirty years and led to mass emigration, especially to the U.S.A. The worst period of Russian persecution was 1905–9, when outrages were organized by the terrorist 'Black Hundreds'; it is estimated there were 50,000 Jewish victims. There was also serious anti-semitic activity in Rumania and, between the wars, in Poland and Hungary as well. Hitler's anti-semitism (which had its origin in pre-war Vienna) used the Jew as a scapegoat for every ill that had befallen Germany. A campaign excluding Jews from positions of influence started in 1933 and forced many leading figures into exile. Hitler developed the theory of an 'Aryan' master-race popularized in the 1900s by H. S. Chamberlain (1855–1927), an English-born writer who became a German citizen. (Chamberlain, in his turn, had borrowed extensively from the Frenchman, de Gobineau, who had written in the 1850s.) In the Nuremberg Laws of September 1935 the Nazis sought to codify their racial myth. Jews were denied German citizenship and forbidden to marry 'Aryan' Germans. A further law in November 1938 confiscated Jewish property. Persecution of Jews increased with the coming of war, and was extended to all lands through which the German armies advanced. Between 1939 and 1945 the Nazis caused the death of six million Jews (over a third of the total Jewish population in the world).

Anzac. A word derived from the initials of the Australian and New Zealand Army Corps, which landed at a cove (subsequently named after them) on the Gallipoli Peninsula (q.v.) on 25 April 1915, and which held out for eight months despite persistent Turkish attacks.

Ardennes Offensive. A last attempt by the Germans in the Second World War to break through the allied front in the West, capture Antwerp, and thus cut off supplies for the British and American armies preparing to invade Germany. The offensive was launched by von Rundstedt on 16 December 1944. Although he succeeded in breaking through on a narrow front, reserves were hastily found to plug the gap. General Eisenhower appointed Field Marshal Montgomery to temporary command of the front even though the heaviest fighting involved American troops. Despite heavy snowstorms, the allies launched a counter-offensive on 3 January 1945, and threw the Germans back. The losses sustained by the Germans were so severe that they subsequently found it impossible to hold the line of the Rhine.

Argentina. At the start of the nineteenth century Argentina formed an important administrative division, the Viceroyalty of La Plata, within the Spanish South American Empire. The Argentinians took a lead in the emancipation of Latin America by overthrowing the Viceroy on 25 May 1810, and finally declared their independence as 'the United Provinces of South America' in 1816. Thereafter, they lapsed into political anarchy, and there developed a long-standing feud between Buenos Aires and the provinces which erupted into civil war, notably in 1861 and 1880. Firm government came only from tyrannical dictators, of whom the most notorious was Juan Manuel de Rosas (1793–1877, dictator 1835–52). A Federal Constitution, based on the American model, was established in 1853, but did not become effective for another eight years. Immigration contributed to an increase of the population from two million in 1869 to eight million in 1914 (expanding to nineteen million in 1955). From 1880 government was in the hands of an oligarchy of some 2,000 landowning families, who, under the guise of the National Autonomist Party, ruled until 1916. Presidents nominated not only their successors but almost every other office-holder as well. A Radical Party, insisting on electoral reform, was created in 1892 and triumphed, under the threat of violent upheaval, in the first free presidential election (1916). The radical leader, Hipólito Irigoyen, was President 1916–22 and 1928–30, but found the comforts of office made him forget his earlier advocacy of progressive reforms. He was overthrown by a bloodless revolution in September 1930, and for thirteen years there was a government of landowners. Fascist ideas rapidly developed within the army. A military coup in June 1943 began a period of extreme corruption, which was to some extent cleaned up by Juan Perón (President 1946–55). Perón's movement afforded an outlet for nationalistic passions but fell foul of the Roman Catholic Church over legislation on divorce and prostitution. Perón's successors, although still military men, appeared to adhere to liberal principles. On 28 June 1957, President Aramburu was able to end the state of military siege that had existed almost continually for over sixteen years.

'Armed Neutrality'. Originally a confederacy of the northern powers, Russia, Denmark, and Sweden, formed in 1780 to ensure rights of neutral shipping during the War of American Independence and to threaten war if the Royal Navy continued to interfere with neutral vessels. This coalition dissolved in 1781, It was, however, resurrected by skilful French diplomacy in December 1800 as a means of defeating the British blockade. By the battle of Copenhagen of 2 April

1801 the British destroyed the Danish fleet, which was the only navy capable of enforcing 'Armed Neutrality' in the Baltic. By the end of 1801 'Armed Neutrality' had proved a failure.

Armenian Massacres. A nationalist movement developed in the Turkish provinces of Armenia in the middle of the nineteenth century. Failure on the part of Sultan Abdul Hamid (q.v.) to carry out promised reforms led the Armenians to form secret terrorist societies in the hope that Turkish reprisals would awaken European sympathy for the Armenian cause, as had happened over Bulgaria 1875–8. An Armenian rising at Sassun (August 1894) was cruelly suppressed by Turkish irregulars. There were protests in Western Europe (particularly from British Liberals) and the Sultan again gave assurances of intended reforms (April 1895). He continued to temporize, even under the threat of coercion from the British fleet, and in August 1896 Armenians seized the Ottoman Bank in Constantinople, thereby causing three days of ferocious slaughter in the capital itself. Forceful protests from the Ambassadors halted this massacre, but incidents continued for another nine months in the provinces. When it became clear that the European Powers would not support the Armenian cause to the extent of demanding independence, Armenian provocation and Turkish reprisals gradually died out. The Armenian nationalists had failed to realize that there was, in reality, no parallel with the case of Bulgaria, for the Russians, who had befriended the Bulgars, were afraid of the repercussions of Armenian nationalism within their own Caucasian territories.

Armistice. A suspension of hostilities pending a definite peace settlement. In modern times the word is especially applied to the Armistice signed in a railway coach at Compiègne between Germany and the Allied and Associated Powers on 11 November 1918, thus terminating the First World War. Earlier armistices had been signed with Bulgaria (Salonica, 29 September), Turkey (Mudros, 30 October), and Austria-Hungary (Padua, 3 November). On 22 June 1940 Hitler made the French sign an armistice with victorious Germany in the same railway coach at the same spot as in 1918.

Arnold, Thomas (1795–1842). Born in the Isle of Wight, educated at Winchester and Corpus Christi, Oxford, and ordained. He was a Fellow of Oriel, 1815–19, and thereafter taught privately for nine years. Arnold disliked all forms of religious dogma and preferred non-liturgical services based upon sermons with high moral purpose. These beliefs shaped his policy as Headmaster of Rugby, 1828–42.

While offsetting some of the brutality of public-school life by giving responsibility to the sixth form, and while reforming the predominantly classical curriculum by the addition of mathematics, modern history, and French, Arnold concentrated above all on producing 'Christian gentlemen', moulding the character of his pupils, especially through his sermons each Sunday in Chapel – which he made the central feature of school life. Many of his methods had been tried elsewhere, but his success in grafting the prefectorial system on to an essentially religious foundation ensured their permanence in British public schools. In 1841 Arnold became Regius Professor of Modern History at Oxford (while continuing to be Headmaster of Rugby). He was the father of the poet, Matthew Arnold (1822–88).

Asquith, Herbert Henry (1852–1928). Created Earl of Oxford and Asquith, 1925. Born in Yorkshire, educated at City of London School and Balliol, became a barrister in 1876 and a Liberal M.P. in 1886. He was a successful Home Secretary in the Gladstone and Rosebery Governments of 1892–5 but incurred the displeasure of many of the Liberal Party by supporting the 'Imperialists' in the Boer War. Nevertheless, he was appointed Chancellor of the Exchequer in 1905 and was the obvious successor to Campbell-Bannerman as Prime Minister in 1908. The first years of his administration were marked by the conflict with the suffragettes (q.v.) and by the dispute with the House of Lords over the 'People's Budget' of 1909, which precipitated the Parliament Act of 1911 (q.v.). Asquith was also faced with severe industrial strife and by the threat of civil war in Ireland over the proposed Home Rule Bill, 1913–14. As wartime Prime Minister in 1915, Asquith was anxious to form a coalition government and thereby secure the maximum amount of political solidarity. He headed a coalition from May to December 1915, but, since it was believed that he lacked vigour, he was ousted by a combination of Lloyd George and the Conservatives. From 1916 to 1925 there was so serious a feud between Asquith and Lloyd George that the whole Liberal Party was weakened and ceased to be the normal 'alternative party' to the Conservatives.

Assignats. A word meaning first-mortgage. The assignats were a form of paper money issued in France by the Constituent Assembly in December 1789. They were used originally to anticipate the sale of confiscated lands and bore a five per cent interest (later abandoned). Assignats were legal tender from April 1790 to May 1797; they were grossly over-issued and produced severe inflation, and, despite attempts by the Directory (q.v.) to relate their value to a specified amount of land, they became worth less than one per cent of their face value and were withdrawn.

Ataturk. See *Kemal, Mustapha.*

Atlantic Charter. A statement of fundamental principles for the post-war world issued jointly by Roosevelt and Churchill after a series of meetings between 9–12 August 1941 aboard the U.S. cruiser *Augusta* and H.M.S. *Prince of Wales* in Argentia Bay, Newfoundland. The main terms were: (i) a renunciation of territorial or other aggrandizement by Britain and the U.S.A.; (ii) opposition to territorial changes contrary to wishes of the people immediately concerned; (iii) support for the right of peoples to choose their own form of government; (iv) support for easing of restrictions on trade, and access to raw materials on equal terms; (v) full collaboration between nations in economic fields after the war; (vi) the future peace must ensure freedom from want and fear; (vii) the future peace must guarantee freedom of the seas; (viii) aggressor nations must be disarmed pending the establishment of a general security system. On 15 September 1941, it was announced that fifteen nations fighting the Germans and Italians (including the Soviet Union) had endorsed the Atlantic Charter.

Atomic Bomb. A weapon of mass destruction by nuclear fission perfected by American and British scientists in the later stages of the Second World War, the first experimental bomb being exploded in the deserts of New Mexico on 17 July 1945. An American aircraft dropped an atomic bomb on the Japanese city of Hiroshima three weeks later (6 August), killing or seriously wounding over 160,000 people. A second bomb was dropped on Nagasaki on 9 August. The Japanese Government accepted terms of surrender on 14 August.

Attwood, Thomas (1783–1856). English political reformer, son of a banker. In January 1830 Attwood founded the Birmingham Political Union and for two years maintained a vigorous campaign for political reform and an equitable system of parliamentary representation. With the passage of the Parliamentary Reform Act of 1832, Attwood was elected an M.P. for Birmingham. Subsequently, he became a fanatical believer in currency reform and was closely associated with the Chartists (q.v.). In July 1839 Attwood presented the Chartist 'monster petition' to the House of Commons.

Ausgleich ('Compromise') of 1867. An agreement between the Austrian Government in Vienna, led by Count Beust, and the moderate

Hungarian politicians (especially Deák and Andrássy) providing for the transformation of the Austrian Empire into the Dual Monarchy of Austria-Hungary, and remaining valid until 1918. By the Ausgleich the territories of the Emperor Francis Joseph were divided into what was generally called 'Austria' (technically, 'the lands represented in the Imperial Parliament') and the Kingdom of Hungary. The two States were to have a common monarch, joint foreign relations, joint military and naval affairs, and a common finance ministry. Each State was to have its own Prime Minister and its own parliament, but sixty members from each parliament were to form the Delegations, a body summoned annually by the Emperor-King to meet alternately at Vienna or Budapest to discuss, independently of each other, matters relating to both States. A commercial union was negotiated at the same time; this was renewable every ten years and frequently produced strained relations between the Austrians and the Hungarians, notably in 1897. Tension was also caused by Hungarian attempts to secure greater independence for the Hungarian section of the Imperial and Royal Army. The Ausgleich left Croatia within the Kingdom of Hungary, and the Hungarians negotiated a separate agreement with the Croats in 1868. The other nationalities of Austria-Hungary (especially the Czechs) greatly resented the privileged position given to the Hungarians by the Ausgleich. An influential group within the Monarchy wished to form a Slav unit of the Empire, so as to keep a balance between the Austrians and the Hungarians, but their plans were cut short by the assassination of their leader, Archduke Francis Ferdinand (q.v.), and the consequent outbreak of the First World War.

Austerlitz. Decisive battle of the War of the Third Coalition, fought in Morávia on 2 December 1805 between Napoleon and the Russians and Austrians. Although Napoleon had forced the surrender of another Austrian army six weeks earlier at Ulm (q.v.), the arrival of fresh Russian troops gave the allies an advantage of 86,000 men to the French 70,000. The Russians planned to outflank the French right, but Napoleon had anticipated the move and made his main thrust at the weakened allied centre, breaking the line in half. The allies were routed, and lost 18,500 men to the French 900. The Austrians sued for peace, which was signed at Pressburg on 23 December 1805.

Australian Colonies Act of 1850. Allowed the four Australian colonies (New South Wales, Tasmania, South Australia, and Victoria) to draft constitutions and, subject to the approval of the

Privy Council, to form their own legislatures on whatever franchise they might choose. The colonies were thus given virtual self-government; the first constitution (for New South Wales) was adopted in 1855. The Act was the work of the second Earl Grey (1802–94), who was Colonial Secretary in Lord John Russell's Liberal Government of 1846–52. A proposal by Grey that the Act should be followed by the establishment of a general assembly for all Australia was rejected because it was thought that the distances were too great and the common interests too few; confederation did not come for another fifty years.

Australian Commonwealth Act (July 1900). Federated the Australian colonies. There had been a demand for federation ever since 1891, caused in part by a fear of French, German, and American imperial ambitions in the Pacific. A federal convention at Hobart worked out a provisional constitution in 1897, but it aroused opposition in New South Wales and was amended by a conference of colonial prime ministers in 1898. The Commonwealth of Australia came into being on 1 January 1901, but friction between the states was so intense that it was not until 1909 that agreement was reached on the site of the commonwealth capital – in 'neutral' Canberra.

Austrian Empire. Dates from 1804, when Francis II, perceiving the approaching end of the Holy Roman Empire (q.v.) had himself proclaimed 'Francis I, Emperor of Austria'. Because of the Napoleonic Wars, the territories comprising the Austrian Empire were not settled until the Treaty of Vienna (1815); as well as present-day Austria and Hungary, the Empire originally included Bohemia, Moravia, Galicia, Silesia, Slovakia, Transylvania, the Bukovina, Croatia-Slavonia, Carniola, Gorizia, Istria, Dalmatia, Lombardy, and Venetia. Eleven nationalities, and the absence of geographic or economic unity, hampered the establishment of effective central government, and throughout its existence the Empire fought a losing battle with those of its subject people (first the Italians, later the Rumanians and South Slavs) who wished to unite with others of their race already in nation-states beyond the frontier. The Habsburg dynasty sought a balance of national power within the Empire, playing off one nationality against another (notably in the Revolutions of 1848, q.v.) until forced in 1867 by the Ausgleich (q.v.) to change the Empire's character by conceding Hungarian demands. The support given by the Allies in the First World War to the aspirations for independence of political exiles (notably Masaryk, q.v.) made the disintegration of the Empire inevitable. The Treaties

37

of St Germain and Trianon of 1919–20 formally recognized the break up of the Empire.

Austrian Republic. With the withdrawal of Emperor Charles (q.v.) a republican government was established in Vienna (November 1918). In March 1919, a constituent assembly (with the socialist, Karl Renner, 1870–1951, as Chancellor) voted Austria an integral part of the German State, but as union with Germany was forbidden by the peace treaties, this vote was invalid, and a new constitution in October 1920 created a federation on the Swiss model. Between the wars, there was little 'Austrian' feeling in the Republic; political affiliations, outside Vienna, were regionally patriotic or Pan-German or nostalgically Habsburg. The Viennese, who formed a quarter of the population, suffered considerable economic privations through the peace treaties. Vienna became socialist, while the provinces were predominantly clericalist: there were frequent clashes between the rival 'private armies', the Heimwehr (fascist) and the Schutzbund (socialist) culminating in serious riots in Vienna in July 1927. All Austria suffered from the economic depression of 1931–2, which was worsened by the failure of a leading bank, the Credit Anstalt (May 1931). Under Chancellor Dollfuss (q.v.) a brief civil war led to the defeat of the socialists (February 1934) and the promulgation of a new, virtually fascist, constitution. An abortive Nazi putsch in July 1934 led to the murder of Dollfuss. His successor was Kurt von Schuschnigg (Chancellor, July 1934–March 1938), whose authority was weakened by increasing Nazi pressure culminating in the Anschluss (q.v.) of March 1938. From 1938 to 1945 Austria formed a province of 'Greater Germany'. With Allied occupation, a second, more stable, republic emerged under the experienced guidance of Karl Renner. By the Austrian State Treaty of 1955 the occupying powers recognized Austria's independence and neutrality; troops were withdrawn by the autumn of that year.

Axis, the Rome–Berlin. The name given to the cooperation of Nazi Germany and Fascist Italy between 1936 and 1945. The metaphor was invented by Mussolini in a speech at Milan on 1 November 1936: 'This Berlin–Rome line is not a diaphragm but rather an axis'. The speech followed a visit by Ciano, the Italian Foreign minister, to Hitler, resulting in a loose understanding for collaboration (the 'October Protocols'). This agreement was strengthened by the formal alliance of the two countries, the so-called 'Pact of Steel', 22 May 1939. Cooperation with Japan came with the Anti-Comintern Pact (q.v.) signed by Germany and Japan in November

1936 and by Italy a year later, and the Tripartite Pact (q.v.) of September 1940.

Babeuf's Conspiracy (1796). The outstanding example of extremist socialism during the French Revolution. François Babeuf (1760–97) had played an insignificant part in the early stages of the Revolution, but emerged as a political journalist in the autumn of 1794. During the Directory (q.v.) he formed, with a group of ex-Jacobins, a 'Society of Equals', which carried out intensive socialist propaganda within Paris. Babeuf believed in a simple social egalitarianism: his manifesto opened with the words: 'Nature has given each man the right to enjoy an equal share in all property'. His ideas thrived in the turmoil of the Directors' economic policy and some of the troops on the outskirts of Paris became disaffected. Babeuf spoke too freely of his plans; secret agents reported his intention of an armed rising on 11 May 1796. He was arrested on the eve of the conspiracy and his group broken up. A year later he was executed, together with one associate. Although his movement was ineffective in his lifetime and although Babeuf was himself uncertain of the precise way to consolidate the 'final revolution', he provided France with a tradition of revolutionary socialism that was to re-assert itself in 1848 and under the Third Republic.

Bagehot, Walter (1826–77). British political scientist. Born in Somerset, educated at Bristol and University College, London. Bagehot was a banker by profession, but he left his imprint on Victorian society as a man of letters. He was an able journalist on the *National Review* and *The Economist* (of which he was editor from 1860 until his death). His most important study was *The English Constitution* (1867), in which he tried to apply the new principle of scientific analysis to political society by penetrating through the forms of government to the realities of administration.

Bakunin, Mikhail (1814–76). Russian anarchist. Bakunin was born into an aristocratic family with estates near Tver and served as an officer in the Imperial Guard, but he resigned his commission in revulsion at Russian treatment of Polish rebels. From 1848 until his death Bakunin was at the centre of revolutionary unrest in many parts of Europe. He took part in the February Revolution of 1848 in Paris, stirred up the Czech demonstrations in Prague in the same year, and encouraged a revolt in Saxony in 1849. Sentenced to death by both the Prussians and Austrians, he avoided execution but spent years of imprisonment before being handed over to the Russians, who sent him to Siberia. He escaped from Siberia after six years (1861) and spent the rest of his life encouraging an anarchist revolt in western Europe. It was at this time that his friend Herzen (q.v.), who supplied him with money, described him as possessing 'the latent power of a colossal activity for which there was no demand'. Bakunin clashed with Marx and Engels in the First International (see *International Socialism*) from 1869 to 1872, and participated in anarchistic revolts in Lyons (1870) and in Spain (1873). His anarchism was essentially a personal emotional rebellion against society, and his impulsive character made him a dangerous colleague, but with his blend of merciless realism and naïve optimism he was the archetype of Russian revolutionary in the pre-Bolshevik era. His famous claim that 'the passion for destruction is also a constructive passion' was echoed by many of the young Russian 'nihilists'.

Balaklava, Battle of (25 October 1854). A battle of the Crimean War (q.v.). The Russians tried to seize the British base at Balaklava, but were repulsed by a Highland regiment and by the Heavy Brigade of cavalry. Confusion between the British commanders then led to the gallant, but militarily unnecessary, charge of the Light Brigade under Lord Cardigan. The commander of the British forces, Lord Raglan, ordered the divisional commander of the cavalry, Lord Lucan, to send his men forward in order to recover certain British-made guns captured by the Russians from the Turks. Lucan, misunderstanding the instructions conveyed by Raglan's emissary, despatched Cardigan's Light Brigade to seize the main Russian positions at the head of the valley and not to recover the guns. The Russian position was taken, but the Brigade lost a third of its men dead or wounded. The valour of the Light Brigade was immortalized in Tennyson's verse.

Balance of Power. The system of international relations based on the assumption that peace can be maintained only by ensuring that the threat of predominance by any one country or alliance is offset by the creation of a group of states of equal strength. This belief in the just equilibrium was a cardinal principle of British foreign policy throughout the nineteenth century, but was abandoned as a discredited device of the old diplomacy when the League of Nations was created in 1919.

Baldwin, Stanley (1867–1947, created Earl of Bewdley 1937). Educated at Harrow and Trinity, Cambridge. He became Conservative M.P. for Bewdley (his birthplace) in 1908, and held minor office in the Coalition Government of 1916–22, attaining Cabinet rank as President of the Board of Trade in 1921. On 19 October 1922 he played a prominent part in the famous meeting of the Carlton Club which took the Conservative Party out of the Coalition. He became Chancellor of the Exchequer under Bonar Law, whom he succeeded as Prime Minister in 1923, being preferred to Curzon (q.v.). On failing to get a clear majority in the 1923 election, Baldwin resigned, but returned as Prime Minister from 1924 to 1929, the period being marked by the General Strike (q.v.) and rising unemployment. He was Lord President of the Council in MacDonald's 'National Government' of 1931, becoming Prime Minister again in 1935. He resigned in 1937 after the Abdication Crisis (q.v.). His apparent political myopia in the face of resurgent German nationalism has been much criticized.

Balfour, Arthur James (1848–1930, created an Earl in 1922). The nephew of Lord Salisbury, for whom he acted as secretary at the Congress of Berlin. He achieved political distinction by his firmness as Chief Secretary of Ireland, 1886–92, and had the unique constitutional experience of becoming First Lord of the Treasury in 1895 while not holding the premiership. He succeeded his uncle as Prime Minister in 1902, but despite success in education reform and foreign affairs soon found his government split by the Tariff Reform (q.v.) proposals of Joseph Chamberlain (q.v.) and suffered a major defeat in the 1906 election. He remained leader of the Conservatives during the disputes over reform of the House of Lords, but by 1911 his habitual unhurried casualness had lost him the support of the party, and he resigned in favour of Bonar Law. During the wartime coalitions he served as First Lord of the Admiralty in 1915 and Foreign Secretary 1916–19. He headed a vital British mission to Washington after the U.S.A. entered the war and played a prominent part in shaping the new Europe; he was a signatory of the Treaty of Versailles and led the British delegation to the Washington Conference of 1921.

Balfour Declaration. A communication made on 2 November 1917 by A. J. Balfour, British Foreign Secretary, to Lord Rothschild, a leader of Zionism (q.v.), declaring British support for the establishment of a Jewish national home in Palestine provided that safeguards could be reached for the rights of the 'existing non-Jewish communities' in Palestine. The Declaration was soon confirmed by all the Allied governments and formed a basis for the League of Nations mandate for Palestine (q.v.) in 1920.

Balkan Wars. In March 1912 the rival Balkan states Bulgaria and Serbia were induced by Russian diplomatists to sign an alliance providing for future partition of Macedonia, then still a Turkish province. Greece and Montenegro duly associated themselves with this alliance and in October 1912 these four states attacked Turkey, gaining swift victories. The Great Powers, meeting in an Ambassadorial Conference in London, tried to end the war and succeeded, in May 1913, in securing a preliminary peace under which the Turks surrendered most of their European territories on the understanding that the Powers would create a new and independent state of Albania – an arrangement distasteful to Serbia and Montenegro, who wished to acquire the Albanian coastline. Friction arose between the Serbs and Greeks on the one hand and the Bulgarians on the other. The Bulgarians, who had suffered three-quarters of the casualties, rightly anticipated that Serbia and Greece were planning to divide Macedonia between them, giving only formal compensation to Bulgaria. The Bulgarians accordingly attacked the Serbs and Greeks (29 June 1913), but found themselves invaded by the Rumanians and the Turks (with whom the Serbs and Greeks were still technically at war!). Inevitably, the Bulgarians were rapidly defeated. The Treaty of Bucharest (August 1913) divided most of the territory claimed by Bulgaria in Macedonia and Thrace between Serbia and Greece, and also made Bulgaria cede southern Dobrudja to Rumania. The general effect of the Balkan Wars was: (i) to limit Turkey-in-Europe to the area around Adrianople and Constantinople; (ii) to create the ill-defined state of Albania; (iii) to double the size of Serbia and of Montenegro; (iv) to make Greece the most important power on the Aegean, possessing the key port of Salonica; (v) to leave Bulgaria bitterly resentful. This settlement was to determine the behaviour of the Balkan States during the First World War.

Ballot Act, 1872. Demands for secret ballot in British parliamentary elections had been advanced ever since the days of Chartism, since it was assumed that only strict secrecy could prevent bribery and intimidation. A select committee report of 1869 led Gladstone to introduce a Bill affording guarantees of secret ballot in 1870. This Bill was thrown out by the Lords. A second Bill a year later met with the same fate, but in the face of staunch opposition from the Commons the Lords gave way. The Ballot Act made it easier for radical politicians to secure election. It had important consequences in Ireland, where voters had been especially liable to intimidation from landowners. Without the Ballot Act there would have been no effective Irish Party.

Barras, Paul François (1755–1829). Member of a French aristocratic family, who adopted revolutionary principles after 1789 and became a Jacobin representative in the provinces, achieving fame when, with Captain Bonaparte, he organized the defence of Toulon. Again with Napoleon, he put down the Paris rising of Vendémiaire (1795); he subsequently became a prominent member of the Directory (q.v.). He arranged Napoleon's appointment as a General in Italy and also his marriage to Josephine de Beauharnais, a cast-off mistress of Barras. Although he assisted Napoleon once more during the Brumaire coup, his personal venality and excessive licentiousness repelled even the society of the Consulate and he was never thereafter given political employment.

Bastille, Fall of the. On 14 July 1789 the workers of the Faubourg St Antoine stormed the Bastille, the royal fortress that commanded the eastern side of Paris. They broke into the keep in the face of volleys from the garrison, butchered the Governor and the chief representative of municipal authority, and proceeded to dismantle the Bastille stone by stone. The fortress had gained exaggerated notoriety as a state prison from pamphlets circulating in France on the eve of the Revolution, and its fall was represented as a supreme gesture of defiance towards royal despotism. Traditionally, the events of this day mark the beginning of the French Revolution, and the 'Quatorze Juillet' is still celebrated as the National Day of Republican France. Modern historical interpretation has modified the legendary importance of these events in two ways: the mob attacked the Bastille, not to release prisoners, but to secure arms; and the attack represents, not the start of the French Revolution (which had been gradually gathering momentum over the previous two years), but the passing of the initiative from the lawyers of the States General (q.v.) to the fickle population of Paris. Nevertheless, it is agreed that no other dramatic event in the Revolution had such important consequences. Political authority was henceforth transferred to the national legislature, foreign regiments that the King could have used for a counter-revolution were withdrawn from the neighbourhood of Paris, and, within a few days, the red and blue colours of the city of Paris were merged with the white of the Bourbons to form the tricolour flag of the new France.

Bavaria. Region in southern Germany. Chief city Munich; became an Electorate in 1623 and a Kingdom in 1805. Bavarian politics in the early nineteenth century reflected popular discontent with the personal extravagance (and frequent lunacy) of the Royal House of Wittelsbach. Thus in Munich the 1848 Revolution was mainly a protest against King Ludwig's subservience to his mistress, the dancer 'Lola Montez' (born Eliza Gilbert). In 1871, Bavaria became a Kingdom within the German Empire, receiving largely illusory guarantees of influencing policy. In 1918 a short-lived Bavarian Soviet Republic was proclaimed in Munich by Kurt Eisner. A few months later Bavaria became an integral part of Republican Germany. An excessive German nationalism developed within Bavaria in the 1920s, encouraged by the chief minister, Gustav von Kahr (1862–1934). This tendency assisted the growth of the Nazis, who tried to seize power by the Munich Putsch (q.v.) of 1923 and who continued to use the Bavarian town of Nuremberg as the scene of their annual party rallies. Since the Second World War Bavaria has become the largest province in the German Federal Republic.

Baylen, Battle of. In the spring of 1808 the Spanish people rose in revolt against French domination. Underestimating the extent of the insurrection in the Spanish provinces, Napoleon ordered General Dupont to march southwards from Madrid with two divisions and restore order in Cadiz. Dupont was trapped by a Spanish force of 30,000 regulars (and supporting guerillas) under Castanos at Baylen (20 July 1808). The French were forced to capitulate. Although Napoleon restored much of his authority by the early campaigns of the Peninsular War (q.v.), he could never remedy the loss of prestige inflicted on his armies at Baylen; a national uprising destroyed the legend of French invincibility.

Beaconsfield, Earl of. See *Disraeli, Benjamin.*

Belgium. Became an independent kingdom in 1831, its people having revolted in August 1830 against the union with Holland imposed after the fall of Napoleon. The neutrality of Belgium was guaranteed by the Treaty of London (q.v.), 1839, reaffirmed during the Franco-Prussian War of 1870 but broken by the German invaders in 1914. The Belgian King, Albert (reigned 1909–34), appealed for the help of the British and French: a small segment of the country remained in Allied hands throughout the war. The rapid development of industry made Belgium between the wars the most densely populated country in Europe, although from the 1880s Belgium possessed a colonial outlet in the Congo (q.v.). On 10 May 1940, the Germans again invaded Belgium; after eighteen days of resistance King Leopold III ordered the Belgian Army to capitulate, thereby putting the British and French troops that had gone to Belgium's assistance in a desperate position. While the King remained a prisoner of war, the Government in exile continued to fight with the Allies. The King's conduct considerably lowered the prestige of the monarchy. He handed over the royal prerogative to his son, King Baudouin, in 1951.

Beneš, Eduard (1884–1948). Czechoslovak statesman. Beneš was born into a peasant family and educated at the Universities of Prague, Dijon, and Paris (where he gained his doctorate). In 1915 he escaped from Austria-Hungary and returned to Paris, where he joined Masaryk (q.v.) in the movement for Czechoslovak unity and independence. He became chief Czech representative in Paris; by his considerable powers of persuasion, he enlisted the support of several leading Frenchmen. He achieved much personal success as Czechoslovak representative at the Paris Peace Conference, and served as Foreign Minister from 1918 to 1935, when he succeeded Masaryk as President. Beneš made Czechoslovakia the lynch-pin of the Little Entente system (q.v.); he developed especially close ties with the French and Russians. The Munich Agreement (q.v.) of 1938 seemed to him to be a betrayal by the West, and he resigned the Presidency. In 1941 he became President of the exiled Czechoslovak Government in London, returning to Prague in 1945. Despite his earlier pro-Russian policy, Beneš now found himself distrusted by Stalin and he was forced to make more and more concessions to the Communists until eventually the party took over the Government in February 1948. Beneš finally resigned in June and died, a broken man, three months later.

Bentham, Jeremy (1748–1832). British philosopher and jurist. After an Oxford education, Bentham was called to the Bar but did not go into practice, concentrating his thought on questions of punishment and prison discipline. In 1776 he published a *Fragment on Government*, a reformer's attack upon the existing form of the law of England. By 1780 he had worked out his theories of philosophical jurisprudence, but he did not publish his *Introduction to the Principles of Morals and Legislation* until 1789. Bentham's philosophy, which is generally termed Utilitarianism, believed in 'the greatest happiness of the greatest number'; punishment is an evil, and can only be justified if it prevents worse evils. Hence Bentham saw in his own day the need to codify and reform criminal law, and he worked, too, for a more logical Poor Law (q.v.). Bentham was a great influence on Chadwick, Francis Place, Brougham, and Peel, and upon a generation of writers who, like him, attacked the abuse of justice and legal circumlocution.

Berlin, Conference of (November 1884–February 1885). A meeting of representatives of fifteen nations called by Bismarck to ease tension between the European Powers over partition of Central Africa. The immediate cause of the tension was British and Portuguese distrust of Belgian and French ambitions in the Congo and of German expansion in East Africa and the Cameroons. The Conference gave recognition to the Congo State (q.v.), affording it access to the sea; agreed on methods to suppress slavery and the slave trade; guaranteed freedom of navigation on the Congo and Niger Rivers; and made other decisions on spheres of influence so as to prevent the scramble for colonies leading to a major war. The Conference is also noteworthy for the cooperation of the Germans and French.

Berlin, Congress of. An international conference held in June–July 1878 under the presidency of Bismarck to revise the Treaty of San Stefano (q.v.) and achieve a balance in south-eastern Europe acceptable to the Great Powers. Most of the arrangements were privately settled in advance by diplomatic negotiations but were confirmed by the Treaty of Berlin: an autonomous principality of Bulgaria was created; a province of Eastern Roumelia, nominally Turkish but with a Christian Governor, was established south of Bulgaria; the independence of Serbia and Montenegro was confirmed, both states receiving territorial compensation; the independence of Rumania was confirmed, the Rumanians obtaining northern Dobrudja in return for ceding Bessarabia to Russia; Russia was confirmed in possession of the Caucasus; Austria-Hungary received the right to occupy Bosnia-Herzegovina and Novi-Bazar (q.v.), and Britain the right to occupy Cyprus. Other European lands ceded by Turkey at San Stefano were restored to her. Although Eastern Roumelia united with Bulgaria in 1885, the main lines of the settlement lasted for thirty years.

Berlin-Baghdad Railway. In 1899 a German company, with official backing, received a concession to construct a railway from Constantinople to the Persian Gulf. As German financial interests already dominated the lines of Central Europe and the Balkans, and had been active in Asia Minor for six years, this project was given the grandiose title 'Berlin-Baghdad Railway'. It was resented by the Russians (who themselves had plans for Persian railways), but met with a divided reception in Britain, some favouring it as a means of entangling Germany and Russia, others seeing a potential menace to India in a German-dominated port on the Gulf. With the adoption of the Entente policy and further Turkish concessions to Germany, British opinion hardened against the project. Russo-German differences were settled by an agreement in 1911, and an agreement early in 1914 satisfied the objections of the British and French, but only a small section of the line had been constructed by the outbreak of war. The project was, on the whole, a comparatively minor irritant in Anglo-German relations.

Bernadotte, Jean-Baptiste (1763–1844). Born at Pau, entered the French Army. Although not entirely trusted by Napoleon, he was made a Marshal in 1804 and created Duke of Ponte Corvo in 1806. He distinguished himself at the battles of Austerlitz and Wagram. When the heir to the Swedish throne died, Bernadotte was elected heir-apparent by the pro-French party in the Swedish parliament (August 1810), and ascended the throne as King Charles XIV in 1818. As Crown Prince he induced the Swedes to negotiate an agreement with the British and Russians, by which, in return for sending an army against Napoleon in Germany, Sweden was to receive Norway in the peace settlement. He accordingly led a Swedish army of 120,000 men in the Leipzig Campaign; Sweden acquired Norway by the Treaty of Vienna. He was an enlightened King, granting concessions to the Norwegians, handing over the control of Sweden's revenue to Parliament, accepting the principle of ministerial responsibility, and encouraging education. The ruling dynasty of Sweden is still the House of Ponte Corvo.

Bevin, Ernest (1881–1951). Born in Devon. After serving as a farm labourer, Bevin moved to Bristol, where he became a carter, working in close touch with the dockers. In 1911 he became Assistant General Secretary of the Dockers' Union, building up its power in the difficult period of syndicalist disturbances. In 1921 he united nearly fifty unions into the largest in the world, the Transport and General Workers' Union. Between the wars Bevin was distinguished by his brilliant presentation of the dockers' case before wage tribunals, by his power of compromise and conciliation within the trade union movement, and by his international outlook. He was a member of the T.U.C. General Council from 1925–40 and Chairman of the T.U.C. in 1937. He undertook a tour of the British Commonwealth in 1938–9 that improved labour relations with the overseas dominions. In May 1940, although not then an M.P., he was appointed Minister of Labour in Churchill's Coalition Government, with responsibility for the organization of the British working effort throughout the war. He became Foreign Secretary in the Attlee Government of 1945 and held the post until March 1951, five weeks before his death. As Foreign Secretary he was responsible for the Brussels Treaty of 1948, for the prompt acceptance of the Marshall Plan and for supporting the creation of N.A.T.O. in April 1949.

Bismarck, Otto von (1815–98, created a prince 1871). Came from a family of Junkers (q.v.) in Brandenburg. After serving in minor diplomatic posts he settled down as a country gentleman, until the political ferment of 1848. Regarded then as a narrowly Prussian reactionary, he temporarily left the country, but in 1851 became a delegate to the assembly of the German Confederation in Frankfurt and afterwards served as Ambassador in St Petersburg and Paris. In September 1862 he was appointed chief minister of Prussia, with the immediate task of completing army reforms despite parliamentary refusal of a grant; characteristically he solved this problem by governing without a budget. Bismarck's policy was ruthlessly realistic and opportunist; he believed in the inevitable unification of Germany, but was determined that it should be done under Prussian Junker leadership. With his Eastern frontier secure through a friendly understanding with Russia, he sought the elimination of Austria as a Germanic state and the replacement of France by Prussia as the arbiter of Europe. To achieve these ends he fought three wars; with Denmark (1864) over Schleswig-Holstein (q.v.); with Austria and the other German states (1866); and the Franco-Prussian War (q.v.) of 1870. On the proclamation of the German Empire at Versailles in January 1871 he became Imperial Chancellor and dominated European diplomacy for nineteen years. During this period he sought peace, as he considered Germany had reached her maximum practical size and he wished to avoid conflicts between other states that might have destroyed the balanced European order he had created; hence his policy of the 'honest broker' at the Congress of Berlin (q.v.). He prevented France from waging a war of revenge, by keeping her in diplomatic isolation through a system of alliances, first the Dreikaiserbund (q.v.) with the Russians and Austrians, later the Triple Alliance (q.v.) with the Austrians and Italians. Except for a brief period in 1878–9, he maintained amicable relations with Russia, culminating in the Reinsurance Treaty (q.v.) of 1887. He was less successful in home affairs, since he regarded parliamentary parties as states in miniature with whom he could make temporary alliances; thus he sided with the Liberals in 1871, but deserted them in 1879 when he thought Germany needed Protection rather than Free Trade. He distrusted movements with international affiliation; hence he was in conflict with the Roman Catholics in the 1870s (Kulturkampf, q.v.) and with the Socialists in the 1880s. He gradually found himself out of sympathy with the Pan-German enthusiasm of the younger generation, and was forced to resign in 1890 by the thirty-year-old William II after disagreements over home and foreign policy – an event generally remembered from the caption to the *Punch* cartoon, 'Dropping the Pilot'.

Björkö, Treaty of (24 July 1905). An abortive personal agreement reached by Kaiser William II and Tsar Nicholas II during visits to each other's yachts on a Baltic cruise; Russia and Germany were to form a defensive alliance against attack by any other power in Europe. The agreement was opposed by the Russian foreign office, on the ground that it betrayed their ally, France, and also by the German Chancellor, Bülow, whose resentment was roused by the independent initiative taken by the Kaiser. The Russians, dependent on French financial aid, declined to go further with the proposed alliance when they saw the start of Franco-German friction during the Moroccan Crisis (q.v.).

Black and Tans. During the Irish troubles of 1920 the British Government decided to recruit additional members for the Royal Irish Constabulary. Because of a shortage of regulation uniforms, the recruits were issued with khaki tunics and trousers and dark green caps, almost black. This dress caused them to be known as the 'Black and Tans' (a familiar breed of Irish hounds). The 'Black and Tans' were active in suppressing Irish national unrest from March 1920 until the formation of a provisional government for the Irish Free State (q.v.) in January 1922. Terrorist activity provoked the 'Black and Tans' into reprisals. The most serious of these were at Balbriggan, near Dublin, in September 1920 (when houses, public houses, and a factory were wrecked, and two Irishmen killed) and in Cork in the following December, when one of the main streets was set on fire and the County Hall and Library destroyed. These undisciplined acts aroused a considerable outcry in Britain, especially in the Liberal press, and in the U.S.A.

Black Hand. The name generally given to the Serbian secret society, *Ujedinjenje ili Smrt* ('Unity or Death') formed, mostly by young army officers, in Belgrade in May 1911 to work for the union of the Serbs living within the Austrian and Turkish Empires with their kinsfolk in Serbia proper. The Black Hand exerted considerable influence on Serbian policy in the Balkan Wars but clashed with the Serbian Government over the administration of the new lands won from the Turks. The leader of the Black Hand, Colonel 'Apis' Dimitriević, authorized the training of a group of young Bosnians in terrorist activity and sent them back into Bosnia to assassinate the heir to the Austrian throne and his wife at Sarajevo (q.v.) on 28 June 1914. During the First World War the Black Hand again fell foul of the Serbian Government (by then in exile), who arrested Dimitrievič and his main associates and accused them of plotting the murder of the Serbian Prince Regent. After a highly irregular trial at Salonica (June 1917) Dimitriević and two other Black Handers were shot and the society was broken up. In 1953 the verdict of the Salonica trial was quashed by the Serbian Supreme Court, and an attempt was made to rehabilitate the reputation of the Black Handers by the Yugoslav Communist authorities.

Blanc, Louis (1811–82). French socialist. Born in Madrid, where his father was in charge of financial administration during the French occupation. Although he had powerful connexions in his mother's family, they gave him no help, and as a law student in Paris, Blanc developed a grievance against society. In 1839 he published *L'Organisation du travail*, in which he preached an idealistic socialist doctrine, concentrating on a theory of equal wages. Two years later his *Histoire des dix ans* bitterly criticized the Orleanist Monarchy; he also undertook the historical rehabilitation of Robespierre as a friend of the labouring class. He was a member of the French Provisional Government from February to May 1848 and presided over the 'Luxembourg Commission' for eliminating unemployment. His personal panacea, 'National Workshops', proved a disastrous failure and, after the riots of June 1848, he fled to England, where he remained until 1871. He was a deputy for Marseilles under the Third Republic, but was not trusted by the French Marxists (although, in fact, Marx had appropriated many of Blanc's earlier theories).

Blériot, Louis (1872–1936). French airman. On 25 July 1909 Blériot became the first person to fly the English Channel, crossing from Calais to Dover in 37 minutes. The significance of the flight was fully appreciated by the British Government and the public. The War Office, for the first time, became interested in the development of aircraft; so, also, did the German General Staff.

'Bloody Sunday'. In Russian history, the term used to describe the incident in St Petersburg on 20 January 1905 when a procession of

workers and their families, led by a priest, Gapon, was fired on by
troops guarding the Winter Palace as it was carrying a petition to the
Tsar (who was not, in fact, in residence) asking for an amnesty for
political prisoners, the summoning of a Constituent Assembly, and
an eight-hour working day. There were several hundred casualties.
The incident led to strikes in many towns, thereby beginning the
'Revolution' of 1905 (q.v.).

Blücher, Gebhard von (1742–1819, created Prince of Wahlstadt,
1814). Prussian soldier. Blücher fought in the last battles of the
Seven Years War (1756–63) and in the campaigns against the French
revolutionary armies. When Napoleon defeated Prussia in 1806
Blücher continued to resist even after the fall of Berlin. He played
a prominent part in the 1813 campaign, gaining a decisive victory on
the Katzbach in Silesia and subsequently fighting at Leipzig. During
this campaign he was made a Marshal. In 1814 he led the Prussian
troops in France and entered Paris. Recalled upon Napoleon's return
from Elba, Blücher was given command of the Army of the Lower
Rhine. He was injured at Ligny by his own cavalry, but two days
after arrived at Waterloo with reinforcements at a vital moment in
the battle.

Blum, Léon (1872–1950). French statesman. Blum, like Dreyfus (q.v.),
was by birth an Alsatian Jew, and it was because of his sympathy for
Dreyfus that in 1899 he joined the socialist group led by Jaurès (q.v.),
abandoning thereby a promising career as a dramatic critic. (His
brother René, of similar tastes, became an outstanding French ballet
impresario, until murdered by the Nazis.) Léon Blum did not become
a Deputy until 1919, but by 1925 had established himself as leader
of the party. When, in June 1936, he became head of the 'Popular
Front' Government (q.v.), he was France's first socialist Prime
Minister. He remained in office for a year, introducing social reforms
which included the much-disputed '40-hour week'. Despite his determination to keep France's military potential up to the level of
Germany's, he had considerable difficulty with the French industrialists and, after his fall, only held office again for a few weeks in
1938. He was imprisoned by the Vichy régime in October 1940. In
1942 he was tried at Riom as a scapegoat for France's military unpreparedness, but he successfully turned the tables on his accusers.
Blum remained in custody until May 1945. At the end of 1946 he
played an important rôle in the formal institution of the Fourth
Republic.

Boer Wars. There were two wars fought between the British and the Boers (descendants of Dutch settlers in South Africa). (1) 1881, a brief conflict in which the Boers sought to recover the independence they had surrendered to the British four years earlier in return for protection against the Zulus. The Boers defeated the British at Majuba (February 1881) before Gladstone restored their independence by the Convention of Pretoria (q.v.). (2) 1899–1902, an attack on Cape Colony and Natal under the political leadership of Kruger (q.v.), the result of Boer irritation at the colonial policy of Chamberlain and belief in sympathetic support in Europe. There were three main phases to the War: (i) October 1899–January 1900, a series of Boer successes with British garrisons besieged in Ladysmith, Mafeking, and Kimberley; (ii) February–August 1900, British counter-offensives under Lord Roberts leading to the relief of the garrisons and the occupation of the Boer capital, Pretoria, on 5 June; (iii) September 1900–May 1902, a period of guerilla warfare with Kitchener trying to prevent Boer Commandos from raiding isolated British units by erecting blockhouses and moving civilian sympathizers with the Boers into concentration camps. The War was ended by the Treaty of Vereeniging (q.v.), May 1902.

Bolivar, Simon (1783–1830). Liberator of South America. Born in Caracas, Venezuela, of upper-class creole descent. He travelled extensively in Europe and was influenced by the French philosophers and Locke. In 1812 he participated in the disastrous first Venezuelan Republican rising led by Miranda (q.v.). He crossed into New Granada (Colombia) and organized forces which recaptured Caracas (1813) but, after bitter warfare, were again thrown out of Venezuela and eventually out of Colombia as well (1815). Three years later, Bolivar returned from Jamaican exile to the Orinoco Estuary, established a base at Angostura (now Ciudad Bolivar) and, with the help of British volunteers, crossed the Andes, proclaiming in December 1819 the independence of what are now Colombia and Venezuela (although, in fact, Venezuela's independence was not assured until 1821). In 1822, Bolivar expanded his activities into Ecuador, and with the retirement to Europe of San Martin (q.v.), assumed responsibility for the armed forces of Peru, leading them to victory in 1825 in the territory that was to be named after him, Bolivia. His plans for a great republican confederation broke on the separatist movements in Venezuela and Colombia (1829–30), and, faced with conspiracies from some of his most trusted lieutenants, he died in disillusionment. Bolivar was also an original political theorist; he was hampered by a naïve optimism that expected a broader vision from his compatriots than they possessed.

Bolsheviks. Originally the more violently revolutionary wing of the Russian Social Democratic Party in exile. At the second Congress of the Party, held in London in 1903, a vote was taken on the composition of the editorial board of *Iskra*, the Party newspaper. The vote gave a majority to Lenin's group, who thereupon assumed the name Bolsheviki (members of the majority), although, in fact, on most other issues at the Congress Lenin was outvoted. The more moderate socialist revolutionaries were known as Mensheviks (q.v.). The Bolsheviks remained a radical group within the Social Democratic Party until 1912, when they established a separate Central Committee at a Congress in Prague. The Bolsheviks came to power in Russia by the October Revolution of 1917. (See *Russian Revolution* and *Communist Parties*.)

Bonaparte Family. The Bonapartes (originally Florentines) settled in Corsica in the sixteenth century. The marriage of Carlo Bonaparte (1746–85) and Marie Ramolino (1750–1836) produced five sons and three daughters; the eldest son, Joseph, became King of Naples and died in 1844; the second son, Napoleon (1769–1821), became Emperor of the French; the third son, Lucien, was made Prince of Canino and died in 1840; the fourth son Louis (died 1846), became King of Holland, married Hortense Beauharnais (daughter of Napoleon's first wife by her first husband), and had three sons of whom the youngest became Emperor Napoleon III (q.v.); the youngest son, Jérôme, became King of Westphalia and died in 1860. Of the daughters, Élise married Felix Bacciochi; Pauline married, first, General Leclerc and, second, Camillo Borghese; and Caroline married Joachim Murat (q.v.).

Borodino, Battle of (7 September 1812). A bitter battle outside Moscow between Napoleon and the Russians under Kutuzov, in which both sides had heavy casualties. Although Kutuzov lost nearly half his men and was forced to abandon the city, the Russians were not routed, and re-formed during the month's lull before the retreat from Moscow (q.v.).

Bosnia-Herzegovina. A region in Yugoslavia. Bosnia-Herzegovina was occupied by the Turks in the fifteenth century and, even today, contains the largest group of Moslems in Europe outside Turkey. In the 1870s the provinces were moved by enthusiasm for union with their Serbian compatriots; in 1785 there was a serious uprising, which was suppressed by the Turks with customary cruelty. At the Congress of Berlin of 1878 Austria-Hungary was given the right to occupy the provinces, although they remained part of the Turkish Empire. The Austrians developed Bosnia considerably, treating the provinces as if they were colonial possessions and reducing Turkish authority to a mere formality. The Young Turk movement (q.v.) made the Austrians fear that their control would be challenged, and in consequence they formally annexed the provinces in October 1908. The annexation precipitated the Bosnian Crisis, since it was particularly resented by the Russians, who wanted compensation for increased Austrian power by concessions over the Straits. Although the menacing attitude of Austria's ally, Germany, forced Russia to accept the annexation (March 1909), it left much international bitterness. Moreover, the Serbs living in Bosnia began a terrorist agitation against Austrian rule which culminated in the 1914 assassination at Sarajevo (q.v.) and so led to war. Between the wars the provinces formed part of the Kingdom of Yugoslavia. From 1941 to 1945 the woods and mountain ravines of the region provided cover for bitter guerilla warfare. Bosnia-Herzegovina now forms one of the federated republics within Yugoslavia.

Bosphorus. The channel of water linking the Black Sea and the Sea of Marmora, on the European shore of which was built the city of Constantinople. The strategic position of the Bosphorus made it a point of dispute, the free passage of its waters forming part of the Straits Question (q.v.). In the 1890s the Russians planned to seize the Bosphorus by what is known, from the name of the Russian Ambassador to Turkey, as the 'Nelidov Project'. They considered the operation seriously in 1895 and again in 1896, but abandoned it because of the obvious hostility of the British Government.

Botha, Louis (1862–1919). Boer statesman and General, was brought up as a farmer and pioneered in new territories. He entered politics in 1897, seeking, in opposition to Kruger, a more moderate policy towards the British settlers. When war came in 1899 Botha rapidly emerged as a Boer leader, distinguishing himself at Colenso and Spion Kop and being placed in command of Transvaal troops in 1900. For eighteen months he conducted a guerilla campaign, but thereafter accepted the Peace of Vereeniging (q.v.) and worked for reconciliation. He was premier of the Transvaal from 1907 to 1910 and was so respected by the moderate Boers and by his former enemies that in 1910 he became the first Prime Minister of the Union of South Africa, a post he held until his death. In 1914 he put down a pro-German Boer revolt with firmness and clemency and subsequently commanded the troops that entered German South-West Africa, which surrendered to him in July 1915. Although he had difficulties at home in his last years with the more nationalistic Boers, he participated in the Paris Peace Conference and signed the Treaty of Versailles, urging on the allied powers a more charitable view of Germany. He died on returning to South Africa.

Boulanger, Georges (1837–91). French political general. Born at Rennes, served in Algeria and Italy, fought in the Franco-Prussian War and was promoted to Brigadier in 1880. Boulanger entered politics in 1884, originally as a protégé of the Radicals, especially Clemenceau (q.v.). As a reforming War Minister (1886) he showed himself to be a good republican, retiring prominent royalists from the Army, improving living conditions for officers and men, and demonstrating his patriotism by ordering the sentry-boxes to be painted red, white, and blue. He was a handsome figure and rapidly became popular; riding astride a magnificent black horse, he seemed a symbol of French military glory to those who were anxious to avenge France's defeat of 1870–1. When the Government fell in May 1887, Boulanger was relegated to a provincial command. Anxious to recover his lost position, he responded to overtures from right-wing groups, including crypto-royalists. By 1888 Boulanger had emerged as a would-be Bonaparte, attracting to his cause all the dissident politicians of the right who wanted a more authoritarian government. With the aid of a group known as the 'League of Patriots', he began a campaign for revision of the constitution. He was especially popular in Paris, and, at the height of the campaign, seemed about to stage a *coup d'état* in the capital (27 January 1889) but, in the last resort, lacked the nerve to overthrow the Government. Many of his disappointed supporters complained that their idol had been too responsive to feminine charms. After two months of hesitancy, he fled to Brussels and was condemned by a French court in his absence for treason. The Boulangist Movement could not survive his flight; although, in the next decade, many Boulangist political figures reappeared as supporters of the Army in the Dreyfus Case (q.v.). Boulanger lived on for two years in Belgium, but in 1891 he turned a revolver on himself over the grave of his mistress, provoking from Clemenceau the characteristic comment: 'He died as he had lived – like a subaltern.'

Boxer Rising. An outbreak of anti-foreign violence in China in 1900. Rapid development of European commerce and the acquisition of Kiaochow by Germany (1897), Port Arthur by Russia, and Wei-hai-wei by Britain (1898) had aroused ill-feeling in Northern China. With the connivance of the Government and the active support of the Dowager Empress Tzu Hsi (q.v.), young Chinese enrolled in a secret organization whose name was translated as 'The Society of Harmonious Fists', popularly termed 'Boxers'. Attacks on converts to Christianity, on missionaries, and on workers on foreign-controlled railways made the European Powers decide to take measures to safeguard their nationals. When reinforcements under Admiral Seymour tried to reach the capital, Peking, they were fired on by the forts at Taku. A Boxer outbreak at once occurred in Peking itself. On 19 June the German Minister was assassinated and the foreign legations placed in a state of siege. On 14 August the legations were relieved by a six-nation force, which thereupon looted the capital. A German expeditionary force, under von Waldersee, arrived later in the year and took strong punitive measures to avenge the murder of the German Minister. Boxer disturbances also occurred in the provinces of Shensi and Manchuria, which the Russians occupied, ostensibly to protect their railway interests. The methods used by the Powers in breaking up the Boxers intensified anti-foreign resentment and drove many young Chinese into the nationalist and republican movements of which Sun Yat-sen (q.v.) was the leader.

Bradlaugh, Charles (1833–91). British politician. The centre of a constitutional dispute during the second Gladstone Ministry. Bradlaugh was a rationalist lecturer who had been sentenced to imprisonment in 1876 for his share in a pamphlet advocating birth control. Although the sentence was quashed on appeal, he achieved an unenviable reputation in Victorian society for 'advanced' views. In 1880 he was elected Radical M.P. for Northampton. As a freethinker he claimed the right to affirm when taking his seat rather than swear the oath. The Speaker, Sir Henry Brand, referred his request to a select committee, which decided against him. Bradlaugh then offered to take the oath, but a group of Conservatives complained that since Bradlaugh was a freethinker, his oath would not bind him. Bradlaugh was thereupon excluded from sitting in the Commons. On three occasions he was re-elected for Northampton but was still excluded; in 1881 he was even forcibly removed by ten policemen. In 1886 a new Speaker, Peel, insisted that Bradlaugh had the right to take the oath. Bradlaugh remained an M.P. until his death and in 1888 secured the passage of an Oath Act, permitting affirmation in both the Commons and the law courts.

Brazil. Formally proclaimed a Portuguese possession in 1500. Napoleon's invasion of Portugal led the Regent, Prince John (King John VI, 1816–26) to move his capital to Rio de Janeiro in 1808 and begin modernizing Brazil. By 1821 the Brazilians had become resentful of Portuguese dominance and forced the King to return to Europe; his son Pedro remained as Regent, declaring Brazil independent and being proclaimed Emperor of Brazil in October 1822. Resistance by Portuguese garrisons was overcome by the Brazilian Navy, led by Lord Cochrane. Discontent in southern Brazil following a frontier dispute with Argentina led to the abdication of Pedro in 1831 in favour of his son, Pedro II, then aged five but ruling in his own right from 1840 to 1889. Under Pedro II there was considerable material progress and a growth of political liberalism; slavery was finally abolished in 1888. In the following year, an army revolt led to the establishment of a republic which adopted a federal constitution as 'The United States of Brazil' in 1891. The main problems facing the Republic were maintenance of good prices for coffee and rubber, and the rise in population (1850, 8 million; 1920, 30 million; 1950, 57 million). Social unrest in the 1920s led to a major revolt in 1930 led by Getulio Vargas. From 1930 to 1945 Vargas controlled Brazil and established a fundamentally fascist régime. Brazil, nevertheless, declared war on the Axis Powers in 1942 and, in sending an expeditionary force to Italy in 1944, became the first South American state to despatch fighting troops to Europe. After civil discord, Vargas returned as President in 1951, but committed suicide in 1954.

Brenner Pass. The lowest pass over the Alps and a route used over the centuries by the Teutonic invaders of Italy. The importance of the pass was increased when the Austrians constructed a railway over it in 1867. By the Treaty of St Germain (q.v.) of 1919, the area south of the Brenner Pass was assigned to Italy for strategic reasons, although 240,000 German-Austrians lived in the new Italian territories (known to the Austrians as 'the South Tyrol'). The Brenner Pass was a convenient meeting-place for Hitler and Mussolini, who conferred there in March 1940, October 1940, and June 1941.

Brest-Litovsk, Treaty of (3 March 1919). A peace conference between the Central Powers and the Russian Bolsheviks opened at Brest-Litovsk on 3 December 1917. By brilliant debating tactics, Trotsky, who headed the Russian delegation, delayed signature of a peace-treaty for nine weeks, in the hope that revolution would spread to

Germany and Austria. On 18 February the Germans, irritated by Russian prevarication, resumed their advance, and penetrated so deeply into Russia that Lenin ordered acceptance of German terms on 28 February. Three days later, the Russians signed the Treaty, which surrendered Poland, the Baltic provinces, the Ukraine, Finland, and the Caucasus. The Treaty was formally invalidated by the German Armistice in the West.

Briand, Aristide (1862–1932). French statesman. Born at Nantes. From 1894 to 1906 Briand was associated with the group of socialists led by Jaurès (q.v.), whom in 1904 he helped to found *L'Humanité*. In 1906 Briand was expelled from the Socialist Party for accepting office as Minister of Public Instruction and Worship in a Radical Coalition Government. He held this office until 1909, completing the separation of Church and State. He then succeeded Clemenceau as Prime Minister, bringing on his head the hostility of his former comrades when, in 1910, he broke a railway strike by calling up striker reservists for military service. Between 1909 and 1929 Briand headed eleven Governments, but was Prime Minister for only 58 months. As wartime Prime Minister (October 1915–March 1917) Briand lacked vigour, but, during the late twenties, his was the dominant voice in French foreign policy. He was a strong supporter of the League of Nations, an advocate of international arbitration and a champion of Franco-German reconciliation (cf. *Locarno Treaties*).

Bright, John (1811–89). British radical leader. The son of a Rochdale millowner and member of a Quaker family. In 1841 Bright left the family business for political work, becoming associated with Cobden in the Anti-Corn Law League (q.v.). He was Liberal M.P. for Durham in 1843 and for Manchester from 1847 to 1857. He was always independently minded and never hesitated to follow an unpopular line if his conscience dictated it – thus he strongly opposed the Crimean War and the Liberal Government's Egyptian venture of 1882. Apart from his agitation against the Corn Laws and his frequent criticism of foreign policy, Bright was partly responsible for securing the admission of Jews to the House of Commons (1858), for the abolition of the East India Company, and for the campaign culminating in the Reform Act of 1867. He held office as President of the Board of Trade in Gladstone's Government of 1868; later he disagreed with Gladstone over Egypt and Irish Home Rule.

Bristol Riots (29–31 October 1831). The worst instance of unrest in the controversy over Parliamentary Reform (q.v.). The narrow streets of old Bristol were ideal centres for mob violence, and there had been three serious outbreaks of disorder there in the eighteenth century. Rioting began with the arrival of a newly appointed Recorder of Bristol, Sir Charles Wetherall, an outspoken opponent of reform in the Commons. The Mansion House was wrecked, the Bishop's palace set on fire, and other public buildings attacked. The magistrates lost their nerve and called in troops. A cavalry charge restored order, after bloodshed. Four of the rioters were executed and twenty-two transported. The riots caused alarm in London, where it was feared that, if they spread to other towns, they might spark off a revolution.

Britain, Battle of. The conflict between the R.A.F. and the German Air Force (Luftwaffe) in British skies between 10 July and 31 October 1940. The Germans, with an initial force of over 1,350 bombers and 1,200 fighters, launched a series of attacks, first against shipping, then against airfields, and finally against the towns, the whole operation being a prelude to invasion. The main air defence was the 'Hurricane' and 'Spitfire' fighters, which were, on the average, outnumbered three to one by the attackers. The climax of the battle fell on 15 September, when 56 German planes were destroyed (confused reports led to an original British claim of 185). When the invasion plan was postponed, the Germans changed their tactics and resorted to indiscriminate bombing of the larger cities, especially London, with the main attacks falling at night. During the twelve-week battle 1,733 German aircraft were destroyed for the loss of 915 British fighters.

British North America Act, 1867. United Quebec, Ontario, Nova Scotia, and New Brunswick in the Dominion of Canada (proclaimed 1 July, 1867). The Act reflected public concern in Canada over religious and racial differences, difficulties of inter-provincial railways, and defence (especially after the start of the American Civil War). Conferences were held in Charlottetown and Quebec in the autumn of 1864; agreement was reached on a confederation with provincial governments and a bicameral federal parliament. These proposals were discussed in London in 1866 and formed the basis of the Act, introduced into Parliament by Lord Derby's Government.

Brougham, Henry (1778–1868, created Baron Brougham and Vaux in 1830). Born and educated in Edinburgh, called to Scottish Bar (1800) and English Bar (1808), helped to found the *Edinburgh Review*, 1802. As an M.P. after 1810 he favoured legal reforms and slave emancipation. His defence of George IV's consort, Caroline, when she returned from abroad to claim her rights as Queen in 1820, won him wide popularity. Throughout his political career he showed interest in education, and helped found London University in 1828. As Lord Chancellor (1830–4) he introduced rational reforms in the legal system and supervised the passage of the 1832 Reform Bill through the Lords. He gave his name to a particular type of carriage which he customarily used.

Brown, John (1800–59). A deeply religious fanatical believer in the emancipation of American slaves. Brown first attracted attention in May 1856 when, with four sons and three companions, he raided Pottawatomie Creek in Kansas and killed five pro-slavery settlers to avenge an attack they had made on anti-slavery headquarters in Lawrence. In the following August, Brown had to defend Osawatomie against a strong force of pro-slavery attackers. He then left Kansas and toured New England as a hero of the abolitionists. There he conceived a plan for a slave rising in Virginia, which was to lead to the formation of a free state in the southern Appalachians. To start the rising, Brown raided the Federal Arsenal at Harper's Ferry (October 1859). No slaves joined the raiders, and, after two days of shooting, Brown surrendered to a force of marines, commanded by Robert E. Lee (q.v.). He was tried for treason and hanged (2 December). Brown's action made the dispute over slavery more bitter; the Southerners complained that abolitionist propaganda was inciting the negroes to massacre, while abolitionists regarded him as a martyr-hero.

Brumaire. The 'foggy month' in the calendar adopted by the French revolutionaries, the period between 21 October and 20 November. Napoleon's *coup d'état* of 18 Brumaire (9 November 1799) established the Consulate (q.v.). The two parliamentary chambers of the Directory (the Council of the Ancients and the Council of the Five Hundred) were summoned to St Cloud, a small town north of Paris, where they were intimidated by troops under Napoleon and Murat. With some difficulty, they were induced to nominate three provisional Consuls (Napoleon, Sieyès, and Ducos) and were then dispersed.

Bulgaria. Slav state in the eastern Balkans. Although there had been a powerful Bulgarian Empire in the tenth century, modern Bulgarian nationalism remained essentially cultural until 1870 when the Turks, who had occupied Bulgaria for 500 years, authorized the establishment of a Bulgarian Exarchate (i.e. separate branch of the

Orthodox Church). With Russian backing, the Exarchate encouraged nationalist agitation which the Turks tried to suppress with cruelty in 1875–6, thereby provoking war with Russia. The resultant Treaty of San Stefano (q.v.) of 1878 re-established a Bulgaria as extensive as it had been in the Middle Ages, but a few months later the Treaty of Berlin limited autonomous Bulgaria proper to the region north of Sofia and made southern Bulgaria a separate province within the Turkish Empire, known as Eastern Roumelia. In 1885 the Bulgarians, under Stambulov (q.v.), defying the Great Powers, united Bulgaria and Eastern Roumelia, defeated the Serbs at Slivnitza, and staked a claim as the dominant Balkan people. Under Ferdinand of Saxe-Coburg (1861–1950; Prince of Bulgaria 1887–1911, King 1911–18) Bulgaria followed a tortuous policy of balance between the rival Great Powers. Disappointed in the Balkan Wars, Bulgaria sided with the Germans in 1915, but was severely defeated on the Salonica Front in September 1918. After a period of peasant dominance under Stamboliisky (q.v.), Bulgaria became virtually a dictatorship under royal nominees, political life being dangerously enlivened by the terrorists known as I.M.R.O. (q.v.). King Boris (1894–1943, reigned from 1918) joined the Germans in occupying Yugoslavia in 1941, but astutely kept out of the Russian campaign. The Russians, however, invaded Bulgaria in September 1944 and set up a predominantly communist régime headed by the veteran international revolutionary, Georgi Dimitrov (1882–1949).

Bull Run (Virginia). Due west of Washington, site of two battles in the American Civil War: (1) 21 July 1861, when the Confederate General Thomas J. Jackson (1824–63) kept off Union forces with such effect that he was thereafter known as 'Stonewall Jackson'; (2) 29–30 August 1862, a Confederate victory which would have endangered Washington had it been properly exploited.

Bülow, Bernhard von (1849–1929). German statesman, son of Bernhard Ernst von Bülow (1815–79), who was Bismarck's Foreign Minister from 1877 to 1879. The younger Bülow entered the German diplomatic service in 1874, eventually becoming Ambassador in Rome (1894) and, in 1897, Foreign Minister. He was, at first, especially favoured by Kaiser William II, who created him Chancellor in 1900, hoping to make him 'a second Bismarck'. Bülow's lack of passionate convictions made him essentially weak, although he was an adroit diplomatist. He had few ideas on domestic policy and, even in foreign affairs, was dominated by others, notably Holstein (the influential Counsellor of the Foreign Office) and Admiral Tirpitz (q.v.). Relations between Bülow and William II deteriorated because of the Kaiser's tendency to take serious steps in foreign affairs without consulting his ministers. After an interview accorded by the Kaiser to the *Daily Telegraph* in October 1908, it was only a matter of time before Bülow resigned. When he did so (July 1909) the ostensible reason was differences with the Reichstag over his budget proposals. In December 1914 Bülow returned to Rome as Ambassador, vainly striving to prevent Italy from joining Germany's enemies.

Burke, Edmund (1729–97). Born and educated in Dublin, became a lawyer, but showed more interest in political journalism. As a Rockingham Whig M.P. he established his reputation as an orator by opposing duties on the American trade. His *Thoughts on the Present Discontents* (1770) attacked the revived power of the Crown under George III. In the seventeen-eighties he concentrated on exposing political corruption and the evils of Indian administration under Warren Hastings. Despite his Whig principles, he reacted against the French Revolution earlier than most of his compatriots, seeing in the new ideas a menace to British traditions. His *Reflections on the French Revolution* (1790) lost him the support of Fox. Burke was the most eloquent speaker in favour of war with France in 1793 and spent the last four years of his life assisting French refugees. Despite his defence of American liberties and his attacks on the East India Company, Burke was an essentially conservative thinker, basing his condemnation of royal power on veneration for the political settlement made by the Whigs in 1688 and his hostility to the Revolution on a distrust of the demagogic elements in democratic representation.

Burma. Although there was a formidable Burmese Empire in the eleventh and twelfth centuries, the country was subsequently in a state of chronic civil war, from which it recovered in the middle of the eighteenth century under the ambitious ruler, Alompra of Ava. In 1824 the threat of a Burmese invasion of Bengal led to the dispatch of a British military expedition, which captured Rangoon in 1826 and forced the cession of territory in southern Burma and a renunciation of Burmese claims on Assam. In 1852, after hostile acts to British traders, a second Burma War led to the annexation of the Irrawaddy Delta. Finally in 1885 King Thibaw, with French encouragement, confiscated the Bombay-Burma Company's property, thus bringing down on his country a force of 10,000 British and Indian troops, who deported the King and occupied the remainder of Burma. In 1886 Burma became a province of the Indian Empire.

It was detached from India in 1937 and given some self-government. The Japanese invaded Burma in February 1942 and were at first welcomed as liberators, since they established an all-Burmese government. When Burma was reoccupied by the British in May 1945, an understanding was reached with the moderate Burmese nationalists. An independent Burma came into being in 1948.

Burns, John (1858–1943). British socialist. Born in Vauxhall of Scottish descent, apprenticed to engineering. Burns learned his socialism from a Communard exile and acquired his gift of oratory from temperance meetings, before becoming a trade unionist. He was arrested in 1886 and again in 1887 for incitement to violence at meetings in the West End of London; on the second occasion he was imprisoned for six weeks. He became a member of the L.C.C. in 1889 and, in the same year, played a prominent part in organizing the first major London Dock Strike. From 1892 to 1918 he was M.P. for Battersea and held office in the Liberal Governments from 1905 to 1914 as President of the Local Government Board and, for a few months, as President of the Board of Trade. He opposed participation in the First World War and resigned from the Government, virtually withdrawing from political life.

Burschenschaften. In 1815 there was disappointment among the younger generation of Germans at the failure of the Congress of Vienna to create a united Germany. A group of students at Jena formed a society pledged to combine personal virtues of sobriety and chastity with the patriotic purpose of achieving national unity. Within two years similar student societies, Burschenschaften, had developed in fifteen other universities. They achieved notoriety by a patriotic festival held at Eisenach in 1817 on the tercentenary of Luther's first act of defiance. The murder of a Russian agent, Kotzebue, in 1819 and other minor crimes afforded Metternich the opportunity of denouncing the Burschenschaften and securing passage of the repressive Carlsbad Decrees (q.v.), which effectively cooled patriotic ardour. The Burschenschaften were the prototype of many patriotic student organizations that flourished in the European countries seeking national unity in the nineteenth century.

Cabinet System. The British Cabinet, as the supreme executive committee of Parliament, emerged out of the more cumbersome Privy Council early in the eighteenth century and achieved a regular, although informal, position in the constitution under Walpole in the 1720s. It remained ill organized and cannot be said to have assumed its modern form until the days of Peel (q.v.). Cabinet discussions remained not only secret but unrecorded until 1916, when a Secretariat was established. At the same time, the Imperial War Cabinet was constituted as an inner executive group to deal with the international emergency; it included Commonwealth statesmen, and its members were free from departmental duties. The U.S. Cabinet was instituted by Washington when he summoned together his departmental heads at the end of 1791. Regular Cabinet meetings began only with the presidency of Adams (1797–1801). The American Cabinet has remained much smaller than its British counterpart; it has never exceeded a dozen members, while most modern British Cabinets have contained about twenty.

Cambon Brothers (Paul, 1843–1924; Jules, 1845–1935). Distinguished French diplomats who in 1914 held the key embassies of London and Berlin. Paul was Ambassador in Madrid 1866–91, Constantinople 1891–8, and London 1898–1920. Although he arrived in Britain during the tension over Fashoda, he worked throughout his mission for cooperation, achieving the Anglo-French Entente of 1904 and the military alliance of the First World War. Jules was Governor-General of Algeria 1891–7, Ambassador in Washington 1897–1903, in Madrid 1903–7, in Berlin 1907–14, and a delegate to the Paris Peace Conference of 1919.

Campbell-Bannerman, Henry (1836–1908, knighted 1895). The son of a Lord Provost of Glasgow, became a Liberal M.P. in 1868, and held various departmental posts before entering the Cabinet as Secretary for War in 1886, a post he also held from 1892 to 1895. Although an indifferent parliamentary orator, he became Liberal leader in the Commons in 1898 and enhanced his prestige and popularity in the ensuing six years by identifying himself increasingly with the progressive wing of his party; thus, he opposed the Boer War and began to call for radical reforms. He became Prime Minister in December 1905, but his health was already bad and he was forced to resign in April 1908. His Government began a series of social reforms at home and reconciliation in South Africa, which culminated in the grant of self-government.

Campo-Formio, Treaty of (October 1797). A peace settlement arranged by Bonaparte between Austria and France, showing many Napoleonic characteristics, particularly the playing off of one potential enemy against another. 'Belgium' was transferred from Austria to France; France gained the Ionian Islands and the establishment in northern Italy of a 'Cisalpine Republic'; the Austrians were to receive Venice and all her territories; a Congress, to be summoned at Rastatt, would settle the future of Germany. Secret clauses promised France large areas of the left bank of the Rhine, while Austria would receive Salzburg and part of Bavaria. It was agreed that Prussia would have no territorial compensation. By allowing France to annex Italian territory, the treaty sowed the seed of future discord.

Canadian Federation. See *British North America Act, 1867.*

Canadian Pacific Railway. When British Columbia joined the Dominion of Canada in 1871, it was agreed that a transcontinental railway should be constructed within ten years. A series of scandals over contracts delayed the project, and it was not until 1881 that a charter was granted to the Canadian Pacific Railway Company for a line linking Upper Canada and Vancouver. The Company took over the 650 miles of track already laid and completed the line, 2,900 miles long, by November 1885, although it was not officially opened until May 1887. It had important consequences on the growth of Canada, facilitating internal migration and opening up the prairies.

Canning, George (1770–1827). British statesman. Born in London, educated at Eton and Christ Church. Although at first a Whig, Canning became a supporter of Pitt during the French Revolution and served him in various minor offices, 1796–1800 and 1804–6. In 1807 he became Foreign Secretary and was largely responsible for ordering the second bombardment of Copenhagen (q.v.) and for the decision to wage the Peninsular War. He remained out of the Cabinet from 1809 to 1816 because of a quarrel with Castlereagh (q.v.), which ended in a duel. He was about to take up the post of Governor-General of India in 1822 when Castlereagh's suicide brought him back to the Foreign Office, where he remained for five years. Canning possessed a felicitous turn of phrase, in contrast to the clumsy oratory of his predecessor, and accordingly there appeared a greater difference between his policies than in fact existed. Canning carried further Castlereagh's abandonment of the Congress System. He openly supported the revolt of the Spanish American colonies, co-operating with the Americans in making the Monroe Doctrine (q.v.) effective. His attempt to settle the Greek War of Independence led, after his death, to the battle of Navarino (q.v.). He was Prime Minister for the last five months of his life, inaugurating a progressive policy of moderate Tory Reform.

Canning, Stratford. See *Stratford de Redcliffe.*

Cape Colony. Cape Town was captured by the British from the Dutch in 1795, restored to the Dutch in 1801, retaken in 1806, and finally ceded to Britain in 1814. During its early years, the two main problems of the Colony were the raids by Kaffir tribes (which necessitated five military campaigns) and the relationship between British emigrants and the Dutch settlers (Boers), culminating in the Great Trek (q.v.) of 1835. A Legislative Council was established in 1837, representative government following in 1853. Cape Colony assumed responsibility for Natal in 1843, but was involved in long disputes with the Boers over the Orange River territory, which was eventually allowed to become a 'Free State' in 1854 by the Bloemfontein Convention. The discovery of diamonds in the hinterland (1867–70) led to a further wave of emigration. Cecil Rhodes (q.v.) as premier from 1890 to 1896 pursued a forward policy towards the Transvaal which contributed to the Boer War of 1899–1902. With the establishment of the Union of South Africa (q.v.) in 1910, Cape Colony became the province of Cape of Good Hope.

Caporetto, Battle of (24 October–4 November 1917). In the first two years of war, the Italians fought some eleven battles with the Austrians along the Isonzo River, but advanced only ten miles. In the autumn of 1917, the Central Powers massed six German and nine Austrian divisions on the Isonzo and broke the Italian line at Caporetto on 24 October, advancing as much in one day as the Italians had in two and a half years. Within three days the Italians were routed and the front was only stabilized early in November with the arrival of British and French reinforcements and through the inability of the Austrian supply services to keep up with the victorious troops. Nearly 300,000 Italians were captured during the battle and as many again deserted; the magnitude of this humiliation had important political repercussions, the Fascists subsequently being anxious 'to wipe out the stain of Caporetto' by over-emphasizing military virtues.

Carbonari (the 'Charcoal-burners'). Most famous of Italian secret societies. Established after the restoration of the Bourbon rulers of Naples in 1815. The Carbonari were republicans aiming at national unity and the overthrow of existing Italian governments. Although based on Christian humanitarianism, the movement borrowed Masonic symbolism and ritual. It was responsible for unsuccessful revolts in Naples and Piedmont in 1820 and 1821, and for a wider series of risings in 1831. The Carbonari lacked clear leadership, and tended to promote isolated and sporadic revolts which could be easily suppressed. After the disappointments of 1831, the movement was absorbed in the 'Young Italy' brotherhood of Mazzini (q.v.). In the years 1816–20 there was also a Carbonari Movement in France.

Cardwell, Edward (1813–86, Viscount 1874). Born at Liverpool and educated at Winchester and Balliol. Cardwell entered Parliament as 'Peelite' Member for Clitheroe in 1842. He held minor offices in the Aberdeen and Palmerston Governments, but achieved distinction as Secretary for War in the Gladstone Government of 1868–74. He expanded and modernized the Army so as to meet the situation created by Prussia's decade of victories. He abolished many of the savage peacetime punishments and the purchase of commissions, introduced a system of short-service enlistment, withdrew troops from self-governing colonies, re-arranged regiments according to geographical districts, established the 'linked battalion system' (one battalion remaining in the home depot while the other was on foreign service), and equipped the infantry with efficient breech-loading rifles. Cardwell's reforms enabled the Army to fight its colonial campaigns during the epoch of imperialism; it was left to another War Minister, Haldane (q.v.), to prepare for a European War.

Carlists. The supporters of the claims of Don Carlos (1788–1855) and his descendants to the Spanish throne. Shortly before his death in 1833, Ferdinand VII of Spain declared that his kingdom was no longer bound by the Salic Law (which excluded women from the throne) and that consequently his daughter Isabella should succeed him. Isabella's rights were challenged by Ferdinand's brother, Don Carlos, who began a full-scale civil war in 1834 with much of the north of the country and the conservative aristocracy supporting him. The Carlist disorders helped to leave Spain in a political backwater while momentous changes were taking place in the rest of Europe. Although the first Carlist War was ended in 1837 and Don Carlos forced to leave the country, disorder continued throughout Isabella's reign (1833–68). In 1870 open war was resumed by the original claimant's grandson, also called Don Carlos (1848–1909), who was recognized as King Charles VII by the Pope. After military defeats in 1872 and 1874, the accession of his cousin, Alfonso XII, deprived him of much of his support, and in February 1876 he was forced to flee to France. Sporadic Carlist disorders continued for another twenty years in the mountainous north.

Carlsbad Decrees, 1819. A series of measures agreed by representatives of the German states meeting under the presidency of Metternich (q.v.) at Carlsbad (now Karlovy Vary) in August 1819, and applied to the German Confederation in the following month. Political meetings were prohibited, a general surveillance of the educational system was ordered, and there was strict press censorship. The decrees were necessitated by the patriotic agitation in the German universities led by the Burschenschaften (q.v.), who were held responsible for the murder of a Tsarist agent, Kotzebue. The Carlsbad Decrees inaugurated a period of thirty years of Austrian domination, during which the German states were, with varying degrees of efficiency, under a repressive police system.

Carlyle, Thomas (1795–1881). British historian. Born in Ecclefechan, Dumfriesshire. Educated at Edinburgh University and became a schoolmaster. He had little literary success in Scotland and came south to London in 1834 where he wrote *The French Revolution*, which established him as a leading man of letters in 1837. His other works included *Sartor Resartus* (1838); *Heroes, Hero-Worship and the Heroic in History* (1841); *Past and Present* (1843); and a life of Frederick the Great (1858–65). His ideas influenced a generation of liberal reformers, although there were inconsistencies between the philosophy of his earlier and later works. His Calvinistic preoccupation with duty made him overrate the element of personal responsibility in history. At the same time, his awareness of evil enabled Carlyle to disturb the conscience of an age dominated by a complacent acceptance of material progress.

Carnarvon, Henry Molyneux Herbert, Lord (1831–90, became fourth Earl of Carnarvon in 1849). An early British enthusiast for colonialism. After serving as Colonial Under-secretary in the Derby Government of 1858–59, he was Colonial Secretary from 1866 to 1867 and again from 1874 to 1878. In this capacity he was responsible for the British North America Act (q.v.) of 1867, for the purchase of Griqualand West by Cape Colony and the annexation of the Transvaal in 1877. His schemes for the federation of South Africa were premature.

Carnegie, Andrew (1835–1919). Archetype of American millionaire industrialist and philanthropist. Born in Dunfermline in great poverty, Carnegie emigrated in 1848 and became a telegraph office messenger in Pittsburgh. By the age of nineteen his initiative had made him private secretary to the Superintendent of Pennsylvania Railroads. Carnegie stayed with Pennsylvania Railroads until 1865, rising rapidly through a series of administrative posts; he did valuable work for the telegraph services of the Union forces in the Civil War. He soon realized that America's industrial future depended on the development of iron and steel. From 1873 he concentrated entirely on the steel industry, and within twenty-five years built up, by purchase or lease, a huge steel 'empire'. By the end of the century, the U.S.A. was producing more steel than either Britain or Germany, and Carnegie's Steel Company controlled the industry. In 1901 he retired, selling his interests to the U.S. Steel Corporation. For the rest of his life Carnegie devoted himself to philanthropy, endowing foundations for educational work and the promotion of international peace.

Carnot, Lazare (1753–1823). As a member of the Committee of Public Safety organized the first of the 'citizen armies' of France, 1793–4. He was so indispensable to the French war effort that he remained as a member of the Directory until 1797, when he fled to Switzerland. Napoleon brought him back as Minister of War in 1800–1, and he served again as Minister of the Interior during the Hundred Days of 1815, being subsequently exiled by Louis XVIII.

Carson, Edward (1854–1935, knighted 1900, life peer 1921). Born and educated in Dublin, entered Parliament as M.P. for Dublin University in 1892. He became a formidable barrister. From 1900 to 1905 he was Solicitor-General. During the Liberal Government of 1905–15 Carson led the British Protestant resistance to Home Rule (q.v.), and in 1911 he set up an Ulster Unionist Council, which prepared a draft constitution for Ulster (q.v.). In 1912 he organized a volunteer force of 80,000 men, a 'private army' pledged to resist Home Rule. Carson entered the Asquith Coalition as Attorney-General in 1915 but soon left the Government and became a leader of dissident Tories. In 1916 he joined Bonar Law and Lloyd George in securing the resignation of Asquith and subsequently became a member of the War Cabinet. After the war, Carson tried to find a compromise solution of the Irish problem; his restraint was in marked contrast to the pre-war period. He was Lord of Appeal from 1921 to 1929.

Cartwright, Edmund (1741–1823). British inventor. Born in Nottinghamshire, educated at Oxford, and took holy orders. While Rector of a living in Leicestershire, he perfected a machine for power weaving (1785). As a Prebendary of Lincoln Cathedral, he tried to open the first factory using power looms (1786) but his venture failed. The

Cartwright loom was, however, adopted by the factories that transformed the weaving industry in Britain between 1800 and 1812.

Casablanca Conference. A meeting in North Africa between Roosevelt and Churchill, 14–24 January 1943, at which it was determined to insist on the eventual 'unconditional surrender' of Germany and Japan. Attempts to overcome friction between Roosevelt and the 'Free French' under de Gaulle met only limited success. The Combined Chiefs of Staff settled strategic differences over the projected invasion of Sicily and Italy.

Casement, Roger (1864–1916, knighted 1911). Born near Dublin, entered the British Consular Service in 1892 and gained distinction by reports in 1903 and 1910 on the harsh conditions predominating in the rubber industries of the Congo and of Brazil. Shortly after his knighthood he retired from the Consular Service and became a fervent Irish Nationalist. In 1914 he was in the U.S.A. and determined to enlist German aid to gain independence for Ireland. He went to Berlin and, for eighteen months, tried without success to induce Irish prisoners of war to form a brigade in the German Army. In April 1916, on the eve of the 'Easter Rising' (q.v.), he was landed from a German U-boat near Tralee but was arrested within a few hours. He was brought to London, charged with high treason, tried, and hanged. Feeling over Casement remains high; the Irish regard him as a patriot martyr. Allegations have been made that, in order to discredit Casement (particularly in the U.S.A.), the British authorities secretly made use of a diary (which was not produced in court) and which contained sordid details of his private life.

Cassino. A small town between Naples and Rome, dominated by a Benedictine monastery on a height above the junction of two rivers. Cassino served as the pivot of the German 'Gustav Line' from January to May 1944. The Germans withstood attacks by British, Canadian, Indian, New Zealand, and U.S. troops, until a fourth offensive led to its capture by the Poles and the British on 18 May, thereby opening the allied route to Rome, which fell seventeen days later. The monastery was destroyed by bombing on 15 February.

Castlereagh, Robert Stewart, Viscount (1769–1822). Son of the first Marquis of Londonderry (whom he succeeded in 1821). In the decade 1790–1800 Castlereagh worked for the union of Britain and Ireland, serving as Chief Secretary for Ireland 1798–1801, but resigning when George III rejected Catholic Emancipation. He was in charge of Indian affairs under Addington and continued as Secretary for War and Colonies (1805–9). In 1809 he quarrelled with the Foreign Secretary, Canning, and, after a duel, both were temporarily retired from office. In 1812 Castlereagh became Foreign Secretary, holding the office until August 1822, when he committed suicide. Castlereagh's austere character and his inability to deliver a clear and concise speech made him unpopular; he was unjustly blamed for the repressive home policy of the Liverpool Government, and his funeral was cheered through the streets of London. His contemporaries did not appreciate his work in forming the Fourth Coalition nor his comprehension of the European Balance of Power. He inherited from Pitt the idea of establishing a diplomatic order in Europe, and was able to put this into practice at the Congress of Vienna. By the time of his death he had become disillusioned with the Congress System, and his policy was coming closer to that later pursued, with more verve, by his successor Canning (q.v.).

'Cat and Mouse Act' (1913). The name popularly given to the 'Prisoners, Temporary Discharge for Health, Act'. By this measure, women suffragettes (q.v.) who refused to take food while in prison for violent offences could be released on a licence, which could be revoked without further trial if the offence were repeated. The Asquith Government hoped by this Act to discourage the suffragettes from further offences. The Act was criticized on humanitarian grounds by many prominent figures, and was not successful as a deterrent.

Catholic Emancipation. The Test Act of 1673 required holders of public office to receive the Anglican sacrament and reject the doctrine of transubstantiation, thereby excluding Roman Catholics and Protestant nonconformists from Parliament and from executive posts. Although many disabilities were removed in the later eighteenth century, the position was made especially difficult in 1800 by the Act of Union (q.v.) with Ireland. Pitt had given a tacit pledge that emancipation would follow union, though George III considered that emancipation would be contrary to his Coronation Oath, and refused to sanction it. In 1823 Daniel O'Connell (q.v.) founded the Catholic Association to press for full emancipation. He was himself elected to Parliament from County Clare in 1828, but was unable to take his seat. Wellington and Peel, although opposed to emancipation, were afraid that Irish unrest would lead to civil war unless the Test Act was repealed. This was achieved in 1828 and, in the following year, a Catholic Emancipation Bill was carried through Parliament despite intense Tory opposition. Roman Catholics were allowed to sit in Parliament and hold any public office (except Lord Chancellor or Lord Lieutenant of Ireland), provided they took an oath denying the Pope's right to interfere in British domestic affairs. Roman Catholics remained unable to take degrees at Oxford, Cambridge, and Durham until Gladstone abolished University Religious Tests in 1871.

Cato Street Conspiracy (1820). An ill-planned venture by extremist radicals to murder members of the Tory Cabinet of Lord Liverpool (q.v.) while they sat at dinner with Lord Harrowby. The conspirators then planned to seize London. The scheme was revealed at an early stage to the authorities – and may, to some extent, have been given its final form by an *agent provocateur*. The conspirators, who were led by Arthur Thistlewood, were arrested in Cato Street, off the Edgware Road in London; five of them were hanged and five transported for life. The conspiracy is historically significant only as a commentary on the general political dissatisfaction with the Tory Government; it coincided with a period of unrest in Europe and with a rapid rise in post-war unemployment at home.

Cavour, Camillo, Count (1810–61). Italian statesman. By birth a member of the Piedmontese aristocracy. Cavour's liberal convictions made him abandon an army career and he became interested in scientific farming, visiting Britain, where he also studied the parliamentary system. In 1847 he founded a newspaper, *Il Risorgimento*, to work for a liberal, monarchical Italy. Although he did not take an active part in the revolutions of 1848 he entered politics soon after and became Minister of Agriculture, Marine, and of Commerce in Piedmont, October 1850, within a few months exchanging the portfolio of Marine for that of Finance. He was Prime Minister of Piedmont from November 1852 until his death in June 1861 (except for the last six months of 1859). In home affairs, his government developed commerce, improved the financial system, re-organized the Army, constructed strategic roads, railways, and canals, and curbed the power of the Church ('a free church in a free state'). Believing that Italy could only be unified with outside help, Cavour brought Piedmont into the Crimean War, in order to raise Italian grievances at the Peace Conference. In July 1858 Cavour made a secret agreement with Napoleon III at Plombières (q.v.) for the joint Franco-Piedmontese War against Austria (April to July 1859). When Napoleon prematurely made peace, Cavour resigned but returned in January 1860 to negotiate the union of Parma, Modena, Tuscany, and the Romagna with Piedmont. Later in 1860, the expedition of

Garibaldi to Sicily and Naples placed Cavour in a dilemma; while favouring Italian unification, he feared that Garibaldi would advance on Rome (see *Roman Question*) and precipitate the hostile intervention of Catholic Europe. To forestall Garibaldi, Cavour marched Piedmontese troops into the Papal States (10 September 1860), halting them on the border of the 'Patrimony of St Peter', which was peculiarly the Pope's possession. The Piedmontese linked up with Garibaldi on the River Volturno, the two leaders having carried through a pincer movement to secure a united Kingdom of Italy, which was proclaimed on 17 March 1861 – only eleven weeks before Cavour's death.

Central Powers. A phrase originally used to describe Germany, Austria-Hungary, and Italy after these states were linked by the Triple Alliance of 1882 (q.v.). With the disaffection of Italy from the alliance in 1914, the phrase was loosely used to distinguish Germany and Austria-Hungary from the 'Entente Powers' (France, Russia, and Britain).

Centre Party. The Roman Catholic political organization in Imperial Germany and the Weimar Republic. It was founded in 1871 by Ludwig Windthorst (1812–91) to defend Catholic interests against the predominantly Prussian Protestant policy of Bismarck. The Centre Party therefore opposed Bismarck during the Kulturkampf (q.v.) but grudgingly lent him support in the 1880s in his disputes with the Social Democrats. From 1893 to 1907 it was the predominant party in a Conservative-Centre Coalition, but it thereafter lost influence to the nationalist groups. In July 1917 the Centre Party, under Mathias Erzberger (1875–1921), carried a Peace Resolution in the Reichstag favouring a negotiated peace, free from annexations. Erzberger subsequently accepted some of the responsibility for the Versailles Treaty, and the Centre Party remained as one of the leading groups in the Republic. Among Centre Party members were Brüning (b. 1885), Chancellor in 1930, and von Papen (b. 1879), Chancellor in 1932 and Vice-Chancellor under Hitler 1933–4. The Centre Party was disbanded on 5 July 1933.

Ceylon. An island in the Indian Ocean, developed by the Portuguese in the sixteenth century, but taken over by the Dutch in the seventeenth century. In 1796 a British force despatched by the East India Company captured the Dutch settlements around the coast. The Dutch formally ceded their territories by the Treaty of Amiens (1802). The interior of the island remained under the King of Kandy, a notoriously cruel despot. When in 1814 a revolution broke out against the King, the British Governor, Sir John Brownrigg, authorized British troops to attack Kandy (1815), and the British took over the island in full sovereignty. From 1815 to 1947 Ceylon was administered as a British colony, with its economy mainly dependent on the production of tea and rubber. It was not until the period 1918–24 that reforms admitted representatives of all classes of Sinhalese and Tamils to the legislative council, although it had long been customary to consult the Sinhalese aristocratic families. Ceylon achieved dominion status within the Commonwealth by the Ceylon Independence Act of 1947.

Chadwick, Edwin (1800–90). Administrator of the Poor Law (q.v.). Chadwick was born near Manchester. He was self-educated and although called to the Bar in 1839, never practised, since he preferred journalism. He became a close friend of Bentham (q.v.). Chadwick was largely responsible for the Poor Law Report of 1834 and was immediately appointed secretary of the Poor Law Commissioners, serving on innumerable commissions dealing with social problems. From 1848 to 1854 he headed the Board of Health. Chadwick was an unfortunately tempered man, full of propellent zeal but brash and tactless. He was not good at delegating authority, and in trying to do too much too swiftly he aroused opposition (especially in the North). Yet Chadwick, more than any other individual, was responsible for the first efforts at slum clearance and for improving sanitary conditions so that cholera was stamped out. He was knighted in 1869.

Chamberlain, Austen (1863–1937). Eldest son of Joseph Chamberlain. Became Conservative M.P. for East Worcestershire in 1892. He was Chancellor of the Exchequer in Balfour's Government 1903–5 and in the Lloyd George Coalition 1919–21. His most constructive work was as Foreign Secretary under Baldwin from 1924 to 1929. He played a prominent part in the discussions leading up to the Locarno Treaties (q.v.) of 1925. In the same year Chamberlain was made a Knight of the Garter.

Chamberlain, Joseph (1836–1914). Son of a shopkeeper. Made his fortune as a Birmingham manufacturer. Achieved fame in 1875 as radical Lord Mayor of Birmingham by pioneering slum-clearance schemes. He became M.P. for Birmingham in 1876 and was President of the Board of Trade in the Gladstone Ministry 1880–5. His radical 'Unauthorized Programme' won the election of 1885 for Gladstone, but he broke with the Liberals in the following year, partly in opposition to Home Rule and partly through personal distrust of Glad-stone. His defection split the Liberal Party and led to the fall of the Government. In 1895 Chamberlain became Colonial Secretary in Salisbury's Conservative-Unionist Government, working especially for expansion in Africa and for imperial federation. Although his policy over the Jameson Raid (q.v.) was of doubtful honesty, his political influence rose rapidly within the Cabinet, and he sometimes intervened on matters of foreign policy, notably in 1898 and 1899 when he sought an alliance with Germany. He left the Colonial Office in 1903, and for two years campaigned for 'Tariff Reform' (q.v.), an agitation that made him split the Unionists as effectively as he had earlier split the Liberals. In 1906 he was struck down by paralysis and took no further part in politics.

Chamberlain, Neville (1869–1940). Son of Joseph and half-brother of Austen. Did not enter Parliament until his fiftieth year, having con-centrated on business and local government. He was a Lord Mayor of Birmingham and represented the city as an M.P. from 1918 until his death. His municipal experience made him a successful Minister of Health in the Conservative Governments between 1923 and 1929. In November 1931 he succeeded Snowden as Chancellor of the Ex-chequer, a post he held until he followed Baldwin as Prime Minister in May 1937. Chamberlain immediately became virtual director of foreign policy, although he knew little about Europe and tended to prefer the reports of his personal adviser, Sir Horace Wilson, to the information given by the Foreign Secretaries; Eden (who resigned, frustrated, in February 1938) and Halifax (q.v.). Chamberlain be-lieved that he could meet German grievances by direct man-to-man discussions with Hitler, and, during the Czechoslovak crisis of 1938, flew to visit Hitler at Berchtesgaden and Godesberg, as well as join-ing in the four-power conference at Munich (q.v.). He abandoned appeasement only at the Nazi occupation of Prague in March 1939, thereafter offering alliances to Poland, Rumania, and Greece. It was in accordance with the first of these that his Government declared war on Germany, in September 1939. Chamberlain's hesitancy and bad handling of personal relations were clear during the first winter of war. He resigned after the German occupation of Norway. He remained Lord President of the Council in Churchill's Coalition Government until his death six months later.

Chanak Crisis. A state of extreme tension, verging on war, between Britain and the Turkish Nationalists under Mustapha Kemal (q.v.), September–October 1922. The crisis arose from the victory of the

Kemalists against the Greeks at Smyrna (q.v.) and from Kemal's intention of carrying the war across the Dardanelles and into the European territories assigned to Greece at the Peace Conference. It was feared in London that Kemal would also attack the Allied occupation force guarding the approaches to Constantinople. Despite French and Italian hesitancy, Lloyd George (the Prime Minister) and Churchill ordered reinforcement of the British detachments in Chanak (the region on the Asiatic shore of the Dardanelles). Eventually, an agreement was reached at Mudania between the British Commander, General Harrington, and Kemal's representative, General Ismet (later known as Ismet Inönü), promising British agreement that Eastern Thrace and Adrianople should be returned to Turkey provided that the Turks accepted neutralization of the Dardanelles and the Bosphorus. This Convention (signed on 11 October 1922) formed a basis for the Treaty of Lausanne (q.v.) of 1923. The Chanak Crisis had the incidental effect of causing the disintegration of the Lloyd George Coalition Government since the Conservative leaders were alarmed at his apparent irresponsibility in bringing the country to the brink of war.

Charles, Emperor of Austria and King of Hungary (born 1887, reigned 1916–18, died 1922). Became heir to the Austrian throne on the murder of his uncle, Francis Ferdinand, in 1914 and succeeded his great-uncle, Francis Joseph, in November 1916 at the height of the War. Charles was anxious to reform the constitutional structure of his territories and to secure a separate peace. Through Prince Sixte of Bourbon-Parma, brother of his wife (Empress Zita), he contacted the British and French, and preliminary peace meetings were held. When the Germans heard of these talks, they tightened their control of their Austrian ally. His hope of reform at home came to nothing because of war conditions, and he was unable to prevent the Empire from disintegrating in 1918. He refused to abdicate but withdrew into private life in Switzerland. In 1921 he twice secretly returned to Hungary and attempted to recover his throne, but he was forced to leave through the hostility of the 'Little Entente' powers and of the Hungarian Regent Horthy (q.v.). Charles died in exile in Madeira in April 1922, his eldest son, Archduke Otto (born 1912), becoming claimant to his titles.

Charles X (1757–1836, King of France from 1824 to 1830). Grandson of Louis XV and brother to Louis XVI and Louis XVIII (whom he succeeded). As Comte d'Artois he was notorious at the Court of

Versailles for his dissolute life and reactionary politics. He fled from France in 1789 and took refuge in Edinburgh. Returning to France in 1814, he became leader of the ultra-royalists. As King he was closely attached to the clerical party, authorizing the imposition of savage penalties for irreligious behaviour. He successively alienated all shades of political opinion, purging the Army of Bonapartist officers, indemnifying former émigrés, and refusing political reform. With his Minister, Prince Jules de Polignac, he issued a series of repressive decrees ('The Four Ordinances of St Cloud') which provoked the Revolution of July 1830. Charles again fled across the Channel to Edinburgh, but died six years later while on a visit to Austria.

Chartism. An English movement for political reform, advocating fulfilment of the People's Charter of 1838: universal male suffrage; annual parliaments; vote by ballot; payment of M.P.s; equal electoral districts; abolition of the property qualification of M.P.s. The Birmingham radical M.P., Attwood (q.v.), was responsible for summoning a National Convention in London in February 1839 and for presenting a petition to the House of Commons in the following July. The Convention revealed dissensions within the movement and marked differences between the Northerners (who were fundamentally anti-industrialist) and the men from the Midlands and London. There were violent outbursts in Birmingham and Newport (Mon.) where 24 Chartists were killed in a full-scale rising (3 November 1839). Between 1840 and 1842 the Chartist movement was widely split, but a second petition was presented in May 1842 and, like its predecessor, rejected. A final outburst of Chartist agitation in 1848 reflected the general unrest throughout Europe. A proposed monster Chartist demonstration in Kennington (10 April) considerably alarmed the Government, which entrusted the Duke of Wellington with defence of the capital, but there were fewer demonstrators than expected and, in the face of resolute action by the police, the meeting ended quietly with a third petition being conveyed to Westminster. Ridicule was subsequently poured on the Chartists when it was found that the petition included numerous facetious signatures ('Pug-nose', 'Mr Punch', and 'Victoria Rex' [*sic*]), and the movement died a natural death. Chartism failed because of its weak leadership, lack of coordination or contact with trade-unionism, and because its objectives lacked the simple direct purpose of its contemporary rival, the Anti-Corn Law League (q.v.). Nevertheless, the four main Chartist demands were enacted within the ensuing seventy years.

Chinese Revolution of 1911. Revolutionary groups aiming at the overthrow of the Manchu Empire had been secretly operating in China since 1905. In October 1911 discovery of the headquarters of the revolutionaries in Hankow led to disturbances which showed the powerlessness of the dynasty to command allegiance. In November, two rival régimes were established: General Yuan Shih-kai being appointed Prime Minister by a National Assembly in Peking and Sun Yat-sen (q.v.) being elected President by a revolutionary assembly in Nanking. In February 1912 the boy-emperor Pu-i (b. 1906) was induced to abdicate and, in order to unite the country, Sun Yat-sen agreed to hand over authority to Yuan Shih-kai, who became provisional President of the Chinese Republic. The 'Nanking Constitution' of March 1912 aimed at the establishment of a democratic republic with a bicameral parliament. Yuan, however, sought to strengthen his personal authority, and had himself proclaimed Emperor in December 1915. His death in the following June allowed the restoration of the 'Nanking Constitution', but the rivalry of ambitious 'war-lords' prevented the national government from exercising any real power until the success of the Kuomintang (q.v.) in 1928.

Churchill, Lord Randolph (1849–94). Third son of the Duke of Marlborough and father of Sir Winston, entered Parliament in 1874 as Conservative M.P. for Woodstock. After 1880 he emerged as the leader of Tory Democracy, heading a progressive group (sometimes called the 'Fourth Party') which sought to secure the working-class vote by maintaining Disraeli's policy of social reform. As Secretary for India in Salisbury's Ministry of 1885–6 he was largely responsible for the annexation of Upper Burma. In 1886 Churchill became Chancellor of the Exchequer and Leader of the Commons in Salisbury's Government. He was the youngest politician to hold either office for over a century, but within five months he resigned in opposition to increased expenditure on the fighting services. Since no political group was prepared to support him against Salisbury, this dramatic gesture was ill-timed. It marked the end of his political career, as he was thereafter dogged by bad health.

Churchill, Winston Leonard Spencer (born 1874; knighted 1953). Son of Lord Randolph Churchill. Educated at Harrow and Sandhurst, saw military service in Cuba and Malakand, and participated in the battle of Omdurman in 1898. He was a war correspondent in South Africa 1899–1900 and was captured by the Boers but escaped. Although elected M.P. for Oldham as a Conservative in 1900, his Free Trade principles made him join the Liberals in 1904. He attained Cabinet rank as President of the Board of Trade in 1908 and carried through important social legislation (including the establishment of the first employment exchanges). He was Home Secretary in 1910 and a dynamic First Lord of the Admiralty in 1911, being largely responsible for the decision in July 1914 to keep the fleet at war stations after a practice peacetime mobilization. In 1915 he was made a scapegoat for failure at the Dardanelles (q.v.) and resigned, serving as a Colonel on the Western Front. He became Minister of Munitions in 1917, was Secretary for War and Air (1918–21), and Colonial Secretary (1921–2). He broke with the Liberals in 1922 and was out of Parliament for two years before returning as Conservative M.P. for Epping in 1924, serving Baldwin as Chancellor of the Exchequer (1924–9). His dislike of concessions to India and his attempts to alert Britain to the new German menace excluded him from office until the outbreak of the Second World War, when he returned to the Admiralty as First Lord. On 10 May 1940, he was appointed Prime Minister of the Coalition Government. He formed a War Cabinet of five (later eight) and acted as his own Minister of Defence. He thus led the British people in 'their finest hour', sustaining them until the collapse of Germany in 1945. With the defeat of the 1945 election, he became Leader of the Opposition, and was Prime Minister again from 1951 to 1955.

Ciano, Galeazzo, Count (1903–44). Italian politician. Son of an Italian Admiral. Himself an airman when not engaged in politics. He married Mussolini's daughter in 1930 and served in various offices connected with propaganda between 1930 and 1936 before becoming Foreign Minister (January 1936). Ciano negotiated the successive 'Axis' agreements with Germany and favoured the annexation of Albania in 1939 and the incursion of Italy into the Balkans in 1940–1. After the Italian defeats in North Africa, he was dismissed from the Foreign Ministry and sent as Ambassador to the Vatican (February to July 1943). After voting for the overthrow of Mussolini on 25 July 1943, he left Italy for Germany, was blamed by Hitler for Mussolini's fall, tried for treason, and shot by Neo-Fascists on 11 January 1944.

Civil Constitution of the Clergy. An Act passed by the French Constituent Assembly on 12 July 1790, providing for the reorganization of the dioceses of France on a more 'rational' basis and for the appointment of priests and bishops by the laity in elections held in a similar way to those for district and departmental officials. The clergy at the same time were ordered to take an oath of loyalty to the national constitution. Less than half the clergy accepted the Civil Constitution, and there developed a split between the *prêtres assermentés* (who had taken the oath) and the *prêtres réfractaires*. The Civil Constitution was condemned by the Pope as interference by the laity in purely ecclesiastical affairs. The breach within the French Church lasted until the Concordat of 1801 (which established a new episcopate).

Civil War. *See American Civil War; Russian Revolution and Civil War; Spanish Civil War.*

Clapham Sect. An important group within the Evangelical Movement (q.v.) among the Anglican clergy. The majority of the members of the group worshipped at the parish church of Clapham (in south London) during the period 1792 to 1813, when the Reverend John Venn was rector. The Clapham Sect emphasized the necessity for religion to express itself in good works. Through one of its members, William Wilberforce (q.v.), it played a prominent part in the movement to abolish the slave trade. It was also concerned with missionary work in India, with 'bettering the conditions and increasing the comforts of the poor', and with religious education.

Clemenceau, Georges (1841–1929). French statesman born in La Vendée of an atheist and republican family, who educated him for a medical career. In 1870 he was appointed Mayor of Montmartre and controlled the area during the siege of Paris, narrowly escaping death in the Commune (q.v.). From 1876 to 1893 he was an iconoclastic Radical deputy and his ruthlessness and caustic tongue won him the soubriquet 'The Tiger'. He was discredited in 1893 by the Panama Scandal but recovered his reputation through his fervent championship of Dreyfus in the press. He became a Senator in 1903 but never held office until March 1906, when he was appointed Minister of Home Affairs. In the following October he became Prime Minister. His Government lasted for two and three-quarter years, the second longest period in the Third Republic. It was marked by violent attacks on the Socialists and attempts to check the growing strike movement. Clemenceau was an outspoken critic of military incompetence and defeatism for the first three years of war. In November 1917 he became Prime Minister of a government of nonentities (whom he himself called 'the geese that saved the Capitol'). His indomitable courage kept France together under the severe blows of March 1918, and enabled him to lead the country to victory in the following November. He presided over the Paris Peace Conference of 1919. Although at the Conference he was harsher to the Germans than Wilson or Lloyd George, it was felt in France that he had been too lenient; this criticism, coupled with parliamentary resentment at his exercise of authority, led to his political eclipse in January 1920. In retirement, he feared a resurgent Germany and even foresaw 1940 as a potential year of danger; the title of his memoirs, *The Grandeur and Misery of Victory*, illustrates his disillusionment with the post-war world.

Cleveland, (Stephen) Grover (1837–1908). President of the U.S.A. Born in New Jersey, admitted to the New York Bar, Governor of New York 1883–4. In the highly scurrilous presidential campaign of 1884, Cleveland stood as Democratic candidate and won, largely through a narrow success in New York. He was the first Democratic President for twenty-eight years. During his administration of 1885–9 he followed a conciliatory policy towards the South and strengthened presidential authority, vetoing some two thirds of the bills presented to him. He caused resentment among ex-servicemen's associations by his scrupulous investigation of pension claims. The opposition of the veterans and of capitalists alarmed by attempts to reduce tariffs led to his defeat by Harrison in 1888, but he was successful again four years later. Domestic disputes in his 1893–7 administration were centred on monetary matters and dominated by a panic on Wall Street in June 1893. Cleveland's anti-inflationary measures and his dispatch of troops to break up a strike in Illinois alienated many of his own supporters, and the Democratic Convention of 1896 chose as candidate the eloquent radical William Jennings Bryan, who lost the election to McKinley (q.v.). In foreign affairs Cleveland was an anti-imperialist, opposing the American forward policy in Hawaii. He wished to settle the longstanding boundary dispute between Britain and Venezuela (q.v.). When Britain refused his arbitration, he authorized his Secretary of State, Olney, to send a strong note to Britain (July 1895) insisting that if she maintained her pressure on Venezuela this would be regarded by the U.S.A. as a violation of the Monroe Doctrine (q.v.). Cleveland also sent a belligerent message to Congress on the same question (December 1895). The British, surprised at this unexpected disturbance of the even tenor of Anglo-American relations, accepted American arbitration and signed a treaty with Venezuela in 1897.

Cobbett, William (1763–1835). Born, the son of a farm labourer, at Farnham, Surrey. From 1784 to 1791 he served in the Army, mostly in Canada. After publishing a pamphlet denouncing military corruption (1792), he left England for France and hastily emigrated to the U.S.A. because of the Revolution. He spent seven years in Philadelphia, where he became widely known as a journalist who defended British policy and as a critic of the views of Tom Paine (q.v.). After being fined for libel in 1800, he returned to England and opened a bookshop in Pall Mall, where he published in 1802 the *Weekly Register*, which soon became an organ of highly individualistic radical criticism. This was followed in 1804 by his *Parliamentary Debates*. In 1810 he was imprisoned for two years and fined £1,000 for attacking flogging in the army, and, fearing further prosecution, spent the years 1817–19 in the U.S.A., bringing back with him to England the bones of his earlier antagonist, Paine. By 1820 he had come to hate the new industrialism and urban life in general. He determined to get away from 'the Great Wen' (as he termed London) and travelled throughout the country observing the old agricultural system and championing the yeoman society that was passing away. The accounts of his tours were published in book form as *Rural Rides* (1830). In the reform agitation of 1831 he was charged with inciting violence, but defended himself skilfully, and the case was dismissed. He became M.P. for Oldham in the reformed Parliament of 1832. Cobbett was an outstanding political thunderer with a vigorous literary style. In his love of an idealized free peasantry he was something of a Tory, but he had a radical zeal for parliamentary reform and a radical hatred of savage injustices.

Cobden, Richard (1804–65). British radical. Although born into a Sussex farming family, Cobden became a calico printer in Manchester. As a political pamphleteer (from 1835) he had two main concerns, Free Trade and Disarmament. In home affairs he always believed in a minimum amount of governmental interference. He became a leader of the Anti-Corn Law League (q.v.) with Bright (q.v.), and spent a considerable private income before securing repeal in 1846. Again with Bright he opposed the Crimean War and lost his seat as M.P. for Stockport, which he had represented since 1841. He was re-elected in 1859 but rejected Palmerston's offer of a Cabinet post, preferring to remain an independent critic ready to champion any cause that would further his ideal of international arbitration. He was responsible for the Commercial Treaty with France in 1860, which reduced tariffs on trade between the two countries. During the American Civil War, he was active in easing the strained relations between Lincoln's Administration and Palmerston's Government.

Code Napoléon. The name given in 1807 to the Civil Code introduced by Napoleon in 1804 and remaining the basis of the French legal system. Before the Revolution, there had been no legal unity in France, with major contradictions between the customs of the north and south. Unsuccessful attempts to formulate a uniform code had been made on five occasions under the Convention or the Directory. The Code Napoléon was worked out at 84 sessions of the Council of State, over 36 of which Napoleon himself presided. It was a compromise between the paternal authority of Roman Law and the egalitarian principles of the Revolution. It was a fundamentally middle-class code, stressing the rights of property. Napoleon introduced the Code into all territories annexed by France and into the French vassal states.

Collins, Michael (1890–1922). The son of a farmer from Cork. Worked in London in the Post Office and a bank, before returning to Ireland as an extreme nationalist in time to assist in organizing the Easter Rising (q.v.) of 1916. He was imprisoned in 1916 and again in 1918 because of his militant views and was elected in 1918 to the first *Dail Eireann*. In 1921 he was one of the representatives sent by the Irish to London to arrange a settlement. He tried, on his return to Ireland, to win support for the new Irish Free State of which, in January 1922, he became Prime Minister. He was faced, however, by a new outburst of terrorism led by the Irish Republican Society, and it was an extremist group of republicans who assassinated him in August 1922 while he was inspecting Irish troops.

Combination Laws. Repressive measures taken by Pitt in 1799 and 1800 against political agitation among industrial workers. All combinations of workers to press their employers for shorter hours or more pay were forbidden, offenders being liable for summary trial before magistrates. These laws remained in force until 1824, when a campaign led by Francis Place (q.v.) and Joseph Hume secured their repeal.

Comintern (more correctly Komintern). Russian abbreviated title of the Third International, March 1919 to May 1943. (See *International Socialism*.)

Committee of Public Safety. On the failure of the war effort of the Girondins (q.v.) in the spring of 1793, the French National Convention appointed a Committee of Public Safety to act as the executive authority throughout the Republic. Originally the Committee comprised nine men, later twelve. The Committee was used by Robespierre as an instrument of Jacobin tyranny, but it also contained a number of less narrowly political leaders, including the 'organizer of victory', Lazare Carnot (q.v). The Committee was abolished in 1795. The idea of a Committee of Public Safety as the executive re-emerged at various times in the nineteenth century, notably in Vienna in the autumn of 1848.

Commonwealth of Australia Act, 1900. See *Australian Commonwealth Act.*

Commune of Paris (1871). After the Franco-Prussian War (q.v.) patriotic radicals in Paris sought to ensure the effective republicanization of the new régime headed by Thiers (q.v.). Paris had endured a four-months' siege and was humiliated at the acceptance by the National Assembly in Bordeaux of peace terms which included the entry of German troops into the city. On 18 March 1871, rioters in Montmartre refused to surrender their guns to 'Bordeaux' troops and seized and hanged the two Generals commanding them. Thiers withdrew all forces from Paris, thereby creating a power vacuum which was filled on 26 March by a central committee calling itself the Commune in emulation of the Jacobin-dominated Assembly of 1793. With German occupation forces inactive in the suburbs, French troops under Macmahon (q.v.) and Gallifet fought their way back to Paris, re-taking the city street by street in merciless fighting (21–28 May). More damage was done to Paris than in any war and more people killed than in the 'Terror' of the Revolution. The Communards, for their part, shot hostages (including the Archbishop of Paris.) The suppression of the Commune left much bitterness, which exacerbated the relations between Paris and the Governments of France for thirty years. Although more Communards were latter-day Jacobins, shadow-acting the great days of the Revolution, than Communists, the fate of the insurrection retarded French socialism by three decades and provided international socialism with its fundamental martyrology. The Commune was the last attempt by Paris to dictate the form of French government to the provinces, a historical process that had begun more than two centuries earlier with the Frondes of 1648–51.

Communist Parties. Although the word 'communist' was used by Marx (q.v.) and Engels (q.v.) in the 1840s, it was not until after the Russian Revolutions of 1917 that the more extreme Marxists broke away from the Social Democrat Parties (q.v.) and formed organizations specifically called 'Communist Parties'. In Russia the Bolsheviks (q.v.) did not formally adopt the term 'Communist' until

1918. Six years later the 'Russian Communist Party (Bolshevik)' became the 'All-Union Communist Party (Bolshevik)', a name retained until 1952, when the word 'Bolshevik' was dropped in favour of 'Communist Party of the Soviet Union'. Except for a brief period from the end of 1918 to the spring of 1921, the Communist Party has been the sole political organization within the Soviet lands. Factions have arisen from time to time within the party, and these have produced conflicts and purges. Since the Russian party has always dominated the Communist International (Comintern, q.v.), these disputes have been echoed within the parties of other states. The most important conflicts have been the rivalry between Stalin and Trotsky (q.v.) that followed the death of Lenin (q.v.), and the elimination of the opponents of Stalin in the late 1930s by the purge known as the '*Yezhovshchina*' (q.v.). At the Party Congresses of 1956 and 1961 a further conflict developed between the Communists who believed in 'peaceful co-existence', led by N. K. Khruschev, and the old 'Stalinists' (especially Molotov, Malenkov and Kaganovich).

Most European Communist Parties outside Russia had a period of intensive activity immediately after the First World War, a phase of quiescence in the 1920s, agitation in the early 1930s (except where banned by right-wing governments), and revival with the Russian military successes at the end of the Second World War. The German Communist Party was founded on 30 December 1918, but suffered a severe setback within a fortnight of its creation when German irregular troops murdered its two moderate leaders, Luxemburg (q.v.) and Liebknecht. The German Communists remained a numerically powerful force until the advent of Hitler, although internal divisions weakened their effectiveness. In Hungary a communist party was formed in November 1918 and had a brief period of office under Bela Kun (q.v.) before being forced underground, re-emerging only with the Russian occupation of Hungary in 1945. The Bulgarian Communist Party (formed early in 1919) staged a successful rising in 1923 but was then outlawed until the arrival of the Russians in 1945. A Yugoslav Communist Party was established in April 1919 and gained considerable successes in municipal elections in 1920, but was proscribed in 1921 after the murder of the Minister of the Interior by a Communist. Communism continued to have a powerful appeal to the Yugoslav intelligentsia, many of whom took the lead in resisting the occupying powers during the Second World War and thereby developed a greater independence of Moscow than most other parties. Yugoslavia became a communist state at the end of the Second World War. There was an influential Communist Party in Czechoslovakia between the wars, which was revived in 1945 and secured control of the Republic in February 1948. In France and Italy communist parties were established in 1918. The Italians were effective in the strike movement that preceded Mussolini's 'March on Rome' (q.v.). The French, too, had greatest influence in the trade union movement and no party member held a governmental post until after the Second World War (although the Communists had been offered a post by Blum, q.v., in 1936). The Spanish Party, formed in 1920, was small in numbers but was able to exercise authority over the Spanish non-communist left-wing movement during the Civil War (q.v.) because of the support it could secure from Russia in resisting the Spanish fascists. The British Communist Party, established in 1918, never became a powerful force.

Outside Europe, communist parties have flourished in Asia, where in many cases they became the first form of organized Marxism (the chief exceptions being India and Indonesia, where the parties developed from groups dissatisfied with trade union activities). The most important organization outside the Soviet Union has been the Chinese Communist Party, established by two Peking University professors, Chen Tu-hsiu and Li Ta-chao, in July 1921. The divided state of China in the 1920s made it a profitable area for communist expansion, and Chen Tu-hsiu received considerable support from the Russians. For a time, however, the Russians were also assisting the Kuomintang (q.v.), to whom they sent military advisers. Conflict between the Chinese Communist Party and a right-wing group in the Kuomintang led by Chiang Kai-shek broke out in 1926 and, within a year, the original party was virtually destroyed. A new party was developed by the survivors under Li Li-san and, when he was accused of 'right-wing deviationism' in 1930, under Mao Tse-tung (b. 1893), a guerilla leader from the Kiangsi region who had attended the founding Congress in 1921. It was Mao who led the 'Long March' (q.v.) of 1934 to Yeman and who organized the '8th Route Army' as part of a united front to resist the Japanese from 1937 to 1945. Once the Japanese had been defeated, civil war broke out between Mao's Communists and the Kuomintang, ending with the creation of a Communist Government in Peking in 1948. Since 1956 the Chinese Communist Party has tended to appear less accommodating in its principles than the Russian Party.

Concentration Camps. The term 'concentration camp' was first applied to the centres in which Boer civilians were interned by Kitchener from 1900 to 1902 to prevent them aiding Boer guerillas. Inefficient administration and bad hygiene made these camps notorious and caused bitterness in South Africa.

In Germany the first concentration camps were established by the Nazis at Oranienburg and Dachau in 1933. By 1939 there were six such camps in Greater Germany, with 21,000 prisoners. During the war, the original purpose of the camps as places of 'preventive detention' for opponents of the régime was replaced by a systematic policy of using them as extermination centres for Jews, in which sadistic medical experiments were authorized. Some camps provided slave labour for the German armaments industry. Members of the Resistance were also sent to them. The most notorious camps were Buchenwald (239,000 prisoners between 1937 and 1945), Belsen and Auschwitz in Poland. Germany's allies also had concentration camps, notably Hungary and Rumania.

Concordat. A treaty between the Papacy and a temporal power concerning ecclesiastical affairs. The most famous was the Concordat between Pius VII and Napoleon in July 1801. This was carried through by Napoleon against the wishes of his advisers, since he wanted to separate Catholicism from Royalism and yet reassure the purchasers of former church lands. Napoleon also saw the value of bishops as 'moral prefects' and of village priests as local representatives of the established political order. The Concordat accordingly recognized Catholicism as 'the religion of the majority of Frenchmen', guaranteed liberty of worship, and provided for the establishment of a new episcopate with bishops nominated by Napoleon and instituted by the Pope. Stipends of bishops and clergy were paid by the State. The Concordat did not become law until April 1802 and then only as part of a 'Law of Public Worship', which permitted the existence of other religious sects. Moreover, Napoleon, without consulting the Pope, included certain 'Organic Articles' subjecting the Church to strict governmental regulation. Relations between Napoleon and the Church remained strained, especially during the period 1809–14 when he imprisoned the Pope in Savoy. Nevertheless, the Concordat was accepted by successive French régimes, except for a period of intense anti-clericalism from 1905 to 1914 under the Third Republic. Other concordats in modern times have been concluded with Spain (1851), with Austria (1855), with Mussolini's Italy (Lateran Treaties, q.v., 1929), and with Nazi Germany (1933).

Confederate States of America. The political organization caused by the secession from the American Union of eleven Southern States (Alabama, Arkansas, Florida, Georgia, Louisiana, Mississippi, North Carolina, South Carolina, Tennessee, Texas, and Virginia) following the election of Lincoln as President. The Confederacy comprised five and a half million whites and three and a half million slaves. The Confederate States framed a constitution based on the U.S. Constitution but stressing the independent character of each State and making specific reference to the institution of slavery. A provisional government was set up at Montgomery, Alabama, on 8 February 1861. Jefferson Davis (q.v.) was elected President and established his capital at Richmond, Virginia. The Confederacy remained in being until formally dissolved by Davis on 24 April 1865.

Confederation of the Rhine. Established by a treaty signed in Paris on 17 July 1806. It was a Napoleonic creation, intended to consolidate the French hold upon western Germany demonstrated by the success of the Ulm-Austerlitz campaign; Bavaria, Würtemberg, Hesse-Darmstadt, Baden, and the territories of twelve other German dignitaries were to unite under the protection of Napoleon, whom they pledged to assist with an army of 63,000 men officered by the French. The Confederation received the advantages of the Napoleonic Codes and a formal constitution on the French model. The Act of Confederation virtually made eight million Germans subjects of the French Empire. The arrangement lasted until after Napoleon's defeat at Leipzig at the end of 1813; with the departure of the French, the Confederation disintegrated.

Congo. In the period 1879–84 a Belgian company, under the direction of King Leopold II (reigned 1865–1909) established trading stations on the lower Congo River. At the same time, the French organized a protectorate north of the river. To ease tension over partition of the region, to stop slavery, and to secure freedom of trade, the Great Powers summoned a Conference at Berlin (q.v.) in 1885, which, *inter alia*, recognized the existence of the 'Congo Free State' as a personal possession of King Leopold. By playing off the British and French, Leopold secured recognition of his claims to a large area of the Congo Basin (1894). In 1903 an agitation in Britain (and later the U.S.A.) against ill-treatment of the natives in the Congo attracted wide attention and, after a commission established by Leopold had reported unfavourably, the Belgian Government assumed responsibility for the Congo in October 1908, the territory organized as the Belgian Congo being eighty times as large as Belgium itself. Although the Belgians removed the most flagrant abuses, they continued to deny the native population any political rights until 1956 when a small group of Africans were given the vote. In 1960 Belgium conceded political independence to the Congo, a precipitate act that led to chaos and an international crisis, a separatist movement developing in the rich mining province of Katanga.

Congress System. A method of diplomacy by conference, instituted by Article VI of the Quadruple Alliance of Britain, Austria, Prussia, and Russia signed in Paris on 20 November 1815. This Article proposed that representatives of the Four Powers would meet at fixed periods to discuss measures that would be 'most salutary for the repose and prosperity of the nations and for maintaining the peace of Europe'. Congresses were held at Aix-la-Chapelle 1818, Troppau 1820, Laibach 1821, and Verona 1822 (q.v.). The British dissociated themselves more · and more from their allies' desire to interfere in the internal affairs of states threatened by revolution; at Verona, the British withdrew from the system entirely. A further Congress, attended only by the three Eastern autocracies, was held at St Petersburg in 1825, but revealed major differences between Russia and Austria, and the system was abandoned. It should be noted that the Congress of Vienna had been concluded before the institution of the system of congresses, from which, indeed, it differed both in composition and function.

Conscription. A compulsory enlistment for military service first used in modern times by the French Committee of Public Safety with the *levée en masse* of August 1793, devised by Carnot (q.v.). Although the decree provided for mobilization of all Frenchmen, it was applied only to those between eighteen and twenty-five. An extended system introduced by Jourdan in 1798 provided recruits for the Napoleonic armies. A method of giving brief military training to civilians in time of peace was established in Prussia by Scharnhorst and Gneisenau in 1808. The Prussian system was modified by further reforms between 1813 and 1815. The citizen army (*Landwehr*) organized to resist Napoleon in 1813 was integrated with the regular forces. Prussian conscripts were obliged to join the regular army at twenty, enter the reserve at twenty-three, and remain in the *Landwehr* from the ages of twenty-five to forty. Most European nations followed the Prussian method in the course of the century, although the Prussians called on only a small proportion of their population, for reasons of economy. In the early 1860s General von Roon reformed the Prussian Army and extended the obligation for service with the colours while, at the same time, increasing the number of conscripts. The Prussian system was extended to the whole of the German Empire in 1871. Conscription in Austria dated from 1868; in Italy from 1873; and in Russia from 1874. France had abandoned conscription in 1815 but formally re-introduced it, in principle, three years later. Nevertheless, an equitable system of military service was adopted in France only under the Third Republic; until 1870 the French Legislature determined annually the size of the Army and an appropriate number of men were called up by ballot, richer conscripts being able to 'buy' substitutes. Conscription was introduced in Britain in January 1916, abolished in December 1920, and re-introduced in June 1939. The British Government announced the ending of conscription in the summer of 1957. The ex-enemy states were forbidden to have conscript forces by the peace treaties of 1919–20, but conscription was restored by Hitler in Germany in March 1935 and by Schuschnigg in Austria in April 1936. A form of conscription ('Selective Service') was introduced in the U.S.A. in May 1917, abandoned after the Armistice, re-introduced in September 1940, and extended in scope in June 1951 (during the Korean War).

Conservative Party. The word 'Conservative' as opposed to the traditional term 'Tory', was first used in Britain by Canning in 1824, but the Party really dates from the Tamworth Manifesto of 1834 in which Peel grafted ideas of moderate reform on the older concept of respect for established institutions. Peel's party split after the repeal of the Corn Laws in 1846, and the Conservatives were in office only for three short periods until the 1870s. Disraeli established the fundamental principles of the Party as 'the maintenance of our institutions, the protection of our Empire, and the improvement of the condition of the people'. After the 1886 split in the Liberal Party over Irish Home Rule, Gladstone's opponents merged with the Conservatives, and the Party was generally known as 'Conservative and Unionist' until the settlement of Ireland in 1922. The Party was in office from 1886 to 1892 and from 1895 to 1905, concentrating on imperial and foreign affairs. Disputes over Tariff Reform (q.v.) – and lack of a social policy – led to the Party's eclipse, until it returned to power under Bonar Law in 1922. Subsequent leaders have included Baldwin, Neville Chamberlain, Churchill, Eden, and Macmillan. The Party has always been more reformist than its right-wing counterparts on the Continent.

Constantinople Agreements. March–April 1915. Secret undertakings given by the British and French to the Russians that after the war Constantinople and the hinterland of the Dardanelles and Bosphorus would be incorporated in the Russian Empire, provided that Britain and France 'achieved their aims in the Near East and elsewhere'. The agreements represented a major change in the traditional policy of both western countries towards the Eastern Question (q.v.); they reflect the growing fear that the Russians would make a separate peace unless offered some valuable prize. The undertaking subsequently proved a considerable embarrassment; for, after the Revolution, the Bolsheviks repudiated all agreements signed by the Tsarist Government but, in the spring of 1918, published the terms of the secret treaties, thereby causing an outcry among liberals in the West and the U.S.A. and stiffening resistance in Turkey.

Consulate. The system of government established by Napoleon after his *coup d'état* of Brumaire (q.v.), November 1799, lasting until the establishment of the Empire in May 1804. The constitutional form of the Consulate was originally devised by Sieyès (q.v.) who wished to have three Consuls of equal status and power so as to prevent Napoleon as First Consul from becoming a dictator. Napoleon, however, modified Sieyès' scheme, making the Second and Third Consuls mere subordinates. In the spring of 1802 Napoleon further modified the constitutional framework of the Consulate; after a popular plebiscite, he secured the Consulate for life, with the right of nominating a successor. It was under the Consulate that Napoleon defeated the Second Coalition (Britain, Russia, Austria, Turkey, Naples, and Portugal), pacified La Vendée, introduced the Code Napoléon (q.v.) and the Concordat (q.v.), and negotiated the Peace of Amiens (q.v.).

Continental System. A blockade of Britain inaugurated by Napoleon in the Berlin Decree of 21 November 1806, and seeking to enforce the closing of continental ports to British commerce. The system was extended to Russian ports after Tilsit (1807) and to Spain and Portugal in 1808. The Milan Decree of December 1807 threatened to treat any neutral vessel trading with Britain as British. The Continental System was effective during 1808 but, by the following year, Spain and Portugal were evading Napoleon's restrictions and Russia was seeking a way of escape. In March 1809 Napoleon was forced to issue licences for trade with Britain. The Continental System was unpopular not only with the peoples of Europe but with the French middle class, hitherto Napoleon's main pillar of strength.

Coolidge, (John) Calvin (1872–1933). President of the U.S.A. The son of a storekeeper in Vermont. He became a lawyer and a prominent supporter of the Republican Party in New England. He attracted nation-wide attention in 1919 when, as Governor of Massachusetts, he crushed a police strike in Boston. The Republicans nominated him as Vice-President in the 1920 Election and he served under Harding, whose death in 1923 led automatically to Coolidge's succession as President. He was elected for a further term in 1924 but did not stand in 1928. The Coolidge Administration was marked in home affairs by the rapid growth of commercial monopolies. Coolidge aptly summed up his whole attitude when he declared: 'The business of America is business'. Although the Republican Party claimed that 'Coolidge prosperity' was 'permanent', much of the company speculation lacked adequate coverage and, within a year of Coolidge's retirement, American business was shattered by the Wall Street Crash (q.v.).

Cooperative Movement. Began with the establishment of the 'Rochdale Equitable Pioneers' in 1844, in an attempt to realize within a capitalist society the cooperative principles earlier practised by Owen (q.v.). A retail store was set up and plans made for a more equitable system of 'production, distribution, education, and government'. The movement spread rapidly, mainly because of the popularity of the method by which members received dividends representing a share in the profits, after deduction of a sum for educational and social purposes. There were 15,000 members by 1851 and 437,000 by 1875. The Cooperative Wholesale Society was established in Manchester in 1864 in a further attempt to challenge the competitive capitalist system. In practice, the C.W.S. assumed the rôle of a national cooperative manufacturer. In pursuance of the original ideals of the movement, Cooperative Congresses were held annually from 1869, and in 1918 the first Cooperative candidates contested parliamentary elections, in alliance with the Labour Party.

Copenhagen, Battles of (1801 and 1807). There were two naval actions at Copenhagen during the Napoleonic Wars. (1) 2 April 1801: a British fleet under Sir Hyde Parker, with Nelson commanding the smaller vessels that bore the brunt of the engagement, destroyed the greater part of the Danish fleet which was preparing to enforce the decrees of 'Armed Neutrality' (q.v.) excluding British vessels from the Baltic. (2) 2–7 September 1807: a combined naval and military expedition bombarded Copenhagen, since British intelligence reported that Napoleon was about to occupy Denmark and commandeer its fleet. This instance of 'English tyranny on the seas' won some support for Napoleon's Continental System (q.v.), since the European states resented intimidation of a neutral, but it effectively prevented a fleet of nearly fifty vessels from supplementing the French.

Corfu Incident. On 27 August 1923 an Italian General, Tellini, and four members of his staff were shot while engaged in determining the Greek-Albanian frontier. Mussolini regarded this as a national insult and decided to demonstrate the Fascist belief in power politics. He sent a strong ultimatum to Greece and followed this up on 31 August by bombarding and occupying the Greek island of Corfu. The Greeks appealed to the League of Nations. Under pressure from the British (and, to a lesser extent, the French), Mussolini evacuated Corfu on 27 September. The Council of Ambassadors, at the request of the League, ordered the Greeks to accept most of the Italian demands, including payment of a considerable indemnity.

Corfu, Pact of. An agreement signed on the Greek island of Corfu, (home of the Serbian Government while their country was occupied) on 20 July 1917, between Pašić (q.v.), Serbian Prime Minister, and Ante Trumbić, president of the Yugoslav Committee, an organization established in 1915 in London by exiles from the South Slav regions of Austria-Hungary and working for the union of all the South Slav peoples in one state. The Pact declared that Serbs, Croats, Slovenes, and Montenegrins should form one kingdom under the Serbian (Karadjordjević) dynasty with a democratic constitution and local autonomy. The Pact thus formed a basic charter of unity for Yugoslavia (q.v.). When, in the 1920s, the Serbs began to dominate Yugoslavia to the exclusion from government of the other races, there were complaints that Pašić had tricked Trumbić to win support at a time of weakness for the Serbian cause.

Corn Laws. A Corn Law was first introduced in Britain in 1804, when the landowners, who dominated Parliament, sought to ensure their prosperity by imposing a protective duty on imported corn. Because of the war and the Continental System, this first Corn Law did not arouse much opposition, but in 1814 a Government Committee recommended that foreign corn should be imported free of duty only when the price of wheat had climbed to 80s. a quarter. This proposal formed the basis of the Corn Law of 1815. In 1828, Huskisson (q.v.) sought to relieve the distress caused by the high price of bread by introducing a sliding scale of duties according to price. A major trade depression in 1839, followed in a few years by bad harvests and a potato famine in Ireland, worsened conditions and gave force to the agitation of the Anti-Corn Law League (q.v.). Peel, who had revised Huskisson's scale in 1842, finally repealed the Corn Laws in June 1846, despite the opposition within his party of a formidable group of protectionists, headed by Lord George Bentinck and Disraeli.

Cracow. The capital of medieval Poland; possesses a university which dates from the fourteenth century. By the third partition of Poland (1795) Cracow became part of Austria but, in 1809, it was ceded by Austria to Napoleon's puppet state, the Grand Duchy of Warsaw. At the Congress of Vienna it was claimed by both the Russians and the Austrians; on 11 February 1815 it was agreed that Cracow and its environs (an area of just over 600 square miles) should be established as an independent republic. Cracow's traditional rôle as an intellectual and spiritual centre for Poland was, however, so great that the republic became the home of national and liberal thinkers seeking to escape from the academic stagnation of the Austria of Metternich. Fearing the influence of the Cracow liberals, Metternich ordered the annexation of the republic in 1846. Cracow remained in Austrian Galicia until the establishment of the Polish Republic in 1918.

Crimean War. The immediate cause of the Crimean War was the refusal of the Turks to accept a Russian demand to protect Christians within the Turkish Empire. The ultimate origins lie in British suspicion of Russia, partly because of her intervention to suppress the Hungarian Revolution of 1848–9 and partly because of the Tsar's proposals for the eventual partition of Turkish territory. At the same time, Franco-Russian relations were exacerbated by a dispute concerning the privileges of Catholic and Orthodox monks at the Holy Places in Palestine. (This dispute had, in fact, been settled before the war began.) The Turks declared war on 23 September 1853, and there was a brief campaign in the Danubian Principalities (q.v.) before Austria secured Russian evacuation of the region. The Turkish fleet was destroyed at Sinope on 30 November and the British and French sent warships into the Black Sea to prevent Russian landings. War between Russia and the British and French followed in March 1854. In September, the Allies landed in the Crimea and besieged Sebastopol (q.v.) for a year, the two most famous battles (Balaklava, q.v., and Inkerman, q.v.) being fought within the first two months of the siege. The war revealed appalling administrative chaos on both sides, relieved for the British only by the nursing activities of Florence Nightingale (q.v.). In January 1855 Cavour (q.v.) sent 10,000 Piedmontese troops to assist the Allies in order to enhance his country's international prestige. The Russians accepted a preliminary peace on 1 February 1856, under threat of an Austrian declaration of war. Final peace was established at the Congress of Paris (q.v.) a few weeks later.

Crispi, Francesco (1819–1901). Italian statesman. Born in Sicily. He became a revolutionary in 1848 and was expelled from Neapolitan territory, later being thrown out of Piedmont as a Mazzinian. In 1860 he was a prominent member of 'the Thousand' under Garibaldi. He became a member of the extreme left in the Italian Parliament but three years later was 'converted' to monarchism, as he regarded the crown as the best unifying force in the new Italy. He opposed Garibaldi's attempts to liberate Rome at the end of the 1860s and achieved fame in the 1870s by his exposure of corruption among some of his colleagues. An unproven accusation of bigamy kept him out of politics for some years, but his fervent patriotic eloquence enabled him to regain influence and he was Italian Prime Minister from 1887 to 1891 and from 1893 to 1896. He strengthened the Italo-German alliance and secured Italy her first overseas possessions, notably Eritrea, but his attempt to annex Abyssinia ended in the disastrous defeat of Adowa (March 1896), and this failure, coupled with accusations of embezzlement from the Opposition, forced him out of politics. He remains, however, the most energetic Italian politician between the founding of the Kingdom and the rise of Fascism.

Croatia. Region of Yugoslavia, capital Zagreb (formerly called Agram). Although there was an independent Croatia in the tenth century, from 1102 to 1918 Croatia was joined to Hungary. During the revolutions of 1848, Josip Jelačić, the Governor (*Ban*) of Croatia, led a movement against the Hungarian rebels and in favour of Croatian autonomy under Habsburg protection. Croatia did indeed gain a limited form of autonomy in 1868, but many Croats were dissatisfied with their political status within Austria-Hungary and, led by Bishop Strossmayer (q.v.), began to work for a South Slav State, a 'Yugoslavia'. In 1917 Croatian exiles signed with the Serbian Government the Pact of Corfu (q.v.) providing for the establishment of a Yugoslav State after the war. Friction arose in the new Yugoslavia between the Croats (Roman Catholics) and the Serbs (Orthodox), the Croats complaining that they were virtually excluded from government until 1939. Croatian fascist fanatics (*Ustaše*), led by Ante Pavelić (1889–1959), resorted to terrorism and, with Yugoslavia's defeat in 1941, proclaimed an independent Croatia with an Italian Duke as titular King (although he never dared visit his territories). The Pavelić régime perpetrated appalling atrocities against Serbs, Jews, and Communists and thereby provoked bitter reprisals. Croatia became a 'People's Republic' within communist Yugoslavia in 1946.

Cromer, Earl of (1841–1917). British imperial statesman. Born Evelyn Baring and raised to the peerage in 1892, taking his title from his birthplace. He was originally an artillery officer but served on the Viceroy's council in India as a financial adviser. He was knighted in 1883 and, in the same year, appointed British Agent and Consul-General in Egypt, a post he was to hold for 24 years. During this period Cromer was virtually ruler of Egypt. He found the country near bankruptcy but, by developing methods of cultivation and irrigation, he improved the position of the Egyptian peasantry and at the same time gave Egypt honest government. Cromer's military reforms made possible Kitchener's reconquest of the Sudan in 1896–9. Although faced by French intrigues and incursions until 1898, Cromer was always anxious for Anglo-French cooperation; he played a considerable part in overcoming objections in London to the Entente Cordiale of 1904. Cromer retired in 1907.

Cuba. An island in the Caribbean Sea, organized as an independent state since 1901. The Spanish occupied Cuba in the sixteenth century. The Cubans remained loyal in the upheavals of the early nineteenth century but waged a civil war for liberal reforms from 1868 to 1878, eventually securing the abolition of slavery in 1886. Spanish misgovernment in Cuba was one of the causes of the Spanish-American War (q.v.) of 1898. Although Cuba then became independent, the Constitution of 1901 confirmed the right of the U.S.A. to intervene militarily in Cuba if the political situation deteriorated. This right, known as the 'Platt Amendment', lasted until 1934, when it was abrogated in return for a trade agreement; U.S. troops or marines intervened in Cuba in 1906, 1913, 1917, and 1933. From 1933 to 1944 and from 1952 to 1958 Cuban politics were dominated by Fulgencio Batista, whose policy was originally inspired by fascist principles. Batista was overthrown in 1958 by a radical movement led by Fidel Castro which showed many of the characteristics of communism. American resentment at Soviet military backing for Cuba led to a major international crisis in October 1862.

Curragh Incident. In March 1914 Ulster opposition to the Irish Home Rule Bill became so acute that the Asquith Government believed it would be necessary to use troops to keep order in Northern Ireland. The officers stationed in the military camp at the Curragh, near Dublin, were informed that if they were unwilling to undertake operations against the Ulstermen, they would be allowed to resign their commissions and be dismissed from the Army. Fifty-seven officers of the Third Cavalry Brigade, commanded by General Hubert Gough, informed the Commander-in-Chief that they would 'prefer to accept dismissal if ordered north'. Some infantry officers followed Gough's example. There was much sympathy for the Curragh officers among the senior military authorities, and they obtained from the chief-of-staff a written assurance that they would not be required to force Home Rule in Ulster. The Curragh Incident was not a mutiny, but a rare instance of the British officer-class putting pressure on the civil government; for although Asquith insisted on his War Minister's resignation, there is little doubt that the dissident officers gained a political victory.

Curzon, George Nathaniel (1859–1925, created Viscount 1898, Earl 1911, Marquis of Kedleston 1921). Educated at Eton and Balliol, Conservative M.P. for Southport 1886–98, travelled widely, and wrote a scholarly study of Persia. He was Under-Secretary for India 1891–2 and for Foreign Affairs 1895–8, achieving such success that he was appointed Viceroy of India while still under forty. He brought with him from the Foreign Office a strong distrust of Russia; this made him pay especial care to the North-West Frontier Province, but he also undertook administrative reforms, most of which made for smoother government, although the partition of Bengal caused ill-feeling among the Hindus. He resigned in 1905 after differences with Kitchener over control of the Indian Army. He was a member of Lloyd George's War Cabinet from December 1916 and was Foreign Secretary from 1919 until January 1924. He was largely responsible for the settlement at Lausanne (q.v.) and for frustrating French encouragement of separatism in the Rhineland. In 1923 he suffered bitter disappointment at being passed over as Prime Minister because he was a member of the House of Lords (in which the Labour Opposition was not then represented). He was the last of the aristocratic administrators whose actions were governed by a sense of imperial responsibility.

Curzon Line. A proposal to settle the disputed frontier between Poland and Russia, put to the Poles by Lloyd George on 10 July 1920. Subsequent correspondence about the proposed frontier was undertaken by Lord Curzon, the Foreign Secretary, who thus gave his name to the line of demarcation. The line stretched from Grodno, through Brest-Litovsk and Przemysl, to the Carpathians; it would have excluded from Poland lands predominantly inhabited by White Russians, Ukrainians, and Lithuanians. The Poles rejected the proposal and subsequently secured territory twice as large as that suggested by Lloyd George. After the Nazi-Soviet Pact (q.v.) of 1939, the Curzon Line (with minor variations) became the boundary between the German and Russian spheres of occupation. In 1945 it was accepted by the Polish Government as the frontier with the U.S.S.R.

Custozza

Custozza, Battles of. Custozza in Lombardy was the scene of two
Austrian victories against Italian troops during the Risorgimento
(q.v.). On 25 July 1848 Marshal Radetzky (q.v.) routed the Piedmontese under Charles Albert; on 24 June 1866 Archduke Albrecht
defeated an Italian Army supporting Bismarck in his war with
Austria.

Cyprus. Island in the Eastern Mediterranean. Strategically situated
40 miles from Turkey and 240 from the Suez Canal. In 1571 the
Turks captured it from the Venetians, and it remained under Turkish
sovereignty until 1914. By the Cyprus Convention of 1878, confirmed
by the Congress of Berlin, the British acquired the right to station
troops in the island in return for guaranteeing Asiatic Turkey from
Russian attack. The British hoped to use Cyprus as a base to cover
the approaches to Egypt and to the Dardanelles, but the value of
the base was lessened by the occupation of the superior harbour of
Alexandria in 1882. The British annexed the island when the Turks
declared war in 1914; in the following year, an offer to cede the
island to Greece in return for a Greek entry into the war was
rejected. Cyprus became a Crown Colony in 1925. In 1931 there were
serious riots caused by the desire of the Greek-speaking community
(four-fifths of the population) for *Enosis*, union with Greece. Demands for *Enosis* began to be pressed with even more vigour in
1954; after numerous acts of terrorism, a compromise solution providing for an independent Republic of Cyprus was worked out in
talks in Zurich and London, 1959, and implemented in August 1960.

Czechoslovakia. A republic created in 1918 from the former western
Slavonic provinces of Austria-Hungary. The Allies recognized the
Czechoslovak National Council (founded in Paris by Masaryk, q.v.,
and Beneš, q.v.) as the provisional government in the autumn of
1918. A constitution, based on the French model, was enacted in
February 1920. The new Republic included the most valuable industrial areas of Austria-Hungary. Racially, it comprised seven
million Czechs, two million Slovaks, three-and-a-quarter million
Germans in the Sudetenland (q.v.), seven hundred thousand Hungarians, and four hundred and fifty thousand Ruthenes. Although
Czechoslovakia enjoyed a high standard of living, internal politics
were marred by latent racial conflicts, ill-feeling being engendered
by the predominance of the industrious Czechs over the other peoples. External policy was marked by a consciousness of the German
danger; Czechoslovakia was the centre of the 'Little Entente' (q.v.)
but failed to improve relations with Poland because of the dispute

98

over Teschen (q.v.). Sudeten German agitation increased between 1935 and 1938. War was prevented only by the Munich Settlement (q.v.), which ceded some 10,000 square miles of the Czech frontier regions to Germany and another 6,000 miles to Poland and Hungary. After Munich, Slovakia became completely autonomous, gaining a tenuous 'independence' when the Germans annexed the Czech provinces of Bohemia and Moravia in March 1939. Ruthenia, which had also become autonomous in October 1938, was annexed by Hungary at the same time. In 1945 a Czechoslovak 'National Front' Government returned to Prague, but was under considerable Russian pressure. The pre-1938 frontiers were restored, but Czechoslovakia was forced to cede Ruthenia to the U.S.S.R. in June 1945. Communist electoral successes in 1946 were followed in February 1948 by the overthrow of the democratic government. Czechoslovakia thereafter became a Russian satellite state.

Daimler, Gottfried (1834–1900). German scientist. In 1886 invented a practical internal-combustion engine using petrol. In the following year, Daimler fitted this engine in the first successful motor car. (The principle of the internal combustion engine had been applied ten years earlier by Nikolaus Otto to his 'Silent Gas Engine'.)

Dalhousie, Lord (James Broun Ramsay, 1812–60, succeeded his father as tenth Earl in 1838, created Marquis 1849). President of the Board of Trade in 1845, being particularly concerned with the development of railways. He was appointed Governor-General of India in 1847, arriving early in the following year and being immediately faced by a rebellion in the Punjab, where the Sikhs offered serious resistance for twelve months. Dalhousie ordered annexation of the Punjab and left it to be brilliantly administered by the brothers Henry and John Lawrence (q.v.). Subsequently Dalhousie also annexed several more states (notably Pegu and Oudh) and the Irrawaddy Delta in Burma. He undertook extensive reforms, constructing the first railway and telegraph systems, but avoiding heavy taxation by proverbially Scottish economies. His health was bad, and he took little part in public life after retiring from the Governor-Generalship in 1856. His reforming energy alienated Indian traditionalists and Brahmin priests and contributed to the Indian Mutiny, which broke out a year after his retirement.

Danton, Georges (1759–94). Born at Arcis-sur-Aube, became a lawyer. He emerged as administrator of Paris in 1791, becoming Minister of Justice in 1792 and being blamed by early nineteenth-century historians for the September Massacres (see *French Revolution*). Later historians praised his inspiring defiance of the invaders as a member of the Committee of Public Safety. By 1794 he had become leader of the right wing of the Jacobins, a servant of France rather than of the Revolution. A generous ruffianly patriot, fundamentally lazy and pleasure-seeking, he was the antithesis of Robespierre, who used revelations of Danton's financial indiscretions to have him arraigned before the revolutionary tribunal and executed, with his supporters, on 6 April 1794.

Danubian Principalities. Moldavia and Wallachia, commanding the mouths of the Danube. Under Turkish vassalage from the middle of the fifteenth century, and remained technically part of the Turkish Empire until the proclamation of Rumanian independence in 1877. By the Treaty of Kuchuk Kainardji of 1774, the Turks admitted the right of Russia to intervene on behalf of the Christian people of the Principalities. Russia occupied the Principalities from 1829 to 1834, securing their complete autonomy, and returned in 1848 to suppress a nationalist revolt in Wallachia, withdrawing in 1851. In July 1853 the Russians reoccupied the Principalities as a method of putting pressure on Turkey during the disputes leading to the Crimean War. From April 1854 to March 1857 the Principalities were occupied by Austria (with the consent of the Russians and Turks), in order to keep the peace on the lower Danube. The Great Powers guaranteed the Principalities by the Treaty of Paris of 1856 and, two years later, sanctioned the establishment of separate, but identical, administrations in Moldavia and Wallachia. The two legislatures united in 1862, adopting the name 'Rumania' (q.v.).

Danzig (Polish, Gdansk). Port at the mouth of the Vistula. Although populated by Germans, Danzig served as Poland's one seaport from the fifteenth century until 1793, when it was annexed to Prussia, remaining German until 1919. The Treaty of Versailles, in order to give Poland an outlet to the sea, constituted Danzig a Free City of some 400,000 inhabitants with an elected senate but administered by a League of Nations Commissioner. Despite the predominantly Germanic population, Poland was given charge of foreign policy, commerce, and customs, although the Poles constructed a new rival port at Gdynia in the 'Polish Corridor'. From 1933 to 1939, the Danzig Senate was Nazi-controlled. Polish-German relations over Danzig deteriorated in March 1939. On 1 September the local Nazi leader, Forster, proclaimed the union of Danzig and Germany, thereby unleashing the Second World War. In March 1945, the Russians captured Danzig and, in May, handed it over to the Poles who expelled the German population, thoroughly Polonizing the city.

Dardanelles. The channel between the Aegean Sea and the Sea of Marmora, and thus the first part of the strategic waterway linking the Mediterranean and the Black Sea. Free passage of the Dardanelles has historically formed part of the Straits Question (q.v.). British ships forced their way up the Dardanelles in 1807, and sailed through to assist Turkey in September 1853 and to threaten Russia in February 1878. On 18 March 1915 an Anglo-French fleet failed to penetrate the main Turkish defences and put the Turks on their guard in anticipation of the Gallipoli Expedition (q.v.).

Darlan, Jean Louis Xavier François (1881–1942). French Admiral and politician. From 1933 to 1940, Darlan, as executive head of the French Navy, raised its standards to an unprecedented height in modern times. Darlan, however, was himself ambitious and an anglophobe. When, after the French Armistice of 1940, the British fired on French warships at Mers-el-Kebir to ensure that they would not be used by the Germans, Darlan believed his old mistrust of Britain fully justified. He served Vichy France (q.v.) as Minister of Marine and acted as its chief minister from February 1941 to April 1942. He sought military collaboration with the Germans, even visiting Hitler at Berchtesgaden (11 May 1941); the Germans did not entirely trust him. By chance, Darlan was in Algiers when British and American troops landed there at the start of the North African campaign (8 November 1942). After initial opposition, Darlan agreed to cooperate with the Americans in return for recognition of his authority, but on 24 December he was assassinated in Algiers by a young fanatic who was apparently linked with the royalists.

Darwin, Charles (1809–82). Born and educated at Shrewsbury, passing on to Christ's College, Cambridge. Darwin sailed on the naturalist expedition to the Galapagos Islands, Tahiti, and New Zealand in the *Beagle* (1831–6). On returning, he settled in Kent and spent twenty years testing and developing his hypothesis that species evolve through the natural selection of those best suited to survive environmental conditions. His theories were published in *The Origin of Species* (1859) and created a major sensation. His views powerfully reinforced naturalistic trends in mid-Victorian thought; their influence went far beyond the purely biological sciences. The philosophical and historical views of the late nineteenth century were dominated by a scientific materialism which owed much to Darwin.

Davis, Jefferson (1808–89). President of the Confederate States (q.v.). Born in Kentucky and educated at West Point. After serving in the Army he became a Mississippi planter. He was a Senator 1847–51 and 1857–61; he served as Secretary of War in the Pierce Administration of 1853–7, being particularly concerned with strengthening coastal defences. When Mississippi seceded in January 1861, he was appointed provisional President of the Confederacy, subsequently being elected for a six-year term of office and formally inaugurated at Richmond in February 1862. The Confederate Generals found him a difficult political leader, as he had a high (and unwarranted) opinion of his own military knowledge. He was captured in Georgia in May 1865, and imprisoned for two years. Plans to try him for treason were dropped, and he lived over twenty years in quiet retreat in Mississippi.

Dawes Plan. The name generally given to a report on the German economic problem issued in April 1924 by a committee presided over by an American, Charles G. Dawes. The plan provided for a scale of annual payments of reparations (q.v.), reorganization of the German *Reichsbank*, and recommended a large foreign loan for Germany. It considerably assisted Germany in meeting her treaty obligations in the period 1924–9.

Deák, Ferenc (1803–76). Member of a distinguished Hungarian family. Studied law, entered politics in the early 1830s. Deák was a calm, undramatic orator of high intellect. He opposed the romantic extremism of Kossuth (q.v.), and did not fight in the Hungarian Revolution of 1848–9. He was, in consequence, able to clear himself when put on trial after the suppression of the revolution and, throughout the 1850s, engaged in a quiet and rational campaign of national political education. By June 1861 it was clear that Deák had assumed the mantle of Kossuth as leader of the Hungarian people. He was summoned to Vienna to assist a committee preparing constitutional changes in the Empire. Wisely, Deák refrained from taking advantage of the Austrian defeat of 1866 to ask for more concessions, and he was thus able to secure the Ausgleich of 1867 (q.v.) by which Hungary received a form of 'Home Rule'. Deák himself always refused political office and left the further championing of Hungarian rights to his chief colleague, Andrássy (q.v.).

Decembrist Conspiracy. An attempt by Army officers in St Petersburg, with support from nobles in southern Russia, to overthrow the Tsar's Government in December 1825. The movement was badly led and divided in objectives. Some conspirators sought to set up a republic, others hoped to saddle the new Tsar, Nicholas I (q.v.), with a perpetual oligarchy. Some worked for emancipation of the serfs, others were anxious to preserve the social order, fearing a general serf uprising. The conspiracy was betrayed by police spies; four of the leaders were executed and 120 exiled to Siberia. The conspiracy had the effect of confirming Nicholas I's distrust of any ideas connected with liberalism.

Delcassé, Théophile (1852–1923). French statesman, became a Deputy in the French Parliament in 1889, and was soon identified with a group favouring expansion in Africa. From 1893 to 1895 he was Minister of Colonies and authorized Marchand's expedition to Fashoda (q.v.). He became Foreign Minister in 1898 at a time of severe Anglo-French tension but, realizing that France could not be simultaneously on bad terms with Germany in Europe and Britain in Africa, he worked for the Anglo-French Entente (q.v.) of 1904. He was forced to resign during the Moroccan Crisis of 1905 by a conspiracy of his colleagues under German pressure. As Naval Minister from 1911 to 1913 he continued to strengthen Anglo-French relations, arranging Mediterranean fleet dispositions with the British Admiralty. After seventeen months as Ambassador in St Petersburg, he returned as Foreign Minister in August 1914, remaining in office until October 1915 and assisting in the negotiating of the Treaty of London which brought Italy into the war.

Delhi Durbar of 1911. 'Durbar' is a Hindustani term for the court, or levée, of a ruler. In 1911 King George V and Queen Mary as Emperor and Empress of India held a Durbar in great pomp in Delhi. After receiving demonstrations of loyalty from Indian princes, they announced the transfer of the Indian capital from Calcutta to Delhi, the ancient seat of the Mogul emperors. The Delhi Durbar was the only state occasion of its kind held by a British Emperor of India in person.

Democratic Party. One of the two main political parties in the U.S.A. The Democrats were really founded by Andrew Jackson (q.v.) in the 1820s, although the term had been used earlier as an alternative name for the Republican Democrats of Jefferson and his successors. (See *Republican Party*.) Jackson – and, even more, his chief political adviser and eventual successor, Martin van Buren – welded together the wild democratic 'grass-roots' habits of the frontier and the mass political instincts of the urban communities in a national chain of conventions, which set the pattern for later party development. The Democratic Party split in 1854, when Northern Democrats failed to follow Stephen A. Douglas (q.v.) on the slavery issue. By 1856 the Democrats had come under the control of Southern interests, and this contributed to the Party's eclipse after the Civil War. They began to recapture Northern support in the 1880s and were in office, under Cleveland (q.v.), from 1885 to 1889 and from 1893 to 1897. Opposition to monopolistic trusts contributed to the success in the 1912 election of Woodrow Wilson (q.v.), who headed the Democratic Administrations of 1913 to 1921. After the economic depression of 1929 the Democrats emerged as the champions of governmental action to end unemployment and stimulate industry. These proposals were embodied in the New Deal (q.v.) of Franklin D. Roosevelt (q.v.). The Democrats were continuously in office from 1933 to 1953 and won the election of 1960. Under Wilson, Roosevelt, and Truman they showed a sense of world responsibility, in contrast to the isolationist trend of their Republican rivals.

Denmark. Formed part of a united Scandinavian kingdom until the fifteenth century and remained linked with Norway until 1815 when, as a result of her alliance with Napoleonic France, Denmark also lost her Germanic possessions in Pomerania. The Danes secured representative government in the 1830s and the country became a constitutional monarchy in 1849. External policy was dominated by the problem of Schleswig-Holstein (q.v.) over which Denmark was at war with the German states in 1848–9 and 1864, being eventually forced to cede the two Duchies and Lauenburg to Prussia. Denmark kept out of the First World War but recovered northern Schleswig at the peace settlement, Iceland being united with Denmark at the same time (remaining so until 1944). The Germans entered Denmark on 9 April 1940, the Danes offering little resistance, and remained in occupation until 1945.

Depression. A decline in trade and general prosperity. There were two main periods of economic depression in the years covered here: (1) 1873–96, characterized by (a) a world fall of prices, caused partly by a demand for gold as a monetary unit at a time when no new supply was available; (b) European agricultural distress, resulting from bad harvests following wet summers, local diseases, and the general effect of the influx of grain from the American Middle West and Canada and of meat from Australasia and South America; (c) collapse of banking houses through over-speculation, notably in Vienna (1873) and Paris (1882). The Depression was felt especially strongly in Britain, whose industrial lead was challenged by the increased productivity of Germany and the U.S.A. The financial depression lifted with the opening up of new gold deposits in Africa, Australia, and Alaska; the industrial depression was relieved by the discovery of new markets during the era of Imperialism (q.v.). (2) 1929–34, the 'World Slump' – (*a*) in agriculture, caused by over-production in certain regions and maldistribution, aggravated by (*b*); (*b*) in finance, caused by (i) in the U.S.A., a fever of speculation, lead-ing first to withdrawal of funds from Europe and later to the panic known as the 'Wall Street Crash' (q.v.) of October 1929, (ii) in Europe, the collapse of the Austrian Credit Anstalt, a bank with interests throughout the Danubian lands, precipitated by French withdrawal of short-term credits; (*c*) in industry, a fall in exports and internal consumption, resulting from shortage of capital, leading to reduced industrial production, less need of transport (hitting the shipbuilding industry) and so producing mass unemployment. The general effect of the Depression was to lead to (i) increased economic planning (see *New Deal*), (ii) intensified economic nationalism (tariffs), (iii) the encouragement of political nationalist movements as an alternative to communism (e.g. the German Nazis, the Austrian Fatherland Front, the Rumanian Iron Guard, etc.).

Derby, Earl of (1799–1869, born Edward George Stanley, succeeded as fourteenth earl in 1851). As Lord Stanley sat in the House of Commons as a Whig from 1820 to 1835 and was a member of Grey's Reform Act Ministry from 1831 to 1834. In 1833 he introduced the proposals to abolish colonial slavery. From 1841 to 1845 he was Secretary for War and Colonies in the Conservative Ministry of Peel. His strongly protectionist views made him oppose Peel in 1846 and, with Disraeli, he headed the Conservative opposition to Lord John Russell (q.v.). Derby was Prime Minister for nine months in 1852 and from February 1858 until June 1859, but he handled his party badly and could not keep his Cabinets together. He became Prime Minister for a third time in June 1866 and, with Disraeli, piloted the Second Reform Act (see *Parliamentary Reform*) through both Houses. He resigned through ill-health in February 1868, and died in the autumn of the following year. His son, the fifteenth earl (1826–93) served as Foreign Secretary in the Government of 1866–8 and was to hold the same office under Disraeli from 1874 to 1878, but he joined the Liberals in 1880, served as Gladstone's Colonial Secretary from 1882 to 1885, and ended his career as a Liberal Unionist.

De Valera, Eamonn. Born 1882 in New York of a Spanish father and Irish mother, educated in Ireland; commanded a battalion of Irish

Volunteers in the Easter Rising (q.v.) of 1916. He was captured and sentenced to death by the British but not executed, because of his American connexions. He presided over Sinn Féin (q.v.) from 1917 to 1926 and fought with the Irish Republican Army against the 'Free State-ers' 1922–3. His political party, Fianna Fáil (founded 1926) was able to form a government in 1932 and he was Eireann Prime Minister 1932–48, cutting all ties with Britain during the Second World War. He was Prime Minister again from 1951 to 1954 and from 1957 to 1959 when he became President.

Diaz, Porfirio (1830–1915). Mexican dictator; of part Indian descent. Although educated for the Church, Diaz entered politics in the mid-1850s as a supporter of Juárez (q.v.), serving in the war against Maximilian (q.v.) and commanding the troops that recaptured Mexico City (June 1867). He broke with Juárez soon after, but was powerful enough to become the real ruler of the country in 1876, a position he retained for thirty-four years. Government was administered, ruthlessly but efficiently, by a hand-picked clique of personal supporters who packed the judiciary and executive. Diaz had considerable prestige with the Great Powers, partly because he supported all schemes of international cooperation (particularly those sponsored by the U.S.A.) and partly because of the attractive terms he offered to foreign investors. Superficially, Mexico prospered as never before; but his followers aroused the resentment of the peasantry by fraudulent seizure of common land, and his régime fell in a wave of xenophobic feeling and agrarian unrest (May 1911).

Directory. The name given to the executive power in France between August 1795 and November 1799 (see *French Revolution*). There were five 'Directors', jointly responsible for the conduct of affairs. They were assisted by a cumbersome bicameral legislature (comprising 'The Council of the Ancients', who were men over the age of forty, and 'The Council of the Five Hundred'). The Directory represents a halt in the re-organization of France after the sweeping changes of the previous six years. It has received a bad press from historians, most of whom have been enthusiasts either for the genuine revolutionaries who preceded it or for the Napoleonic era which followed it. Many of the Directors were personally corrupt, and the provincial administration was chaotic. Nevertheless, it was during the Directory that France gained her first major victories in the Revolutionary Wars, culminating in the Treaty of Campo-Formio (q.v.). Renewed revolt in the Vendée (q.v.) and the defeats of the War of the Second Coalition (q.v.) completed the alienation of the majority of Frenchmen. On 9 November 1799 Bonaparte overthrew the Directory by the *coup d'état* of 18 Brumaire (q.v.), and established the Consulate (q.v.).

Disarmament Conference of 1932–4; a meeting of sixty nations (including non-members of the League such as Russia and the U.S.A.) at Geneva to secure reduction of national armaments in accordance with the Covenant of the League of Nations. The Conference sat for five months in 1932, eight in 1933, and a fortnight in 1934. It failed, partly because of the insistence of the French that some system of general security should precede disarmament, and partly because of the change in international relations resulting from the advent of Hitler as German Chancellor in January 1933. (The Germans walked out of the Conference in October 1933.)

Disestablishment Acts. One of the chief grievances of the Irish throughout the ninteenth century was the obligation of the Roman Catholics to help support the established Episcopal Church of Ireland (i.e. 'the Church of England in Ireland'), of which less than one seventh of the population were members. In 1869 the first Gladstone Government passed an Act disestablishing and disendowing the Irish Church from 1 January 1871. The Irish clergy were allowed to keep over £13 million of their property, the rest being used for educational purposes or the alleviation of distress. The Church of Ireland remained in existence as an entirely independent, protestant body. Passage of the Act aroused deep feeling in England, where it was interpreted as the prelude to a general attack upon the idea of an official church (which was far from Gladstone's intention). Unsuccessful Bills for disestablishing the episcopal church in Wales were introduced by the Liberals in 1895 and 1909. With the removal of the Lords' power of permanent veto, a Welsh Church Disestablishment Act was carried in 1914, but did not become operative until 1920.

Disraeli, Benjamin (1804–81, created Earl of Beaconsfield 1876). The son of a Jewish author who had been converted to Christianity. After three unsuccessful attempts to enter Parliament, Disraeli was elected for Maidstone in 1837. He was a Tory radical supporting the 'Young England Movement', and these views are reflected in his political novels, *Sybil* and *Coningsby*. He opposed Peel over Free Trade in 1846, and for twenty-two years led the Protectionists in the Commons. He was Chancellor of the Exchequer in 1852, 1858–9, and 1867. As Leader of the Commons he introduced the 1867 Reform

107

Bill. He was Prime Minister for ten months in 1868, and then led the Opposition for six years. He was Prime Minister again from 1874 to 1880, advocating a vigorous foreign policy (which culminated in his attendance at the Congress of Berlin), undertaking social reforms designed to improve housing conditions and hygiene, and promoting the concept of Empire. Colonial rebuffs in Afghanistan and South Africa contributed to his defeat in 1880. He was the 'second founder' of the Conservative Party, imposing on it his own beliefs in domestic reform and imperial development. His personal initiative enabled Britain to purchase 40 per cent of the shares in the Suez Canal (q.v.) in 1875.

Dogger Bank Incident (21 October 1904). During the Russo-Japanese War (q.v.), the Russian Baltic Fleet passing through the North Sea encountered vessels which, from faulty intelligence reports, it believed to be Japanese torpedo boats. The Russians opened fire; in reality, they were firing on Hull fishing boats and sank one trawler, killing two of the crew. Indignation in Britain was so intense that the two countries were almost plunged into war. British warships trailed the Russians across the Bay of Biscay until the Russians agreed to put the responsible officers ashore at Vigo and accept international arbitration. The rest of the fleet resumed the voyage to the Far East, eventually being annihilated at the battle of Tsushima. The incident represents a nadir in Anglo-Russian relations, but the obvious regret in St Petersburg at the naval error, and the Russian acceptance of claims for compensation, eased tension between the two countries, thus indirectly facilitating the Anglo-Russian Entente (q.v.) of 1907.

Dollfuss, Engelbert (1892–1934). Leading politician in the Austrian Republic. After war service Dollfuss, a devout Catholic, joined the Austrian Christian Social Party led by Monsignore Ignaz Siepel. Dollfuss became Austrian Chancellor in May 1932. He was bitterly opposed to socialism, which he believed was favoured by the Austrian democratic constitution. He accordingly suspended parliamentary government in March 1933. In February 1934 a demonstration by socialist workers led Dollfuss to order the Austrian Army to attack the huge socialist housing estates in the suburbs of Vienna, and for five days there was a fierce civil war before the socialists were crushed. Three months later he promulgated a constitution that was fundamentally fascist, but, before it became fully operative, he was murdered (25 July 1934) in his Chancellery, the *Ballhaus*, by Austrian Nazis, trying unsuccessfully to stage a *coup d'état*. In foreign policy, Dollfuss relied on the friendship of Mussolini and co-operation with Hungary. He was succeeded as Chancellor by Kurt von Schuschnigg.

Douglas, Stephen A. (1813–61). Born in Vermont, settled in Illinois at the age of twenty, vigorously working for the development and assimilation of the territories. From 1843 to 1847 he was an active champion of 'Manifest Destiny' (q.v.) in the House of Representatives. As a Senator, he was largely responsible for Bills extending territorial government in Utah and New Mexico (1850), and became leader of the 'Young America' group of Democrats, an aggressively nationalist movement which sought to adapt the republicanism of Mazzini to transatlantic conditions. In 1854 he introduced the Kansas-Nebraska Act, based on the principle of 'popular sovereignty' and formally denying Congress the right to intervene in the slavery dispute in new territories. In 1858 Douglas was challenged as senatorial candidate for Illinois by Abraham Lincoln; a series of seven joint debates between the candidates over slavery helped crystallize the views of both parties on this issue. Douglas, in formulating a moderate Democratic policy over slavery, offended the Southern Democrats. Although Douglas defeated Lincoln in the senatorial election of 1858, he lost to Lincoln in the presidential election of 1860. Once the Civil War began Douglas gave Lincoln his full support.

Dreadnought. A class of 'all-big-gun' battleship, deriving its name from H.M.S. *Dreadnought*, laid down in October 1905, launched in February 1906 and at sea by October 1906. The *Dreadnought* (with ten 12-in. guns and a speed of 21 knots) could outrange and outpace any other type of battleship; she represented a revolution in naval architecture. Although first in service in the Royal Navy, foreign designers were already planning such a vessel when *Dreadnought* was laid down, and there was soon a full-scale naval armaments race. The coming of Dreadnoughts weakened Britain's naval lead, which had been based on the Two-Power Standard (q.v.) of 1889. Since earlier battleships were rendered obsolete, rival fleets could start the construction of the new capital ships on almost level terms. The first German Dreadnought, the *Nassau*, was laid down in July 1907. In 1914, Britain had 19 Dreadnoughts at sea and 13 under construction, compared with Germany's 13 at sea and 7 building. Other countries with Dreadnoughts at sea by 1914 were the U.S.A. (8), France (8), Japan (4), Austria-Hungary (2), and Italy (1). The only major battle in which Dreadnoughts were engaged was Jutland (q.v.). The supremacy of the Dreadnought capital ship was challenged by the Washington Conference of 1921–2 (q.v.) and by the development of air and underwater weapons.

Dred Scott Case (1857). Dred Scott was a negro who was taken from a slave state to 'free soil' in Illinois and Wisconsin, where he remained for four years (1834–8). After returning to Missouri, Scott claimed that he was no longer a slave because he had lived in a free state. Over a period of eleven years, the Case was carried from local courts to Federal District Courts and finally to the Supreme Court. By a majority of 3 to 2 (with 4 non-committal votes) the Supreme Court judges declared that, since a negro slave was not an American citizen, Dred Scott had no right to sue in Federal Courts. They also declared that Scott's status was determined by the laws of the state in which he resided when he raised the question of freedom (i.e. Missouri, a slave state). At the same time, the Supreme Court maintained (by a majority of 6 to 3) that the Missouri Compromise (q.v.), under which Wisconsin was free territory, was unconstitutional since it deprived an owner of his lawful property (in this case, a slave). The Supreme Court's decision was hotly contested by Northern abolitionists and considerably intensified feeling over slavery throughout the Union.

Dreikaiserbund ('League of the Three Emperors'). A diplomatic system for cooperation between Germany, Austria-Hungary and Russia devised by Bismarck after the Franco-Prussian War to maintain peace in Eastern Europe and prevent defeated France securing an ally for a war of revenge. The first Dreikaiserbund was based upon agreements in May and June 1873 (after a preliminary meeting of the Emperors William I, Francis Joseph, and Alexander II in Berlin in September 1872). It was little more than a vague understanding, emphasizing the importance of monarchical solidarity against subversive movements, and did not survive the Eastern Crisis of 1875–8. In 1881 Bismarck negotiated the more formal, but secret, Dreikaiserbund Alliance. This provided for prior consultation about changes in the *status quo* in Turkey, and guaranteed benevolent neutrality if one of the contracting powers was at war with a fourth power (except Turkey). It was valid for three years, renewed in 1884, but lapsed in 1887 because of Austro-Russian tension in the Balkans. Bismarck thereupon maintained his link with Russia through the Reinsurance Treaty (q.v.).

Dreyfus Case. In October 1894 Captain Alfred Dreyfus (1859–1935), an Alsatian Jewish officer on the French General Staff, was court-martialled for treason, degraded, and sentenced to imprisonment on Devil's Island. The evidence consisted of military information, apparently in Dreyfus's handwriting, intended for the Germans. In 1896 a new Chief of Intelligence, Colonel Picquart, discovered that secrets were still being betrayed and that the handwriting of the new source was identical with the handwriting of 1894; his attempts to re-open the Dreyfus Case were frustrated, and he was transferred to Tunisia. In 1897 Dreyfus's brother, independently, made a similar discovery to Picquart's and named the traitor as Major Esterhazy, who was tried and acquitted by a military court. The French Radicals were now aroused, believing that the General Staff (clericalist, royalist, and anti-semitic) was guilty of a prejudiced error and would not admit it. The Dreyfusard cause was taken up by the novelist Zola (who openly denounced the General Staff) and Clemenceau (q.v.). It was found that Dreyfus's original accuser had forged evidence. Dreyfus was retried at Rennes (September 1899), found 'guilty with extenuating circumstances' but pardoned. The Dreyfusards pressed for his acquittal, and in July 1906 the court-martial verdict was quashed, Dreyfus was readmitted to the Army, promoted, and given the Legion of Honour. He rendered distinguished service in the First World War. The *affaire* went far deeper into French life than any ordinary court case. Throughout 1898–9 there was a violent press campaign and frequent street clashes, with the Dreyfusards (intellectuals, Socialists, and radicals) accusing the Anti-Dreyfusards (the Army leaders and the Church) of discrediting the Republic and seeking an excuse for an authoritarian régime. The latent hostility of these two factions continued throughout the Third Republic.

Dual Alliance usually signifies the Franco-Russian Alliance (q.v.) of 1893–4, but may also be applied to the secret Austro-German Alliance of 1879, the keystone of Bismarck's international system, by which the two powers promised each other support if attacked by Russia. The Austro-German Dual Alliance remained valid until 1918; it was expanded in 1882 into a Triple Alliance (q.v.), including Italy.

Duma. The name given to the Russian Parliament created by Nicholas II in response to demands in the Revolution of 1905 (q.v.). The First Duma was elected on a broad suffrage in the spring of 1906 and sat from 10 May to 21 July. Since the Tsar reserved the prerogative to legislate by decree, and limited the Duma's financial powers, the session was occupied by an extensive campaign for recognition of rights, and ended in deadlock. The Second Duma (5 March–16 June 1907) was even more radical and, on its dissolution, a new electoral law increased the representation of the middle classes at the expense of the commonalty. The Third Duma, elected on this basis, sat from the end of 1907 to 1912 and achieved some basic reforms. The Fourth Duma (1912–16) was less effective, because of the international crisis and the War, but in November 1916 gave clear warning of the impending revolution unless there was a fundamental change in the régime. (See *Russian Revolution*.)

Dunkirk. Port in Northern France from which over 200,000 British troops and 120,000 French were evacuated, 27 May–4 June 1940, when the capitulation of the Belgian Army in the north and the thrust of German tank forces in the south cut off the British Expeditionary Force and the French First Army. Over 850 vessels took part in the evacuation, half of them small craft hurriedly sent across from England. All heavy equipment was abandoned.

Durham, Earl (1792–1840, born John George Lambton, created a Baron 1828, Earl 1832). As 'Radical Jack' Lambton, he was one of the main champions of parliamentary reform and a supporter of Earl Grey, whose daughter he married. He was Lord Privy Seal in 1830, and was sent as Ambassador to St Petersburg in 1832, but returned home to help found the Colonization Society, seeking a just and active policy of colonial development. In 1838 Melbourne sent him to Canada as Governor-General to examine the causes of the rebellion of Mackenzie (q.v.) and Papineau. His high-handed treatment of former rebels lost him the support of the Government, and he was recalled after only six months in Canada. On his return, however, he presented the Colonial Office with the famous Durham Report (1839), which, by advocating the granting of responsible government to colonial territories, revolutionized the British concept of empire.

Easter Rising. A rebellion in Dublin from 24 to 29 April 1916, to secure immediate Irish independence. The rising was led by P. H. Pearse of the Irish Republican Brotherhood and James Connolly of the Sinn Féin (q.v.). There was serious street fighting and loss of life around the Dublin General Post Office. Hopes of German aid were not realized. Fourteen leaders were subsequently executed;

others were spared because of possible adverse reactions in the U.S.A. Rebel prisoners were amnestied in June 1917.

Eastern Question. A collective term for the problems raised in south-eastern Europe by the weakness of the Ottoman Turkish Empire and the rivalry of its successors. The problems fell into three main groups which, on occasions, overlapped – especially in the 1870s.

(i) *Attempts by neighbouring supra-national empires to benefit at the expense of Turkey.* (*a*) Russia: began to encroach on the Ottoman Empire with the wars of Catherine the Great (1768–74 and 1787–92), securing the Crimea, obtaining rights in the Danubian Principalities (q.v.) and recognition of protective rights for the Orthodox Church in Constantinople (Treaty of Kuchuk-Kainardji, 1774). The Russians fought an indecisive war with Turkey from 1806 to 1812, and, intervening on behalf of the Greeks in 1828, advanced across the Balkan Mountains and imposed the lenient Treaty of Adrianople (1829). Religious rights and a desire to anticipate the apparently imminent disintegration of the Empire led to the Crimean War (q.v.). Russia renewed her pressure on Turkey in the 1870s through Panslavism (q.v.), and, in the war of 1877–8, reached the suburbs of Constantinople, where the abortive Treaty of San Stefano (q.v.) was signed. Russian expansionist tendencies revived under Izvolski (q.v.) in the period 1907–10, gaining British and French recognition in the Constantinople Agreements (q.v.) of 1915, which were rendered invalid by the Bolshevik Revolution. (*b*) Austria: was mainly interested in the acquisition of the western Balkans, achieving success with the occupation of Bosnia-Herzegovina (q.v.) in 1878, annexing the provinces in 1908, and thereafter being troubled by national hostility that had earlier been directed at the Turks. This hostility was a contributory cause of war in 1914.

(ii) *Attempts to prevent the disintegration of the Ottoman Empire.* Although Austria (under Metternich) and Russia (between 1829 and 1841) sought to preserve the Empire, the role of protector was normally reserved for Britain until 1897. The British had tried to prevent the Russians acquiring the naval base of Oczakov as early as 1792, and except during the Greek War of Independence (see *Navarino*) opposed Russia consistently throughout the century, aiding the Turks militarily in the Crimean War and by diplomatic pressure in 1878, and seeking to prevent Russian domination of the Straits (q.v.) by the Convention of 1841 closing the Dardanelles and the Bosphorus to foreign warships in time of peace. At the same time, the British sought to induce the Turks to reform their oppres-

sive governmental methods. With the visit of Kaiser William II to
Constantinople in 1898, Turkey tended to rely more and more on
Germany, rather than Britain, for support and gave the Germans
valuable railway and commercial concessions, receiving in exchange
military instructors and becoming Germany's ally in 1914.

(iii) *The rise of independent national states.* In the later Middle
Ages the Ottomans had conquered all the nationalities of the
Balkans. The first of these subject nationalities to revolt against the
Turks were the Serbs (in 1804 and again in 1815), but it was Greece
(q.v.) which aroused European sympathy by the War of Independence (1821–30). The Rumanians received international support,
especially from the French, after the Crimean War; their independence was confirmed in 1878. The Bulgarians rose in 1875, eventually securing recognition as an autonomous united principality in
1886, with formal independence following in October 1908. The
Balkan peoples combined against Turkey in the Balkan War (q.v.) of
1912, resulting in a considerable enlargement of Serbia and Greece
and the creation of an independent Albania (q.v.). Bitter rivalry developed between Serbia and Bulgaria; the two countries opposed
each other in the First World War.

The last phase of the traditional Eastern Question was marked by
the attempt of Mustapha Kemal (q.v.) to save the nucleus of a
Turkish national state after the defeat of 1918. The old Eastern
Question may be said to have ended with the Treaty of Lausanne
(q.v.) of 1923.

Education Acts. Although the first grant of public money for educational purposes was made in 1833, it was not until Forster's Education Act of 1870 that education was recognized as a public service,
existing Church schools receiving increased grants and locally
elected boards being empowered to establish schools (maintained in
part by local rates) in other areas. School attendance became compulsory in 1880, while all fees in elementary schools were abolished
in 1891. Balfour's Education Act of 1902 placed 'board schools'
under borough or county councils (Local Education Authorities),
authorizing them to establish secondary and technical schools as
well as developing the existing elementary schools. The Education
Act of H. A. L. Fisher of 1918 provided valuable ancillary services
(medical inspection, nursery schools, special centres for defectives,
etc.) and declared in favour of compulsory part-time education for
young people aged fourteen to eighteen, a scheme never carried out
for reasons of economy. The R. A. Butler Act of 1944 transformed
the Board of Education (established in 1899) into a Ministry, raised

the school-leaving age to fifteen, and re-organized the system of state-aided education by subdividing it into primary, secondary, and further educational stages. The basic principle behind the 1944 Act was that every child should have the education 'appropriate to his age, aptitude and ability'.

Edward VII, King-Emperor (born 1841, reigned 1901–10). The eldest son and second child of Queen Victoria. In 1863 he married Princess Alexandra (1844–1925), daughter of King Christian IX of Denmark. As Victoria thought him indiscreet, she denied him access to Cabinet papers until 1892. He was forced, as Prince of Wales, to become a man of the world, in striking contrast to the austerity of his mother's court. His natural liking for ceremonial pomp and circumstance created the illusion that, as King, he enjoyed a power he did not possess. His influence on foreign policy has been curiously exaggerated, especially by German writers, who have read into his personal dislike of the Kaiser and his delight in European travel some fiendish policy of 'encirclement'. His rôle in bringing about the Anglo-French Entente (q.v.) was limited to exercising his felicitous gift of unruffled urbanity on determinedly republican ears during a visit to Paris in 1903. In home affairs, he interfered much less than his mother, or indeed his son George V.

Egypt. Became part of the Ottoman Empire in 1517. It was invaded by the French under Bonaparte in 1798 but formally restored to the Sultan in 1802. From 1805 to 1848 the country was ruled by Mehemet Ali (q.v.) as Governor (Khedive) under the Sultan. French advisers helped Mehemet establish an orderly economy and a powerful army. Khedive Mehemet Said (1854–63) also encouraged French influence, granting the concession to construct the Suez Canal (q.v.). Further efforts to modernize Egypt were undertaken by Khedive Ismail (1863–79), but his son Tewfik (Khedive 1879–92) was weak, and after anti-European demonstrations British troops occupied Egypt (1882). From 1883 to 1907 the country was administered by Sir Evelyn Baring (created Lord Cromer, q.v., in 1892). When Britain went to war with Turkey in 1914 Egypt was declared a British protectorate, becoming the main base for land operations against Turkey. Post-war disturbances led to formal recognition of Egypt's independence in 1922, with Fuad I (a brother of Tewfik) as King. Nationalist agitation led by the Wafd Party continued throughout the inter-war period. Fuad's son, Farouk (born 1920), succeeded him in 1936. In the same year, an Anglo-Egyptian Treaty provided for the gradual withdrawal of British forces (except from the Canal

Zone). The Italian invasion of Egypt in September 1940 and the subsequent Libyan campaigns postponed the British departure. Nationalist feeling was intensified after the war by the creation of the state of Israel (against whom the Egyptians fought a disastrous war in 1948). The monarchy was overthrown in 1952, a Republic being proclaimed in February 1953 and passing under the control of Colonel Nasser in the following year. The withdrawal of the last British troops was followed in July 1956 by the nationalization of the Suez Canal and by Anglo-French military intervention (November 1956). Egypt formed the 'United Arab Republic' with Syria 1958, but the Syrians re-asserted their independence in September 1961.

Eldon, Earl of (1751–1838, born John Scott, raised to peerage 1799). Entered the Commons in 1782 and became Solicitor-General 1788, Attorney-General 1793, and Lord Chancellor in 1801, holding the office until 1827 except for a few months in 1807. Eldon was associated in the public mind with the repressive policy of the period 1815–19, when he vigorously opposed the political manifestations of the new radicalism. He was widely respected among the legal profession as an equity judge.

Elgin, Lord (James Bruce, 1811–63, succeeded his father as 8th Earl in 1841). Son of the distinguished diplomat who in 1816 had induced the Sultan to authorize the removal of the so-called 'Elgin Marbles' from the Parthenon. The son married a daughter of Lord Durham (q.v.) and, as Governor-General of Canada from 1847 to 1856, did much to implement his father-in-law's famous Report, thereby ensuring the responsibility of the executive in Canada to the representatives of the Canadian peoples. He was also able to improve relations between French Canadians and the British. In 1857–8 Elgin led an expedition to China and was able to secure the Treaties of Tientsin (q.v.). He became the second Viceroy of India in 1862, but died after only a year in India.

Emancipation of the Serfs (March 1861). The most far-reaching reform of Tsar Alexander II (q.v.), liberated twenty million serfs who had been bound to perform duties for their masters and to work their holdings in open field strips organized in village communes. (Another million serfs, whose duties put them technically in a different category, were freed by separate edicts at the same time on slightly better terms.) All serfdom was abolished, the peasants becoming free citizens and receiving land from the landlords. The state compensated the landlords, recovering the money over forty-nine years from the peasants. The main faults of the reform were: (i) it imposed a crippling burden of 'Redemption Debts' on the peasants (which they could not pay in times of bad harvests); (ii) the distribution of land varied, so that in the more fertile areas the peasant received less than his fair share; (iii) the peasantry were still treated as a class apart, with specific obligations to the commune. Yet although emancipation modified the form rather than the character of Russian farming, it helped change the economy by increasing the mobility of labour and thereby enabling industrialists to use ex-serfs in the new factories or on the railways. A further twenty million serfs on state lands had already been freed from bondage under Nicholas I and had their remaining restrictions removed in 1866.

Empire of France, The First. The rule of Napoleon I from May 1804 to April 1814 and from March to June 1815. It is important to note that Napoleon was crowned (in December 1804) 'Emperor of the French' the title implying dominion over territory greater in extent than the old boundaries of the Kingdom of France. Thus, at its zenith in 1811 the French Empire stretched from Lübeck on the Baltic to Gaeta, south of Rome, and included a stretch of the Dalmatian coast. The description *First* Empire was adopted during the *Second* Empire (q.v.) of 1852–70.

Ems Telegram. On 13 July 1870, the French Ambassador had an interview with the King of Prussia at the German spa of Ems in which he asked for assurances that Prussia would never support a Hohenzollern candidate for the Spanish throne, a request refused by the King. A telegram reporting the interview was sent by the King to Bismarck in Berlin, who doctored the text so that it appeared as if the King had insulted the Ambassador and the Ambassador the King. In this form, the telegram was released to the press, where it had the effect of exciting national feeling in Paris and Berlin to such an extent that the French declared war on Prussia on 19 July. (See *Franco-Prussian War*.)

Enclosure Acts. The enclosing of land for improved tillage had begun in Tudor times, but by 1790 only two fifths of the cultivated land of England was enclosed. From 1793, when Pitt established the Board of Agriculture, the enclosure movement developed rapidly, sometimes by common agreement among owners but often by parliamentary action. In order to meet the need for corn, over 1,500 Enclosure Acts were passed in the period 1795–1812. Farms increased in size and were able to maintain better stocks, but the

Enclosures took a heavy toll of the old yeoman class. General Enclosure Acts, cheapening the process of enclosure and guarding against injustices, were passed in 1801 and 1837, while the Act of 1845 set up Enclosure Commissioners to safeguard the rights of the smaller men and to set aside land for recreation or for allotments. At its peak the Enclosure Movement represented a deep social revolution, forcing the smaller cottager, who depended on customary rights, to become a hired farm labourer if he were to continue to work on the land.

Encyclical. A circular letter sent to all churches within a certain area; normally a letter of major importance from the Pope. Although many encyclicals are concerned with specifically theological questions, others have formulated the political and social theories of Roman Catholicism. Among these have been: *Mirari Vos* (Gregory XVI, 1832) and *Singulari Nos* (Gregory XVI, 1834) against the Catholic Liberalism of Lamennais (q.v.).; *Quanta Cura* (Pius IX, 1864), condemning rationalistic and liberal philosophy; *Rerum Novarum* (Leo XIII, 1891), rejecting socialism but stressing the importance of social justice in the industrial state; *Quadragesimo Anno* (Pius XI, 1931) confirming *Rerum Novarum* and emphasizing possible evils from free competition or excessive centralization; *Domini Redemptoris* (Pius XI, 1937) 'on the false doctrines of the bolshevistic atheists'; and *Mit brennender Sorge* (Pius XI, 1937), an encyclical in the German language read from all pulpits in Germany on Palm Sunday and condemning Nazism as fundamentally unchristian.

Engels, Friedrich (1820–95). Joint-founder with Marx of modern communism; was born in Germany, where his father was a textile manufacturer. After military training in Berlin, Engels became Manchester agent of his father's business and became interested in Chartism (q.v.), writing a study of working conditions in 1844. His political interest brought him into contact with his fellow German exile, Karl Marx, with whom he cooperated on the *Communist Manifesto*, 1848. After participating in the revolutionary movement in Baden, Engels returned to Mancunian commerce and saw to it that Marx was supplied with money while he carried out his researches into economic history and philosophy. From 1860 to 1869 Engels was a partner in his father's business and thereafter had a large private income. From 1870 to Marx's death in 1883, Engels spent all his time assisting Marx with his writings and continued work on Marx's *Das Kapital* after Marx's death, completing it only in 1894.

Enghien, Louis Antoine de Bourbon Condé, Duc d' (1772–1804). Last member of the distinguished French family of Condé and, through his mother, first cousin of the later King Louis Philippe (q.v.). Enghien was born at Chantilly and fought in the émigré French Royal Army from 1792 to 1801. He subsequently settled near Baden, whence he was kidnapped in March 1804 by agents of Napoleon, who wrongly believed that he had been implicated in a conspiracy to assassinate him. Enghien was brought to Vincennes, tried by a military court for having taken up arms with the enemies of France, and shot (21 March). The execution of Enghien effectively prevented any further Bourbon plots, but it caused revulsion among the Courts of Europe, where it was felt that, because of Enghien's royal blood, Napoleon had made himself a regicide.

Entente Cordiale. Name frequently applied to the Anglo-French Entente (q.v.) of 1904.

Erfurt Conference (October 1808). An elaborately staged meeting of Napoleon and Tsar Alexander I in the presence of the German Princes. Napoleon's object was to demonstrate publicly the friendship between the French and Russian Emperors established fifteen months earlier at Tilsit (q.v.). At the same time, he hoped to make Alexander induce Austria to stay out of the war; he also wished to settle differences with the Russians over the future of Turkey. Alexander, secretly informed of Napoleon's plans by Talleyrand (q.v.), played for time and skilfully avoided committing himself. The Conference fell far short of Napoleon's expectations.

Estonia. The most northerly of the three independent Baltic Republics created in 1917 during the Bolshevik Revolution and receiving general recognition in 1920. Estonia, which covers some 18,000 square miles, was formerly a Russian province, but its people were Lutheran in religion and had closer racial and linguistic affinities with the Finns than with their immediate neighbours. Between the wars, agrarian reforms permitted the emergence of a predominantly prosperous peasant community, governed by a virtual dictator, Paets, from 1934 to 1937. The Nazi-Soviet Pact (q.v.) exposed Estonia to Russian penetration. Naval bases were ceded to Russia in September 1939, the whole country being occupied in June 1940 and proclaimed a constituent republic of the U.S.S.R. in August 1940, an act never recognized by either Britain or America. Estonia was in German occupation from 1941 to 1944.

Ethiopia. See *Abyssinia*.

Evangelical Movement. The name given to a group within the Church of England in the middle of the eighteenth century which sought to combat the apathy of the English clergy by emphasizing the importance of moral earnestness and of proclaiming salvation by faith. The movement subsequently became particularly powerful in Cambridge, where one of its leaders, the Reverend Charles Simeon, was Vicar of Holy Trinity from 1783 to 1836. Simeon and his followers helped to found the Church Missionary Society in 1797 and influenced the Clapham Sect (q.v.). A later supporter was Lord Shaftesbury (q.v.), who cherished the philanthropic traditions of the movement until his death in 1885.

Eylau, Battle of (8–9 February 1807). An indecisive battle in East Prussia. Napoleon with a force of 60,000 men attacked 80,000 Russians and Prussians under Bennigsen; both sides lost about 20,000 men, but the Russians were able to retire in good order. One wing of the French Army, Augereau's corps, had been thrown into confusion and almost wiped out. Although technically a Napoleonic victory, Eylau was the worst blow to French prestige on land for eight years. Bennigsen was subsequently defeated in the following June at Friedland.

Eyre, Edward John (1815-1901). British explorer and colonial administrator. Eyre emigrated from his native Scotland in 1832 and settled in Australia. At the age of 25 he explored the area around Lake Torrens, discovering the lake that is named after him. With an aborigine as his sole companion, he then turned westward and became the first white man to cross the formidable desert known as the Nullarbor Plain to western Australia. Throughout his period of residence in Australia he gained a reputation as a protector of the native peoples. As Governor of Jamaica in the 1860s, however, Eyre was forced to deal with a negro rising which had broken out in the Morant Bay area in 1865 because of resentment of squatters at having to pay rent. Eyre put down the revolt swiftly but with excessive cruelty, ordering the execution of 450 natives, the flogging of many more, and the burning of 1,000 native homes. There was widespread indignation in Britain, with the leading figures of Victorian intellectual life taking up positions for or against Eyre. An attempt to prosecute Eyre for the manslaughter of a wealthy mulatto failed, but he was censured and dismissed. The Negro rising led, in Jamaica, to the temporary suspension of representative government (which was not restored until 1884).

Fabian Society. A movement of predominantly middle-class intellectuals established in January 1884 to spread socialist ideas among the educated public and to work out the application of socialist principles to Britain. Among early Fabians were Bernard Shaw (1856–1950) and Sidney and Beatrice Webb (1859–1947, 1858–1943). The Fabians rejected revolutionary Marxism. They believed that socialism must eventually triumph as a sequel of universal suffrage, but only as the climax of a long period of political evolution – a belief that Sidney Webb later termed 'the inevitability of gradualness'. Meanwhile, the Fabians devised schemes for municipal socialism and for improved labour conditions. The Society achieved prominence in 1889 with the publication of *Fabian Essays* and was one of the constituent elements of the Labour Representation Committee (later Labour Party, q.v.) in 1900. Subsequently the Society tended to act as a specialized research agency for the Labour Party. The name of the Society was derived from Quintus Fabius Maximus, the Roman General of the Second Punic War, who sought to avoid pitched battles with the Carthaginians, preferring to weaken them by harassing operations.

Factory Acts. In the late eighteenth century the rapid growth in Britain of a factory system unrestricted by state regulations led to numerous social evils – child labour, long hours, etc. – and an eventual demand for remedial legislation. The first Bill, prohibiting the employment of apprentices for more than 12 hours a day, was passed by Parliament in 1802 on the initiative of Sir Robert Peel, father of the later Prime Minister. In 1819 a Factory Act forbade employment of children under nine. Employers found easy ways of evading further regulations imposed in 1820, 1825, and 1830. In 1833 the great Factory Act of Shaftesbury (q.v.) re-affirmed the ban on children under nine and limited those between nine and thirteen to nine hours work a day and between twelve and eighteen to twelve a day. It also appointed inspectors to ensure that the Act was effective. Another Act of Shaftesbury's in 1840 banned the employment of children for chimney-sweeping, while an Act of 1844 limited women to twelve hours a day and imposed safety regulations for dangerous machinery. The Mines Act of 1842 forbade the employment of women or boys under thirteen in the mines. There was further legislation in the 1850s and 1860s, and in 1874 women and children were limited to ten working hours a day. In 1891, legislation forbade the employment of children under eleven; this was raised to twelve in 1901 and fourteen in 1920.

Faraday, Michael (1791–1867). English chemist and physicist. From 1812 to 1823 he assisted Sir Humphry Davy in chemical research on gases. Subsequently he made possible the development of electrical energy by his discovery in 1831 of electro-magnetic induction and in 1845 of diamagnetism. Faraday was also the originator of the theory of the atom as the centre of force.

Fashoda. Small town in the Sudan (q.v.) on the Upper Nile, centre of a crisis in Anglo-French relations, September-November 1898. British troops under Kitchener (q.v.), advancing up the Nile after the victory of Omdurman, encountered a French force led by March-and, which had penetrated across the continent from Brazzaville in an eighteen-month journey. The British feared that the French in-tended eventually to dam the Nile and thereby hamper the irrigation of British-occupied Egypt. The French claim to the Fashoda region by right of prior conquest was denied by the British, who prepared for a general war. As France was weakened by the Dreyfus Case and unable to rely on her Russian ally she gave in, withdrew Marchand and, by an agreement of March 1899, renounced all claims to the Nile Valley. The incident was regarded in France as a severe defeat; during the Anglo-French negotiations of 1904 Lord Cromer ordered Fashoda to be renamed Kodok in order to remove a word of national humiliation to the French.

Fenian Brotherhood. An Irish revolutionary movement formed originally among Irish immigrants in the U.S.A. in 1858 by James Stephens, but spreading to Ireland in 1865. The name was derived from the *Fianna*, legendary Irish heroes. The American Fenians staged a raid across the Canadian border in May 1866, while Irish Fenians attempted to seize Chester (February 1867), attacked police barracks, and tried to blow up Clerkenwell Jail (killing 12 people). Differences between Stephens and other, wilder, leaders (and de-nunciation of the Fenians by the Catholic hierarchy) prevented the movement becoming a major rebellion and it dissolved in the course of 1868. The Fenians were, however, largely responsible for awaken-ing Gladstone to the urgency of the Irish problem.

Ferry, Jules (1832–93). French statesman, born in the Vosges, studied law and entered politics in the late 1860s with a series of attacks on the alleged peculation of Baron Haussmann (q.v.). Ferry was elected a Republican Deputy for Paris in 1869 and served as Prefect of the Seine throughout the Siege of Paris and the Commune of 1871. He was a member of the Republican Governments of the period 1879–85, being Prime Minister in 1880–1 and 1883–5. His chief concerns were education and colonial development. He curbed the power of the Church and passed the momentous law of 28 March 1882, which made primary education in France free, non-clerical, and compulsory. At the same time, he left a permanent mark on the French educational system by insisting on the teaching of essentially Christian ethics without the propagation of a religious faith. In the colonies, Ferry was responsible for the acquisition of Tunis (q.v.) and the completion of the conquest of Indo-China. He also enabled France to acquire a share of the Congo and Mada-gascar. He was unique among French politicians in collaborating with Bismarck (at the Berlin Conference), but his preoccupation with imperialism led to attacks from the radical nationalists, who were fundamentally anti-German, and so precipitated his fall in April 1885. Ferry was shot by a lunatic in March 1893 and died from his wounds.

Finland. United with Sweden from the early Middle Ages until 1809, when, following a Russian invasion in the previous year, it was created a Grand-Duchy within the Russian Empire and guaranteed constitutional government. The Russians respected Finland's auton-omy until 1898, when they began a policy of deliberate Russification, formally suspending the constitution in 1903. After the Revolution of 1905 (q.v.) the Finns regained their autonomy and in 1906 were allowed to elect a Diet chosen by universal suffrage of both sexes. A further period of repression bgan in 1910, and the Finns seized the opportunity of the revolutionary chaos of 1917 in Russia to pro-claim their independence (20 July). Throughout 1918 there was civil war in Finland between Bolsheviks and 'Whites' (led by Mannerheim, q.v.). Conservative groups, headed by Svinhufvud, had favoured a German connexion in 1917–18, but with the end of the war this faction disintegrated, and in July 1919 Finland adopted a demo-cratic and republican constitution. Living standards between the wars remained high. Foreign policy was marked by frontier disputes with Sweden (over the Aaland Islands, q.v.) and with Russia (over Karelia). In 1930 and 1932 a fascist movement (the *Lapua* organiza-tion) attempted a *coup d'état* and secured the passage of anti-com-munist laws. Russian demands for bases and for cession of part of the Karelian Isthmus were rejected by the Finns in November 1939, and there followed a fiercely fought fifteen-week war before the

Finns surrendered some 16,000 square miles of territory to Russia. In 1941 the Finns joined the Germans in attacking Russia in the hope of recovering their lost lands, but they were forced to sue for a separate peace in 1944. Although Finland ceded Petsamo to Russia in the 1947 Peace Treaty and gave the Russian fleet facilities at Porkkala (which, in fact, the Russians evacuated in 1955), the country never became a communist satellite state.

Fisher, John Arbuthnot (1841–1920, created a Baron 1909). British Admiral; began his naval training afloat at the age of thirteen and saw action in China five years later. Although trained under sail, Fisher was always alive to the importance of new techniques and became an early enthusiast for the torpedo. His drive (and capacity for self-publicity) won him rapid promotion, and he gained an international reputation as a somewhat bellicose delegate to the Hague Peace Conference of 1899. As Commander-in-Chief, Mediterranean, from 1899 to 1902, Fisher revolutionized training and tactics. He served as First Sea Lord from 1903 to January 1910 and was thus responsible for preparing the fleet to meet the German menace in the North Sea. He also identified his fiery personality with the race to construct Dreadnoughts (q.v.). Although generally recognized as the greatest British Admiral since Nelson, his ferocious zeal made him many enemies; he had a serious dispute with the Commander-in-Chief, Channel Fleet, Lord Charles Beresford. Fisher retired in 1910, but was brought back as First Sea Lord by Churchill in October 1914. Fisher and Churchill were, however, too similar in temperament to collaborate. Fisher resented Churchill's insistence on moving ships to the Mediterranean for the Gallipoli operation, and resigned in a huff in May 1915.

Fiume. A port on the northern Adriatic, now called Rijeka. Fiume was developed as a Hungarian commercial port in the nineteenth century, although the population was predominantly Croatian and partly Italian. When the future of the port was under discussion at the Paris Peace Conference, the Italian nationalist poet Gabriele d'Annunzio seized Fiume with a band of fanatics (September 1919) and defied the peacemakers until ejected in January 1921. A plan for establishing a Free City in Fiume (Treaty of Rapallo, q.v., 1920) was abandoned after Mussolini came to power, and in January 1924 the Yugoslavs recognized the incorporation of the greater part of Fiume in Italy, although they retained the adjoining small harbour of Sušak. The trade and prosperity of Fiume declined considerably under the Italians, and in 1946 the port was formally ceded to Yugoslavia.

Five-Year Plans. The Stalinist organization of the economy of the U.S.S.R. so as to expand industry and collectivize agriculture. The First Five-Year Plan (1928–32 inclusive), a gigantic social revolution involving considerable suffering, developed heavy industry, and organized a centralized agricultural economy. The Second Five-Year Plan (1933–7) enabled more consumer goods to be produced. The Third (1938–42) again imposed heavy burdens on the people, as it concentrated on armaments and defence. Typical products of the Five-Year Plans were the steel-city of Magnitogorsk in the Urals and the hydro-electric power installation at Dnepropetrovsk in the Ukraine.

Foch, Ferdinand (1851–1929, Marshal of France 1918). Born at Tarbes, the son of a civil servant. Entered the army on the outbreak of the Franco-Prussian War. He became an artillery specialist on the General Staff in the 1880s and spent ten years at the École de Guerre as lecturer or commandant. He commanded a division in 1911 and an army corps in 1912. He led the French Ninth Army in the first battle of the Marne (September 1914) and commanded an Army Group on the Somme in July 1916. After a spell of retirement, he returned in May 1917 as chief of staff to the French C.-in-C., Pétain (q.v.). Foch showed more initiative than Pétain and so won the confidence of his allies that in April 1918 he was appointed Supreme Generalissimo of the Allied Armies on the Western Front. He mounted the counter-offensive to the Germans on 15 July 1918 (Second Battle of the Marne), following this up in August by the operations that led the Germans to request an Armistice in November. After playing a prominent part in the Paris Peace Conference, he retired from public life.

Ford, Henry (1863–1947). American industrialist, born and died in Dearborn, Michigan. He served as a machine-shop apprentice in Detroit for five years. He built his first car in 1892–3, but it was not until 1903 that he organized the Ford Motor Company at Detroit, producing in 1909 the first cheap standardized car constructed on a mass-production assembly line. These methods inaugurated a world-wide technique of production that made possible the rapid expansion of the motor-car industry. Ford was in many ways a social pioneer – thus in 1914 he introduced an eight-hour day, with a minimum daily wage equivalent to £1 and a profit-sharing scheme for his employees.

He made several abortive excursions into politics, the most controversial being the despatch of a much-publicized 'Peace Ship' to Scandinavia in 1915 to seek neutral mediation in the war. After the U.S.A. became a belligerent, Ford mass-produced motor vehicles for the Army. He was president of the Ford Motor Company in 1903–19 and 1943–7.

Fouché, Joseph (1759–1820, created Duke of Otranto 1806). French politican, born at Nantes. He was a zealous supporter of Robespierre in 1792–3, touring the provinces on behalf of the Jacobins and achieving notoriety because of his harshness at Lyons. He turned against Robespierre in 1794 because of the cult of the Supreme Being (which he regarded with contempt). Fouché helped Tallien overthrow Robespierre and subsequently became a supporter of Barras (q.v.) under the Directory. He became Minister of Police in July 1799, and continued to hold the office under Napoleon until 1802. His internal spy system was of such value to Napoleon that Fouché was again made Minister of Police (and Minister of the Interior) in July 1804, remaining in office for six years and being dismissed for alleged contacts with the British. He returned a third time as Police Minister in the Hundred Days of 1815, but safeguarded himself by secretly keeping in touch with Metternich and Louis XVIII. After the Bourbon Restoration he served for a time as Ambassador in Dresden.

Fourteen Points. A statement of war aims made by President Wilson of the U.S.A. in a speech on 8 January 1918. Briefly, the points were: (1) A renunciation of all secret diplomacy ('Open covenants openly arrived at'); (2) Freedom of the seas; (3) Removal, as far as possible, of economic barriers; (4) Reduction of armaments; (5) Impartial adjustment of colonial claims; (6) Evacuation of Russian territory; (7) Restoration of Belgium; (8) Liberation of France and return of Alsace-Lorraine; (9) Re-adjustment of Italian frontiers 'along clearly recognizable lines of nationality'; (10) Autonomous development for the peoples of Austria-Hungary; (11) Evacuation of Rumania, Serbia, and Montenegro, with Serbia receiving access to the sea; (12) Self-development for non-Turkish peoples of the Ottoman Empire and free passage of Dardanelles; (13) Creation of an independent Poland with free and secure access to the sea; (14) Formation of a general association of nations to guarantee the political independence of all states. These principles were accepted by the Allied Powers as a basis for peace in November 1918, subject to reservations on the meaning of Point 2 and the imposition on the ex-enemy states of Reparations (q.v.). In practice, too, the Allies were bound by secret agreements made prior to America's entry into the war, the most famous of which, the Treaty of London (q.v.), was a contradiction of several of Wilson's principles. Nevertheless, it was on the basis of the 'Fourteen Points' that Germany and Austria-Hungary asked for armistices in November 1918 (Wilson having made it clear that he had amended Point 10 to 'complete independence for the people of Austria-Hungary'). Subsequently, the Germans maintained that the Allied statesmen at the Paris Peace Conference (q.v.) had violated the principle of self-determination implicit in the Fourteen Points, especially by forbidding the union of Germany and Austria, as the majority of Austrians desired at that time.

Fox, Charles James (1749–1806). The second son of Henry Fox, Lord Holland (1705–74), who, in the course of a devious political career, had amassed a considerable fortune. The younger Fox was educated at Eton and Oxford and began his political career as a supporter of Lord North in 1768, being elected M.P. for Midhurst shortly after his nineteenth birthday. His naturally tempestuous spirit rapidly turned him into a critic of the administration, and in 1774 he joined the Rockingham Whigs in opposing the Government's policy on America. He was in charge of foreign affairs for a few months in 1782 and again in 1783, when he temporarily allied with North under the nominal leadership of the Duke of Portland. The failure of Fox's India Bill in 1783 marked the start of more than twenty years in opposition to the younger Pitt (q.v.), a political duel deepened by Fox's enthusiasm for the early stages of the French Revolution and his persistent hostility to British military participation. In the course of these debates, Fox emerged as the champion of the liberty of the subject and of the press, and thereby established a tradition of political values that was to develop under his friend Grey (q.v.) into nineteenth-century liberalism. His disapproval of the French War led Fox to withdraw from parliamentary life from May 1797 to January 1800. On Pitt's death, Fox returned as Foreign Secretary but died himself nine months later. Fox was no classical orator but he was supreme as debater and critic, triumphing over personal scandal and political errors and achieving eminence in the Commons without a powerful following in the country. He entranced the House by his histrionic talents. A foreign observer once told Pitt that he could not understand how Fox maintained his political influence: 'Ah,' Pitt replied, 'you have not been under the wand of the magician.'

Francis Ferdinand, Archduke of Austria (1863–1914). Nephew of Francis Joseph and heir to the Austrian throne from 1889. Francis Ferdinand was a man of strong character; he distrusted the political power given to the Hungarians in the Dual Monarchy after the Ausgleich (q.v.), and wished to give more influence to the Slav peoples of the Monarchy, especially the Czechs. In 1900 he morganatically married the Countess Sophie Chotek (a Czech); the insults and affronts to which his wife was exposed by the petty restrictions of antiquated etiquette made Francis Ferdinand hostile to the régime, and he became on bad terms with his uncle the Emperor. Speculation on the extent to which Francis Ferdinand would have been a reforming monarch is, however, vain; on 28 June 1914 he was assassinated, with his wife, on a ceremonial visit to Sarajevo (q.v.), by a Bosnian Serb fanatic, an event that precipitated the First World War.

Francis Joseph, Emperor of Austria (born 1830, reigned 1848–1916). Succeeded to the throne on the abdication of his uncle, Ferdinand, during the revolution of 1848, crowned King of Hungary in 1867. Francis Joseph once described himself as 'the last monarch of the old school'. His political ideas were formed in the four years after his accession, during the autocratic régime of Prince Schwarzenberg (q.v.). Although forced to accept a major change in the character of his empire by the Ausgleich (q.v.) of 1867, he continued throughout his life to distrust all notions of party government, preferring bureaucratic administration under a benevolent dynasty. He strove conscientiously to turn the Habsburg dynasty into an impersonal institution, thereby steeling himself to survive military defeat and personal tragedy. His brother Maximilian (q.v.), Emperor of Mexico, was executed (1867); his son Rudolf committed suicide at Mayerling (1889); his wife Elisabeth was murdered by an anarchist at Geneva (1898); his nephew was assassinated at Sarajevo (1914). He reigned in full sovereignty for a longer period than any other European monarch, and was succeeded by his great-nephew, Charles (q.v.).

Franco-Prussian War of 1870. Caused by the rival pretensions for European leadership of the French Second Empire and the Prussian-dominated North German Confederation (q.v.). Relations had worsened over reports that the Prussians were supporting the candidature of a Hohenzollern prince for the Spanish throne. The immediate cause of the war was French resentment at alleged insults in the 'Ems Telegram' (q.v.). The French, overestimating their state of preparedness, declared war on 19 July. The main French Army under

Macmahon received a series of defeats along the eastern frontier throughout August and was forced to capitulate at Sedan on 1 September, the Emperor Napoleon III being himself captured. Marshal Bazaine, with another French Army of 173,000 men, was besieged in Metz and surrendered at the end of October. Paris withstood a grim siege from 19 September to 28 January 1871. Resistance was maintained in the provinces by hastily improvised forces, organized by Gambetta. With the fall of Paris, peace talks began and terms were formally accepted on 1 March. France was to surrender to the Germans the province of Alsace and most of Lorraine; France was to pay an indemnity of five billion francs; a German army of occupation would remain until the indemnity was paid. These terms were incorporated into the definitive Treaty of Frankfurt, 10 May 1871.

Franco-Russian Alliance (the 'Dual Alliance'). In 1891 the Russians, resenting ostentatious demonstrations of Austro-German friendship and anxious to float considerable loans in Paris, accepted a French proposal for joint consultation in case of a war crisis. This loose agreement was extended in December 1893 and January 1894 to a formal secret military convention aimed against the Triple Alliance powers (Germany, Austria-Hungary, and Italy). It was re-affirmed in August 1899 and strengthened by a naval convention in 1912. Although the exact nature of the alliance was not known until after the war, the Germans were so convinced that France would come to Russia's aid in 1914 that they seized the initiative by declaring war on France less than 48 hours after their declaration of war on Russia.

A second Franco-Russian Alliance, made with the Soviet Government in May 1935, provided for mutual aid in case of unprovoked aggression. The Russians subsequently considered that the circumstances of 1939 did not warrant action.

Frankfurt, Treaty of (1871). See *Franco-Prussian War*.

Frankfurt Parliament. Early in the German Revolution of 1848 (q.v.) a provisional parliament of the German people met in Frankfurt and organized elections by direct male suffrage throughout Germany and Austria. The resultant assembly, generally known as the Frankfurt Parliament, sat from 18 May 1848 to 18 June 1849. It was predominantly a middle-class body, containing over 200 magistrates and lawyers, 100 university or higher-school teachers, and only one peasant. The Parliament was particularly concerned with the pre-

paration of a federal constitution for all the German lands. After
lengthy debates, a constitution was adopted in March 1849, and King
Frederick William of Prussia was elected Emperor. When, at the end
of April, he refused the offer of a crown from an elected assembly
on the ground that it was inconsistent with his Divine Right, the
majority of the delegates withdrew from the Parliament, as they considered its efforts to secure German unity a failure. An attempt to
continue the Parliament at Stuttgart in June 1849 was prevented by
soldiery. Although the Frankfurt Constitution remained inoperative,
it served as a basis for the constitution of the North German federation (q.v.) in 1867.

'Free French'. The name given to the Frenchmen of the Second
World War who supported General de Gaulle (b. 1890) when he flew
to London in June 1940 and called on his countrymen to reject the
armistice and continue resistance. The 'Free French' represented not
only a rallying-point of French patriotism, but a political alternative
to 'Vichy' (q.v.). They were organized first through a Conseil de
Défense de l'Empire (27 October 1940), including representatives
from French Africa, then as the Comité National Français (24
September 1941), a 'pre-government' with underground contacts with
the French Resistance. During the invasion of North Africa (November 1942), American pressure temporarily weakened 'Free French'
authority, but de Gaulle succeeded in securing Allied recognition of
his Comité Français de la Libération Nationale at Algiers in June
1943, and a year later this was proclaimed as the French Provisional
Government.

Free Trade. A system under which foreign imported goods are
exempted from excise duties, on the assumption that imports pay for
exports (including money invested overseas) and that free exchange
of goods promotes international cooperation. The term became
current after the publication in 1776 of Adam Smith's *Wealth of
Nations*. The younger Pitt attempted to free British trade in the
period 1783–93, and further tariffs were reduced by Huskisson (q.v.)
in the 1820s, but it was the work of Peel and Gladstone in the 1840s
and 1850s that established Free Trade as the dominant British
economic doctrine. Most European countries adopted Free Trade at
the same time, but many abandoned it during the economic depression (q.v.) of the late 1870s and 1880s. (Thus the Germans turned to
Protection in 1879.) Free Trade was not seriously called in question
by either of the main British parties until Chamberlain's unsuccessful Tariff Reform League (q.v.) of 1903. Severe Protectionist policies

were adopted almost everywhere after the reorganization of trade markets following the First World War. Free Trade was not finally abandoned by Britain until 1932.

French Revolution. Is normally assumed to have lasted from the summer of 1789 to the autumn of 1799, but some historians ante-date it to Calonne's reform plans of 1787 and many consider that it had run its course by August 1794. It is convenient to regard the Revolution as having eight periods, although it must be remembered that chronological divisions are generally artificial and that some characteristics overlap.

(i) *The Political and Economic Bankruptcy of the Old Order* (1787–89). By 1787, the system established a century earlier by Louis XIV was no longer able to run the country efficiently. Long wars had led to an accumulation of debt; political authority was exercised by a small group of privileged nobility; and the peasantry was impoverished by antiquarian agricultural methods, the persistence of feudal traditions of land tenure, and uncontrolled inflation. Attempts by the King's ministers, Calonne and Necker, to reform the system (1787–8) provoked strong resistance from the aristocrats, who induced Louis XVI to summon the States General (q.v.) in the belief that they would be able to dominate it and thus safeguard their rights. But many of the middle-class representatives in the Third Estate knew the ideas of the eighteenth-century political philosophers (especially Montesquieu and Rousseau), and with the American example in mind, had no intention of surrendering rights to the nobility.

(ii) *The Revolution at Versailles* (5 May to 15 October 1789). When the States General met at Versailles, the Third Estate, led by the Abbé Sieyès (q.v.), sought to have itself recognized as a National Assembly, a claim conceded by the King in the third week of June, the title being changed to 'Constituent Assembly' on 9 July. Agrarian distress, the fall of the Bastille (q.v.), and the 'Great Fear' (q.v.) hastened the promulgation of fundamental revolutionary decrees such as the formal Abolition of Feudalism (4 August) and the Declaration of Rights (q.v.). Meanwhile, the rising cost of bread, and rumours of a royalist counter-revolutionary conspiracy, led to demonstrations in Paris culminating in the 'Bread March of the Women' to Versailles on 5 October to demand the King's return to Paris. The Assembly followed him there in the middle of the month. Thenceforth the control of the Revolution by Paris was never seriously challenged.

(iii) *The Mirabeau Period* (October 1789–April 1791). This period of eighteen months saw long debates on the Constitution, the transformation of the internal system of France by the substitution of departments for the old provinces, the growth of anti-clericalism culminating in the 'Civil Constitution of the Clergy' (q.v.), and the beginning of the sale of church and crown lands to the smallholders. Although he was never in office, the dominant personality was the moderate constitutionalist, Mirabeau. His death in April 1791 widened the breach between Louis and the Assembly.

(iv) *The Growth of Republicanism* (April 1791–September 1792). The Revolution was not originally anti-monarchical, but it became so with the King's obvious attachment to the traditional religious system, the abortive attempt of the royal family to escape from Paris ('Flight to Varennes', 20–21 June 1791), and the King's insistence on vetoing anti-clerical legislation even after he had accepted the Constitution limiting his authority (September 1791). Tension was made worse by the hostility of Austria, the birthplace of Queen Marie Antoinette, and by the sympathy shown by the German rulers for the French émigré nobility. On 20 April 1792 France declared war on Austria. The King of Prussia and the Austrian Emperor prepared a joint invasion plan. The imminence of invasion sparked off disturbances in Paris. On 10 August the Tuileries Palace was attacked, and three days later the royal family was imprisoned in the Temple. News of the fall of Verdun to the invaders led to a panic massacre of suspected 'traitors' held in the prisons (2 September), and it was against this background that the Revolutionary Convention gathered, formally abolishing the monarchy on 21 September 1792.

(v) *The Conflict of Girondins and Jacobins* (October 1792 to October 1793). The winter of 1792–3 saw the invading army repulsed and political power passing to the group known as Girondins (q.v.). It was under their lead that the King was tried and executed (21 January 1793) and that war was declared against Britain, Holland, and Spain (February and March 1793). The more radical group, the Jacobins (q.v.) used the failure of the French Army in the Low Countries and the treachery of its commander, Dumouriez (April 1793), as an excuse for throwing out the Girondins and establishing an emergency revolutionary government. The Girondins were tried and executed on 31 October 1793.

(vi) *The Rise and Fall of Robespierre* (November 1793 to July 1794). During these nine months the Jacobins tried to set up a system of government based on the absolutist aspects of Rousseau's *Contrat Social*. In the struggle for political power, Robespierre (q.v.) triumphed over Hébert (q.v.) and Danton (q.v.), both of whom, with their supporters, were executed. It was a period of success in war but butchery at home; 2,600 people were guillotined in Paris alone, and there were other 'Terrors' elsewhere, notably in Nantes. Encouragement of a non-Christian religious 'Cult of the Supreme Being', laws providing for a radical redistribution of confiscated property, and a decree abolishing the last safeguards against unjust accusations of political treachery, all served to stir the remaining members of the Convention to overthrow the Robespierrists on 27–28 July 1794 ('Thermidor').

(vii) *Moderate Republicanism* (August 1794–October 1795). After the execution of Robespierre and the closing of the Jacobin Club, the republicans returned to the fundamentally liberal principles of the Declaration of Rights, despite attempts by the Paris mob to restore revolutionary rule. The Constitution, providing for bicameral government on a limited franchise and an executive 'Directory' of five elected leaders, was voted on 22 August 1795, but before it became effective there was one more Parisian insurrection ('Vendémiaire'), crushed by Barras (q.v.) and Napoleon Bonaparte (q.v.).

(viii) *The Directory* (October 1795–November 1799). The Directors, of whom the most important were Barras and Carnot (q.v.), won great military and diplomatic successes for France in their first two years of power, thanks, for the most part, to the skill of Bonaparte in Italy. From 1797–9 they tended to fall out among themselves, the French countryside lapsed into anarchy, there were serious royalist revolts in the outlying provinces, and, in the summer of 1799, a series of military defeats undid the work of earlier years. The Directory added nothing to the achievement of the Revolution. It showed the need to consolidate and clarify; that opportunity was given to France by Bonaparte's *coup d'état* of Brumaire, 1799 (q.v.).

The French Revolution was an event of fundamental importance not only to France but to Europe. The constitutional experiments and the conflict of rival factions tend to obscure the permanent achievements. In France, the Revolution established the political supremacy of the middle class in the towns and transferred the bulk of landed property to the peasantry in the countryside. For Europe, despite the dictatorial tendencies of Jacobinism, it represented an ideal of popular sovereignty and equality before the law while, for the first time, identifying the whole people with the Nation. Its legacy was the two cardinal features of nineteenth-century Europe – liberalism and nationalism.

Fry, Elizabeth (1780–1845). British reformer; maiden name Gurney. Born in Norwich, married Joseph Fry (a London merchant) in 1800. She first became known as a Quaker preacher and leader, but her fame rests upon her record as a prison reformer. In 1817–18 she led the agitation for better conditions in women's prisons and secured improvements in the transportation of convicts to New South Wales. She was a pioneer of a more responsible order of nursing sisters and worked for women's education, particularly in the East End of London. In 1838–9 she made an extensive tour of French prisons at the request of King Louis Philippe, and her reports secured reforms. She also visited prisons in Belgium, Holland, Denmark, and Prussia.

Gallipoli. A peninsula forming the southernmost European shore of the Dardanelles (q.v.). On 25 April 1915 an Allied force (predominantly British and Australasian) was landed on the peninsula in an attempt to seize forts guarding the approaches to Constantinople and thereby open up a route to assist Russia. The Turks, who had expected the landing for six weeks, had brought up reinforcements, and the invaders encountered stiff resistance. The British Empire troops were commanded by General Sir Ian Hamilton and the Turkish defenders by Mustapha Kemal (q.v.), under the direction of the German General, Liman von Sanders. There followed several months of trying fighting without appreciable results. A second landing at Suvla, higher up the peninsula, on 6 August was no more successful. Kitchener (q.v.) visited Gallipoli in November, and, seeing there was little hope of capturing the heights in the peninsula, ordered preparations for evacuation. Between 10 December and 9 January 1916 the allied force was withdrawn without loss. The expedition suffered from poor coordination, confused leadership, and opposition from Allied military commanders who believed the war could only be decided on the Western Front (see *Anzac*).

Gambetta, Léon (1838–82). French republican politician; born in southern France, called to the Bar in 1859. As a lawyer Gambetta showed bitter hostility to Napoleon III; he was elected to the Assembly as a member for Marseilles in 1869. It was Gambetta who proclaimed the Third Republic from the Paris Hôtel de Ville in September 1870. He stayed in Paris for the first part of the siege of 1870, escaping by balloon to Tours, where he organized the later stages of the Franco-Prussian War as Minister of the Interior and War. He resigned when peace was made, and for six years used his powers of oratory to denounce the crypto-royalism of the conservative politicians, taking a leading part in the defeat of President Macmahon (q.v.) in 1877, but, at the same time, restraining the extremists. From 1879 to 1881 Gambetta was the most important power behind the Republican Governments, but when he became Prime

Minister in 1881 his ministry lasted for only nine weeks, since all the other politicians suspected him of dictatorial ambitions. His most famous speech was delivered on 4 May 1877; by suggesting that clericalism was '*the* enemy' of the Republican way of life, he made the Church the main target of subsequent radical criticism. He died suddenly in 1882 from wounds incurred in a revolver accident.

Gandhi, Mohandas Karamchand (1869–1948). Born in India, studied law in London, practised as a barrister in Bombay, but went to South Africa to organize the Indian population there in its struggles with the Boers. In March 1907 he began a campaign of passive resistance to the Transvaal Government's attempts at discriminating against Indians. Eventually in July 1914 Gandhi received assurances of just treatment from the Union Government (Smuts) and returned to India with the reputation of a moderate but effective leader. During the 1920s Gandhi developed his African methods in India as leader of the Indian National Congress, a largely Hindu body demanding a legislative assembly at that time. By boycotting British goods, Gandhi helped develop India's village industries, while, by preaching passive resistance, he curbed (although he could not prevent) terrorist outrages. He was imprisoned in 1922, 1930, 1933, and 1942, resorting to the hunger strike as part of his campaign of civil disobedience. He came to London in 1931 for the abortive Round Table Conference. By 1942 he had reached a position where he saw independence as the only possible solution for India's grievances. He cooperated with the last Viceroys (Wavell and Mountbatten) in producing plans for the independence and partition of India (15 August 1947). Although many of his followers regarded him as a saint (the Mahatma), some Hindus resented his acceptance of partition, and on 30 January 1948 he was assassinated by a fanatic.

Garibaldi, Giuseppe (1807–82). Italian patriot. Born in Nice (then part of Piedmont) and became a supporter of the Young Italy movement of Mazzini (q.v.). He was forced to flee to South America (1834), where he gained fame as a military commander defending Montevideo against the Argentinians. In 1848 he returned to Italy and in April 1849 organized the defence of the Roman Republic against the French, sustaining a two-months' siege before undertaking a courageous retreat across the peninsula and into exile. In 1859 he led a guerilla force against the Austrians around Lake Como and in May 1860 sailed from Genoa with his Thousand Redshirts to invade Sicily and Naples in the name of a United Italy. After defeating the Neapolitans at Calatafimi (Sicily) and on the Volturno, Garibaldi handed over his conquests to the Piedmontese (whose King was proclaimed ruler of Italy) and retired to Caprera. In 1862 and 1867 Garibaldi made unsuccessful attempts to capture Rome (see *Roman Question*). He fought for Republican France in the Franco-Prussian War. Garibaldi was the heroic idol of mid-Victorian England, the supreme example of romantic patriot-leader.

General Strike. The British General Strike of 4–12 May 1926 was the climax to several years of industrial unrest and of attempts by the miners' unions, led by A. J. Cook, to secure sympathetic support for their grievances from workers in the other major industries. The miners, threatened by further wage cuts, asked the T.U.C. to bring out all major industries, thus conforming to a resolution supporting the miners carried at the 1925 Congress. The T.U.C. accordingly called out transport workers, printers, builders, and workers in heavy industries (and, later, engineers). The Baldwin Government recruited special constables, volunteers to run essential services, and used troops to maintain food supplies, thus avoiding paralysis of the country. The Government's monopoly of information services, including the radio, helped prevent any general wave of panic from disturbing the calm of the public. After nine days the T.U.C. ended the strike, because it realized that the Government had been better prepared for the strike than had the unions. The miners, who felt betrayed by the T.U.C., stayed out in vain until August. The General Strike left a legacy of bitterness on all sides. The Baldwin Government passed a Trade Disputes Act in 1927 making general strikes illegal; this was repealed by the Labour Government in 1946.

George IV (1762–1830, Regent 1811–1820, King from 1820). Eldest son of George III, with whom he was habitually on bad terms, partly because of his association with the Whig Opposition and partly because of his moral laxity. His marriage to Mrs Fitzherbert in 1785 was declared invalid as she was a Roman Catholic. Ten years later he married Caroline of Brunswick, who left him shortly after the birth of their only child, Princess Charlotte (1796–1817). In 1820 the King's unsuccessful attempt to secure a divorce made him widely unpopular. Despite his earlier attachment to the Whigs, his political attitude as Regent and King was hostile to all reform, and he consented to Catholic Emancipation (q.v.) in 1829 only on perceiving that his ministers were singularly undismayed by a threat of abdication. He was a selfish and extravagant hedonist, fortunately possessing some artistic taste; his best memorials are the Pavilion at

Brighton and the grandiose town-planning scheme by which he enabled John Nash to enrich the West End of London.

George V (1865–1936, King-Emperor from 1910). The second son of Edward VII. He served in the Navy from 1877 to 1892, when the death of his brother, the Duke of Clarence, made him second in succession to the throne. In 1893 he married his late brother's fiancée, Princess May of Teck. George V's reign was notable for the growing affection shown towards the monarchy by the ordinary people; this was due in part to the evident felicity of his family life and to the personal touch of the Christmas Messages he broadcast in his later years, but it also reflected his care in fulfilling the duties of a constitutional monarch. When he intervened in politics – over the Parliament Act of 1911, or the Irish Crisis of 1914, or the appointment of Baldwin (q.v.) as Prime Minister in 1923, or the formation of the National Government of 1931 – he did so only at the suggestion of his constitutional advisers. George V had a particular attachment to his Indian Empire and was the only British Emperor to visit his territories as sovereign (see *Delhi Durbar*). The Silver Jubilee celebrations of 1935 were a moving demonstration of loyalty towards both the King and Queen Mary.

George VI (1895–1952; King 1936–52; Emperor of India 1936–47). The second son of George V. Succeeded to the throne on the abdication (q.v.) of his brother, Edward VIII. He served in the Navy from 1909 to 1916 and fought at Jutland; he then served for three years in the Air Force and spent a year at Cambridge. In 1923, as Duke of York, he married Lady Elizabeth Bowes-Lyon. He was keenly interested in promoting social welfare, especially for young people of all classes. As King he remained above politics to an even greater extent than his father. In 1939 he became the first reigning British sovereign to visit the U.S.A. During the war years his sense of service won him universal esteem, which was heightened by his courage in overcoming physical disabilities.

George, David Lloyd. See *Lloyd George*.

George, Henry (1839–97). American economist and political thinker. George, who was virtually self-educated and had been a land prospector along the Pacific coast, developed theories of taxation while serving as a newspaper-man in San Francisco in the 1870s. His classic work, *Progress and Poverty* (1879), maintained that there should be a single tax based on the rent derived from land or from unearned increments, which he condemned as unproductive to society. In the early 1880s George came to Britain as a newspaper correspondent, and made a special study of the Irish land problem while achieving fame as a lecturer. He played only a minor role in American politics, but made probably a greater contribution to British political thought than any of his compatriots, for, although *Progress and Poverty* may have been naïvely overcharged with emotion, its simple catchwords were a more formative influence on British socialism than the ponderous tomes of Marx and Engels. Many of the founders of the Fabian Society (q.v.) owed their first acquaintance with socialist theory to George's lectures.

Gettysburg. Town in southern Pennsylvania, scene of a three-day battle in the American Civil War (1–3 July 1863), when Confederate forces under Lee (q.v.) tried to carry the war into northern territory by crossing the Potomac. Lee was repulsed by General George C. Meade, defending Gettysburg. Meade lost over 3,000 men and Lee nearly 4,000. The defeat of Lee constituted the turning-point in the war. In the following November, Lincoln attended the dedication of the military cemetery at Gettysburg, delivering there his oration on 'the new birth of freedom', with its famous eulogy of 'government of the people, by the people, and for the people'.

Gioberti, Vincenzo (1801–52). Italian patriot and philosopher, born in Turin, ordained priest in 1825. His nationalist views led to his expulsion from Piedmont and he settled in Brussels, where in 1843 he wrote *Del Primato morale e civile degli Italiani* – a plea to the Papacy to reorganize and unite the states of the Italian peninsula. The book had a considerable influence on the supporters of the 'Liberal Pope', Pius IX (q.v.). Gioberti was able to return to Piedmont in 1847 and enter politics. He headed the Piedmontese Government from December 1848 to March 1849. He retired a disillusioned man, condemned by the Church both for his political activity and for some aspects of his philosophical teachings.

Giolitti, Giovanni (1842–1928). Italian politician; was born in the province of Cuneo and educated in Turin. He became a civil servant until, in 1882, he entered the Italian Parliament as a liberal. He served as Minister of Finance under Crispi (q.v.) in 1889. His first Ministry (May 1892 to November 1893) was short-lived because of the so-called 'Tanlongo Scandal', the discovery by a parliamentary commission that a director of the Bank of Rome whom Giolitti had created a Senator had been guilty of major financial irregularities.

After the Tanlongo revelations, Giolitti had to leave Italy for a short period, but he returned and re-entered political life during a period of violent radical unrest at the turn of the century. Giolitti was Prime Minister again from October 1903 to March 1905 and from May 1906 to December 1909. In home affairs he tried to combat left-wing strikes and disorders by financial economies and by seeking a reconciliation with the Catholic Church (which had hitherto stood aloof from the internal politics of the Italian Kingdom). In foreign affairs he strengthened Italy's ties with Austria-Hungary. In his fourth Ministry (1911 to 1914) he was responsible for the annexation of Tripoli and the prosecution of a war against Turkey from which Italy gained, not only Libya (q.v.), but Rhodes and the Dodecanese. The cost of the war necessitated heavy taxation, which contributed to Giolitti's unpopularity, and he was forced to resign in March 1914 after a General Strike had paralysed the country. He remained an influential politician in opposition, vainly striving to preserve Italy's neutrality in 1915. He headed a fifth ministry in June 1920, when Italy was rent by civil disorder and disappointed by the results of the peace settlement. He was unable to satisfy the nationalist groups over Fiume (q.v.) and resigned in June 1921. An astute parliamentary manager, devoid of principle, Giolitti headed a government for more than eleven years in all, a longer period than any other Italian except Mussolini.

Girondins. A group of deputies in the French Legislative Assembly of 1791 and subsequently in the Convention of 1792. Many of them (but not all) came from the region of the Gironde, around Bordeaux; their leaders were Brissot, Roland and his ambitious wife, Pétion, and Vergniaud. They tended to be more idealistic than their political rivals, the Jacobins (q.v.); they believed in a rational legal code and a predominantly middle-class state. In the early months of 1793, they recklessly rushed France into war with Britain, Holland, and Spain and, with the first setbacks, were attacked for incompetence by the Jacobins. The Girondins became afraid of the Jacobin appeal to the masses, but in belatedly seeking to arrest the Jacobin leaders they were themselves outmanoeuvred and overthrown on 2 June 1793. On the following 31 October all the prominent Girondins were executed.

Gladstone, William Ewart (1809–98). The son of a Liverpool merchant, educated at Eton and Christ Church, Oxford. He entered the Commons in 1832 as Tory M.P. for Newark, represented Oxford University as a 'Peelite', 1847–65, and, as a Liberal, South Lancashire 1865–8, Greenwich 1868–80, Midlothian 1880–95. He attained Cabinet rank as President of the Board of Trade under Peel in

1843, was out of office because of his Free Trade views from 1846 to 1852, but served as Chancellor of the Exchequer 1852–5 and 1858–66, introducing a remarkable series of budgets which cut tariffs and reduced governmental expenditure. He became Leader of the Liberal Party in 1866 and Prime Minister in 1868. His first Ministry was responsible for a series of overdue reforms – in the Army, education, and the legal system – as well as the rectification of injustices (Disestablishment of the Irish Church, Irish Land Act, Secret Ballot Act). Although defeated in the election of 1874, Gladstone returned to power in 1880 after the Midlothian campaign (q.v.). His second Ministry carried the Third Reform Act (1884) but failed to solve the Irish problem and was discredited by the death of Gordon and the first Boer War (q.v.). His third Ministry (1886) was short-lived, because Gladstone's conversion to Home Rule (q.v.) alienated the radical wing led by Chamberlain (q.v.) and so split the party. The fourth Ministry (1892–4) was absorbed with an unsuccessful attempt to pass a second Irish Home Rule Bill despite opposition in the House of Lords. Gladstone, more than any other person, determined the form of the later Victorian Liberal Party, although as a classical scholar and High Churchman he differed in many ways from the majority of his supporters. His chief weaknesses were a tendency, as he became older, to concentrate on one topic to the exclusion of other pressing problems, and to take drastic action on the questions that absorbed him without consulting his Cabinet colleagues. Both of these failings contributed to the decisive breach with Chamberlain in 1886. He was an eloquent speaker with deep sympathy for oppressed peoples – some of his most effective work was his championship of political prisoners in the old Neapolitan Kingdom or his pleas for the victims of Turkish atrocities in Bulgaria and Armenia. He was, above all, a parliamentarian, and his political rivalry with Disraeli (q.v.) enabled debates in the Commons to attain a rare pre-eminence in the interest of the general public.

Glenelg, Lord (Charles Grant, 1778–1866, raised to the peerage 1831). British Colonial Secretary. Glenelg was the son of a director of the East India Company. He became president of the Board of Control for India in 1830 and, in 1833, was responsible for ending the trading rights of the Company. He served as Colonial Secretary under Melbourne, 1835–9. By his moderate policy towards the Kaffirs, he alienated the Boers in Cape Colony, thus forcing them to undertake the Great Trek (q.v.). During the Canadian rebellions of 1837 (see *Mackenzie*) his apparent hesitancy and vacillation incurred much criticism.

Gneisenau, August Wilhelm von (1760–1831, created a Count in 1814). After mercenary service with the British in the American War of Independence, Gneisenau achieved a reputation in the Prussian campaigns of 1806–7. Subsequently, with Scharnhorst (q.v.), he supervised the organization and training of a new Prussian Army which, as second-in-command to Blücher (q.v.), he successfully led in the War of Liberation of 1813–14, personally preparing the Prussian invasion of France. He participated in the Waterloo Campaign (where he was on bad terms with Wellington) and was subsequently made a Field-Marshal.

Goebbels, Joseph (1897–1945). Nazi leader, born in the Rhineland, became a Doctor of Philosophy at Heidelberg in 1920, and was an early follower of Hitler. He was appointed Nazi leader in Berlin in 1926 and was given charge of the party propaganda machine in 1929, becoming a member of the Reichstag in the following year. From 1933 to 1945 he was Minister of Enlightenment and Propaganda, his cynical understanding of mass psychology making him a formidable figure. In the last days of the war he committed suicide in Hitler's bunker after killing his wife and children.

Goering, Hermann (1893–1946). Nazi leader, an air ace of the First World War, gaining the highest military distinctions and commanding the crack Richthofen Squadron in 1918. He became an early Nazi, and was wounded in the Munich Putsch (q.v.) of 1923. In 1932 he became President (i.e. Speaker) of the Reichstag. Hitler appointed him Air Minister in 1933, and the Luftwaffe (German Air Force) was his creation. He was also Prussian Minister President and Prussian Minister of the Interior and was sometimes entrusted by Hitler with special diplomatic missions. The rank of Reichsmarshal was created for Goering after the victories of 1940. His personal vanity and ostentation, coupled in the later stages of the war by indolence and inefficiency, made him many enemies among the Nazi hierarchy but, when brought to trial at Nuremberg in 1946, he still showed some character and, in the end, cheated the gallows by committing suicide a few hours before he was due to be executed.

Gorchakov, Alexander (1798–1883). Russian Chancellor; a member of the old aristocracy. He entered the diplomatic service, participating in a minor capacity at the Congresses of Laibach and Verona, but not reaching ambassadorial status until 1854, when, from Vienna, he played an important role in maintaining Austria's neutrality in the Crimean War. He was in charge of Russian foreign policy from 1856 to 1882, setting himself the task of freeing Russia from the restrictions of the Treaty of Paris, an objective attained in 1870, largely through cooperation with Prussia. Gorchakov was prepared to work with Bismarck in the Dreikaiserbund, but was jealous of Bismarck's international position and appears at the Congress of Berlin to have been no more than a senile and cantankerous schemer, so filled with envy of Germany that his last years witnessed the worst wave of Russo-German friction in the nineteenth century.

Gordon, Charles (1833–85). British General; joined the Royal Engineers in 1852 and served with distinction in the Crimean War. From 1860 to 1865 his remarkable success in China won him the soubriquet 'Chinese Gordon', by which he was thereafter known. He explored parts of China and commanded the force that suppressed the Taiping Rebellion (q.v.). He then entered the service of Khedive Ismail of Egypt, administering the Sudan from 1874 to 1880 and having great success in stamping out the slave trade, despite the opposition of powerful native interests. After two years in South Africa he was sent back to the Sudan in 1884 at the time of the Mahdi's revolt, with instructions to rescue isolated Egyptian garrisons. Gordon was, however, reluctant to withdraw before a native revolt and, underestimating his enemies and overestimating his own resources, he found himself cut off in Khartoum. After a siege of ten months Gordon was killed, two days before the arrival of a relief force. Gordon's evangelical Christianity and obvious strength of character had made him a respected hero of the Victorian public, and his death led to an outburst of indignation against the Gladstone Government (a feeling which Queen Victoria openly shared) for not having despatched a relief force earlier.

Gorham Judgement. In 1847 the Bishop of Exeter refused to institute the Reverend G. C. Gorham to Brampford Speke, a living in his diocese but in the gift of the Lord Chancellor, regarding Gorham's views on baptism as unsound. Gorham appealed against the Bishop's decision to the Judicial Committee of the Privy Council, which in March 1850 declared that his views were not contrary to the teachings of the Church of England. Since the Bishop still refused to accept Gorham, he was instituted at Brampford Speke by the Archbishop of Canterbury. The whole incident aroused considerable feeling. Members of the Oxford Movement (q.v.) regarded Gorham's views as heretical, and protested that the Privy Council, being a lay body, was not a valid court of ecclesiastical appeal. Several prominent Anglicans seceded to Rome as a result of the Gorham decision;

among them was H. E. Manning (1808–92), who was to become Cardinal Archbishop of Westminster. Other members of the Church of England interpreted the Gorham Judgement as evidence that the Church needed its own court. The incident accordingly contributed to the decision in 1852 to revive the Convocation of Canterbury, the ancient assembly of the clergy of southern England, which since 1717 had held only formal meetings.

Grand National Consolidated Trades Union. The first attempt to unite skilled and unskilled workers, a joint design of Robert Owen (q.v.) and John Doherty (1797–1854). The Union was formed in January 1834 and rapidly acquired half a million workers, pledged to strike for an eight-hour day. The Government became alarmed, and after persecuting the 'Tolpuddle Martyrs' (q.v.), so intimidated Owen that the Union was dissolved (October 1834).

Grant, Ulysses S. (1822–85). American soldier, President of U.S.A. Born in Ohio, served in the Mexican War and in California, spent six years farming, and returned to the Army on the outbreak of the Civil War, being made a Major-General early in 1862. He won the victories of Vicksburg and Chattanooga (1863) and was appointed commander of the Union Armies in March 1864. In a costly three-month campaign he wore down Lee's reserves and eventually forced him to surrender at Appomattox in April 1865. He served as Secretary for War 1867–8 and was elected President in 1868, being re-elected in 1873. While his Administration was responsible for initiating long-overdue civil service reform and for improving relations with Britain, it was also faced by a bad financial depression (1873) and by a series of monetary scandals, with acts of bribery committed by leading members of the Cabinet. After retiring from politics in 1877, Grant, an essentially simple man, was impoverished by a common swindler, being saved from formal bankruptcy only by the sale of his Memoirs.

Grattan, Henry (1746–1820). Irish politician. Born and educated in Dublin, was elected to the Irish Parliament in 1775. By his brilliant oratory he became the leader of the movement to repeal 'Poyning's Law' (subjecting the actions of the Irish Parliament to the approval of the Privy Council in London). Grattan was successful in 1782 and for eighteen years 'Grattan's Parliament' enjoyed virtual independence. Grattan himself refused office and was largely responsible for the negative attitude to the English authorities adopted by the Irish in this period, a policy of critical hostility that contributed to the

Act of Union (q.v.) of 1800. Grattan represented Dublin in the British House of Commons from 1806 to his death.

Great Exhibition of 1851. An attempt to show the world the technical achievements of the first half of the nineteenth century. In Hyde Park, Paxton's Crystal Palace – more than 600 yards long – housed 7,000 exhibitors from Britain and as many from abroad. The idea of the Exhibition and the choice of site derived from the Prince Consort. The Exhibition demonstrated Britain's material prosperity and, by serving as a model for later international exhibitions, showed for the first time the way in which science could enhance national prestige. The Crystal Palace was subsequently re-erected in South London: it was destroyed by fire on 30 November 1936.

Great Fear (*'La Grande Peur'*). A movement of mass hysteria that swept through provincial France in the second half of July and early August 1789. It seems to have originated, independently in six different places, as a local rumour that gangs of brigands in the pay of aristocrats were coming to 'restore order' in the countryside. There were no provincial newspapers and, with the breakdown of local authority, reports spread with astounding speed. Thus one of these panics originated in Franche Comté in north-eastern France and spread southwards along the Rhône to Provence, westwards to the central plateau, and eastwards to the Alps. Only the most distant provinces – Alsace, Lorraine, and Brittany – did not experience the phenomenon. As the rumour travelled, cottagers drove their cattle in from the fields and barricaded doors, while townsfolk closed city gates and prepared to ward off an attack. No attack materialized, but the sense of insecurity intensified the peasant outrages against landowners that had convulsed France in the preceding four months.

Great Purge (in U.S.S.R., 1936–8). See *Yezhovshchina.*

Great Trek (1836–7). A mass migration from Cape Colony of ten thousand Boers (settlers of Dutch descent) who wished to form new settlements not under the authority of the British crown. The Boers particularly resented charges of cruelty towards natives and complained of inadequate compensation for the abolition of slavery in 1834. They also maintained that the British were not affording them security against Kaffir raids. Some of the migrant Boers settled immediately north of the Orange River, others moved across the Vaal River, and a third group, led by Andrius Pretorius (1799–1853), crossed into Natal, where they established an independent republic with a capital at Pietermaritzburg. In 1843, Natal was annexed to Cape Colony and Pretorius moved his group into the Orange Free State. Five years later, a British force drove them beyond the Vaal. Eventually, the Sand River Convention of 1852 (q.v.) allowed them to settle permanently in Transvaal (q.v.), the capital of which was named after their leader. Among the children on the Great Trek was the future Boer President, Paul Kruger, then eleven years old.

Greece. Passed under Turkish rule in the mid fifteenth century. The Greek Church retained considerable spiritual powers, and the Greek aristocracy was able to form an important administrative class within the Ottoman Empire. A cultural renaissance in the late eighteenth century, coinciding with support from Russian agents, made the Greeks plan a rising against the Turks. In 1821 the Greek War of Independence began with a revolt (unsuccessful) of the Greeks in the Danubian Principalities (q.v.) and a more serious in-surrection in the Morea. The Greek Cause aroused enthusiasm in Western Europe; philhellenic sentiment was crystallized by the death of Byron at the siege of Missolonghi (April 1824). Greek independence was proclaimed at Epidauros on 13 January 1822, but heavy fighting continued between the Greeks and the Turks (and, more particularly, the Egyptians) until 1829, when the Great Powers intervened to establish a Greek Kingdom, limited to the area south of the Gulf of Volo. Otto of Bavaria ruled as King 1832–62 but was deposed after a military revolt; the Danish Prince George accepted the crown and reigned from 1863 to 1913. Greek territory was extended in 1863 by cession of the Ionian Islands (a British protectorate since 1815); in 1881, by the acquisition from Turkey of Thessaly and part of Epirus; and in 1913, by union with Crete and the occupation of part of Macedonia and Thrace. Greece followed a tortuous policy in the First World War, until forced by Venizelos (q.v.) to join the Allies in 1917. An attempt to secure Anatolia in the peace settlement failed disastrously at Smyrna (q.v.) in 1922. A republic was proclaimed in May 1924 but the monarchy restored in November 1935. In August 1936 King George II accepted the establishment of a fascist-type dictatorship by General Metaxas, in power until his death in February 1941. The Italians invaded Greece in October 1940 but were defeated and thrown back into Albania. In April 1941 the Germans overran Greece. Rival monarchist and communist groups maintained a guerilla war with the Germans from 1942 until the British liberated Athens in October 1944, when the two resistance groups started fighting each other. Bitter civil war lasted from May

1946 until October 1949, when the monarchists were successful. Greek politics in the 1950s were dominated by the question of Cyprus (q.v.).

Grey, Charles (1764–1845, became second Earl Grey in 1807). British statesman; educated at Eton and King's, Cambridge, became M.P. for Northumberland in 1786, supporting Fox, opposing war with republican France, and advocating parliamentary reform. With the establishment of the Consulate, Grey began to support the war, and succeeded Fox as Foreign Secretary in the Coalition Government of 1806–7. Attempts to secure Catholic Emancipation caused friction between George III and his ministers and led to the fall of the Government in March 1807, beginning a period of twenty-three years in which Grey was out of office. In opposition, he continued to urge parliamentary reform and Catholic Emancipation but, by supporting Queen Caroline's cause in 1820, made George IV a personal enemy. In 1830, William IV, perceiving the temper of the country, invited Grey to form a Whig Government, which, two years later, duly carried the first Parliamentary Reform Act (q.v.). Grey retired in 1834.

Grey, Edward (1862–1933, baronet 1882, created Viscount Grey of Fallodon in 1916). Came from the same family as the Reform Bill Prime Minister. He was Liberal M.P. for Berwick for thirty-one years from 1885, serving as Under-Secretary for Foreign Affairs, 1892–5. From December 1905 until May 1916 he was Foreign Secretary, the longest ever continuous tenure of that office. During this period Grey continued the policy begun by the Conservatives, concluding the Anglo-Russian Entente (q.v.) of 1907 and authorizing military conversations (q.v.) with the French, Belgians, and, subsequently, the Russians. While hating the idea of war and maintaining that Britain must be free to remain at peace, he nevertheless made it clear to Parliament in August 1914 that he considered Britain had an obligation to help Belgium, thus taking the country into the First World War. He was a believer in international arbitration (which he had used successfully during the Balkan Wars) and, despite failing eyesight, did all he could in later years to champion the League of Nations. In 1919 he went to the U.S.A. on a special diplomatic mission. Grey was a keen fisherman and ornithologist; he remained in politics from a sense of duty rather than from personal choice.

Grey, Sir George (1812–98). Colonial administrator; educated at Sandhurst and served in the infantry 1828–39. In 1841 Grey became

Governor of South Australia, a continent in which he had already carried out exploration; in four years he reorganized the administration, putting it on a sound financial basis. He was moved to New Zealand as Governor in 1845–53, gaining the respect and admiration of the Maori people. After serving as Governor of Cape Colony 1853–9 (whence he was recalled for favouring a South African federation) he returned as Governor of New Zealand 1861–7, successfully ending the Maori War (q.v.) but getting on bad terms with the military authorities, for whom he showed scant respect. After a spell in England campaigning for state-aided emigration, he settled in New Zealand and was a member of the House of Representatives from 1874 to 1894, serving as Prime Minister 1877–9. He was largely responsible for a number of reforms (actually carried after his period of office): adult suffrage; triennial parliaments; and a land tax. He returned to England in 1894.

Guizot, François (1787–1874). French politician born at Nîmes, a Huguenot. He became Professor of History at Paris in 1812 and did not enter politics until 1830, becoming a Minister in 1832. In 1833 he introduced the first Primary Education Law in France. From 1840 to 1847 he was Foreign Minister in the Soult Government, and its key figure. He was Prime Minister from 1847 to February 1848. His policy was narrowly conservative and, in his relations with Britain, maladroit. By refusing political concessions to the class that had benefited from his own Education Law, he precipitated the revolution that overthrew the July Monarchy (q.v.) and forced him into exile (1848). His last years were spent in historical writing, including a study of seventeenth-century England.

Habsburg Dynasty. The imperial family of Austria, descendants of the German Count Rudolf of Habsburg (Holy Roman Emperor 1273–9) who, in 1282, bestowed the Duchy of Austria on his son, Albrecht. The male line died out in 1740, when Emperor Charles VI was succeeded by his only daughter, Maria Theresa. She was married to the Duke of Lorraine and, from 1745, the dynasty was known as the House of Habsburg-Lorraine. The Habsburgs reigned in Vienna until 1918, when Emperor-King Charles (q.v.) went into exile.

Hague Conferences (1899 and 1907). In August 1898 Tsar Nicholas II proposed an international peace conference to limit armaments. The Conference met at the Hague from May to July 1899. The Tsar's proposal was treated with suspicion in many countries; it was known that Russian finances were feeling the strain of the armaments race. Nevertheless, representatives came from 26 states. Little was achieved on disarmament, but it was decided to institute a Permanent Court of Arbitration at the Hague to settle 'disputes involving neither honour nor vital interests'. The International Court was established in 1901. A second Hague Peace Conference met in June 1907 and produced a series of conventions designed to limit the horrors of war.

Haig, Douglas (1861–1928, created Earl 1919). Born in Edinburgh, entered the Army in 1885, serving as a cavalry officer with the Egyptian Army in the Sudan in 1898 and distinguished himself in South Africa 1899–1902. He then served in India, except for the three years 1906–9, when he helped put Haldane's reforms into practice at the War Office. He crossed to France with the 1st Army Corps of the B.E.F. in August 1914 and fought at Mons, on the Meuse, and at Ypres. At the end of 1915 he succeeded Sir John French as British Commander-in-Chief on the Western Front. Haig was an orthodox and unimaginative professional soldier, distrustful of new ideas but enjoying enormous prestige among his brother officers. He was on bad terms with the Prime Minister, Lloyd George, who considered that he wasted lives without tangible success. He sustained a severe defeat by the Germans in March 1918. Haig possessed, however, determination and tenacity and, with disaster threatening, secured the appointment as Generalissimo over the Allied Armies in France of Marshal Foch, with whom he collaborated until the victory of November 1918. Haig spent his last years in work for the disabled soldiers, instituting the 'Poppy Day' Appeal associated with his name.

Haldane, Richard Burdon (1856–1928; Viscount 1912). Born and educated in Edinburgh and studied at Göttingen, where he specialized in German philosophy. He sat as a Liberal M.P. 1885–1911, and was War Secretary 1905–12. Lord Chancellor 1912–15 and again in the Labour Government of 1924. At the War Office, his most important decision was the creation of a General Staff (1906). He also inaugurated the Territorial Army (1907) and Officers' Training Corps. He cut military expenditure but made mobilization swifter and provided for an Expeditionary Force of six infantry and one cavalry divisions (with auxiliaries). In 1912 he went to Berlin in an unsuccessful effort to halt the naval armaments race. Haldane was unjustly attacked by the cheap press in 1915 for his knowledge of Germany and was forced out of public life. He was never a popular personality, probably because of his tendency to obscure practical politics with metaphysical erudition. Haig thought him 'the greatest Secretary of State for War England has ever had'.

Halifax, Earl of (Edward Wood, 1881–1959, created Baron Irwin 1925, succeeded his father as Third Viscount Halifax in 1934, created Earl of Halifax in 1944). Became Conservative M.P. for Ripon in 1910 and held ministerial posts from 1922 to 1926, when he was appointed Viceroy of India. His five years in India coincided with a period of unrest on the North-West Frontier and of civil disobedience from the followers of Gandhi (q.v.), with whom the Viceroy succeeded in reaching an agreement in March 1931. After three years as President of the Board of Education (1932–5) and a brief spell at the War Office, Halifax became Lord President of the Council in November 1935, with special responsibility for foreign affairs. In November 1937 he visited Hitler and was appointed by Chamberlain (q.v.) to succeed Eden as Foreign Secretary in February 1938. He played an important part in inducing Chamberlain to take a stronger line with the Germans after March 1939. In the political crisis of May 1940, he was considered as a possible Prime Minister by both Chamberlain and George VI but he refused the office and continued to serve at the Foreign Office for seven months under Churchill. In January 1941 he was sent to Washington as Ambassador, a post he held for ten years and in which he achieved considerable success.

Hamilton, Alexander (1775–1804). Born in the West Indies, studied law in New York, organizing artillery regiments there in 1776. He served as secretary and aide-de-camp to Washington (1777–81), and fought at Yorktown. In 1783 he began practising as a lawyer in New York, but became increasingly concerned with political questions, drafting the report that led to the summoning of the Constitutional Convention of 1787, where he urged the establishment of a strong central government, putting his views on paper in contributions to the *Federalist*. From 1789 to 1795 he was Secretary to the Treasury, devising the American system of internal revenue, securing the establishment of a Federal Bank, and thereby provoking the opposition of Jefferson (q.v.) and his followers. He resumed his legal work in 1795 but became Federalist leader in New York, urging war against France in 1798 and 1800. His last years were marked by a growing antipathy towards Aaron Burr, one of the Democratic-Republican leaders in the New York Assembly. Hamilton was largely responsible for Burr's defeat both in the Presidential election of 1800 and the New York election of 1804. Burr challenged Hamilton to a duel and fatally wounded him (11 July 1804).

Hanover. Although the Elector of Hanover became King of Great Britain in 1714, in accordance with the Act of Settlement (1701), Hanover never became a British dependency, and the union remained purely dynastic. Queen Victoria was debarred from exercising sovereignty in Hanover, which accepted the 'Salic Law' excluding a woman ruler. Hanover, which had had its status raised from Electorate to Kingdom in 1815, accordingly passed to Victoria's uncle, the Duke of Cumberland (George Ernest of Hanover, 1837–51). He was succeeded by his son George, who reigned until Hanover was annexed by Prussia in September 1866.

Hardie, James Keir (1856–1915). Born in Lanarkshire, the son of a ship's carpenter. More than any other man, he shaped the political history of the Labour movement. He started work in Glasgow as a newspaper-boy at the age of seven and became a miner three years later, educating himself at night school. He gained experience of public speaking in temperance societies, but moved into trade unionism, organizing the miners first in Lanarkshire and later in Ayrshire. Hardie formed the Scottish Parliamentary Labour Party in 1888, and was elected Independent Socialist M.P. for West Ham South in 1892, shocking the Commons by driving to Westminster in cloth cap and tweed jacket and escorted by a trumpeter. Hardie founded the I.L.P. (q.v.) in 1893, played a leading part in the establishment of the Labour Representation Committee in 1900 and became chairman and leader of the Parliamentary Labour Party in 1906. He was defeated at West Ham in 1895 but sat as M.P. for Merthyr Tydfil from 1900 to 1915. He was a fervent nonconformist and pacifist, and opposed participation in the First World War.

Harding, Warren Gamaliel (1865–1923. President of the U.S.A. 1921–3). Born in Ohio and became a lawyer and newspaper owner. As a Senator (1900–4 and 1915–21) he was an orthodox Republican, consistently opposing the attempts of Wilson to secure for the U.S.A. the role of supreme international arbitrator. In the 1920 Election, Harding's pledge of a 'return to normalcy' secured his success with an overwhelming majority. His administration was notable for the Washington Conference (q.v.), the return to international isolation, and a high degree of major political corruption. He died suddenly in San Francisco and was succeeded by Vice-President Calvin Coolidge (q.v.).

Hatt-i Humayun (February 1856). A reforming edict forced on the Turkish Government by the British, French, and Austrian ambassadors at Constantinople after the Crimean War, guaranteeing the civil rights of the Christian subjects of the Sultan and promising the abolition of torture and the reform of prisons. Although the provisions of the Edict were, at first, observed by Sultan Abdul Aziz (1861–76), the revival of Balkan (and later Armenian) unrest led to their increasing neglect by the Turkish authorities.

Haussmann, Georges Eugène (1809–91). French financier and town planner. Haussmann (of German Protestant descent) was born in Paris. In 1853, under the Second Empire, he was appointed Prefect of the Seine with orders to rebuild Paris, making the crowded slums give way to broad avenues and increasing the number of open spaces around the city. Haussmann was responsible for the Bois de Boulogne, for the first network of boulevards, for supplying water, constructing sewers, and erecting new bridges, and a new Opera House. His plans were taken further by later Prefects. Haussmann fell from grace early in 1870, when the Liberal Opposition accused him of peculation. For a time under the Third Republic he sat as Bonapartist Deputy for Ajaccio.

Hébert, Jacques René (1757–94). French revolutionary; born in Alençon, forced to seek a livelihood in Paris when his family was reduced to poverty by an unsuccessful lawsuit. Hébert became a caustic pamphleteer. He joined the Cordelier Club in 1791 and was a prominent member of the Paris Commune 1792–3. In his pamphlets and his journal, *Père Duchesne,* Hébert attacked all forms of religious belief. His thinly veiled contempt for Robespierre's theism brought about his arrest. He was guillotined on 24 March 1794.

Hegel, Georg Wilhelm Friedrich (1770–1831). German philosopher; born at Stuttgart, educated at Tübingen, was successively Professor of Philosophy at Jena, Nuremberg, Heidelberg, and Berlin. Hegel first achieved fame while at Jena with his *German Constitution* (1802), a criticism of the weakness of the German states and a plea for some episodes of heroic war which would enable the stamp of nobility to be put on people who were by nature too easy-going for political leadership. His later work (e.g. *The Philosophy of Right* of 1821) expounded his theory of Idealism, that all historical experience must be dominated by a sense of some abstract Spirit greater than material forms. Hegel also developed the law of the Dialectic, that progress results from the interaction of two conflicting half-truths. As a Prussian nationalist with a totalitarian reverence for the State, Hegel was the master-mind of German thought for much of the nineteenth century. His theory of Dialectic, purged of metaphysics, was adapted by Marx to explain the historical cycle of class-wars.

Heligoland. A small island in the North Sea. The British gained Heligoland after the Napoleonic wars but never fortified it. In 1890, Lord Salisbury's Government ceded the island to Germany in return for colonial concessions in East Africa. The Germans converted Heligoland into a fortress during the period of Anglo-German naval rivalry, and used it as an advance naval base in the First World War. After 1919 the Germans evaded their treaty obligations to destroy its fortifications, and it was again turned into a formidable base in 1936, becoming a frequent target of R.A.F. bombers in the subsequent war. In 1946 the island was fully evacuated and its fortifications were blown up. Heligoland was fully restored to Western Germany in 1952.

Herzen, Alexander Ivanovich (1812–70). Russian man of letters and revolutionary thinker. Herzen was educated at Moscow University and served in the civil administration from 1835 to 1842, but, as a westernizer, was suspected of liberal ideas and unable to secure advancement. He left Russia in 1847, having inherited a private income, and spent the rest of his life in western Europe, mostly in London and Geneva. Originally, Herzen shared many of the optimistic assumptions of the romantic revolutionaries, but later he became a critic of their incompetence, partly because of what he had seen in Paris in 1848 (see *Revolutions of 1848*). He sought to impress upon the exiles the need for a genuinely realistic appreciation of the nature of revolution. Most of his writing took the form of essays in periodicals which were printed in London and smuggled into Russia. Herzen was a brilliant publicist with the rare gift of the vivid and concise phrase. His London home became a centre for revolutionary exiles, many of whom he supported financially (notably Bakunin, q.v.). He was particularly influential on the development of Russian liberal thought in the opening years of Alexander II's reign; but his ideas continued to shape developments long after his death. He was the first political writer to argue that Russia, with her primitive rural communes, was better suited than the industrialized West to become the first socialist state.

Himmler, Heinrich (1900–45). Nazi police chief. Born in Munich. He became deputy leader of the S.S. (Schutz Staffeln, storm troopers) in 1927 and leader in 1929. He was made commander of the unified German police forces in 1936, head of Reich Administration in 1939, and Minister of the Interior in 1943. His ruthless direction of the secret police (Gestapo) made him a sinister figure among the Nazi leaders, responsible for many atrocities. He was arrested in hiding by British troops on 21 May 1945, and committed suicide two days later.

Hindenburg, Paul von (1847–1934). German soldier and President; born at Posen (Poznan), a member of a Prussian military family. He was wounded at Sadowa in 1866 and represented his regiment at the proclamation of the German Empire at Versailles in 1871. He served in the Army for another forty years without particular distinction, retiring as a General. In August 1914 he was recalled and sent to halt the Russian advance in East Prussia, where, largely because of the brilliant work of Ludendorff (q.v.) and Hoffman, he gained the decisive victories of Tannenberg (q.v.) and the Masurian Lakes. Hindenburg remained as Commander-in-Chief on the Eastern Front until August 1916. Although unable to deliver a final blow to knock Russia out of the war, he was built up by German propaganda as a massive legendary Titan. In December 1914 he was made a Field-Marshal and in August 1916 became Chief of the General Staff, with Ludendorff as his Quartermaster-General. Hindenburg and Ludendorff controlled German military and civil policy from July 1917 until the Armistice. Together they were responsible for the harsh terms imposed on Russia by the Treaty of Brest-Litovsk (q.v.) and for mounting the final offensive against the British sector of the Western Front in March 1918. After the defeats of the autumn of 1918, it was Hindenburg who advised the Kaiser to leave Germany. Hindenburg remained in charge of German troops until July 1919, when he retired. Although at heart a monarchist, he was induced to stand for President of the German Republic by nationalist politicians, and was elected (April 1925). Hindenburg personally had little influence on policy during the nine years he was President, showing increasing signs of senility. He was at first contemptuous of the 'Bohemian Corporal' Hitler, but in 1933 appointed him Chancellor on the assurances of politicians whom he trusted. He died at Neudeck in August 1934 and was buried at Tannenberg.

Hitler, Adolf (1889–1945). Born in Braunau-on-the-Inn, Upper Austria; at school in Linz; lived in Vienna 1909–13, absorbing anti-semitic prejudices and eking out a miserable existence as a third-rate commercial artist; crossed the frontier and enlisted in the Bavarian infantry, 1914, serving as a Corporal on the Somme and twice gaining the Iron Cross. In September 1919 he joined a small nationalist group which shortly took the name 'National Socialist German

Workers' Party' (N.S.D.A.P., soon derisively nicknamed 'Nazi'), and discovered his power of demagogic oratory in open-air tirades in Munich against Jews and the Treaty of Versailles. The unsuccessful Munich Putsch (q.v.) of 1923 gained him national fame and thirteen months' imprisonment (during which he wrote *Mein Kampf*), but it was the World Depression that made him a prominent figure. The Nazis became the second largest German party in September 1930, their success resulting from general disillusionment with existing parties, rising unemployment, provision of a scapegoat in the 'treacherous Jew', superior propaganda organization, and the backing of leading industrialists afraid of increasing communism. After the successive failure of three Chancellors in as many years, Hindenburg appointed Hitler on 30 January 1933, believing that the non-Nazi Vice-Chancellor, Franz von Papen, would curb excesses. Four weeks later, the Reichstag Fire (q.v.) provided Hitler with the opportunity of establishing a one-party régime, and on 30 June 1934 he eliminated possible rivals by liquidating the Sturm Abteilungen group of Ernst Roehm and the supporters of Gregor Strasser, at the same time securing von Papen's resignation. On Hindenburg's death, Hitler was proclaimed 'Führer of the German Reich' (2 August 1934), to whom, as Head of State and Supreme Commander, all officers had to take an oath of loyalty. For three years Hitler concentrated on rearmament at home. He secured the military reoccupation of the Rhineland (q.v.) in March 1936, and achieved success in foreign policy by playing off potential enemies against each other and gaining an ally in Mussolini by the Axis (q.v.) of 1936. On 5 November 1937 Hitler secretly instructed his commanders to prepare for an expansionist policy abroad, occupying Austria by the Anschluss (q.v.) of 1938 and Czechoslovakia in October 1938 and March 1939. His demands on Poland led to the Second World War (September 1939), which he considered he had won in the West when German troops entered Paris (22 June 1940). In 1941 he moved his troops eastward, but in attacking Russia he encountered heavy opposition, and personally assumed command in the field on 19 December 1941. A series of failures after Stalingrad, culminating in the Allied landings in Normandy, undermined the Army's confidence in Hitler and led to the attempted assassination of 20 July 1944 (q.v.). At the end of the war Hitler was cornered in the ruins of Berlin, where, after marrying his mistress, Eva Braun, he shot himself (30 April 1945).

Hohenzollern Dynasty. The royal family of Prussia from 1701 to 1918 and the imperial family of Germany from 1871 to 1918, claiming descent from one of Charlemagne's Generals who was Count of Zollern in Swabia. The last Hohenzollern Emperor was William II (reigned 1888–1918). A cadet branch of the family (Hohenzollern-Sigmaringen) ruled in Rumania from 1866 to 1947. The Hohenzollern Candidature of 1870 was an abortive proposal by a group of Spanish politicians that Prince Leopold of Hohenzollern-Sigmaringen should accept the crown of Spain. Although the candidature was forbidden by the King of Prussia, it caused such alarm in France as to contribute to the Franco-Prussian War (q.v.).

Holland. See *Netherlands, Kingdom of the.*

Holy Alliance. A phrase frequently, but erroneously, used to describe the reactionary policy of Russia, Prussia, and Austria in the period 1815–48. In reality, the Holy Alliance was a document drawn up by Tsar Alexander I under the influence of the religious idealist, Baroness von Krüdener (1764–1824), declaring that 'the precepts of Justice, Christian Charity and Peace . . . must have an immediate influence on the Councils of Princes and guide all their steps'. In this form, the document was signed by the Tsar, the Austrian Emperor, and the King of Prussia, 26 September 1815. Other European sovereigns, with three exceptions, subsequently signed the declaration: the Pope would not associate himself with heretics; the Prince Regent had constitutional objections, but concurred in its 'sacred maxims'; the Sultan was not invited to sign because he was a non-Christian. To Metternich, the Holy Alliance was 'a loud-sounding nothing' and to Castlereagh, 'a piece of sublime mysticism and nonsense', but European liberals identified the Holy Alliance with the general repression instituted by the three Eastern European autocracies and more properly associated with the Congress System (q.v.) and the Quadruple Alliance of 1815.

Holy Roman Empire. The largely Germanic and North Italian territory organized under Otto I, crowned Emperor by the Pope in 962. In the Middle Ages the Emperor represented an attempt to maintain ancient Roman traditions of European unity blessed by a Christian conception of divinely ordained authority, but constant friction with successive Popes meant that by the fifteenth century the Empire was little more than a legal term for the trusteeship of the German states. From 1273 the Empire was dominated by the Habsburg family (q.v.) who preferred to concentrate on dynastic expansion and included in their territories many lands outside the boundaries of the Empire. When Napoleon sought to establish a French-dominated Empire, he insisted on the formal abolition of the Holy Roman Empire (June 1806). The last Emperor, Francis II, thereafter reigned as Emperor of Austria.

Home Rule. The Home Rule Association, a movement in favour of repeal of the 'Act of Union with Ireland and the establishment of a parliament in Dublin responsible for domestic affairs, was formed in 1870 by Isaac Butt (1813–79) and won over fifty seats in the 1874 Election. Butt was succeeded as leader by the more militant Parnell (q.v.), who began the policy of obstructing the work of the Commons so as to concentrate attention on Ireland's grievances. Gladstone decided in favour of Home Rule in December 1885; when he sought to carry a Home Rule Bill through the Commons in June 1886 he was defeated by thirty votes, including nearly a hundred of his Liberals. Gladstone's second Home Rule Bill of 1893 passed the Commons but was rejected in the Lords. Once the power of the Lords had been limited by the Parliament Act of 1911, the Liberals introduced a third Home Rule Bill (1912). This aroused great opposition in Protestant Ulster, which did not wish to be dominated by Catholic Dublin. When the Bill had its third reading in May 1914, Ireland seemed on the verge of civil war. Home Rule was not put into operation, because of the First World War. By 1920 the Coalition Government had changed the character of the Irish settlement; the Government of Ireland Act provided for separate parliaments in Northern and Southern Ireland. The Northern Ireland Parliament opened in June 1921 but the South now demanded more than Home Rule. Eventually, by an agreement of December 1921, Southern Ireland gained dominion status.

Hong Kong. A British colony at the mouth of the Canton River. The nucleus of the colony, the island of Hong Kong itself, was seized by the British in 1841 during the 'Opium War' (q.v.); the peninsula of Kowloon was acquired in 1860. The colony was rapidly developed as an entrepôt port and as a naval base. In 1898 the British secured a 99-year lease of the 'New Territories', an area of about 300 square miles on the Chinese mainland behind Kowloon. The Japanese attacked Hong Kong in December 1941 and forced it to surrender on Christmas Day, after a fortnight's valiant resistance. The British fleet and civilian administration returned to Hong Kong in September 1945. It has subsequently received over a million refugees from communist China.

Hoover, Herbert (b. 1874). President of the U.S.A. Born into a Quaker family in Iowa, studied geology and engineering at Stanford

University. After mining experience in Nevada and Australia, he became technical adviser to the Chinese Engineering and Mining Company (1899–1901). Between 1902 and 1915 Hoover made a fortune as director of mining companies. During and after the First World War he directed relief work in Belgium, Central Europe, and Russia. He also served as Food administrator in the U.S.A. He was Secretary of Commerce in the Harding and Coolidge Administrations (1921–8) and was nominated as Republican candidate in the 1928 Presidential Election, defeating the Roman Catholic Democrat, Al Smith. Within a few months of taking office, Hoover's administration was in the grip of a major financial depression (see *Wall Street Crash*), which many critics felt had been exacerbated by the unrestrained speculation of the years in which Hoover had been Secretary of Commerce. As President, Hoover was reluctant to extend Federal responsibilities, believing that natural economic forces would bring about a revival of trade. With the spread of the Depression to Europe he announced a one-year moratorium on debts between governments (June 1931), a measure that relieved the reparations (q.v.) burden for Germany. In the 1932 Presidential Election, Hoover was decisively defeated by Franklin D. Roosevelt (q.v.).

Horthy de Nagybanya, Miklós (1868–1957). Hungarian Admiral and Regent. Born into the Protestant landed gentry and trained for the Navy. He became aide-de-camp to Francis Joseph and served throughout the First World War in the Adriatic, distinguishing himself in action off Otranto in 1917 and becoming the last Commander-in-Chief of the Austro-Hungarian Navy. On returning to Hungary he organized from Szeged a counter-revolution to the communist regime of Béla Kun (q.v.) and entered Budapest in November 1919. He became Regent of Hungary in March 1920, a dignity he held for twenty-four years, refusing to surrender his office to King Charles (q.v.) who returned to claim the crown in 1921. Horthy's policy was maintenance of the established social order at home and revision of the Treaty of Trianon (q.v.) abroad. Although he secured recovery of parts of Czechoslovakia and Rumania in 1938–40 by grace of the Germans, he was constantly on bad terms with Hitler. He joined in the Axis occupation of Yugoslavia in 1941 and duly declared war on the U.S.S.R., but he maintained feelers with the Western Allies and on 15 October 1944 unsuccessfully sought a separate peace, being subsequently imprisoned by the Nazis. The Americans refused, after the war, to hand him over to the Yugoslavs as a 'war criminal' and he went into exile in Portugal.

Hudson's Bay Company. The Company, which was created by Royal Charter in 1670 to discover and develop northern Canada, was in a difficult position by the end of the eighteenth century. New lands, farther to the west than the territories covered by the Charter, were being exploited by fur traders, and there was intense friction between the Hudson's Bay Company and the new North West Company. Eventually in 1838 the Hudson's Bay Company took over its rival, but was immediately faced by new problems, since its wish to keep huge areas undeveloped for hunting purposes conflicted with the pioneering instincts of the rapidly increasing settlers in Canada. Finally, in 1869, the Company surrendered its territorial rights to the Canadian Government in return for a £300,000 indemnity.

Huskisson, William (1770–1830). Tory reformer. Born near Wolverhampton, and lived in France from 1783 to 1792, his experiences of the disintegration of the monarchy influencing his political views. He witnessed the fall of the Bastille and assisted the Controller of the Tuileries to escape from the mob in August 1792. On returning to England he was patronized by Pitt and became M.P. for Morpeth in 1796. He held junior offices in the Governments of 1804–5 and 1807–9 and acted as colonial agent for Ceylon from 1811 to 1823, when he entered Liverpool's Cabinet as President of the Board of Trade, an office he held for over four years, modifying commercial policy by abolishing a number of protectionist duties, thereby continuing the work of fiscal reform begun by Pitt. After a nine-month period as Secretary for War and Colonies, Huskisson found himself at variance with the Prime Minister, Wellington, and resigned. At the opening of the Liverpool and Manchester Railway, Huskisson was knocked down and killed by a locomotive when crossing the line to greet Wellington.

Ibn Saud (1880–1953). Arabian king, of the Wahabi dynasty. Organized the Bedouin tribes of the central Arabian plateau (Nejd) into communities, and waged rebellion against the Turks from 1901 to 1915, but refused to join the Arab Revolt sponsored by T. E. Lawrence, because of rivalry with Hussein of the Hejaz, whom the Allies recognized as King of the Arabs. From May 1919 to December 1925, Ibn Saud fought against Hussein and the rulers of Asir, Hail, and Jauf, eventually defeating all four adversaries and capturing the key towns of Mecca, Medina, and Jidda (1924–5). He was proclaimed ruler of the Hejaz and Nejd in January 1926, changing the name of his kingdom (an area more than four times the size of France) to Saudi Arabia in September 1932. He gained recognition of the unity and independence of his territories in a series of treaties with the Great Powers between 1927 and 1936, at the same time negotiating commercial agreements with American oil interests. He was succeeded by his son Saud (b. 1905).

Immigration Laws in the U.S.A. Between 1820 and 1900 there were $19\frac{1}{4}$ million immigrants to the U.S.A., of whom $17\frac{3}{4}$ million came from Europe. Between 1900 and 1920 there were $14\frac{1}{2}$ million, $12\frac{1}{4}$ from Europe; and between 1920 and 1940 there were $4\frac{1}{2}$ million, $2\frac{7}{8}$ from Europe. Federal immigration laws in the early nineteenth century had mostly been concerned with improving conditions on the transatlantic crossings. The first attempts to exclude immigrants were taken against the Chinese in 1882 and against the Japanese in 1900 and 1908. In 1917, despite a presidential veto, Congress passed an act imposing a literacy test on immigrants. Hostility towards immigrants increased under the Republican Administrations of the 1920s. The Quota Law of 1921 limited the intake in any one year to 3 per cent of the number of each nationality in the Census of 1910, with a maximum quota of 357,000. The 1924 Quota Law was even more drastic, halving the number to be admitted each year and amending the quota so as to allow only 2 per cent of the Census of 1890, a device which restricted immigration from Eastern Europe and Italy. The law was modified in 1929.

Imperialism. A term often abused by serving as a pejorative for political speakers. Historically, it may be applied to numerous epochs, in each of which it has a slightly different significance. In the nineteenth century Imperialism represented the urge of a nation to acquire, administer, and develop less materially advanced territories, primarily for purposes of trade or prestige, but sometimes to offset a strategic danger (real or imaginary). Among the causes of this phase of Imperialism were overpopulation of the home country, the need for markets for mass-produced goods and for new sources of raw materials. At the same time, the imagination of the newly educated millions was excited by the prospect of world empire. In Britain this attitude was encouraged by the Imperial Federation League (founded in 1884) and by the books of Sir Charles Dilke (*Greater Britain*, 1870) and Sir John Seeley (*The Expansion of England*, 1883). It received a further impetus from the historical work of J. A. Froude (1818–94), the novels of Rider Haggard (1856–1925), and above all from the verse and prose of Rudyard Kipling (1865–1936, first book published in 1890). Improved methods of communication and better medical knowledge enabled the European Great

Powers in the 1880s and 1890s to follow up the routes of earlier explorers and indulge in a 'scramble for Africa'. These African territories were sometimes developed by chartered companies (a method followed by Britain in Nigeria, Kenya, and Rhodesia), sometimes by direct governmental action (as by Germany in the Cameroons), and sometimes by private treaty (Leopold II of Belgium in the Congo, q.v.). An attempt was made by Bismarck to ease the tension caused by the partition of Africa, through the Conference of Berlin (q.v.) of 1884–5. The rival Imperialist ambitions of Britain and France in Africa brought the two countries to the verge of war in 1898 over the Fashoda Crisis (q.v.). Imperialist development was not limited to Africa: the U.S.A. acquired a ring of Pacific bases in the late 1890s; the French developed Indo-China; and the Russian overland expansion to Manchuria and northern China led to a conflict with the Japanese, who had begun to encroach on Korea and Formosa (see *Russo-Japanese War*). Since the First World War, Imperialism has more frequently taken the form of economic penetration than of political domination.

Imperial Preference. An economic doctrine believing in a modified form of Protection by which the British Dominions and Colonies would become a self-contained economic unit. The idea was warmly supported by Joseph Chamberlain (q.v.), first at the Colonial Conference of 1897 and later in the Tariff Reform League (q.v.). Imperial Preference involved too severe a break with Free Trade (q.v.) for the majority of Chamberlain's colleagues. In September 1903, failing to convert them to his beliefs, he resigned from the Conservative-Unionist Government, causing a severe split in the party by his subsequent campaign. Imperial Preference was adopted by the National Government of 1931, when Free Trade was abandoned during the World Depression. It was applied to the Dominions by the Ottawa Agreement of 1932, being extended to the Crown Colonies in 1933.

I.M.R.O. (Internal Macedonian Revolutionary Organization). Established in 1895 as a movement for the autonomy of Macedonia within either the Ottoman Empire or a federation of Balkan States. From the first it was challenged by the 'Supreme Macedonian Committee', which sought to annex Macedonia for Bulgaria. This group gained control of I.M.R.O. in 1921 and began terrorist operations in the Yugoslav section of Macedonia, subsequently securing considerable influence over Bulgarian politics. In 1924 I.M.R.O. split into two militantly hostile factions, which indulged in an orgy of assassination, tempered by raids across the Greek and Yugoslav frontiers that seriously endangered Balkan peace. I.M.R.O. activities died down after 1934, partly because of the opposition of a new Bulgarian Government and partly because of the high casualty rate among its leaders.

Independent Labour Party. In the 1880s working-class political representatives stood in parliamentary elections as 'Liberal-Labour'. In 1893 Keir Hardie (q.v.) formed the Independent Labour Party to secure the return of representatives free from any connexion with the Liberals. The I.L.P. did not have any connexion with the Trade Union Movement until in 1900 it became one of the affiliated organizations in the Labour Representation Committee (see *Labour Party*). The I.L.P. remained in existence until 1946; despite its links with the main body of the Labour Movement, its parliamentary representatives were never bound to obey the Labour Party Whip in the Commons.

India Act, 1858. An attempt to settle the internal discord in India after the Mutiny by a change in the form of government. The Act abolished the powers of the East India Company, transferring authority to the Crown and the Company's troops to the Army. The British Government created the post of Secretary of State for India, giving him an advisory council of fifteen members. At the same time, the Governor-General was given the title of Viceroy.

India Act, 1919. Implemented the Montagu-Chelmsford Report (q.v.). An all-Indian parliament of two houses was established, although the Viceroy reserved the right to issue emergency laws without reference to the chambers, and the legislature still had no power to remove the executive. In the provinces, however, the Act made some concessions to the principle of responsible government by instituting a dyarchy (i.e. rule by two bodies); 'reserved subjects' remained the prerogative of the permanent officials, but 'transferred subjects' were handed over to the responsibility of the elected Legislative Councils. The Act was experimental and subject to review after ten years; it was, in fact, criticized in the Simon Report (q.v.) of 1930 and virtually superseded in 1935.

India Act, 1935. Based on the decisions of the London Round Table Conferences of 1931–2 and the 'White Paper' of 1933. The Act proposed the transformation of the Indian Empire into a federation which would include native states as well as the provinces of British India. The federal administration was to be a dyarchy, with responsible government for certain selected subjects but with the Viceroy retaining rights on others. The Act gave greater authority to the provincial assemblies, allowing eleven of them fully responsible government within their areas. The section of the Act dealing with provincial government came into force on 1 April 1937, but divisions among the various Indian communities prevented the initiation of a federal government before the outbreak of war in Europe, and, with the decision to give India dominion status after the war, the federal section of the 1935 Act remained a dead letter.

Indian Councils Act, 1892. For the first time, admitted some Indian members to the Viceroy's Legislative Council and the provincial legislative councils, giving them the right of interpellation and criticism. Although the Indians were nominated and not elected, the Act enabled them to gain valuable experience of political work.

Indian Councils Act, 1909. The Morley-Minto Reforms (q.v.). Gave India a considerable amount of representative government. Indians were allowed a greater share in the work of the Legislative Councils (on which elected members were to predominate) and were eligible for appointment to the Viceroy's Executive Council in India and the Secretary of State's Council in London. Although these reforms did not imply responsible government (since the legislature could not eject the executive), they were a first step towards a self-governing India.

Indian Mutiny (1857–8). Originally a mutiny of the Bengal Army, but turned into a civil war because of grievances in particular provinces, especially Oudh. The revolt was caused by: (i) resentment at the reforms of ancient Indian institutions carried out by Dalhousie (q.v.) as Governor-General from 1847–56; (ii) fear of forcible conversion to Christianity; (iii) the issue of cartridges greased with cow-fat, which offended Hindus, or pig-fat, which offended Muslims. (The authorities had tried to remedy this grievance before the outbreak of the actual mutiny.) The outbreak occurred on 10 May 1857 at Meerut, whence mutineers of three regiments marched on Delhi, seized the city, and proclaimed the aged Moghul Emperor Bahadur Shah II (1775–1862) as their leader. The insurrection spread through the summer of 1857 into the Ganges Valley, Oudh, Rohilkhand, and Central India. British troops and their families were cut off in Cawnpore and Lucknow. In late June a force of 4,000 British seized a ridge facing Delhi, but they could not retake the city until September. At Cawnpore the British surrendered

(26 June) to Nana Sahib, who broke his word and murdered the prisoners. In the autumn, General Havelock fought his way back into Cawnpore and the Lucknow Residency. Sir Colin Campbell drove the rebels back throughout the winter, and Sir Hugh Rose recovered Central India in the spring of 1858. Peace was proclaimed on 8 July 1858. In August 1858, the Government passed an India Act (q.v.) transferring the administration from the East India Company to the British Crown. The Mutiny provoked excesses on both sides and left a legacy of resentment.

Inkerman, Battle of (5 November 1854). The battle took place during the siege of Sebastopol in the Crimean War (q.v.). A Russian force of 15,000 men from Balaklava tried to break through the British lines, held at first by 3,600 men. There was fierce hand-to-hand fighting before, with the arrival of reinforcements, the Russians were thrown back, having lost 12,000 men killed, captured, or wounded, against 3,400 Allied casualties.

International Socialism. The First International Workingmen's Association was established by Marx in London in 1864 to coordinate the attempts of the workers to achieve socialism in various countries. Its activities were hampered by disputes between Marxists and Anarchists, which culminated in a final break between Marx and the Anarchist leader, Mikhail Bakunin (q.v.) in 1872. The First International removed its headquarters to the allegedly calmer atmosphere of New York but was dissolved in 1876. The Second International Workingmen's Association was formed in Paris in 1889. Unlike its predecessor, it was not highly centralized, and did not establish a formal secretariat until 1900. The early Congresses of the Second International were especially concerned with controversy over 'revisionism' (see *Kautsky*) and at Amsterdam in 1905 condemned the participation of socialist parties in 'bourgeois coalitions'. Although at Stuttgart (1907) and at Copenhagen (1910) the International had approved resolutions demanding joint action by the workers to prevent war, the various national parties failed to respond in 1914, thereby fatally weakening the movement. After the Bolshevik Revolution, the Russians established the Third International (Comintern) in March 1919 to work for communist revolutions; this body was dissolved in May 1943, as a gesture of reassurance to Russia's capitalist allies. The Second International was revived in the 1920s as a loose association of social democratic parties and, in this form, still survives.

Iraq. A state between the rivers Tigris and Euphrates, forming, until the end of the First World War, the Turkish provinces of Mosul, Baghdad, and Basra and generally known as Mesopotamia. Iraq became a British mandated territory in 1920. In August 1921 the Emir Feisal, a member of the Hashemite dynasty who had assisted Lawrence (q.v.) in the Arab Revolt, was proclaimed King by the British High Commissioner. The early years of the Kingdom were hampered by revolts of the Kurds (1922–32), disputes with the frontier tribes of the Nejd, and attempts to negotiate a favourable treaty with Britain ending the mandate and securing full independence (finally signed 1930). Economic resources were considerably improved by the construction of oil pipelines to the Syrian coast in 1934 and 1935. King Feisal died in 1933 and was succeeded by his son, Ghazi, who was killed in a car crash in 1939. King Ghazi had supported Pan-Arab political parties, which attained great influence during the dictatorship of General Sidqi, 1936–7. In May 1941 a pro-German group in Baghdad tried to control the government and secured the assistance of about a hundred German and Italian aircraft. British troops intervened and forced the Iraqi leader, Rashid Ali, to flee to Germany. Iraq declared war on the Axis Powers in January 1943. British troops were withdrawn in October 1947, although the R.A.F. maintained a base at Habbaniya. King Feisal II, who had come to the throne in 1939 aged three, assumed full powers in 1953 and, supported by the veteran politician Nuri es Said, sought to organize Iraq as an alternative centre of Arab feeling to Cairo, but was overthrown and murdered in July 1958 by a military coup, headed by General Kassim. A further military coup in February 1963 led to the execution of Kassim by a group of his former followers, alarmed at his apparent sympathy with the communists.

Irish Famine. In the 1840s some four million people in Ireland lived almost entirely on potatoes. In October 1845 a serious blight began among the Irish potatoes, ruining about three quarters of the country's crop. The blight returned in 1846. Conditions were made worse by the concurrent failure of the corn harvest in Britain and Western Europe, and by the inability of the British administration to cope with the unexpected catastrophe. Suffering was so great that huge numbers continued to die throughout the four years 1847–51, despite good potato crops. Estimates of death through the famine vary considerably but the Census Commissioners of 1851 gave the figure over five years as 'nearly one million'. The Famine led to the peak period of emigration: over two million Irish crossed the

Atlantic between 1847 and 1861, with bitter prejudice against the British.

Irish Free State. Created by a treaty signed on 6 December 1921, by Lloyd George and the Irish representatives, Michael Collins (q.v.) and Arthur Griffith; it gave Southern Ireland dominion status. The treaty was denounced by a section of the Republicans, led by de Valera (q.v.), but a constitution was adopted in October 1922 and the Free State officially proclaimed on the first anniversary of the treaty. An electoral victory of the Republicans in 1932 led to an increased disregard of the British connexion (and to a disastrous tariff war with Britain until 1936). A revised constitution was issued in November 1936; the name 'Irish Free State' was replaced by 'Eire'. The link with Britain was further weakened by Irish neutrality in the Second World War. The Republic of Ireland was proclaimed in April 1949, the British Parliament formally accepting the independence of Southern Ireland in an Act passed in the following month.

Irish Home Rule. See *Home Rule*.

Ito, Hiroboumi (1841–1909). Japanese statesman. Leader in the movement for westernization. Ito was born into a peasant family but adopted by members of the aristocracy. Although at first identified with an 'anti-foreign' movement, he was sent to England in 1863 and returned to Japan anxious to adapt aspects of British government to Japanese conditions. Thus, as Governor of Kobe Province, he introduced a modern fiscal system, before being sent in 1871 on a two-year world tour to establish influential contacts of benefit to Japan. He served as chief minister from 1884 to 1888, 1892 to 1896, and in 1900–1. He was largely responsible for summoning the first Japanese Parliament (February 1890) and for building up the modern fleet that enabled Japan to gain a rapid victory in the war against China, 1894–5. After 1901, Ito (now created a Prince) found himself at variance with the military party under Marshal Yamagata. As Ambassador in St Petersburg he tried to prevent the Russo-Japanese War, and on returning to Tokio, voted against the war in the Imperial Council. He was, in consequence, forced to spend the last three years of his life as Governor of Korea, vainly seeking to introduce liberal reforms. He was assassinated by a Korean nationalist fanatic on 26 October 1909.

Izvolski, Alexander (1856–1919). Russian statesman. A member of the lesser Russian nobility. Entered the diplomatic service in 1875 and, after various minor posts, was given a key position at Tokio in 1899, being moved on to Copenhagen in 1903, where the links between the Russian and Danish royal families brought him to the attention of the Tsar, who amid general surprise appointed him Foreign Minister in 1905. During the five years he was in charge of Russian foreign policy Izvolski had two valuable achievements – the improvement of Russo-Japanese relations and the completion of the Anglo-Russian Entente (q.v.). He suffered a severe setback over the Bosnian Crisis of 1908–9; he considered that the Austrian Foreign Minister, Aehrenthal, had broken a verbal understanding by precipitately annexing Bosnia-Herzegovina instead of waiting until Russia could gain 'compensation' by a new solution of the Straits Question (q.v.). From 1910 to 1916 Izvolski was Ambassador in Paris, where he played a considerable part in strengthening the military alliance between France and Russia and in the diplomatic negotiations culminating in the abortive Constantinople Agreement (q.v.) of 1915.

Jackson, Andrew (1767–1845). President of the U.S.A. Born in South Carolina, served briefly in the American Revolution, being taken prisoner by the British. Between 1788 and 1797 he practised as a lawyer in Tennessee, serving as a Senator 1797–8. He withdrew from public life in 1806, partly because of his fiery reputation as a duellist and partly because of conflict with President Jefferson. He became a popular hero, almost overnight, when in January 1815 he repulsed a British landing at New Orleans in the Anglo-American War (q.v.). He led occupation forces in Florida in 1818, governing the territory 1821–3, returned to the Senate 1823–5, and was elected President of the U.S.A. in 1828, securing re-election in 1832 (when he was nominated by the newly styled 'Democratic Party'). Jackson, popularly termed 'Old Hickory', secured support as a hero of the wild frontier, the image of the new American common man, a boisterous champion of states' rights against federalism. His administration was marked by attacks on the Bank of the U.S. (including the withdrawal of federal funds), by the growth of the 'spoils system' of patronage, by wars with the Indians and expansion in Texas, and by an attempt (in the 'Specie Circular') to insist on gold and silver payment for land in place of paper money, so as to combat inflation and land speculation. When he retired in 1836, his candidate, Martin van Buren (1782–1862), succeeded him as eighth President.

Jacobins. The most radical group among the French revolutionaries 1790–4, particularly associated with Robespierre. The Jacobin Club was the name applied to the 'Society of Friends of the Constitution'; it was derived from the fact that the club's premises were the former Dominican Monastery of St Roch in rue Saint Honoré, Paris. (Dominican monks were nicknamed 'Jacobins' because their original Paris home was dedicated to St Jacques.) During 1793 Jacobin Clubs sprang up in all the large cities, acting as the voice of the revolutionary conscience and suppressing alleged counter-revolutionary activities. Jacobin power was destroyed by the execution of Robespierre at Thermidor (q.v.); the Paris Jacobin Club was closed on 12 November 1794.

Jameson Raid. On 29 December 1895 Dr L. Storr Jameson (1853–1917), an administrator in the British South Africa Company, led a force of 470 mounted men from Bechuanaland into Transvaal, intending to advance 180 miles to Johannesburg and join the non-Boer European workers (Uitlanders) in overthrowing the government of Paul Kruger (q.v.). The conspiracy failed; the Uitlanders did not revolt, and Jameson's force was captured four days after crossing the frontier. The raid had important political consequences: Rhodes (q.v.) was forced to resign as Premier of Cape Colony, because of his knowledge of the conspiracy; and the Boers exaggerated their ability to deal with British forces, believing, because of the encouraging 'Kruger Telegram' (q.v.), that they had German support in resisting the British. A Parliamentary Inquiry exonerated the British Colonial Secretary, Joseph Chamberlain (q.v.), from participation in the conspiracy, although later evidence suggests that he knew and approved of a revolt in Johannesburg, if not of the actual raid. Jameson served a prison sentence in Britain, but subsequently returned to South Africa and was Premier of Cape Colony from 1904–8, being made a baronet in 1911.

Janissaries. From the fourteenth century until 1826, the élite military corps of Ottoman Turkey. They were originally recruited by forced levy from Christian-born youths, whom strict discipline turned into fanatical Moslems. Their power to make or unmake Sultans made them a formidable body in palace politics; the last occasion upon which they intervened was in July 1807, when they dethroned Selim III. The arbitrary exactions imposed by Janissaries in non-Turkish provinces did considerable harm to the Ottoman Empire; it was resentment at Janissary oppression that led to the first revolt in Serbia (1804). An incipient rising by Janissaries in 1826 led to their total liquidation by Sultan Mahmud II. The personal bodyguard of the Sultan, assisted by an angry mob, attacked the Janissary barracks in Constantinople and massacred somewhere between 6,000 and 10,000 members of the corps.

Jaurès, Jean (1859–1914). French socialist leader. Born into a bourgeois family at Castres and, after a brilliant career at the École Normale, became lecturer in philosophy at Toulouse (offering his doctoral thesis, in Latin, on 'The Origins of German Socialism in the works of Luther, Kant, Fichte, and Hegel'). He was a Deputy in 1885–6, 1893–8, and 1902–14. Jaurès was always a *French* socialist rather than a Marxist, seeking inspiration in the French revolutionary tradition. Although the outstanding socialist writer and orator of his time, his emphasis on the rights of the individual brought him into conflict with his more doctrinaire comrades. Yet, by championing Dreyfus (q.v.) against their wishes, Jaurès won over hundreds of converts to socialism. Jaurès was, however, forced to accept the ruling of the 1905 Amsterdam Congress of the Socialist International condemning the participation of socialists in 'bourgeois coalitions', and he personally never held political office. For the last eight years of his life he campaigned against excessive nationalism, calling for a new 'Citizens Army', which he thought would be less the tool of the warmongers than the existing conscript forces. On 28 July 1914 Jaurès went to Brussels, seeking vainly to induce the German socialists to strike rather than accept war mobilization. On his return, he was assassinated (31 July) by a fanatical French nationalist. Jaurès was a prolific writer of works on philosophy and history; in 1904 he founded the leading French left-wing newspaper, *L'Humanité*.

Jefferson, Thomas (1743–1826). President of the U.S.A. Born in Virginia, studied law, and became a delegate to the Continental Congress. He drafted the Declaration of Independence (1776). In Congress (1783–4) he was responsible for the Land Ordinance (which formed a basis for the later organization of the territories) and devised a decimal monetary system. From 1785 to 1789 he was American Minister in Paris, witnessing the early stages of the French Revolution and being consulted over the drafting of the Declaration of the Rights of Man (q.v.). He returned to America as the first Secretary of State (September 1789), serving until 1793, when he resigned in protest at the centralizing tendencies of Hamilton (q.v.). As Vice-President under Adams (1797–1801), he continued to urge devolution, even proposing in 1798 that a state had the right to nullify Federal legislation. In the Presidential Election of 1800, he tied with Aaron Burr, securing office only with the support of Hamilton from the House of Representatives. He was President from 1801 to 1809; his Administrations were marked by economy at home, by the Louisiana Purchase (q.v.), and by desperate measures to maintain American neutrality. After his retirement, he founded the University of Virginia (1819) and encouraged the spread of neo-classical architecture throughout the Southern States.

Jena, Battle of (14 October 1806). A victory for Napoleon over the Prussians, who were led by Hohenlohe. At the same time, a few miles to the north, at Auerstadt, the main Prussian Army was routed by a French force, under Davout. The two victories led to the fall of Berlin and marked the eclipse of Prussian military prestige.

Johnson, Andrew (1808–75). President of the U.S.A. Born in North Carolina. He participated as a Democrat in Tennessee state politics 1835–57 and was Governor from 1853 to 1857, when he was elected to the Senate. In the Civil War he was the only Southerner Senator to support Lincoln, who secured his adoption as Union-Republican candidate for Vice-President in 1864. Upon Lincoln's death, Johnson automatically became President but found it impossible to carry through the conciliatory reconstruction policy for which Lincoln had striven. The Radical Republicans passed, over his own veto, a Reconstruction Act of 1867 which enfranchised Negroes and disfranchised ex-Confederates. They also passed a Tenure of Office Act (March 1867) prohibiting Presidents from dismissing high executive officials without senatorial approval. Johnson saw this as an attack on the presidential prerogative and, as a test case, dismissed his Secretary of War, Stanton. The House of Representatives thereupon made use, for the only time in American history, of the constitutional right to impeach the President before the Senate. On 16 May, 1868 the Senate voted 35 for conviction and 19 for acquittal; since this fell one vote short of the necessary two-thirds majority, the impeachment failed.

Juárez, Benito (1806–72). Mexican republican leader. Of Indian descent. Led a Liberal revolt against clerical and aristocratic domination in 1854, and was chief minister from August 1855 to December 1857. A series of sweeping judicial reforms and anti-clerical legislation aroused much opposition, and from 1857 to 1860 there was a civil war, in which Juárez was forced to take refuge at Vera Cruz, where he formed a 'Liberal' Government to lead against the Conservative-Clericals in Mexico City. As soon as his forces were successful, Juárez suspended payment of foreign debts. This action provided the French with an excuse for mounting an expedition which, from 1861–7, sought to establish a satellite empire in Mexico, under the Austrian Archduke Maximilian (q.v.). Juárez, with increasing support from the U.S.A., maintained resistance in the mountains until the French withdrew and Maximilian was captured and shot (June 1867). Juárez continued to hold office as President until his death but was unable to accomplish the necessary major reorganization that Mexico needed, a task undertaken by his former lieutenant, Diaz (q.v.).

July Monarchy. The period of French history covered by the reign of Louis Philippe (q.v.), July 1830 to February 1848. Although the monarchy gave prosperity to the commercial class until the depression of 1846–7, it disappointed almost every section of French political life. The Radicals were alienated by the conservative character of the Ministries appointed by the King; there were insurrections in Lyons (1831 and 1834) and in Paris (1834), which were severely repressed. Social discontent caused by bad factory conditions led to the emergence of a strong socialist movement in the 1840s (see *Louis Blanc*). Attempts to represent military successes in Algeria as the equivalent of Napoleonic victories aroused widespread contempt. Neither the monarch nor his régime captured the imagination of the French people and when, in February 1848, the Government prohibited a campaign to extend the suffrage, there were demonstrations in the streets of Paris, culminating in the flight of the King and the proclamation of the Second Republic. (See *Revolutions of 1848*.)

July 20 Conspiracy, 1944. Climax of the attempts by anti-Nazi groups in Germany to overthrow the régime and secure a negotiated peace. A General Staff Officer, Colonel von Stauffenberg, left a bomb at Hitler's conference table in his headquarters at Rastenburg and, believing Hitler had been killed by the explosion, flew to Berlin where Field Marshal von Witzleben and General von Beck proposed to take over the capital, eliminate the S.S. troops, and proclaim a government headed by Carl Goerdeler, formerly Lord Mayor of Leipzig. The conspiracy failed, partly because Hitler was only injured and no one had cut telephone communications with his headquarters, and partly because of energetic counter-measures taken in Berlin by S.S. Major Ernst Remer. Ironically, anti-Nazi German officers succeeded in gaining control in occupied Paris but were unable to take action because of the failure in Germany itself. The Nazis subsequently took savage reprisals; some 150 alleged conspirators were executed (including Witzleben, Beck, twelve other

Generals, and two former ambassadors) and fifteen other leading
figures committed suicide, including Field-Marshal Rommel. 20
July was more than a military conspiracy. Stauffenberg had contacts
with a group of young German liberals known collectively as the
'Kreisau Circle'. Other conspirators had been influenced by the consistently anti-Nazi teaching of a thirty-seven-year-old Lutheran
pastor, Dietrich Bonhoeffer, who had urged resistance to Hitler as
early as 1938. Nazi vengeance fell as heavily on the 'Kreisau Circle'
and on Bonhoeffer and his friends as on the dissident officers.

Junker Class. A name applied to the group of Prussian landowners
with great estates east of the Elbe who provided Prussia with her
leading administrators and who formed the main sources of the
Prussian and later German officer-corps. They tended to be narrowly
conservative in politics, tenaciously defending their agrarian interests
against all forms of liberalism. The term 'Junker' was originally
Jungherr, and was applied to sons of the nobility serving as officer-
cadets. Many Junker estates remained in existence until the Russian
invasion of 1945.

Jutland, Battle of (31 May–1 June 1916). Principal naval engagement
between the British Grand Fleet (C.-in-C., Admiral Jellicoe, 1859–
1935) and the German High Seas Fleet (Vice-Admiral Scheer, 1861–
1928). There were two distinct actions; the battle cruiser squadrons,
commanded respectively by Admiral Beatty (1871–1936) and Rear-
Admiral Hipper (1863–1932), engaging each other in the afternoon
of 31 May, while the main fleets met in the early evening, lost contact in the dark and resumed action briefly in the early hours of the
following day. The British lost 3 battle-cruisers, 3 cruisers, and 8
smaller vessels; the Germans, 1 battleship, 1 battle-cruiser, 4 cruisers,
and 5 smaller vessels. As the Germans were able to return to port,
despite British preponderance in ships and gunpower, the battle was
tactically indecisive, but Jutland is generally regarded as a British
victory since the Germans never again ventured to seek out the
British fleet and, except for minor sorties, remained in harbour until
the fleet mutinied in November 1918.

Kanagawa, Treaty of (31 March 1854). An agreement between the
U.S.A. and Japan, negotiated by Commodore Perry, and providing
for the opening of two Japanese ports for trade with America and for
the better treatment of American castaways. The Treaty had been
preceded by three years of difficult negotiations. It was followed,
within eighteen months, by treaties in which the Japanese gave privi-

leges to Britain, Russia, and Holland. These agreements represent the beginning of intercourse between Japan and the Occident.

Kapp Putsch (1920). A conspiracy by right-wing Germans under the American-born journalist Wolfgang Kapp (1868–1922), with military dispositions organized by General von Lüttwitz (1859–1942). The disbanding of irregular military forces that had been fighting in the Baltic Provinces provided the conspirators with potential followers, and on 13 March 1920 Lüttwitz seized Berlin and proclaimed a new Government with Kapp as Chancellor. The legal Government escaped to the provinces, where it denounced the Putsch as an attempt to restore the monarchy and ordered a General Strike. Although Ludendorff (q.v.) supported Kapp, the Army generally remained uncommitted. Kapp, failing to gain foreign recognition, hampered by the strike, and opposed by the Security Police, found that he had no authority and fled (17 March). Although a fiasco, the Putsch has historical significance; it showed the existence of a group of disgruntled militarists anxious to destroy 'Bolshevik republicanism'. The Erhardt Brigade, who formed Lüttwitz's main force, brought with them from the Baltic a new symbol on their helmets – the swastika.

Károlyi, Count Mihály (1875–1955). A member of one of the greatest families of the Hungarian landed aristocracy. Entered the Hungarian Parliament in 1905 with liberal views, which became increasingly radical. Throughout the First World War, he led the pro-Entente Independent Party in Budapest. He was appointed Prime Minister by Emperor-King Charles (q.v.) on 30 October 1918, and immediately sought an Armistice, hoping in vain that the Allies would treat his independent Hungarian state as a democratic victim of Austro-German domination. On 16 November he became provisional President of the Hungarian Republic and tried to carry through a number of reforms, personally supervising the distribution of his own estates to the peasantry. In March 1919 he was forced out of office and a communist régime established under Béla Kun (q.v.). Károlyi went into exile, and as he was regarded as a traitor by the Horthy Government that overthrew Kun, he did not return to Hungary until 1946. Károlyi served as a Hungarian diplomat from 1946 to 1949, when the increasingly totalitarian character of the communist government made him return once more to exile.

Kautsky, Karl (1854–1938). Central European socialist. Born in Prague. As a young man, Kautsky was a friend of Marx. He became prominent as a German socialist leader at the Lübeck Party Congress of 1901, when he opposed Bernstein's 'revisionism' (i.e. plea for the gradual achievement of socialism through parliamentary reform). In the First World War, Kautsky remained a pacifist, politically well to the left of the majority of German socialists. His independent character induced him to oppose the Bolshevik Revolution, and he effectively denounced the 'dictatorship of the proletariat' as a distortion of Marxism. After the war he helped edit a collection of German Foreign Office papers discrediting the Hohenzollerns and then settled in Vienna, where he was established as the most formidable social-democrat theorist in Europe. In 1934 he protected himself against the Dollfuss dictatorship by becoming a Czechoslovak citizen, but he continued in Vienna until the eve of the Nazi occupation. He died in Holland.

Kellogg Pact (1928). In April 1927 the French Foreign Minister, Aristide Briand (1862–1932), proposed to the American Secretary of State, Frank B. Kellogg (1856–1937), that their two countries should sign a pact which would renounce war as an instrument of national policy. Kellogg urged that the Pact should be, not bilateral, but increased in scope, and in August 1928 a nine-power conference in Paris formally condemned recourse to war in the terms of Briand's original proposal, although admitting that a signatory had a right to defend its interests (including regional undertakings such as the Monroe Doctrine, q.v., and the obligations of an overseas empire). Other countries rapidly adhered to the Pact. It was signed, in all, by 65 states. The Kellogg Pact was regarded as a considerable advance towards the pacific settlement of disputes, especially since its sponsors included not only Germany but the U.S.A. and the U.S.S.R. (who were not members of the League of Nations). The Pact was, however, limited, for it made no provision for punishing aggressors. In reality it in no way restricted the sovereignty of a signatory, and the intensification of political nationalism in the following decade rendered it nugatory.

Kemal, Mustapha (1880–1938; adopted the name 'Kemal Ataturk' 1935). Born in Salonica, entered the Turkish Army. He supported the Young Turks (q.v.) but subsequently disagreed with their leader, Enver. Kemal fought against the Italians in Libya (1911) and in the Balkan Wars. He distinguished himself as Turkish commander at Gallipoli (q.v.) and in the final battles with Allenby in Syria. When in May 1919 he was sent to Samsun (Anatolia), he began to organize resistance to the dismemberment of Turkey and, in particular, to Greek attempts to secure Smyrna (q.v.) and its hinterland. By the end of 1919 his nationalist movement had become a revolution, and on 23 April 1920 he set up a provisional government in Ankara. War continued against the Greeks until September 1922, when they were ejected from Smyrna. Kemal secured revision of the Turkish peace settlement by the Treaty of Lausanne (q.v.) and proceeded to modernize Turkey. The Sultanate was abolished in November 1922, the Caliphate in March 1924, the Turkish Republic (q.v.) being formally set up in October 1923. Kemal ruled Turkey as a ruthless dictator until his death on 10 November 1938. He secularized the state, encouraged western modes of dress, emancipated women, introduced a Latin alphabet, developed industry, and substituted a narrowly Turkish national pride for the older Islamic loyalties of the past.

Kenya. British colony and protectorate in East Africa. British trade with the East African coast developed in the 1840s and by the middle of the 1870s dominated the region around Mombasa. Spheres of interest between the British and the Germans (who were developing what is now Tanganyika) were settled by treaty in 1886. In May 1887 the British East Africa Company, under Sir William Mackinder, secured formal lease of the coastal region from the Sultan of Zanzibar. The Company was granted a royal charter in the following year and controlled the territory until 1893, when its possessions were taken over by the British Government and organized as the East Africa Protectorate. Executive and Legislative councils were established in 1906 (and extended in 1919 and 1934) and white settlement was encouraged. In 1920 British East Africa was renamed 'Kenya' and became a Crown Colony. Railways penetrated the interior in the middle of the 1920s. Serious disturbances occurred between 1952 and 1954 as a result of the activities of the African secret society, Mau Mau. A multi-racial constitution was introduced in 1960. Independence was promised by the end of 1963.

Kerensky, Alexander. Born in 1881 in Simbirsk (where his father was the schoolmaster of a pupil later known as Lenin). Kerensky studied law in St Petersburg and entered the Fourth Duma in 1912 as a democratic socialist. After the March Revolution of 1917, he became War Minister (16 May) and Prime Minister (25 July) in the Provisional Government, urging the vigorous prosecution of the war. His attempts to mount a formidable offensive in the summer ran counter to the feelings of the Russian people, who were anxious for peace. He was pushed out of office by the Bolshevik *coup d'état* of 7 November. After seeking vainly to organize resistance, Kerensky escaped abroad, and has since lived mainly in the U.S.A. (See *Russian Revolution*).

Keynes, John Maynard (1883–1946, created a Baron 1942). British economist. Keynes was born and educated at Cambridge. He served as chief treasury representative at the Paris Peace Conference and achieved fame with his *Economic Consequences of the Peace* (1919), a brilliant analysis of the leading statesmen of the Conference and an attack on the policy of reparations. In the 1920s and 1930s he became the leading critic of established economic theory, seeking a synthesis between socialism and capitalism by insisting that full employment could be attained by the production of capital goods, the adoption of a cheap money policy, and a programme of public investment. Keynes expressed the definitive version of his thesis in the *General Theory of Employment, Interest, and Money* (1936). During the Second World War he became a financial adviser to the Government; he was a strong advocate of a World Bank which would eliminate international financial crises.

Kiaochow. A bay in the Gulf of Pechili, northern China. In November 1897 German naval units seized Kiaochow in revenge for the murder of two missionaries. They established a formidable naval base at Tsingtao, acquiring, in all, some 200 square miles on a ninety-nine-year lease. At the same time, German capitalists secured mining rights and subsequently developed the neighbouring province of Shantung, constructing a railway from Tsingtao to Tsinan. The German action precipitated a rush for Chinese bases, the Russians seizing Port Arthur (q.v.) and the British Wei-hai-wei, in 1898. In an altimatum to Germany on 15 August 1914 the Japanese demanded the handing over of the Kiaochow leasehold; when this was refused, they captured Kiaochow early in November. China's protest at the Japanese move induced the Japanese to present the Twenty-One Demands (q.v.) to China in January 1915. Despite serious disputes with China, the Japanese continued to hold Kiaochow until 1922, when they withdrew in accordance with arrangements made at the Washington Conference (q.v.). The Japanese reoccupied the bay in January 1938 and remained there until 1945.

King, W. L. Mackenzie (1878–1950). Canadian statesmen. Born in Ontario, descended on his mother's side from W. L. Mackenzie (q.v.). Mackenzie King became a Liberal M.P. in the Canadian Parliament in 1908. He was particularly interested in industrial relations and served as Minister of Labour under Laurier, whom he succeeded as Liberal leader. He was Canadian Prime Minister from 1921 to June 1926, from September 1926 to 1930, and from 1935 to 1948. He was responsible for a reciprocal trade agreement with the U.S.A. (1935)

to ease the effects of the Depression. He raised the international influence of Canada, especially during the War. Against the wishes of many in his party, he secured conscription in 1944. He favoured a reform of the Constitution so that Canada would have greater power to decide her own future.

Kitchener, Horatio Herbert (1850–1916, created Baron 1898, Viscount 1902, Earl 1914). Gained his baptism of fire with an ambulance unit attached to the French Army in 1871. He was commissioned in the same year in the Royal Engineers and undertook important survey work in Palestine and Cyprus, 1874–82. He served in the Sudan (1884–5) and was appointed Sirdar (commander-in-chief) of the Egyptian Army in 1890 as a Major-General. From 1896 to 1899 he undertook the reconquest of the Sudan (q.v.), advancing after Omdurman to Fashoda (q.v.). In the Boer War he was chief of staff to Lord Roberts (December 1899–November 1900), succeeding him as commander-in-chief and organizing the much criticized system of blockhouses and concentration camps that gradually wore down Boer resistance. From 1902 to 1909 he was commander-in-chief in India, engaging from 1903 to 1905 in a bitter quarrel with the Viceroy, Curzon (q.v.), over the administrative control of the Indian Army. He was British Agent in Egypt, virtually ruler of the country, from 1911 to 1914. On 5 August 1914 he was appointed War Minister in Asquith's Government, the first serving officer to hold the post. Although he was invaluable as an inspiration for morale and for recruiting ('Your Country needs YOU'), he could not understand the political attitude of his Cabinet colleagues, distrusted the Territorial Army, and was on bad terms with some of the field commanders. He was drowned on 5 June 1916 when H.M.S. *Hampshire*, in which he was travelling to Russia, struck a mine off the Orkneys.

Knownothings. A short-lived American political party active in the period 1854–9, particularly in the urban centres of the Eastern seaboard and in the South. The Knownothings were opposed to immigration (and especially to Catholic immigrants) and supported slavery. Officially their movement was called the 'American Party'; the more usual name was derived from the reply 'I know nothing' which its members were supposed to give to inquisitive questions. The Party unsuccessfully contested the 1856 election. Although the movement as such died out rapidly, the narrowly bigoted 'Knownothing' attitude remained as a force in American politics.

Königgrätz, Battle of (3 July 1866). German name for the battle of Sadowa (q.v.).

Korea. Became a tributary state of the Chinese Empire in 1637. It was opened to trade with Japan in 1876, and became a centre of Sino-Japanese intrigue and rivalry, culminating in the War of 1894–5. The Treaty of Shimonoseki (q.v.) formally established Korea's independence, but the Japanese sought to dominate the country. From 1898 to 1904 the Russians penetrated northern Korea, securing commercial concessions along the Yalu River. This forward policy precipitated the Russo-Japanese War (q.v.) of 1904–5. In November 1905 Japan assumed responsibility for Korea's foreign relations, formally annexing the country in August 1910 and settling Japanese families there, especially around Seoul. The Russians invaded Korea on 8 August 1945. Friction between Russian-dominated North Korea and American-sponsored South Korea led to war in June 1950. The South Koreans were supported by United Nations contingents, the North Koreans by Chinese 'volunteers'. Peace was restored in July 1953, with Korea again uneasily divided along a line slightly north of the 38th Parallel.

Kosciuszko, Tadeusz (1746–1817). Polish patriot leader. Born at Mereczowszczyno, but trained as a soldier in Prussia and France. He volunteered for the American Army in 1776, fought at Yorktown as a Colonel of Engineers, and was given honorary citizenship by Congress. He returned to Europe in 1791 and, foreseeing the further designs of the eastern autocracies on his country, endeavoured to win the support of the French revolutionaries for the Polish cause. With the Second Partition of Poland (1793), he returned to the Warsaw district and planned an insurrection. The Poles rose against the Russians in March 1794, and Kosciuszko defeated a Russian Army at Raclawice (3 April). Six months later his troops were broken in front of Warsaw and he was wounded and taken prisoner. The Russians sent him back to the U.S.A. but he settled in France in 1798. He refused to assist either Napoleon or Tsar Alexander I to create Polish puppet states, continuing to demand full Polish independence with a constitution on the British model. He died in France.

Kossuth, Lajos (1802–94). Hungarian revolutionary. Kossuth came from a family of the poorer Hungarian nobility, originally of Slovak descent. He became well known in the 1820s and 1830s as a liberal writer of patriotic pamphlets and as a lawyer. He was imprisoned for treason from 1837 to 1840, but, on his release in 1841 became editor of a nationalistic newspaper, *Pesti Hirlap*, which confirmed his leadership of the Hungarian people. In 1847 he was elected a member of the Hungarian Diet; his speeches revealed him as a narrowly Hungarian patriot, bitterly opposed to Austrian rule and to the aspirations of the Slav peoples within the Hungarian lands. His speech of 3 March 1848 with its claims of Hungarian independence, began the revolution of 1848. In July Kossuth organized the Honved, the citizen army of self-defence against the Austrian and Croatian forces that were being sent against Hungary. He became President of the Committee of National Defence two months later and, on 19 April 1849, formally declared the deposition of the Habsburgs and the independence of Hungary. In August, however, Russian intervention sealed Hungary's fate and Kossuth was forced to flee, first to Turkey, later (1851) to France, Britain (where he was rapturously received), and the U.S.A. He was never allowed to return to Hungary.

Kruger, Paulus (1825–1904). Boer statesman. Born in Cape Colony into a family of strict Puritans and remained, throughout his life, dominated by the religious principles of the Old Testament. At the age of eleven, he accompanied his parents on the Great Trek (q.v.) and settled in the Transvaal. He was one of the main political opponents of the British in the first Boer War (q.v.) of 1881. Two years later he became President of the Transvaal. Although his administrative ability was limited, the Transvaal underwent a considerable change in the early years of his Presidency because of the discovery of a large goldfield on the Witwatersrand (1886). Kruger welcomed foreign labour to develop the mines but denied the newcomers all political rights, and imposed heavy taxation on them. His anti-British feeling was shown by a number of incidents in the period 1884–94, and was intensified by the Jameson Raid (q.v.). He purchased arms from Germany and launched an attack on Cape Colony and Natal in September 1899. With the British successes of the second phase of the Boer War, Kruger left his country (May 1900) to seek aid in Europe. He found the Germans no longer interested and the French sympathetic but disinclined for action. He settled in Holland and died in Switzerland.

Kruger Telegram. A message sent by the German Kaiser, William II (q.v.), to President Kruger in January 1896, congratulating him on repulsing the Jameson Raid (q.v.) and preserving the independence of the Transvaal 'without appealing to the help of friendly powers'. The Kaiser's action aroused considerable resentment among the

British, who had not hitherto been unsympathetic to Germany; the telegram was regarded as impertinent meddling in British colonial affairs, and it was thought to be couched in needlessly aggressive language. The telegram also encouraged the Boers in the mistaken belief that they could expect German aid in case of a conflict with Britain.

Ku Klux Klan. An American secret society, originally founded in 1866 to re-establish white supremacy in the Southern states of the U.S.A. by terrorizing Negroes and their sympathizers. Although formally disbanded in 1869, it continued its activities until investigated by a Congressional Committee in 1871. It was re-founded in 1915 and was very active in the period 1922–30, showing hostility towards Negroes, Roman Catholics, Jews, internationalism, and 'Darwinism'. The movement revived slightly in the mid-1950s.

Kulaks. A class of former peasants who were able to become the proprietors of medium-sized farms in Russia as a result of the agrarian reforms of Stolypin (q.v.) in 1906. By assisting the more ambitious peasant to withdraw his land from the commune, Stolypin hoped to create a stable middle class of prosperous farmers who would form a naturally conservative group in society. To a large extent Stolypin succeeded, but only 15 per cent of the Russian peasants had become *kulaks* by 1914. After the Bolshevik Revolution, the class was a considerable embarrassment to Lenin and Stalin, vigorously opposing collectivization until 1929, when Stalin ordered 'the liquidation of the *kulaks* as a class' as part of the First Five-Year Plan (q.v.).

Kulturkampf ('Conflict of Beliefs'). A term originating in an anti-Catholic election address of 1873 but generally used to describe the conflict between Bismarck and the Roman Catholic Church, 1871–87. Bismarck feared that the decrees of the Vatican Council (q.v.) implied that the Church was asserting a prior claim to the State on the obedience of the citizen. He was, too, considerably alarmed by the creation of the Roman Catholic Centre Party (q.v.) which was avowedly anti-Prussian. The Kulturkampf was worse in Prussia than in other parts of Germany, for, while priests throughout the Reich were forbidden to refer to politics in their sermons and the Jesuits were expelled, the Prussian 'Falk Laws' of May 1873 led to the complete subordination of the Church to state regimentation. Many priests preferred to be imprisoned rather than accept the Prussian laws, and their plight aroused general sympathy. Bismarck, seeing

179

his opponents were flourishing under persecution, realized that his policy was inept, and with the election of a new Pope (Leo XIII) in 1878 began negotiations which restored most of the Roman Catholic rights by 1887.

Kun, Béla (1886–?1936). Hungarian communist leader of Jewish origin. While serving with the Hungarian Army in the First World War, Kun was captured by the Russians. After the Revolution he was sent back to Hungary as a Bolshevik agitator and secured the fall of the hesitant Károlyi (q.v.) in March 1919. For four and a half months Kun ruled Hungary as a communist state, carrying through radical reforms but arousing fear and resentment by the cruelty of many of his supporters. Kun was faced by Czech and Rumanian invasions and by the establishment at Szeged of ·a counter-revolutionary government, of whom the effective leader was Admiral Horthy (q.v.). Early in August 1919, the Rumanians occupied Budapest, forcing Kun to flee to Vienna and later to return to Russia and obscurity. His régime disintegrated with his flight. Kun is believed to have perished in the Great Purge of the thirties.

Kuomintang. Chinese nationalist party. Formed in 1891, as a movement devoted to a political democracy and social reform, by Sun Yat-sen (q.v.), played a prominent part in the Chinese Revolution (q.v.) of 1911, but was forced by the power of war-lords to concentrate in southern China until 1926–7, when Sun's successor, Chiang Kai-shek (b. 1886), succeeded, with Russian aid, in advancing north to Nanking. The Kuomintang established an effective government on 10 October 1928, and adopted a formal constitution in May 1931. Throughout the 1930s the Kuomintang headed the Chinese resistance to Japanese pressure and invasion but it departed from many of the principles of its founder and, by 1945, had become riddled with corruption. In the Civil War of 1945–8, the Communists defeated the Kuomintang, forcing its leader to flee to Formosa.

Kut-el-Amara. A town in a key military position on the River Tigris in Mesopotamia (Iraq). In 1915 a British force from India, originally sent to protect oil supplies at Basra, advanced into Mesopotamia under General Townshend, defeated the Turks at Kut (28 September), but failed to penetrate further towards Baghdad. From 7 December Kut was besieged for four and a half months by the Turks, three attempts to relieve it failing (partly because of floods). When Townshend surrendered on 29 April 1916 the Turks captured 10,000 men, many of whom died through ill-treatment as prisoners.

A third battle was fought at Kut in January–February 1917, and the city was recaptured by Sir Stanley Maude, who went on to take Baghdad a fortnight later.

Labour Party. Formed as the 'Labour Representation Committee' in 1900, but working-class members had sat with the Liberals in the Commons since 1885. Labour political groups had been formed by Keir Hardie (q.v.) in 1888 (Scottish Parliamentary Labour Party) and 1893 (Independent Labour Party), but these lacked any connexion with the trade union movement. In February 1900 representatives of all the socialist groups in Britain (the I.L.P., q.v., the near-Marxist 'Social Democratic Federation', and the Fabian Society, q.v.) joined trade unionists in setting up the Labour Representation Committee to establish 'a distinct Labour Group in Parliament'. The first secretary of the L.R.C. was Ramsay MacDonald (q.v.). Early resolutions of the L.R.C. were moderate in tone; they demanded better living conditions and condemned inequality of wealth but carefully avoided committing supporters to 'socialism' or the doctrine of the class war. In consequence, the S.D.F. seceded in 1901, but the movement expanded rapidly, being influenced by the conflict between the Government and the trade unions over the Taff Vale (q.v.) decision of 1901. In the 1906 Election 29 out of 50 L.R.C. candidates were successful and it was decided later in that year to rename the L.R.C. 'The Labour Party'. The Party supported the social reforms of the Liberal Governments but was hampered by lack of funds, especially after the Osborne Judgement of 1908–9 in which the Law Lords decided against the use of trade union funds for political objects. The introduction of payment of M.P.s (1911) helped the Party considerably. During the war, one Labour leader, Arthur Henderson, sat in Lloyd George's War Cabinet and six other members gained administrative experience in governmental posts. Under the spur of the Russian Revolution, the Labour Party adopted in 1918 a new constitution aiming at 'the gradual building up of a new social order based ... on deliberately planned cooperation in production and distribution'; this more openly socialist creed determined Labour's policy until after the Second World War. Postwar disillusionment and unemployment, coupled with feuds within the Liberal Party, allowed Labour to become the official Opposition Party in 1922. A year later its leader, Ramsay MacDonald, was asked to form a Minority Government (1923 figures: Cons. 258; Labour 191; Liberals 158). MacDonald's Cabinet, which included one ex-Tory and two ex-Liberals, struggled on for ten months but was defeated in the Election of November 1924, largely because of the

so-called 'Zinoviev Letter' (q.v.). Economic depression and rising unemployment enabled Labour to emerge from the 1929 Election as the
largest party, though still in a minority. The resultant MacDonald
Government could introduce no radical measures and was hampered
by the world financial crisis; and in August 1931 the Cabinet split
over a proposal from the Chancellor of the Exchequer, Snowden,
to cut unemployment benefits. MacDonald formed a 'National Government' (4 Labs., 4 Cons., and 2 Libs.) and although repudiated by
most of his former colleagues, went to the country and won the election with 558 'National' members to 56 Labour. Lansbury (q.v.) was
elected leader of the Labour Party in 1932 and was succeeded by
Attlee in 1935. During the thirties the Party was weak at Westminster
and divided over foreign affairs and defence, but powerful in local
government, especially on the L.C.C., where (under Herbert Morri-
son) it had secured a clear majority in 1934. In May 1940 Churchill
brought two Labour members (Attlee and Greenwood) into his War
Cabinet and appointed five others to ministerial posts. In the 1945
election, Labour won a clear majority for the first time. (1945 figures:
Lab. 393; Cons. etc. 213; others 30.) Labour narrowly won the election of 1950 and was defeated in 1951, 1955, and 1959.

Lafayette, Marquis de (Marie Joseph Paul Yves Roch Gilbert
Motier, 1757–1834). French aristocrat. Enlisted in the American
revolutionary armies in 1777, subsequently being sent back to Paris
on a diplomatic mission in 1780, returning to America to participate
in the Yorktown campaign of 1781. Although lacking political sense,
Lafayette enjoyed great prestige in Paris and was appointed first
commander of the National Guard in 1789. In 1792 his military
failure against the Austrians led to his impeachment and pro-
scription by the Convention, but he fled to the Austrian lines and
returned to France in 1799. At the Restoration of 1815 he became
the figurehead of the Liberals. His international renown saved him
from arrest after the failure of a clumsy military conspiracy in 1821,
and he attached himself to the Orleanist opposition, giving support
to Louis Philippe (q.v.) in 1830. Lafayette was never a leader, only a
symbol. His achievements are less important than his legend, a bond
of friendship that has effectively linked France and the U.S.A. for a
century and a half.

Laibach (Ljubljana), Congress of (January 1821). This conference
was really a resumption of the adjourned Congress of Troppau (q.v.).
In the intervening three months, the Austrians had amassed 80,000
troops to restore order in the disaffected regions of Italy and the

Russians, too, were ready to send a military force to stamp out revolts. The Congress widened the gulf between the British and their former allies (Russia, Austria, and Prussia). The British protested and withdrew. The outbreak of revolt in Greece and the worsening of the situation in Spain prevented any precipitate military moves outside Italy. It was agreed to hold a further congress in the autumn of 1822; eventually this met at Verona (q.v.).

Laissez-faire. The economic doctrine of individualism, as opposed to collectivism. Belief in non-interference of the State in economic affairs was a fundamental principle of British Liberalism for most of the nineteenth century. It was derived both from the teachings of the classical economists (Adam Smith, Malthus, q.v., and Ricardo, q.v.) and from the tradition of Bentham (q.v.) and the Philosophical Radicals. (See also *Manchester School.*)

Lamartine, Alphonse de (1790–1869). French poet and politician. Born in Mâcon into an aristocratic family. He won national renown, and a place in the Académie Française, as the outstanding Romantic poet of the 1820s, a French Byron. He became a Deputy in 1833 and followed a strongly individualistic policy of opposition, at the same time writing a sympathetic study of the Girondins. In February 1848 he emerged as the typical moderate radical opponent of the Orleanists. With the proclamation of the Second Republic, he became responsible for foreign affairs and the idol of Paris. Within a few months it was clear that he could not control the conflict of moderates and socialists in the Provisional Government. His refusal to allow French military support to other revolutions focused discontent on social conditions for which he could offer no panacea. By June 1848 he was discredited; when he stood for President in December he polled only 0·2 per cent of the national vote. He resumed his literary work but never again achieved distinction.

Lamennais, Félicité de (1782–1854). French Catholic priest and writer. The son of a shipowner, born in St Malo and not ordained until 1816. His influence, which was considerable in the period 1817 to 1835, depended on his writings, in which, while attacking eighteenth-century rationalism, he sought to win the sympathetic support of his Church for political liberalism. The views of Lamennais and his chief followers (Montalembert and Lacordaire) were condemned by Pope Gregory XVI, who feared liberal unrest in the Papal States, in the encyclicals *Mirari Vos* (1832) and *Singulari Nos* (1834). Lamennais defended his views with passionate anger in

Paroles d'un croyant (1833), which led his enemies to denounce him as 'Robespierre in a surplice'. He withdrew his allegiance to the Roman Catholic Church and spent the last twenty years of his life in poverty. Although unsuccessful in his own day, he was the prophet of later Christian Democratic movements.

Lansbury, George (1859–1940). British socialist. Lansbury was born in Suffolk but played a prominent part in local government in Bow and Poplar before becoming a Labour M.P. from 1910 to 1912. His support of the suffragettes and his wartime pacifism then kept him out of the Commons until 1922 although he was an influential writer in the *Daily Herald,* of which he was editor 1919–23. As a member of the Labour Government of 1929–31, he refused to join the Mac-Donald-Baldwin Coalition and was the only ex-Minister still in the Labour Party to keep his seat in the 1931 election. He led the Labour Party from 1932 to 1935, but his simple pacifist Christian socialism alienated many trade unionists, including Bevin (q.v.). After resigning the leadership, he visited Hitler (April 1937) in a vain attempt to assist an Anglo-German understanding.

Lansdowne, Lord (Henry Petty-Fitzmaurice, 1845–1927). Became Fifth Marquess of Lansdowne in 1866). Descended through his mother from Talleyrand. Lansdowne was originally a Liberal, and was sent by Gladstone as Governor-General of Canada in 1883. His association with the Liberal Unionists led to his nomination by Salisbury as Viceroy of India (1888–94). In 1895 he became War Secretary in Salisbury's Government and was blamed by the press for British unpreparedness in the early stages of the Boer War (1899). He succeeded Salisbury as Foreign Secretary in 1900 and conducted the difficult negotiations with France that culminated in the Anglo-French Entente (q.v.) of 1904. From 1905 to 1915 he led the Conservative Opposition in the Lords, arousing much criticism by his use of the Conservative majority to reject measures passed by the Liberals in the Commons. He held non-departmental office in the Coalition Government of 1915–16. In November 1917 he made an appeal for a negotiated peace in a letter to the *Daily Telegraph,* an act that aroused considerable hostility.

Lateran Treaties (1929). Between the Italian Government and the Papacy. Ended the friction that had existed since Italian troops entered Rome in 1870. The treaties established the Vatican City as an independent state and included a Concordat regulating the position of the Roman Catholic Church in Fascist Italy. The Pope (Pius XI,

pontiff 1922–39) received a considerable indemnity for papal possessions seized by the Italian State in the 1870s and gave up his status as
a 'prisoner' within the Vatican.

Latvia. One of the three independent Baltic Republics, 1921–40,
covering an area of some 25,000 square miles and comprising parts of
the former Tsarist provinces of Livonia and Courland. The Latvians
had to struggle against both the Bolsheviks and German irregular
troops before securing recognition of their independence in January
1921. Economic depression led in May 1934 to the establishment of
an authoritarian dictatorship under Ulmanis, which sought, in vain,
to secure German protection against the increasing power of Russia.
The Republic was occupied by the Russians in June 1940 and became a constituent state in the U.S.S.R. two months later.

Laurier, Sir Wilfrid (1841–1919). The first French Canadian to become Prime Minister of the Dominion. Educated in Montreal, became a lawyer and a journalist, and entered the House of Commons
in Ottawa in 1874 as a Liberal, becoming leader of his party in 1887.
He was Prime Minister continuously from 1896 to 1911, and was a
considerable influence in imperial affairs. He helped create a greater
sense of Canadian unity, improved relations with Britain (whom he
favoured with preferential tariffs), and was responsible for the decision to send Canadian troops overseas in the Boer War. His Government was eventually defeated because of opposition to his attempt
to improve trade relations with the U.S.A. While supporting
Canadian participation in the First World War, he refused to join
the Coalition Government of 1917 because he disapproved of
conscription.

Lausanne, Treaty of (24 July 1923). Final peace settlement for
Turkey, necessitated by the refusal of the Turkish Republic under
Kemal (q.v.) to consider the Treaty of Sèvres (q.v.) binding. By the
Lausanne Treaty, Turkey surrendered all claim to territories of the
Ottoman Empire occupied by non-Turks. The Greeks were con-
firmed in possession of all the Aegean islands except Imbros and
Tenedos, which were returned to Turkey. The Greeks surrendered
Smyrna (q.v.). Italian annexation of the Dodecanese and British
annexation of Cyprus was confirmed. The Bosphorus and Darda-
nelles were demilitarized. Turkey recovered Eastern Thrace in
Europe, but there was an exchange of populations between Greece
and Turkey, over a million Greeks being forced to leave in return for
350,000 Turks expelled from Greece.

Laval, Pierre (1883–1945). French politician. Born in Auvergne, became a lawyer and joined the Socialist Party in 1903. In 1914 he was elected socialist Deputy for Aubervilliers, a working-class suburb of Paris, which he represented as Deputy or Mayor for thirty years irrespective of his political vacillations. After narrowly escaping imprisonment for his anti-war policy, he left the socialists in 1920 and attracted some support as an independent by his astute management of the smaller political factions. He became Minister of Public Works in 1925, Minister of Justice in 1926, and a 'National Republican' Senator in 1927. He was Prime Minister from January 1931 to February 1932 and Foreign Minister from October 1934 to January 1936, serving as Prime Minister again for the last six months of the period and being forced to resign because of his apparently cynical plan to appease Mussolini by partitioning Abyssinia. He remained out of the forefront of politics for the next four years, industriously championing the political ideas of Pétain (q.v.), and emerged as the main spokesman of Vichy France (q.v.) in the autumn of 1940. Although superseded by Darlan in 1941, Laval returned as chief minister from April 1942 to January 1944 and managed to avoid giving any military undertakings to the Germans. In the summer of 1944, foreseeing an Allied victory, he tried to convene the National Assembly as the only legally representative body in France, but was arrested by the Germans, who had never trusted him. After fleeing to Spain in 1945 he returned to France to face charges of treason and was shot after a trial of questionable legality.

La Vendée. See *Vendéan Revolt.*

Law, Arthur Bonar (1858–1923). Born in New Brunswick, the son of a Presbyterian Minister. Educated in Glasgow, and entered the Scottish iron trade. He was elected Conservative-Unionist M.P. for a Glasgow constituency in 1900, and became widely known through his speeches in support of Tariff Reform (q.v.) 1902–5. He was defeated in the 1906 Election but returned to the Commons after a by-election in Dulwich and gained a following among the rank and file of the Party, many of whom found Balfour, their leader, remote. In 1911 Bonar Law succeeded Balfour as Party Leader. He strongly supported the Ulstermen in the Irish crisis of 1912–14. In the Asquith Coalition of 1915–16 he served as Colonial Secretary, becoming Chancellor of the Exchequer and Leader of the Commons under Lloyd George (1916–19) and Lord Privy Seal (1919–22). He became Prime Minister in October 1922, when he was already a sick man; ill-health forced him to resign after seven months in office.

Lawrence, John (1811–79, created Baron Lawrence in 1869). Indian administrator. Lawrence was born in Yorkshire. He first went to India in 1830, and held civic posts in Delhi until 1840, when his health broke down and he returned home. After Dalhousie (q.v.) annexed the Punjab in 1849, he assisted his brother, Sir Henry Lawrence (1806–57), to organize the province, being responsible for its administration from 1853 to 1859. He played a considerable part in the recapture of Delhi from the mutineers (his brother, Henry, having been killed defending Lucknow). After recovering from a further breakdown in health, he returned to India as third Viceroy in 1863. He was able to put Indian finances on a firm foundation and did much to end the bitterness that had lasted since the Mutiny. He also adopted a moderate policy towards Russian expansion in Central Asia, which was in marked contrast to the 'forward' policy of the Viceroys from 1876. Lawrence retired and returned to England in 1869.

Lawrence, Thomas Edward (1888–1935). 'Lawrence of Arabia.' While an undergraduate at Jesus College, Oxford, Lawrence became an enthusiastic archaeologist and undertook excavations in Syria and Mesopotamia between 1910 and 1914. His knowledge of the Arabs led him to be sent from Cairo to Jedda (December 1916), where he joined King Hussein in organizing the Arab Revolt against the Turks, which had begun six months earlier. His military expeditions consisted partly of raids on the Damascus–Medina Railway and partly of the conquest of key centres of contact with the main Allied base in Egypt (e.g. the capture of the port of Akaba in July 1917). Throughout the winter of 1917–18 Colonel Lawrence led the Arabs on the right flank of Allenby's Palestine Army, eventually entering Damascus itself in October 1918. Lawrence considered that the Arab cause had been betrayed by the Peace Treaties (and in particular by the decision to administer Syria as a French mandate), and he sought to withdraw from the public eye by enlisting in the R.A.F., first as Aircraftman Ross and, when this deception was discovered, as Aircraftman T. E. Shaw, a name he assumed by deed poll in 1927. He also served for a time in the Tank Corps. He was killed in a road accident in Dorset. He had written his account of the Arab Revolt, *Seven Pillars of Wisdom*, as a Fellow of All Souls in 1919–20; it was privately printed in 1926 and published for general circulation in 1935.

League of Nations. An international organization created in 1920 to preserve the peace and settle disputes by arbitration or conciliation.

Its headquarters were at Geneva. Such a League had been advocated during the war by a number of leading figures in Britain (notably Viscount Cecil of Chelwood) and by President Wilson of the U.S.A., who had made formation of a League one of his Fourteen Points (q.v.). The Covenant (i.e. constitution) of the League was incorporated in each of the peace treaties. When Congress refused to ratify the Treaty of Versailles, the U.S.A. dissociated itself from the League and never became a member. Germany belonged to the League only from 1926 to 1933, Russia from 1934 to 1939, Turkey from 1932. Brazil withdrew from the League in 1926, Japan in 1933, Italy in 1937. The League had no armed force to coerce recalcitrant members; it relied on the boycott known as 'Sanctions' (q.v.), which was rendered ridiculous by the half-hearted way in which it was applied in the Italo-Abyssinian War of 1935–6. The League succeeded in settling a number of international disputes, notably in the Balkans and South America. It was able to assist the refugees from Russia and Turkey in the 1920s, although the general refugee problem of the 1930s was beyond its resources. It also helped the Danubian states to obtain reconstruction loans, and, through the International Labour Organization, secured more equitable working conditions among its member-states. The League was ultimately responsible for the system of mandates (q.v.), for the judicial administration of Upper Silesia, and for the maintenance of the Free City of Danzig (q.v.). It failed to prevent Japanese aggression in Manchuria and China, Italian aggression against Abyssinia, or the Russian attack on Finland in 1939, despite the fact that all six of these countries were member-states. In the pre-war crisis of 1938-9 the Great Powers tended to ignore the existence of the League. During the war the League sought to continue its non-political activities so far as was possible. It was formally dissolved in April 1946, handing over its remaining responsibilities to the United Nations Organization.

League of the Three Emperors. See *Dreikaiserbund*.

Lee, Robert E. (1807–70). American soldier. Commissioned in the Engineers, later serving with cavalry in the Mexican War. He was responsible for the capture of John Brown (q.v.). When the Civil War began, Lee was offered a field command by Lincoln but preferred to serve as commander of the Army of Northern Virginia for the Confederates. He gained a series of victories in the first part of 1863, but was defeated at Gettysburg (q.v.) in July. Throughout 1864 and the early part of 1865 he opposed Ulysses S. Grant (q.v.), being appointed Commander-in-Chief of Confederate Armies in February 1865. His surrender to Grant at Appomattox (9 April 1865) virtually ended the Civil War. He later became president of Washington College, now Washington and Lee University, Virginia.

Leipzig, Battle of (16–19 October 1813). Culmination of the campaign of 1813 in the War of the Fourth Coalition (q.v.). Forces of Austrians, Russians, and Prussians advanced on Leipzig from north and south and outnumbered Napoleon's defenders by two to one. Even so, the French had the advantage of the first day's fighting, although they sustained heavier losses than they could afford. On 18 October the Saxons, who were fighting as allies of Napoleon, deserted to the other side. Napoleon had difficulty in retreating, because there was only one bridge across the River Pleisse. He eventually withdrew to the Rhine with only 70,000 men, many of whom had typhus. The battle of Leipzig completed the liberation of Germany; German historians subsequently named it 'The Battle of the Nations'.

Lenin, Vladimir Ilyich (1870–1924, family name Ulyanov). Born at Simbirsk on the middle Volga, the son of a school inspector. When he was sixteen his elder brother was hanged for complicity in a plot to assassinate the Tsar. Lenin graduated in law as an external student at St Petersburg University while living under restrictions in Samara, a thousand miles away. He studied Marx, contacted political exiles, was arrested, and spent three years in Siberia. He left Russia in 1900 and settled in Germany, later living for a time in Brussels, Paris, and London. Through his pamphlets, with their penetrating analysis of post-Marxian socialism, and through his newspaper, *Iskra* (*The Spark*), Lenin became recognized as the leader of the militant wing of the Russian Social Democrats, a group known as the Bolsheviks (q.v.) from 1903. Lenin returned to Russia in November 1905, and for three months organized the resistance of the workers in St Petersburg, but he was forced abroad again in 1906. In 1914 he settled in Switzerland. After the Revolution of March 1917 Lenin returned to Petrograd passing through Germany in a sealed train provided by the German General Staff, who counted on Lenin and his followers spreading disaffection among the Russian soldiery. Lenin remained in Petrograd from 16 April to 18 July 1917, when an abortive Bolshevik *coup d'état* forced him to flee to Finland. He returned in October and, from his headquarters in the Smolny Institute, led the rising that captured the government offices (6 November). Lenin became head of the new government, the Council of Peoples' Commissars. He carried through a major distribution of land and the nationalization of the banks and property. He also ordered an armistice between Russia and the Central Powers and in March 1918 authorized signature of the Treaty of Brest-Litovsk (q.v.). Lenin's attempt to achieve a communist economic revolution while waging civil war led to the virtual collapse of the Russian economy by the end of 1920. In March 1921 he adopted the New Economic Policy (q.v.), which represented a retreat from his 'War Communism'. Lenin's health deteriorated in 1923, after an attempt on his life by a Social Revolutionary. He died on 21 January 1924. The city of Petrograd was renamed Leningrad in his honour five days later.

Lesseps, Ferdinand de (1805–94). French engineer. Born at Versailles and entered the foreign service in 1825. In 1849 he was entrusted with delicate negotiations with the Italian Republicans in Rome but, after being abruptly recalled, left the diplomatic service. As a consul at Alexandria, he had considered the possibility of a canal through the Isthmus of Suez, a project that he now sought to realize. He was a personal friend of Khedive Said and a cousin of the Empress Eugénie of France; he was thus able to secure powerful backing for his enterprise. The concession for the Suez Canal (q.v.) was granted to him in November 1854 and it was officially opened in November 1869. He then planned the construction of a Panama Canal. In this instance he made four serious errors: he underestimated the cost; he permitted the Panama Canal Company to be controlled by dubious financiers; he envisaged a sea-level canal where, in reality, locks were required; and he did not allow for the ravages of yellow fever among his labourers. When the Company went bankrupt, de Lesseps was involved in the 'Panama Scandal' (q.v.) of 1892 and was sentenced to imprisonment, although this judgement was set aside by a court of appeal.

Lewis, Meriwether (1774–1809). Born in Virginia, served in the American infantry, and became private secretary to Jefferson (q.v.), who in 1803 appointed him to command an expedition to explore the Missouri River and find if it was possible to establish a transcontinental water route. In the spring of 1804, Lewis set out from St Louis with the geographical expert William Clark (1770–1838) as his chief adviser and having 27 other men under his command. The explorers blazed a trail across the present states of Nebraska, the Dakotas, Montana, and Washington, reaching the Pacific after eighteen months of difficult pioneering, including a crossing of the

Rockies. Although the expedition had shown that there was no water route, Lewis and Clark had opened the way for internal migration and, by skilful handling of the Indian tribes, had left a high standard for the settler. Lewis was appointed Governor of Louisiana Territory on his return, but died mysteriously while travelling in Tennessee in October 1809.

Liberal Party. The Liberals were the successors of the Whigs, a name too closely associated with the aristocracy for the democratic leaders of the nineteenth century. In the Grey and Melbourne Governments of the 1830s the political heirs of Adam Smith and Fox came to refer to themselves as Liberals, a term already in use on the Continent, but the first distinctly Liberal Ministry was not formed until 1868, when Gladstone became Prime Minister. A centralized party organization, the National Liberal Federation, was established in 1877. Gladstonian Liberalism comprised Free Trade budgets, financial economy, political reform, and a pacific attitude towards foreign and imperial problems. In 1886 the Party was split over Irish Home Rule (q.v.) and remained weak and ineffective for the rest of the century. There were great differences within the Party over the Boer War, but Campbell-Bannerman (q.v.) succeeded in bringing the conflicting groups together and won an overwhelming victory in the election of 1906. The Campbell-Bannerman and Asquith Ministries placed greater emphasis on social legislation than Gladstone had done. Internecine disputes between Asquith and Lloyd George weakened the Party during the First World War, and it has never subsequently secured an electoral majority, although individual Liberals sat in the National Government of 1931 and in Churchill's Coalition of 1940–5. The Liberal Party in the late nineteenth century was predominantly a party of religious non-conformity; between the wars it remained strongest in the areas with a Free Church tradition.

Libya. Formerly the Turkish province of Tripoli. Occupied by Italy after a war with Turkey in 1911–12 undertaken for purposes of national prestige and expansion. Civil government was established in Libya in 1919 and emigration from Italy encouraged, but from 1922 to 1930 the Italians had to undertake military expeditions against Arab forces, headed by the Senussi tribesmen who controlled the inner oases of Cyrenaica. Although Mussolini constructed military roads in the colony, his power suffered severe setbacks from the two British advances to Benghazi of December 1940–January 1941 and December 1941–January 1942. Finally, the major British offensive against the German Afrikakorps and the Italians led to the conquest of Libya by the Eighth Army (October 1942–24 January 1943). Libya was under military administration until 1951, when it was recognized as an independent constitutional monarchy under the leader of the Senussi, King Idris.

Licensing Act (1872). In an attempt to curb excessive drunkenness, Henry Bruce (Home Secretary in Gladstone's Liberal Government of 1867–74) carried through the Commons a Licensing Act strictly limiting the hours and places at which alcoholic liquor could be sold. The Act was extremely unpopular in some towns and there were even riots. Quite apart from its social significance, the Act had important political repercussions. Gladstone himself thought that it was the prime cause of the Liberal defeat in the election of 1874. ('We have been borne down in a torrent of beer and gin', he wrote to his brother.) Moreover, the Act had the long-term effect of rallying the brewing industry and the publicans to the Conservatives.

Limited Liability. Expansion of capital in the middle of the nineteenth century necessitated a revolution in methods of business enterprise. The earliest joint-stock companies had suffered from the perils of unlimited liability, which, in its simplest form, could render an individual liable to loss of all his property if a company failed in which he had an interest, even a small one. Demands for the registration and regulation of joint-stock companies arose in Britain in the 1840s, coinciding with the political advance of the middle-class businessman. Select Committees reported on the situation in 1850 and 1851, and their recommendations were partly incorporated in the Limited Liability Act of 1855 and the Joint Stock Companies Act of 1856, but anomalies remained. General Limited Liability came in Britain with the consolidating Act of 1862. A similar process was going on in the continental countries at the same time: the French Limited Liability laws date from 1863 and 1867; and in Germany the principle was incorporated in the Prussian Commercial Code of 1861 and rapidly adopted by the other states. This legislation, in Britain and the Continent, had the effect of providing safeguards against a disproportionately crippling loss. The investment of capital by the Victorian middle class (and its continental equivalents) was thus stimulated, not only for domestic concerns but in major projects overseas. Without the security offered by limited liability, the late nineteenth-century development of economic imperialism would have been impossible.

Lincoln, Abraham (1809–65). Born in Kentucky into an illiterate and wandering frontier family, settled eventually at New Salem (Illinois), where he ran a store, served as postmaster, and studied law. After being admitted to the Bar in 1836, he moved to Springfield, where he became an outstanding advocate and served four terms in the state legislature, representing Illinois as a Whig in Congress from 1847 to 1849. He came to the forefront of national politics when, in 1854, the Kansas-Nebraska Act of Stephen Douglas (q.v.) re-opened the question of slavery. Lincoln joined the Republicans in 1856 and stood against Douglas for the Senate in 1858, holding seven widely publicized debates with Douglas during the campaign in which he attacked the institution of slavery (although admitting that he saw no method of ending it). Lincoln lost the Senatorial Election, but his reputation ensured his nomination as Republican candidate for the Presidency in 1860, a choice partly determined by his moderation and apparent conservatism. He won the presidential campaign, largely because of splits among the Democrats, but his record in the debates with Douglas was sufficient to induce seven slave states to secede before he assumed office in March 1861. It was his desire to provision Fort Sumter (against the advice of his Cabinet) that precipitated the American Civil War (q.v.). As President, his greatest qualities were his personal integrity, his noble oratory (as at Gettysburg, q.v.), and the adroit way in which he handled his Party and his generals. The historical legend that represents him as an ardent champion of slave emancipation is misleading. Even as late as August 1862, he said, 'My paramount object is to save the Union, and not to save or destroy slavery', and emancipation was not proclaimed until 1 January 1863. Throughout the last year of war, he kept at bay the politicians who desired harsh treatment of the South, urging a lenient plan of Reconstruction 'with malice toward none, with charity for all'. A week after the surrender of the main Confederate Army, he was shot by John Wilkes Booth in Ford's Theatre in Washington, on Good Friday 1865, dying the next morning (15 April).

List, Friedrich (1789–1846). German economist. Born in Saxony. List was originally a champion of economic and political freedom, and was imprisoned for his views and forced to spend a period of exile in the U.S.A. On his return in 1833 he developed a theory of protection which stressed national welfare rather than the success of any individual undertaking. His book *The National System of Political Economy* (1846) maintained that during the transition from an agrarian to a manufacturing economy it was essential to impose tariffs even though, at a later stage, Free Trade might be established. List influenced the economic policy of the Zollverein (q.v.), which gradually imposed heavier and heavier duties on manufactured goods. List was also the first advocate (1833) of a planned all-German railway system, radiating from Berlin.

Lithuania. Southernmost of the three Baltic States created after the First World War. Lithuania had been a large state in the fifteenth century, stretching from the Baltic to the Black Sea. From 1569 it was united to Poland, sharing the fate of the Polish lands when they were partitioned. Nearly all of Lithuania was submerged in the Russian Empire. A Lithuanian cultural and national movement began in the 1880s. In 1917 the Lithuanians received encouragement from the Germans, who recognized a Lithuanian Kingdom (with a German Duke as ruler) in March 1918. A republican Government was established in November 1918 and was immediately faced by a Bolshevik invasion. The Russians captured the ancient Lithuanian capital of Vilna in January 1919 but lost it soon after to the Poles, who held on to it for over twenty years, a cause of considerable friction. Lithuania ended her war with Russia in July 1920, but was not recognized by the Great Powers until 1922. In 1923 the Lithuanians seized the predominantly German port of Memel, which they administered as an autonomous region until it was 'liberated' by Hitler in March 1939. From 1926 Lithuania was governed by a nationalist dictatorship headed by Antanas Smetona. In October 1939 the Russians induced the Lithuanians to sign a mutual assistance pact, ceding them Vilna (which had formed part of the Russian-occupied section of Poland), which became the capital in place of Kaunas. Russia continued to put pressure on Lithuania and in July 1940 a packed assembly voted for incorporation in the U.S.S.R.

'Little Entente'. A term originally coined in derision by a Hungarian journalist to describe the system of alliances between Czechoslovakia and Yugoslavia (1920), Czechoslovakia and Rumania (1921), and Yugoslavia and Rumania (1921), which were consolidated in a single treaty signed in Belgrade in May 1929. The alliances were intended to maintain the *status quo* in Central Europe and to prevent a Habsburg restoration or any change in the frontiers laid down by the Treaties of St Germain and Trianon (q.v.). In February 1933 the Little Entente was converted into an international community with a Permanent Council and Secretariat; a high degree of economic cooperation was envisaged. From 1929 to 1937 regular military conversations were held and war plans made, but these were basically concerned only with a possible Hungarian war of revenge and did not face up to the growing German menace. Yugoslavia's tendency to work with Germany after 1935 weakened the alliance, which disintegrated once Czechoslovakia had been abandoned by the Western Powers in the Munich Agreement. The Yugoslavs and Rumanians formally ended the Little Entente at the end of February 1939. Despite its ineffectiveness at the moment of crisis, the Little Entente remains as an early example of the type of international organization which was to develop after the Second World War.

Litvinov, Maximilian (1876–1952). Soviet Russian statesman. Born in Bialystok, as Meier Wallakh, became a revolutionary as a young man, and, after imprisonment, escaped abroad in 1902. He smuggled arms into Russia in 1906, was deported from France in 1908, and settled in London, where he worked for a publisher and married an Englishwoman. He was appointed first Bolshevik representative in London at the time of the Revolution but was deported in September 1918. From 1926 onwards he was in effective control of the Soviet Foreign Ministry, although he did not officially succeed Chicherin as Foreign Commissar until 1930. Throughout the thirties, Litvinov worked for better relations with Russia's western neighbours and was largely responsible for Russia's vigorous support of the League of Nations from 1934 to 1938 and for the Franco-Soviet Pact of 1935. In May 1939, when Stalin wished to reach an agreement with the Germans, Litvinov was dismissed and replaced by Molotov. Litvinov served as Russian Ambassador in Washington from December 1941 until the summer of 1943.

Liverpool, Earl of (Robert Banks Jenkinson 1770–1828, Lord Hawkesbury 1803, Lord Liverpool 1808). British Prime Minister for nearly fifteen years, a period of continuous office exceeded only by Pitt and Walpole. He entered the Commons as a Tory in 1790 and held governmental office from 1793 to 1827, except for a period of fourteen months in 1806–7. He was responsible for foreign affairs from 1801 to 1804 (including the period of the Treaty of Amiens, q.v.), and for home affairs 1804–6 and 1807–9. From 1809 to 1812 he was Secretary of War, becoming Prime Minister on the assassination of Perceval (q.v.) in May 1812. He remained as head of the Government until February 1827, when he resigned after suffering a paralytic stroke. Although it was during these years that final victory was achieved in the Napoleonic Wars, Liverpool's lack of personality prevented him from winning the interest of his countrymen. At the same time, hostility in the post-war period was directed at his Foreign Secretary, Castlereagh (q.v.), or the Home Secretary, Sidmouth, rather than at Liverpool. He thought in terms of parliamentary votes rather than of general principles. Although he was a poor orator, he possessed all the qualities of a capable chairman of committees, holding together Cabinets that contained strong and discordant personalities.

Livingstone, David (1813–73). Scottish missionary and explorer. Born in Lanarkshire, worked in a cotton mill but saved enough money to study at Glasgow and took a medical degree in 1840. He was then sent by the London Missionary Society to Bechuanaland, where he did much to combat disease and keep down slavery. Between 1849 and 1856 he discovered Lake Ngami and the Victoria Falls and explored the Zambesi. From 1858 to 1864 he led an expedition which explored the eastern tributaries of the Zambesi and discovered Lake Nyasa. In 1865 he went in search of the sources of the Nile. Nothing was heard of him for over five years, but in October 1871 he was found by the American newspaper-correspondent H. M. Stanley at Ujiji on Lake Tanganyika. He continued to explore Central Africa but died at Ilala (Northern Rhodesia) in May 1873. He was greatly revered by the natives, who respected his deep Christian humility, his medical care and the fervour with which he tried to maintain the dignity of man, whether black or white.

Lloyd George, David (1863–1945, created an Earl a few months before his death). Born in Manchester and brought up in North Wales. He became a solicitor and in 1890 was elected Liberal M.P. for Carnarvon, a constituency he represented for fifty-five years. He was denounced as a 'pro-Boer' for his anti-war speeches of 1899–1902 but, as a representative of the radicals, was brought into the Cabinet in 1905 as President of the Board of Trade, becoming Chancellor of the Exchequer in 1908. Lloyd George successfully advocated a series of social reforms (e.g. Old Age Pensions Act 1908, National Health Insurance Act 1911) and was responsible for the 'People's Budget' of 1909, which, largely because of the creation of a super-tax and of Land Value duties, was rejected by the Lords, thus beginning the quarrel between the two Houses that led to the Parliament Act (q.v.) of 1911. In July 1915 he was made Minister of Munitions in the Asquith Coalition, but he combined with the Conservatives to overthrow Asquith in December 1916 on the ground that he lacked vigour. Lloyd George then became Prime Minister himself, and remained in office until 1922. He showed great energy as a war leader and attended the Paris Peace Conference (q.v.) in person.

He achieved a settlement of the Irish problem (see *Irish Free State* and *Ulster*). His Coalition Government became increasingly dominated by Conservatives and he was distrusted by his former Liberal colleagues, partly because of his treatment of Asquith. His Government fell over the Chanak Crisis (q.v.), and he remained an isolated figure, never again in office. Lloyd George also did much to encourage the cultural renaissance of the Welsh people.

Local Government Acts of 1888 and 1894. Extended the principle of democratic control to the small community. In 1888 the so-called 'County Councils Act' of the Salisbury Government provided for the election of county councils which would take over and extend the powers of local administration formerly held by Justices of the Peace at Quarter Sessions. Certain larger counties (e.g. Yorkshire and Lincolnshire) were subdivided into smaller administrative districts and 60 towns were given greater independence, with the status of 'county borough' (originally a town with more than 50,000 inhabitants). The Act also created the administrative County of London. Six years later the Liberals established urban and district councils within the counties, assigning to them questions of housing, sanitation, etc. At the same time, parish councils were created within the rural districts, for communities of more than 300 people.

Locarno, Treaties of (1925). An international conference was held at Locarno in October 1925, which produced a number of treaties, signed on 1 December. The most important of these was an agreement confirming the inviolability of the Franco-German and Belgo-German frontiers and the demilitarized zone of the Rhineland (q.v.). This treaty was signed by France, Germany, and Belgium and guaranteed by Britain and Italy. At the same time, the Germans concluded arbitration conventions with France, Belgium, Poland, and Czechoslovakia; Franco-Polish and Franco-Czech Treaties of Mutual Guarantee were also signed. The Locarno agreements were a triumph for Austen Chamberlain (q.v.), Briand (q.v.), and Stresemann (q.v.), all of whom were seeking a period of international cooperation. The Locarno Treaty was violated by Hitler in March 1936, when he sent his troops into the Rhineland; but, as the other signatories were then preoccupied by the Abyssinian Crisis, they contented themselves with formal protests.

Loi Falloux. An educational law proposed by the liberal Catholic, Falloux, a deputy in the French Legislative Assembly, in June 1849. The law was enacted in March 1850, and considerably extended the influence of the Church over education by permitting State funds to be used for the foundation and continuance of Church schools. The passage of the law shows the extent to which the Bonapartists under the Second Republic were anxious to retain Roman Catholic support. By perpetuating a division between the private schools of France (nearly all in the hands of the Church) and the State *lycées*, the Loi Falloux became a special target of Radical criticism, but it was not repealed until 1905, during the anti-clerical Ministry of Émile Combes, himself the product of a Jesuit school that had benefited under the provisions of the Loi Falloux.

Loi le Chapelier. A measure carried by the French National Assembly on 14 June 1791, prohibiting the meeting of associations of workers or employers and declaring any form of strike illegal. The law is characteristic of the insistence of the French revolutionaries that sectional interests should be subordinated to the necessities of the nation as a whole, and that the liberty promised by the Declaration of the Rights of Man (q.v.) did not include the right of an unprivileged class to assert its grievances by resort to strike action (as the workers of Paris were threatening to do in the spring of 1791). The measure was introduced into the Assembly by a Breton lawyer, Isaac Le Chapelier. In a modified form the law was incorporated into the Napoleonic Penal Code. Freedom of association for the workers was not finally granted in France until 1884, although certain restrictions had been removed twenty years earlier.

London, Treaty of (April 1839). A final settlement of the dispute between the Dutch and their former Belgian subjects, who had set up an independent monarchy after overthrowing Dutch rule in 1830. The Treaty represented a diplomatic triumph for Palmerston (q.v.). The King of the Netherlands accepted Belgian independence; the Belgians recognized that Luxemburg should remain a Grand Duchy, with the Dutch King as Grand Duke; the River Scheldt was declared open to the commerce of both Belgium and Holland. Article VII affirmed that Belgium was 'an independent and perpetually neutral state' under the collective guarantee of Britain, France, Prussia, Russia, and Austria. It was the breach of this guarantee by Germany in 1914 that led to the British declaration of war, the Treaty being the famous 'scrap of paper' to which the then German Chancellor contemptuously referred when informed of the British attitude.

London, Treaty of (26 April 1915). A secret agreement signed between Britain, France, and Russia on one hand, and Italy on the other, guaranteeing territorial compensation for Italy provided she became an Allied belligerent within one month. The Treaty provided for an eventual peace settlement assuring Italy of *Italia Irredenta* (Trentino, South Tyrol, Istria, Gorizia, Gradisca, Trieste), a large stretch of the Dalmatian coast and its islands, a segment of Albanian territory around Valona, full sovereignty over the Dodecanese Islands, the Turkish province of Adalia in Asia Minor, colonial expansion in Africa, and a share in any war indemnity. The Allies accepted Italy's demands because they believed that Italian intervention would rapidly destroy Austria-Hungary and 'open the back-door to Germany'. The full terms were revealed by the Bolsheviks when they repudiated all the international obligations of Tsarist Russia early in 1918. The Treaty aroused the special ire of President Wilson (q.v.) because of its flagrant disregard of the ethnic principle, and the U.S.A. refused to consider its terms as binding. At the Paris Peace Conference (q.v.) of 1919 the British and French also turned against Italy, and she received far less than she had originally demanded.

Long March (1934–5). An epic migration of Chinese Communists (see *Communist Parties*) in the course of their conflict with the Kuomintang (q.v.). In 1931 the Communists, under Mao Tse-tung, had established a Chinese Soviet Republic in Kiangsi Province. After three years of military operations against Mao by the forces of General Chiang Kai-shek, the Communist position became untenable. The Communists accordingly evacuated Kiangsi and undertook a march of some 8,000 miles, heading north-westwards for a year through difficult mountain country to Yenan (Shensi Province) on the Yellow River. Thousands perished on the march. Once in Yenan the survivors were able to organize a stronger defensive position. They continued to resist the Kuomintang until the beginning of 1937, when a truce was made to enable both Chinese groups to combine in the face of Japanese aggression. (See *Sino-Japanese Wars*.)

Louis XVIII (1755–1824, King of France from 1814). Brother of Louis XVI. In 1791 he escaped to Brussels, later fleeing eastwards to Brunswick and Warsaw before taking refuge in Buckinghamshire in 1807. In 1814, when Napoleon's fall seemed imminent, he crossed to Ghent and there negotiated with Talleyrand (q.v.) a Charter guaranteeing the principal gains of the Revolution in return for recovery of the throne. Louis sincerely tried to observe these conditions as King, and his reign represents a period of growing prestige for the parliamentary system. He was opposed to the ultra-royalists and sought to restrain the White Terror that followed Waterloo. Although not a strong character, Louis was able to pursue a moderate policy, first under the Duc de Richelieu and later Duc Decazes, until ill-health forced him to hand over effective control to his brother, the Comte d'Artois (Charles X, q.v.). Under Louis, French industry prospered, the Army was reformed, and France recovered international confidence after suppressing a revolt in Spain (1823).

Louis Philippe (1773–1850, King of the French 1830–48). A descendant of Louis XIII and eldest son of Philippe, Duc d'Orléans, who remained in France during the Revolution, adopted the cognomen Égalité but was, nevertheless, guillotined. Louis Philippe fought in the revolutionary armies at Valmy and Jemappes but fled to the Austrians in 1793 and remained in exile in Switzerland, the U.S.A., and England until 1815. His Paris home, the Palais Royal, was a centre of middle-class opposition to the restored monarchy, and when Charles X fell in 1830 he was chosen King, beginning the régime known as the July Monarchy (q.v.). Louis Philippe dressed like the bourgeoisie who were his chief supporters and shared their political attitudes, a grave weakness in the economic depression of the 1840s. Although an intelligent man, he suffered from three disadvantages: a desire to secure thrones, through marriage, for his large family; a tendency to rule through a puppet prime minister, despite the elective quality of the constitutional monarchy; and a figure that became the butt of every caricaturist in Paris. When the barricades went up in February 1848, following his ban on a meeting for franchise reform, he fled to England and died at Claremont in Surrey.

Louisiana Purchase (April 1803). The biggest land sale in history. Doubled the size of the U.S.A. by securing from France the whole of the Mississippi Valley up to the Rocky Mountains, an area of 828,000 square miles, purchased for 15 million dollars. Louisiana had been French until 1762, when it was ceded to Spain; it was returned to France in 1800. Napoleon, after rejecting the idea of a new American Empire, determined to sell the territories, and President Jefferson (q.v.) was anxious to acquire them. The treaty was negotiated by the American Minister in Paris, Livingston, and the future President, James Monroe. The agreement left the boundaries ill defined, and this was to cause further trouble, especially over Texas.

Luddites. The term applied to hand-workers who, feeling themselves displaced by the new machinery, banded together to wreck the machines. The Luddites originated among the hosiers of Notting-hamshire, Derbyshire, and Leicestershire in 1811 and rapidly spread to the woollen-cloth workers of Yorkshire and Lancashire. The Government applied savage penalties, but Luddite riots continued intermittently until 1818, when the discontent was absorbed by the new political radicalism. The name Luddite is derived from the sig-nature 'King Lud' or 'Ned Lud' attached to public letters denounc-ing the introduction of machines.

Ludendorff, Erich (1865–1937). German soldier. Like Hindenburg (q.v.), with whom his career was closely linked, Ludendorff was born in Posen (Poznan). He entered the army in 1882 and by 1914 had become a Major-General. After participating in the Belgian offen-sive, he was moved to the East as Chief of Staff to Hindenburg, sub-sequently sharing with him the exaggerated popular adulation for the victories of Tannenberg and the Masurian Lakes. Ludendorff re-mained Hindenburg's adviser until October 1918; from August 1916, when Ludendorff became Quartermaster-General, they dominated German civil and military policy. Ludendorff bears much of the responsibility for resorting to unrestricted U-boat warfare, for assist-ing Lenin (q.v.) to return to Russia, and for the harsh terms of Brest-Litovsk (q.v.). After the Allied offensive of July-August 1918 Luden-dorff's nerve broke. As early as 29 September he urged the Govern-ment to open peace negotiations, and on 27 October, resigning his post, fled to Sweden, disguised by coloured spectacles and false whiskers. He later attached himself to the extreme nationalist and anti-republican groups, participating in both the Kapp Putsch (q.v.) of 1920 and Hitler's Munich Putsch (q.v.) of 1923. After gaining less than one per cent of the vote in the first presidential election of 1925 as a Nazi candidate, he broke with Hitler and entered into a some-what querulous retirement.

Luxemburg. Independent Grand-Duchy of about 1,000 square miles, situated between Germany, France, and Belgium. Luxemburg was part of the Holy Roman Empire until the Napoleonic conquests. In 1815 the King of the Netherlands was made Duke of Luxemburg in compensation for his lost estates in Nassau, which became Prussian. In 1839 the western part of Luxemburg was assigned to Belgium but the rest of the Duchy remained attached to the Dutch Crown until 1890 when, as a woman could not then succeed to the Luxemburg title, it became independent. Luxemburg was invaded by the Ger-mans in 1914 and 1940 and formally annexed to Germany from 1942 to 1945. Since the First World War it has had close economic links with Belgium.

Luxemburg, Rosa (1870–1919). Socialist leader. Born in Russian Poland but became a German citizen in 1895 when she married a German worker. Luxemburg had a strong and independent personality; she was contemptuous of the nationalistic trends within the socialist movements and critical of even the most eminent of her fellow socialists. She herself worked for the union of all socialist groups, not only from the three regions of partitioned Poland but from Lithuania as well. She influenced the development of both Russian and German Communism, participating in the Russian disturbances of 1905 and, on her return, founding with Karl Liebknecht the German Spartacus League. She was imprisoned throughout the First World War but, with the fall of the Empire, became a formidable political figure. She had scant respect for the Social Democrats in the Republican Government but she was a restraining influence on the more violent extremists. Despite this, she, along with Liebknecht, was arrested by German officers and murdered with atrocious brutality (15 January 1919).

Lyautey, Louis Hubert (1854–1934). French soldier and colonial administrator. Born at Nancy, entered the Army through the military college of St Cyr and saw service in Algeria, Madagascar, and Indo-China. When Morocco became a French protectorate in March 1912, General Lyautey was appointed Resident-General, responsible for military and civil administration, a post he held until September 1925. Lyautey, who was made a Marshal of France in 1921, was in many respects a model Governor, respecting the Sultan of Morocco's authority, carrying out major engineering schemes (notably in Casablanca), and making bare lands fertile by expert farming. He was personally a sincere Catholic, to whom many of the features of the Third Republic were antipathetic. He believed that it was possible to assimilate the Catholic culture of France and the traditions of Islam, and he sought to train a new type of colonial administrator who would accept his ideas. Many, however, failed to distinguish between assimilation and domination and Lyautey's political legacy was almost exclusively to the extremists of the Right.

Macaulay, Thomas Babington (1800–59, created a Baron 1857). Born in Leicestershire, the son of a colonial governor and leading opponent of slavery. Macaulay, a precocious schoolboy and brilliant undergraduate, was educated privately and at Trinity, Cambridge. He became a Whig M.P. in 1830 and gained a wide reputation for his speeches defending the 1832 Reform Act. From 1834 to 1838 he was a member of the Supreme Council of India, assisting with the formulation of the penal code and introducing educational reforms. Although he sat in Russell's Cabinet of 1846 for a year, he spent the rest of his life in historical writing. The first two volumes of his *History of England* were published in 1848, the third and fourth in 1855. The classic character of the *History* was at once recognized; the measured dignity of his style and the simplicity of his moral judgements reflected the comfortable optimism of the prosperous middle class which formed his reading public.

MacDonald, J. Ramsay (1866–1937). Born in poverty in a small Scottish fishing village. He joined the I.L.P. (q.v.) in 1894 and was a first-rate organizer, although fired by ambition for social success. He became an M.P. in 1906 and was chairman of the I.L.P. 1906–9, but he had already helped to found the Labour Representation Committee, and from 1911 to 1914 he led the Parliamentary Labour Party, with considerable dexterity. He lost influence during the war and was defeated in the 1918 election. In 1922 he was successful at Aberavon; he was promptly re-elected leader of the Parliamentary Labour Party (largely through Scottish support), and thus became Leader of the Opposition, since Labour had 25 more seats than the Liberals. After the indecisive 1923 election, he agreed to head a Labour Minority Government (January 1924), and was his own Foreign Secretary. The election of November 1924 (held under the shadow of the 'Zinoviev Letter', q.v.) led to MacDonald's defeat, but he was again Prime Minister in 1929. The worsening financial situation precipitated a split in his Government in August 1931, and he formed a coalition (the National Government), which the majority of the Labour Party refused to support. He led the coalition for four years but was a mere figurehead for a predominantly Conservative administration. He resigned in June 1935 and was succeeded by Baldwin (q.v.).

Mackenzie, William Lyon (1795–1861). Canadian journalist and rebel. Born in Dundee, emigrated 1820, sat as a fiery member of the Upper Canada legislative assembly (1828–36). He had a passionate hatred of what he considered to be unjust privilege, and, impatient for social reform, joined the French-Canadian Louis-Joseph Papineau in a rebellion (November–December 1837). For five weeks there was a series of armed riots while Mackenzie, from an island in the Niagara River, proclaimed a provisional government and, with help from anti-British Americans, raided Canadian outposts. There were incidents between Canadian militia and the Americans, which worsened the relations of the two countries and lost Mackenzie sympathy. Mackenzie incorporated sections of the American Declaration of Independence in his 'Declaration of the Toronto Reformers' and his 'Draft Constitution', borrowed extensively from American models. He was forced to flee to the U.S.A. in January 1838. The rebellion prompted the British Government to send out the Earl of Durham (q.v.) to report on Canadian conditions.

McKinley, William (1843–1901). President of the U.S.A. Born in Ohio, became a Major in the Union Army in the Civil War and subsequently an attorney. As a Republican Congressman, McKinley became well known for his advocacy of high tariffs. He was elected Governor of Ohio in 1891 and 1893. As a result of a campaign directed with great skill by the big-businessman Marcus Hanna (1837–1904), McKinley secured Republican presidential nomination in 1896 and defeated Bryan in an election fought mostly over tariffs and fiscal policy. His administration saw the highest tariffs in American history and the growth of expansionist policies. In July 1898, Hawaii was annexed. As a result of the Spanish-American War (q.v.) over which McKinley yielded to the demands of the press, the U.S.A. acquired the Philippines, Puerto Rico, and Guam. Although McKinley again defeated Bryan in 1900, he was assassinated on 6 September 1901 by an anarchist, and was succeeded by Theodore Roosevelt (q.v.).

Macmahon, Patrice (1808–93, created Marshal of France 1859, Duke of Magenta 1859–70, President of France 1873–9). Descendant of an Irish soldier who settled in France after 1688. Entered the Army under Charles X and served in Algeria, always remaining at heart a supporter of the Bourbons. His military reputation was made, however, under the Second Empire; he distinguished himself in the Crimea in 1855 by capturing and holding the Malakoff Fort and was the victor of Magenta (q.v.) in 1859. After serving as Governor-General of Algeria, he returned to France in 1870, was defeated at Wörth and wounded and captured at Sedan (q.v.). On repatriation, he commanded the troops that suppressed the Commune (q.v.) in 1871. Two years later he was elected President of the Republic by a predominantly royalist assembly, which hoped that he would achieve a restoration of the monarchy. On 16 May 1877 (in what is known as the crisis of *Seize Mai*), he dismissed the Prime Minister. When his own nominee, the Orleanist Duc de Broglie, failed to secure a majority, he used the presidential prerogative of dissolving the Chamber and holding an election. Despite governmental interference in the election, the royalists did not gain the majority that

Macmahon had wished. He continued in office until January 1879, when, seeing the royalist influence declining, he resigned and was succeeded by the genuine republican Jules Grévy. Macmahon was the last of the Presidents of the Third Republic to attempt to use his office as a strong executive power; no subsequent President dared to dismiss a prime minister or dissolve the Chamber.

Macquarie, Lachlan (?1760–1824). Colonial Administrator. After military service in India, Macquarie was sent as a Colonel with his regiment to New South Wales, being appointed Governor in 1809, the first non-naval man to hold the post. In his twelve years of office, he did much to remove the stigma associated with penal settlement from New South Wales. Sydney was developed as a city, roads were constructed, a town (Bathurst) founded in the interior, civil courts and a bank were set up, and attempts were made to secure social equality for ex-convicts with free settlers.

Madison, James (1751–1836). President of the U.S.A. Born in Virginia, played a prominent rôle in the politics of the state from 1775 to 1780, when he served in the Continental Congress. He was responsible for the content of the American Constitution to a greater extent than any other man, and his articles in the *Federalist* (a joint compilation with Hamilton, q.v., and Jay) form a commentary on his views. Madison broke with Hamilton over financial questions and served under Jefferson as Secretary of State from 1801 to 1809, being particularly involved with both Britain and France over the rights of neutrals in the Napoleonic Wars. He succeeded Jefferson as President in 1809, serving two terms of office. His fumbling leadership of the Anglo-American War of 1812–15 (q.v.) lost him much prestige. At home his Second Administration saw a move towards Hamilton's ideas on tariffs and banking. Madison was succeeded by Monroe in 1817.

Magenta, Battle of (4 June 1850). A French victory in the Franco-Piedmontese War against Austria that had been planned at Plombières (q.v.). There were heavy casualties on both sides, but the Austrians subsequently withdrew deeper into Lombardy, being brought to battle again three weeks later at Solferino (q.v.).

Maginot Line. The name given to the fortifications constructed in the period 1929–34 along the eastern frontier of France from Longwy (facing Luxemburg) to Switzerland. The name is derived from a Minister of War, André Maginot (1877–1932). The fortifications were not continued along the Franco-Belgian frontier, because of Belgian objections and because a group of French strategists held that the Germans could not penetrate the Ardennes. In 1940 the Germans turned the Maginot Line by their thrust through Belgium and around Sedan. When France signed her armistice with Germany, all the Maginot Line forts were intact, except for some outlying defences facing Saarbrücken. The last fort surrendered, unassailed on 30 June. The Maginot Line is often taken as a symbol of the defensive mentality of the French High Command between the wars.

Mahan, Admiral Alfred T. (1840–1914). Served as an active officer in the U.S. Navy from 1859–66, thereafter becoming a lecturer on naval history and subsequently the president of Newport War College, retiring from the Navy in 1896. His two major historical works, *The Influence of Sea Power upon History, 1660–1783* (published 1890) and *The Influence of Sea Power upon the French Revolution, 1793–1812* (published 1892), were best-sellers, although written only on the study of a few secondary works. They helped to convince public figures in the U.S.A. and Europe of the vital importance of sea-power. In the U.S.A. Mahan's arguments led to a demand for a large Navy with overseas bases and colonial possessions, and thereby stimulated the passion for imperialism. In Britain, his writings were taken as proof of the need for absolute command of the sea; a contemporary review said they represented 'a scientific inquiry into the causes which have made England great'. He also had considerable influence on German thought, especially on Kaiser William II. With glorious incongruity, Mahan was a delegate to the Hague Conference (q.v.) on Disarmament of 1899.

Mahdi. The title of the Moslem Messiah. Several Moslem fanatics have assumed this style, the most famous of them being Mohammed Ahmed of Dongola (1840–85), who roused the Sudan in revolt against Egyptian rule in 1882 and was responsible for the siege and capture of Khartoum in 1885, massacring General Gordon (q.v.) and the garrison. When the Mahdi died six months later, his followers, the Dervishes, held all the Sudan except for Red Sea ports. The Mahdi was succeeded by the Khalifa, Abdullah el Taashi, who ruled the Sudan for thirteen years until his defeat at Omdurman (q.v.) in September 1898 by Kitchener, who ordered his troops to destroy the Mahdi's tomb.

Mahmud II (1785–1839, Sultan of Turkey from 1808). His mother was a French creole captured by pirates, and he was the most successful Turkish sovereign for two centuries. He was brought to the throne by Bairakdar Pasha after the Janissaries (q.v.) had weakened the power of the Sultanate by their predominance in palace politics. Mahmud disciplined rebellious pashas in the provinces, destroyed the Janissaries (1826), and re-asserted the absolute power of the Sultan. Although successful in giving vigour to the central government, he could not prevent the breaking away of outlying provinces where Turkish control had been weak (notably in Serbia and Greece, q.v.). In the 1830s he was menaced by the aspirations of his vassal, Mehemet Ali (q.v.) of Egypt, whose troops he had used in Greece but who now demanded control of Syria. Mahmud's mental powers failed rapidly in his later years.

Malta. A fortified island in the narrowest part of the Mediterranean. The population is believed to be Carthaginian in origin, and the language is Semitic. Malta was given by the Emperor Charles V to the Knights of the Order of St John of Jerusalem in 1530, and the Knights fortified and administered the island until it was captured by Bonaparte in 1798. The British blockaded Malta, which surrendered to them in 1800. By the Treaty of Amiens (q.v.), the British undertook to return the island to the Knights, but failed to do so and in 1814 annexed it to the British Crown. Malta was developed as the main base of the Mediterranean Fleet. A Legislative Assembly was established in 1921. Serious disputes followed between the Roman Catholic Church and the British administration and, at the same time, Mussolini demanded that Malta should be united with Italy. The constitution was suspended on three occasions. Between 1940 and 1943 Malta withstood severe bombing by German and Italian aircraft and faced the threat of starvation; the island was awarded the George Cross in 1942 in recognition of the valour of its people. In 1957–8 the naval economy programme produced economic distress; rioting followed and the constitution was again suspended.

Malthus, Thomas Robert (1766–1834). British economist. Born in Surrey, was ordained in 1797, and as a curate anonymously published in 1798 his *Essay on the Principle of Population as it affects the Future Improvement of Society*, in which he maintained that population increases more rapidly than food supplies and is limited only by war, finance, poverty, and vice. Wages should accordingly sink to subsistence level, to check the natural prolificacy of the labouring classes. This theory had considerable influence during the early nineteenth century. Malthus himself subsequently became Professor of Political Economy at the East India College, Hailey-bury.

Manchester School. A name applied to the radical politicians of the 1840s, who believed in Free Trade, international collaboration, and *laissez-faire* (q.v.). Cobden (q.v.) and Bright (q.v.) were the acknow-ledged leaders of the group.

Manchu Dynasty. Proclaimed the Imperial Dynasty of China at Mukden in 1636, and reigned until 1912, when, after the Chinese Revolution (q.v.), the last Emperor Pu'I (born 1906, Imperial title Hsuang Tung) abdicated. From 1932 to 1945 Pu'I was Japanese puppet ruler in Manchukuo.

Manchuria. Province of north-eastern China, finally conquered by the Chinese in 1644. It was penetrated by Russian commercial in-terests at the end of the nineteenth century. Russians constructed the Chinese Eastern Railway through Manchuria to Vladivostok (1896–1900) and occupied the province after the Boxer Rising (q.v.) of 1900. In February 1904 the Japanese attacked the Russian occupation forces, and heavy fighting continued throughout Manchuria for eighteen months. By the Treaty of Portsmouth (q.v.) of 1905, the Japanese and Russians agreed to restore Manchuria to China (al-though the Russians retained their rights over the Chinese Eastern Railway) and the Japanese were given the South Manchurian Rail-way (to Port Arthur), along which they were allowed to station troops. The Japanese improved their position in Manchuria in 1916–17, benefiting both from the weakness of the Chinese Government and the withdrawal of the Russians following the Revolution. In 1931 the Japanese used the Mukden Incident (q.v.) as an excuse for occupying the whole of Manchuria and expelling the Chinese authorities. In February 1932 the Japanese established the state of Manchukuo in the province, a puppet régime recognized only by Germany and Italy, but one which made the Japanese do much to develop the industrial resources of the region. In 1945 Manchuria reverted to China. (See also *Port Arthur.*)

Mandates. Territories formerly in the German colonial empire or the non-Turkish regions of the Ottoman Empire which, by the peace treaties of 1919–20, were ceded to the Allied Powers under the ultimate responsibility of the League of Nations, to whom annual reports on conditions were submitted. Some mandated territories were intended to receive independence at an early stage (Palestine, Iraq, and Transjordan of British mandates; Syria and the Lebanon of French mandates). Others were seen as requiring longer administration because of the backward state of the peoples (Togoland, Cameroons, Tanganyika, South-West Africa, Samoa, and New Guinea). Detailed questions were settled by the Permanent Mandates Commission of the League; in 1945 the functions of this Commission were taken over by the Trusteeship Council of the United Nations.

'Manifest Destiny'. A phrase used by Americans in the mid nineteenth century to justify territorial expansion. It appears to have originated in an unsigned article in *The United States Magazine and Democratic Review* for July 1845, referring to 'the fulfilment of our manifest destiny to overspread the continent allotted by Providence for the free development of our yearly multiplying millions'. Within a few months, the phrase became popular with expansionist members of Congress, anxious for war with Mexico, settlement of the Oregon Question (q.v.), and the acquisition of California.

Mannerheim, Baron Carl Gustaf Emil (1867–1948). Finnish soldier and statesman of Swedish descent; served in the Russian Imperial Army, attaining the rank of General. When, in the spring of 1918, Finnish communists seized Helsinki, Mannerheim recaptured the city for the 'Whites' and drove the 'Reds' out of the country, with German assistance. In 1919–20, acting as Head of State, Mannerheim commanded the Finnish Armies against the Russians, eventually securing recognition of Finnish independence by the Soviet Government. Mannerheim, who had been created a Marshal, retained considerable influence as President of the Defence Council. He returned to active service when the Russians attacked Finland in November 1939; his fortifications in the Karelian Isthmus (the Mannerheim Line) kept out the Red Army for thirteen weeks. He allied with the Germans for a third war with Russia in June 1941. Faced by a strong Russian offensive, the Finnish Parliament elected Mannerheim President in August 1944. He secured an armistice in the following month and belatedly brought Finland into the war against Germany (March 1945). Despite a political swing to the left in Finland, he remained President until March 1946, resigning 'for reasons of health'.

Maori Wars. The First Maori War in New Zealand broke out in 1843 over land disputes in South Island and apparent breaches by the settlers of the Treaty of Waitangi (q.v.). The insurrection spread to North Island, where it was more serious. The outbreaks were ended by the wise policy of Sir George Grey (q.v.), who won the confidence of the Maori chiefs. The Second Maori War took the form of sporadic guerilla attacks between 1860 and 1870 in North Island. It was precipitated by the Government's acquisition of native lands and included a religious movement (the Hau-hau) which led to some fanatical atrocities. Order was eventually restored with the help of fresh troops from Britain and Australia.

Marat, Jean Paul (1743–93). French revolutionary. Born near Neu-châtel, having a Swiss mother and a Spanish Calvinist father. Marat travelled extensively in Holland and Britain, where he secured a medical degree at St Andrews, showed an interest in science, and dabbled in politics, mostly in support of Wilkes. In the decade before the Revolution he was a successful medical practitioner in Paris. In 1789 he flung himself into journalism, editing *L'Ami du Peuple*, which contained searing denunciations of those in authority and called for a dictatorship 'in the name of the people'. In September 1792 he became a member of the Vigilance Committee and bears much responsibility for the massacres in the Paris prisons. He attached himself to the Jacobins, and was engaged in a bitter conflict with the Girondin-dominated Convention when on 13 July 1793 he was murdered in his bath by Charlotte Corday, a beautiful twenty-five-year-old aristocrat with royalist sympathies.

'March on Rome', 1922. A Fascist-inspired legend of the way in which Mussolini (q.v.) came to power in Italy. Throughout the summer of 1922 there was a danger of civil war in Italy, with the Fascists seizing control of several cities. In the last week of October, Mussolini demanded the formation of a Fascist Government and concentrated his supporters on the approaches to the capital. King Victor Emmanuel III gave way before the Fascist threat, dismissed the Prime Minister, and invited Mussolini to come down from Milan to Rome and form a Government (30 October). The phrase 'March on Rome' over-dramatizes the order of events. Mussolini himself came to Rome by express train; his followers dispersed after a ceremonial parade.

Marconi, Guglielmo (1874–1937). Italian inventor. Born at Bologna. In 1895 his experiments enabled him to send messages by wireless telegraph over a mile. He took out the first patent for wireless telegraphy in the following year and by 1901 was able to transmit and receive signals between Newfoundland and Cornwall. Throughout the rest of his life Marconi played a leading part in the commercial development of wireless telegraphy and radio.

Marmont, Auguste (1774–1852). Like Napoleon, an artillery officer, and served with him in Italy and Egypt, being made a General at the age of twenty-six and a Marshal at thirty. From 1805 to 1810 he administered Dalmatia for Napoleon, and was created Duke of Ragusa (now Dubrovnik) in 1808. For a year he was Governor-General of the Illyrian Provinces (see *Yugoslavia*), but in 1810 he resumed military service as commander in Spain. Although he fought well in the final French campaign in 1814, he surrendered Paris to the Allies without Napoleon's authorization, thereby precipitating the Emperor's downfall. Subsequently, Marmont served the restored Bourbons as a General but was very unpopular in France. He went into exile in 1830, settling in Vienna, where for a time he was tutor to Napoleon's son, the Duke of Reichstadt (1811–32).

Marne, Battles of the. The River Marne is a tributary of the Seine, which it joins some ten miles west of Paris. Two decisive battles were fought along the Marne in the First World War, representing the point of greatest penetration by the Germans in France. The first battle lasted from 5 to 19 September 1914; under the orders of General Joffre, the French and British counter-attacked the German armies of Kluck and Bülow, who received orders from German G.H.Q. (in Luxemburg) to fall back on 9 September, at a time when their troops could see the Eiffel Tower in the distance. The second battle, 15 July to 7 August 1918, was Ludendorff's last offensive; the Germans crossed the Marne west of Rheims and advanced to Chateau-Thierry but were checked by a Franco-American force under the command of Marshal Foch and driven back, the allied counter-offensive marking the beginning of a general advance that forced Germany to sue for peace.

Marx, Karl (1818–83). Born at Trier of a German-Jewish family which had accepted Christianity. As a student at Bonn and Berlin (1835–41) Marx was influenced by the ideas of Hegel (q.v.) on the dialectic, but he reacted against Hegel's idealism and found himself in sympathy with the exiled German socialists, for whom in Brussels he wrote (in collaboration with Engels, q.v.) the *Communist Manifesto*, published in 1848. During the revolutionary disturbances Marx returned to Cologne but, faced with a charge of high treason, fled in 1849 to London, where he spent the remainder of his life. Marx and his family lived in considerable poverty, helped out by allowances from Engels. For some years Marx was a correspondent of a New York newspaper, but he spent most of his time carrying out research in the library of the British Museum, developing his theories of the class struggle and the economic laws of capitalist society. The first volume of Marx's most important work, *Das Kapital*, was published in 1867. Marx took little part in specifically British politics, but in 1864 he helped found the International Workingmen's Association (see *International Socialism*), which he led through a series of factious quarrels until its formal dissolution in 1876.

Masaryk, Tómaš (1850–1937). Czechoslovak philosopher and statesman. Masaryk was born in Moravia, the son of a coachman on an Imperial Habsburg estate. He was educated at Brno, Vienna, and Leipzig and when a separate Czech University was established in Prague (1882) he was appointed Professor of Philosophy, a post he held for 32 years. He sat in the Austrian Parliament as a representative of the Young Czech Party from 1891 to 1893 and as leader of the 'Czech Realists' from 1907 to 1914. As a Professor in Prague he influenced not only Czechs and Slovaks but other Slav students, especially Croats and Serbs; he sought to reconcile Western European empiricism with the heritage of Slavonic thought, purged of mysticism. He achieved European political fame by his defence of Croats accused of treason at Agram (Zagreb) in 1908 and by the evidence that he produced in 1909 of forged documents used by the Austrian Foreign Office to discredit the political leaders of Austria's South Slav peoples. In December 1914 he escaped to London, where he became chairman of the Czech National Council (and a lecturer at King's College). His academic reputation enabled him to receive a sympathetic hearing from leading politicians and journalists, to whom he stressed the need for nation-states to replace the multi-national anachronism of Austria-Hungary. From October 1916 he disseminated these views through an influential monthly periodical, *The New Europe*. In 1917 Masaryk went to Russia, where he organized a Czech Legion from among prisoners of war. Later he crossed Siberia and went to the U.S.A., where he influenced the formulation of President Wilson's views on the post-war world. While in America, Masaryk received considerable backing from Czech and Slovak immigrants and secured official recognition as leader of an Allied country from the U.S. Government (3 September 1918). In December 1918 he returned to Europe as President-elect of Czechoslovakia. He was twice re-elected President, although remaining aloof from party politics. He resigned in December 1935, when his health began to give way, and died in September 1937. His son Jan, Czech Foreign Minister 1941–8, died in mysterious circumstances shortly after the Communists seized power in 1948; his body was found in the courtyard of the Foreign Ministry, beneath an open window.

Matteotti, Giacomo. An Italian socialist Deputy, murdered by a gang of Fascists on 10 June 1924. Matteotti had courageously denounced fascist acts of violence in a book, *The Fascisti Exposed.* His murderers were not tried until 1926, and then received light sentences. The crime led to a domestic crisis in Italy; the majority of non-Fascist Members of Parliament refused to participate in parliamentary business (the 'Aventine Secession'), and Mussolini was forced to ban their meetings and apply a strict press censorship. The murder and its repercussions alienated a number of foreigners who had originally sympathized with Mussolini.

Maurice, (John) Frederick Denison (1805–1872). English Christian Socialist. The son of a Unitarian Minister, but was converted to the Church of England, largely through the influence of the poet S. T. Coleridge. Maurice held the Professorships of History, Literature, and Divinity at King's College, London, in the 1840s, but was deprived of his Chairs for his unorthodox attitude to religion and politics. From 1860 to 1869 he was Vicar of a London parish (St Peter's, Vere Street) and became Professor of Moral Philosophy at Cambridge in 1866. In the early 1850s Maurice was closely associated with the novelists Charles Kingsley and Thomas Hughes in a movement generally known as 'Christian Socialism'. They sympathized with many of the points in the programme of the Chartists (q.v.), and sought to win over some of its former supporters to the Churches while at the same time trying to establish a social-reform group within the Church itself. In 1854 Maurice and Hughes founded the Working Men's College, to educate the workers in one of the tougher slum districts of North London. Maurice played a leading part in the development of adult education and in awakening the social conscience of the Victorian Church.

Maximilian (1832–67). Archduke of Austria and Emperor of Mexico. A brother of the Emperor Francis Joseph (q.v.). Appointed Governor of Lombardy-Venetia in 1857, but was made a scapegoat for the failure to retain Lombardy against the Piedmontese-French attack of 1859, and retired to his castle at Miramare (Trieste), where he specialized in botanical studies. In 1863 he was induced to accept the crown of the Catholic Empire which, with Napoleon III as patron, French troops were seeking to establish in Mexico. He went to Mexico City and set up an orderly government (which was, in fact, not sufficiently clericalist for some of his supporters). His power depended entirely on the French, and when, under American pressure, Napoleon III was forced to withdraw his troops (March 1867) Maximilian soon fell into the hands of the Mexican 'Liberals' under Juárez (q.v.), who had him shot at Querataro (19 June 1867). The episode considerably weakened the international prestige of Napoleon III.

Maynooth Grant. In 1844 Peel, anxious to conciliate the influential Irish priesthood, proposed to increase the subsidy to the Roman Catholic College at Maynooth. This subsidy had originally been granted before the Act of Union and had been continued by successive parliaments in Westminster since 1800. Peel's proposal would have increased the amount from £9,000 a year to £26,000. The Cabinet was divided, and Peel delayed a decision for many months. Gladstone (q.v.) considered an increased subsidy to Maynooth as against his principles, and resigned as President of the Board of Trade (February 1845). A Bill incorporating the increased subsidy was carried in the following April, when, to Peel's mystification, Gladstone voted for the grant. The Maynooth Question also divided the 'Young England' group (q.v.).

Mazzini, Giuseppe (1805–72). The apostle of Italian republicanism. He was born in Genoa, the son of a doctor, and enlisted in the Carbonari (q.v.) in the 1820s. Despairing of this movement's sporadic conspiracies, he established in March 1831 a new revolutionary society, 'Young Italy', in which he sought not only to unite Italy through a general uprising but to elevate Italian patriotism by moral fervour. His plans for an insurrection in June 1832 collapsed when the Piedmontese arrested some of his principal collaborators; 'Young Italy' resorted to the isolated risings which its leader had earlier condemned. From his headquarters in Marseilles (and, from 1837, London) Mazzini encouraged the idea of a republican brotherhood of nations, establishing a 'Young Europe' movement based upon non-sectarian principles of Christian charity. In 1848 he returned, briefly, to liberate Milan and in March 1849 became head of the triumvirate which served as an executive for the Roman Republic. When Rome fell, he went back to exile but never again enjoyed the same prestige, many of his earlier supporters (notably

Garibaldi, q.v.) supporting the unification of Italy under the House of Savoy. As he would not retract his republicanism, Mazzini never openly returned to Italy, although he made abortive journeys there to promote conspiracies among his followers. In 1868 he settled in Lugano, only 15 miles inside Switzerland, and in 1872 he slipped across the frontier, disguised as an Englishman, to die at Pisa in his homeland. Mazzini was far more than an Italian thinker; his words helped to shape the liberal ideal throughout continental Europe and influenced immigrant groups in the U.S.A.

Mediterranean Agreements (1887). Mainly the work of Salisbury (q.v.), who was both Prime Minister and Foreign Secretary. The first agreement was an exchange of notes between Britain and Italy (12 February) providing for joint consultation to preserve the *status quo* in the Mediterranean area (which included the Aegean and Black Seas). Austria-Hungary and Spain adhered to the agreement a few months later. The second agreement (12 December) was a treaty between Britain, Italy, and Austria-Hungary for action to prevent Turkey surrendering her rights in the Balkans or Near East. Both agreements were secret and were intended to prevent any change in the Mediterranean or Near East to the advantage of Russia or France. Although Germany was not a signatory, Bismarck knew and approved of the agreements, and they thus represent the nearest point of contact between Britain and the Triple Alliance (q.v.). When Rosebery became Foreign Secretary in 1892 he allowed the agreement to lapse.

Mehemet Ali (1769–1849). An Albanian tobacco-merchant from Kavalla, entered Turkish service and commanded Albanian troops fighting for the Sultan against the French in 1799. Subsequently, he intrigued against Turkish officials in Egypt with such effectiveness that the Sultan reluctantly appointed him Governor in 1805, conceding him supreme authority throughout Egypt in 1811. With French help, Mehemet Ali built up a powerful Army and fleet and developed the Egyptian economy. He also conquered the Sudan (1820–2) in search of gold and slaves, founding the city of Khartoum in 1823. From 1823 to 1828 his troops (led by his son, Ibrahim) helped the Turks in the Greek War of Independence. For his services Mehemet was given the Governorship of Crete, but he wanted more, and waged a successful war against the Turks from 1832 to 1833, securing Syria and Adana. After a second war in 1839–41, he was forced by the Great Powers (especially Britain) to surrender his earlier conquests, being compensated by recognition as hereditary ruler of Egypt. Mehemet was thus the founder of the Egyptian dynasty that reigned until 1952. He was mentally deranged for the last two years of his life, Egypt being governed by a Council of Regency, originally headed by Ibrahim (who pre-deceased him by nine months). Mehemet Ali was succeeded by his grandson Abbas (1848–54).

Meiji Period. The name given by the Japanese to the years 1868–1912, in which the Emperor Mutsuhito (accession February 1867) broke the seven-hundred-year-old rule of military feudatories and assumed personal control of Japan. Restrictions on foreign trade were removed, and the Japanese borrowed heavily from Western methods. A new Army was modelled on the German; a new Navy on the British. A centralized bureaucratic government was set up, and the country began a swift process of industrialization. A Cabinet was created in 1885, with Ito (q.v.) as the first Prime Minister, and in 1889 the Emperor accepted a new constitution which, while preserving his prerogatives, created a bicameral system of representation. The second half of the period saw the beginning of Japanese expansion on the Asiatic mainland, marked by the penetration of Korea (q.v.) and Manchuria (q.v.) and by victory in the Russo-Japanese War of 1904–5. On the Emperor's death in July 1912 Japan passed into the Taisho Period (q.v.).

Melbourne, Viscount (William Lamb, 1779–1848, succeeded his father as second Viscount in 1828). Educated at Eton and Trinity, Cambridge, called to the Bar in 1804 and entered the Commons as Foxite M.P. for Leominster in 1806. He later became a Canningite Tory and served Canning as Secretary for Ireland in 1827. In 1828 he reverted to his Whig principles and took office as Home Secretary under Grey in 1830, succeeding him as Prime Minister from July to November 1834 and returning to power from April 1835 to September 1841. He was thus responsible for initiating Queen Victoria into public affairs, virtually acting as her private secretary. His grace of manner and political indolence belonged essentially to the eighteenth century, of which in social habits he was the last exemplar in high office.

Mensheviks (Mensheviki). The moderates of the Russian Social Democrat Party and opponents of the Bolsheviks (q.v.). The Party split at a Congress in London in 1903, and, although outwardly reunited in 1906, became deeply divided in 1912. The leading Menshevik was an Odessa Jew, Julius Cedarbaum, known by the conspiratorial name of Martov. Trotsky (q.v.) was associated with the Mensheviks in 1905. The Mensheviks were themselves divided: some favoured participation in the Duma (q.v.) and in 1917 some were prepared to support Kerensky in his efforts to defend Russia against the Germans.

Metternich, Klemens (1773–1859, created a Prince 1813). Born at Coblenz, fled to Austria in 1792, served as Austrian Minister at Dresden 1803–6, and Berlin 1806–9. He became Foreign Minister in 1809 and Chancellor in 1821, holding both posts until driven into exile in London and Brighton by the revolutions of 1848 (q.v.). He returned to Austria in 1849, becoming a respected elder statesman in retirement and giving advice, among others, to Bismarck. Metternich always regarded the years 1809–15, in which he led Austria into the Fourth Coalition and presided over the Congress of Vienna (q.v.), as the valuable period of his life and the succeeding thirty-three years of the 'Metternich System' as an epilogue. Although considered an arch-reactionary by European liberals, he was in reality a conservative, anxious to preserve the equilibrium of government and seeing aristocratic control menaced by the pretentious claims of the 'Jacobin' middle classes. Because he was born a 'foreigner', he was not allowed to control Austria's internal affairs – in old age he complained, 'I governed Europe sometimes, Austria never' – but it was largely through his influence that the Austrians developed their Italian possessions rather than concentrating on their traditional interests in Germany.

Mexican War, 1846–8. Relations between the U.S.A. and Mexico had been bad for over ten years, partly because of frontier incidents but more especially because of American expansionist policy in Texas (q.v.), which was annexed in 1845, and in New Mexico. President Polk sent American troops into a disputed area along the frontier, and, when they were attacked, accused Mexico of shedding 'American blood on American soil' (April 1846). General Zachary Taylor invaded Mexico across the Rio Grande and captured Monterey, while General Winfield Scott landed at Vera Cruz and captured Mexico City (September 1846). By the Treaty of Guadeloupe Hidalgo (February 1848) Mexico renounced claims to Texas, recognized the Rio Grande frontier and, in return for 15 million dollars, ceded New Mexico and California (where gold had recently been discovered).

Mexico. Secured independence from Spain in 1821 when Agustin de Iturbide (1783–1824), with the support of the Church and the land-owners, proclaimed Mexico a constitutional monarchy, ruling as 'Emperor' from July 1822 to March 1823. A federal republic was set up in 1824. For the next thirty years the dominant figure was Antonio de Santa Anna (1797–1876), who tried to centralize the government but was faced by frequent separatist insurrections and by American intrigues culminating in the loss of Texas and the Mexican War (q.v.). In 1855 a liberal movement, associated with Juárez (q.v.), finally drove out Santa Anna but was involved in civil war and the French attempt to set up a Mexican Empire under Maximilian (q.v.). Mexico did not have peace until the end of 1867. From 1876 to 1911 the country made considerable economic progress under Diaz (q.v.), but with his overthrow a series of short-lived régimes struggled for recognition. Punitive action against the Mexicans for frontier incidents was undertaken by the United States in 1914 and 1916. A new constitution was adopted in January 1917, which formed the basis of drastic social reforms. From 1924 to 1935 Mexico was virtually under the control of Plutarco Calles. He improved relations with the U.S.A., but his radicalism alienated the Church, which was in conflict with the state from 1927 to 1929. In 1938 Mexico nationalized the foreign oil companies; this led to strained relations with the U.S.A. until 1947.

Midlothian Campaign. The series of election speeches made by Gladstone (q.v.) in southern Scotland and northern England at the end of November 1879 and again in March 1880, condemning the foreign, imperial, and financial policy of the Beaconsfield Govern-ment in an unprecedented torrent of eloquence. These speeches played a considerable part in the Liberal electoral victory of April 1880; they also have a wider historic significance as the first occasion upon which a leading statesman wooed the British electorate.

Midway Island, Battle of (4 June 1942). Decisive naval engagement between the U.S. fleet (Admiral Nimitz) and the Japanese (Admirals Yamamoto, Nagumo, and Kondo) resulting in a victory for the Americans that ended Japanese expansion into the Central Pacific and marked the turning-point in the war. The battle was remarkable in being fought almost entirely between naval aircraft, with the fleets out of sight of each other: the Japanese lost four carriers to the Americans' one.

Military Conversations, 1906–14. On 10 January 1906 (in the first Moroccan Crisis and shortly after the Liberal Government of Campbell-Bannerman had assumed office), the French Ambassador, Paul Cambon, asked the Foreign Secretary, Grey, to authorize conversations between the military staffs of Britain and France in order to decide on the form of cooperation between the two countries should they find themselves at war with Germany. After consulting the Prime Minister, the War Minister, and the Chancellor of the Exchequer, Grey authorized the conversations. The first was held on 17 January, and others of a similar kind continued until 1914. Cabinet approval was not obtained until 1912, when naval conversations were also authorized, but an exchange of letters emphasized the hypothetical nature of all undertakings. Despite these reservations, the conversations extended the scope of the Anglo-French Entente (q.v.). Unofficial talks between the British military attaché in Brussels and the Belgian Staff also began in 1906. Anglo-Russian naval conversations were authorized in June 1914, but had made no progress by the outbreak of war.

Mill, John Stuart (1806–73). British philosopher, economist, and humanist. Born in London, the son of the utilitarian philosopher James Mill (1773–1836). J. S. Mill worked in London for the East India Company from 1833 to 1856, publishing two important works while in their service, *A System of Logic* (1843) and *Principles of Political Economy* (1848), an analysis of the classical economists which showed much more sympathy towards human suffering than they had themselves. Mill's political theories marked a transitional point in British liberalism, for he saw the need for state interference to prevent the abuse of *laissez-faire* principles; in his later years he regarded himself as a socialist. His great plea for respecting minority convictions, *On Liberty*, was published in 1859. Mill was Liberal M.P. for Westminster, 1865–8. In 1867 he introduced a motion proposing to enfranchise women on the ground that taxation necessarily carried a right of parliamentary representation. The motion, the first of its kind in Britain, was defeated by 196 votes to 73. Mill developed his views on women's rights in *The Subjection of Women* (1869). He spent a considerable part of each year in France, and his thought was influenced by French traditions.

Milner, Alfred (1854–1925, created a Viscount 1902). British imperialist. Born in Hesse-Darmstadt. His father was German, although of British descent, and his mother was British. Milner was educated at Tübingen, before going up to Balliol. He was a Liberal journalist for three years and then a civil servant in Britain and in Egypt, before being appointed High Commissioner in South Africa and Governor of Cape Colony in 1897. He remained in South Africa until 1906; he found the situation on his arrival so serious that he began to prepare for what he regarded as an inevitable Boer attack (see *Boer Wars*). From 1902 to 1906 he was Governor of the Transvaal and Orange River Colony, accomplishing much material reconstruction. On his return, he became a prominent critic in the Lords of Lloyd George's 'People's Budget' and of Irish Home Rule. Nevertheless, in December 1916 he agreed to enter Lloyd George's War Cabinet, where he served both as an important link with the overseas empire and as a brake on the rasher actions of the Prime Minister. Available evidence suggests that he was second in influence only to Lloyd George. He headed an important delegation to Petrograd in February 1917, to encourage the Russian war effort, and eased the obstacles preventing Anglo-French military cooperation in March 1918. His basic hostility to a major reshaping of Europe led to his omission from the delegation to the Paris Peace Conference, although he was Colonial Secretary from 1919 to 1921. With his fundamental belief in the need to educate colonies to assume the responsibilities of self-government, while at the same time envisaging some super-imperial council, Milner was the inspiration of the last generation of servants of empire. His principal defects were a rigidity of outlook, which isolated him from the masses, and a partiality for bureaucratic methods. Both, perhaps, reflected his German upbringing.

Minorities Treaties. As part of the Peace Settlement of 1919–20 most of the states of Central and Eastern Europe were required to sign treaties, or make declarations, ensuring their racial minorities equal treatment in law, religious freedom, and the use of their languages. These treaties were guaranteed by the League of Nations. The German undertaking was limited to Upper Silesia. Italy did not have to sign such a treaty, since it was assumed (mistakenly) that, as a great and victorious power, she was sufficiently virtuous to give these rights to her German-Austrian and Slovene minorities without formal obligation. Several of the other states disregarded their undertakings, notably Poland and Rumania. The League proved powerless to enforce the treaties.

Miranda, Francisco de (1756–1816). Controversial figure in the liberation of South America. Miranda was born in Caracas, Venezuela, of creole descent. He fought in the American War of Independence and in the French revolutionary army of 1793–4. He developed plans for a new Inca Empire, in which he tried to interest the British, Americans, or French. He made several raids on Venezuelan towns, sometimes with British support, but it was not until the declaration of Venezuela's independence in 1811 that he returned from London to his birthplace and, because of his European military experience, was given command of its army. He was hampered by limitations of personal character and by the activities of (nominally) loyalist Spanish irregulars led by Monteverde. Morale was lowered in Caracas by an earthquake in March 1812. Miranda was made dictator, but, dejected by a series of failures, he capitulated to Monteverde in July 1812 in return for a promise of amnesty – which Monteverde promptly disregarded. Miranda sought to escape to Britain but was allowed to fall into Spanish hands, partly through the hostility shown to him for his capitulation by other Venezuelan leaders, including Bolivar (q.v.). Miranda was shipped to Cadiz, where he died in prison.

Missouri Compromise. For the first two decades of the nineteenth century a precarious political balance was maintained between Northern and Southern interests in the U.S.A. by admitting 'slave' and 'free' territories alternately to statehood. This balance was endangered by the creation of new states out of the Louisiana Purchase (q.v.), where, under the Spaniards and French, slavery had been permitted even in the northernmost regions. In March 1820, after a bitter conflict between the Senate and House of Representatives, Congress authorized the admission of Missouri as a slave-state to be counterbalanced by Maine as a free state, but, at the same time, prohibited slavery in those regions of the Louisiana Purchase running north of the line 36° 30′. This settlement, known as the 'Missouri Compromise', was regarded as contrary to the Constitution by the majority of Southerners, since it infringed future state rights. It remained a subject of dispute for a quarter of a century, the Supreme Court eventually deciding against the Compromise (as robbing a slave-owner of his property) in the Dred Scott Case (q.v.) of 1857.

Mohammed Ali. See *Mehemet Ali.*

Moltke, Helmuth von (1800–91). German Field-Marshal. Entered the Prussian Army in 1822 and served in it for 66 years, although from 1835 to 1839 he was seconded as adviser to the Turks. Moltke became Chief of the Prussian General Staff in 1857 and, in collaboration with Bismarck and General von Roon (1803–79, Prussian Minister of War 1859–73), completely re-organized the Prussian Army. He was responsible for the strategic planning that defeated Denmark in 1864, Austria in 1866, and France in 1870. From 1870 to 1888 he was the first Chief of the Great German General Staff.

His nephew, also called Helmuth von Moltke (1848–1916), became Chief of the General Staff in 1906, a post he held until 14 September 1914. He commanded the invasion of Belgium and France, but was made a scapegoat for the failure to capture Paris and the repulse on the Marne (q.v.). (See also *Schlieffen Plan*.)

Monroe Doctrine. Contained in the annual message to Congress of President James Monroe (1758–1831, President 1817–25), although it was actually drafted by his Secretary of State, John Quincy Adams (q.v.). The message was prompted by the threat of European intervention to suppress the revolt of the Spanish-American colonies. Originally, joint Anglo-American action had been proposed by Canning (q.v.), but this was unacceptable to the Americans because of the persistence of anti-British sentiment. The Doctrine maintained: (i) that the American continent was no territory for future European colonization; (ii) that there was an essentially different political system in the Americas from Europe; (iii) that the U.S.A. would regard any attempt by European powers to extend their influence in the Americas as dangerous to its peace and security; and (iv) that the U.S.A. would not interfere with existing European colonies, nor participate in purely European wars. The Doctrine remained the basis of American foreign policy for over a century. At various times it was modified, notably by President Polk in 1845 – who declared 'The people of this continent alone have the right to decide their own destiny' – and by President Theodore Roosevelt (q.v.) in 1904, when he announced that the U.S.A. was 'an international police power' for the American continent. In 1912 Senator Lodge carried through Congress a resolution extending the Monroe Doctrine to non-European powers (i.e. Japan).

Montagu-Chelmsford Report (1918). Recommended the establishment of partially responsible government in India. The report took its name from the Secretary of State, Edwin Montagu (1879–1924), and from Lord Chelmsford, Viceroy 1916–21. It formed the basis of the Government of India Act (q.v.) of 1919.

Montenegro. The Latinized name of Crna Gora, a mountainous region in south-western Yugoslavia. Montenegro became a principality in the late fourteenth century. Although Turkish armies twice occupied it, the Montenegrins were able to maintain practical independence because of the difficult terrain; their independence was confirmed by the Sultan in 1799. The native dynasty of Petrović produced a remarkable succession of warrior princes, of whom the most distinguished was the poet and philosopher, Petar Njegos (1813–51), Prince-Bishop 1830–51. The last ruler, Nicholas I (Prince, 1860–1910, King 1910–18) modernized his state. Although ruling with the arbitrary unpredictability of an (almost) enlightened despot, he did give Montenegro a formal constitution (1905) and elevated it to the dignity of a Kingdom (1910). He created at Cetinje a passable imitation of a capital city and considerably extended his territories by judicious intervention in the Balkan Wars (q.v.). He went to war in 1914 in support of Serbia and, when his Kingdom was overrun at the end of 1915, he escaped to France (where he died in 1921). The Allies believed that Nicholas had not resisted the Austrians as energetically as he might, and when in 1918 a packed assembly at Podgorica deposed the dynasty and voted for union with Serbia, the Allies, with many qualms, accepted the decision. Between the wars Montenegro was engulfed in Yugoslavia. After the Axis invasion of 1941, the Montenegrin people resorted to fierce guerilla resistance; their brave defiance of the invaders ensured that, by the communist constitution of 1946, Montenegro re-appeared as one of the federated republics within Yugoslavia.

Montreux Convention (20 July 1936). In 1936 the Turks, fearing that Mussolini intended to build up an Italian colonial empire in Asia Minor as well as in Africa, requested an international conference to reconsider the clauses in the Treaty of Lausanne (q.v.) demilitarizing the Dardanelles and the Bosphorus. The Montreux Convention, which was the fruit of the Conference's deliberations, was signed by representatives of Britain, France, Greece, Yugoslavia, and the Black Sea countries: Turkey was allowed to refortify the Straits; new regulations controlled the aggregate tonnage of warships passing through the Straits in time of peace. (See *Straits Question*.)

Morley, John (1838–1923, created a Viscount in 1908). Liberal politician, man-of-letters, and biographer of Gladstone. Born in Blackburn. He had considerable influence as a journalist 1867–83, and then became M.P. for Newcastle. A strong believer in Irish Home Rule (q.v.), he was partially responsible for converting Gladstone to this cause, and served as Irish Secretary in 1886 and from 1892 to

1895. As Secretary for India 1905–10 he was largely responsible for the Indian Councils Act of 1909 (q.v.). He served as Lord President of the Council 1910–14 but resigned on the outbreak of war, the last of the Gladstonian Liberals.

Morley-Minto Reforms. A name frequently applied to the Indian Councils Act of 1909 (q.v.). Lord Morley was Secretary for India in the Asquith Government and Lord Minto was Viceroy of India from 1905 to 1910.

Morny, Charles Louis Joseph (1811–65). French politician. A half-brother of Napoleon III, being the son of Queen Hortense and the Comte de Flahaut, who was himself an illegitimate son of Talleyrand. Morny served with distinction in the French Army in Algeria in the 1830s, and was a friend of the Orleanist princes. He became a Bonapartist in 1848 and planned Napoleon's *coup d'état* of December 1851. He served the Second Empire as Minister of the Interior, Ambassador to Russia, and President of the Legislative Assembly. He blatantly abused his public position to foster private speculations, the most serious tragically involving France (and the Archduke Maximilian q.v.) in Mexico. He was created a Duke by Napoleon III in 1862.

Moroccan Crisis, 1905. Agreements between France and Britain (April 1904) and France and Spain (October 1904) had secretly provided for the eventual partition of Morocco (q.v.). Although the Germans had earlier stated that they had no interest in Morocco, Bülow (q.v.) determined in 1905 to demonstrate to France, by insisting on the independence of Morocco, that the Anglo-French Entente (q.v.) was of no permanent diplomatic value. Accordingly, during a Mediterranean cruise, Kaiser William II landed at Tangier (31 March 1905), and in a speech declared Germany's support for the Moroccans. The Germans demanded an international conference on Morocco, believing that they would be able to achieve the diplomatic isolation of France. The French Government were alarmed by the German attitude, and, as a gesture of appeasement, jettisoned the Foreign Minister who had made the Entente, Delcassé (q.v.). The British encouraged the French, and when France discovered that she could also count on the support of the U.S.A., she agreed to the international conference. This was held at Algeciras (q.v.) January to April 1906, and resulted in a strengthening, rather than a weakening, of the Entente. A second Moroccan Crisis occurred in 1911 over Agadir (q.v.).

Morocco. A Moslem state in north-west Africa, independent since the Middle Ages, but by the late nineteenth century backward, in permanent revolt against its Sultan, and with ill-defined frontiers. By the beginning of 1905 France was ready to add Morocco to her North African Empire but the Moroccan Crisis (q.v.) and the Conference of Algeciras (q.v.) retarded French policy, and it was not until 1912 that France partitioned Morocco with Spain. Southern Morocco became a French Protectorate and was developed rapidly under the genius of Lyautey (q.v.). Moroccan rebels, Riffs, led by Abd-el-Krim, began attacking the Spanish garrisons in northern Morocco in 1921 (destroying a large force at Anual) and the French garrisons in April 1925. A Franco-Spanish Army under Pétain (q.v.) checked the Riffs and eventually defeated and captured Abd-el-Krim in May 1926. The city of Tangier, which faces Gibraltar, was within Spanish Morocco from 1912 to 1923 but was then neutralized and declared an international zone, a status it enjoyed until 1956, except for the years 1940–5 when it was occupied again by the Spanish. In November 1934 Moroccan nationalism (as distinct from the tribal ambitions of the Riffs) influenced French politics for the first time, a reform programme by a group of young Moroccans being rejected out of hand in Paris. Nationalism was stimulated by the Spanish Civil War (q.v.), in which Franco made great use of Moroccan troops, and by the decline in French prestige. Consultative Assemblies were authorized in French Morocco in 1948. Serious anti-French riots continued from 1953 to 1955. In March 1956 the French withdrew from the administration of the country, an example followed by Spain shortly after.

Morris, William (1834–96). English idealistic socialist, poet, artist, and craftsman. Morris came from a comfortable middle-class family, and won distinction for his poetry and his attempts to improve domestic art in England, before throwing in his lot with the Social Democratic Federation in 1883. In the following year he helped to establish the semi-anarchist 'Socialist League', leaving that too in 1890 to form a small socialist group in Hammersmith. His utopian *News from Nowhere* was published in 1891. Although he accepted the Marxian analysis of the class-struggle, his socialism sprang from the heart rather than the mind; it was essentially a protest against the ugliness of capitalism. This association of art and socialism remained a powerful influence in British domestic life for many years after his death.

Morse, Samuel F. B. (1791–1872). American inventor. The son of a distinguished geographer, who was also a Congregational minister. Educated at Yale and subsequently as an art student in London, he became a portrait painter and professor of painting at what was to become New York University. At the age of forty he became interested in the transmission of signals by electricity, and in 1837 he abandoned art for science. In 1838 he invented the code of dots and dashes named after him. He was responsible (in collaboration with Alfred Vail) for the first practical electrical telegraph line, from Baltimore to Washington (1844).

Moscow, Retreat from (1812). After a twelve-week campaign, culminating in the battle of Borodino (q.v.), Napoleon entered Moscow on 14 September only to find it in flames, three quarters of the city being destroyed in five days. He remained in Moscow until 18 October, hoping to induce the Russians to accept peace; when they refused, he decided to withdraw to winter quarters, but the cold weather descended earlier than usual and caught Napoleon's 100,000 men in its grip, killing first the horses and later the poorly equipped and famished troops. The Russians harried the retreating French and nearly captured Napoleon crossing the Beresina; they too suffered considerably from the weather. When the French rearguard withdrew from Russian territory on 14 December, only one thousand of the *Grande Armée* were fit for action.

Mukden Incident (1931). Japanese troops, guarding the South Manchurian Railway in accordance with treaty rights, used an explosion on the railway while they were on night manoeuvres as an excuse for seizing the city of Mukden (18 September 1931). Within five months, despite the condemnation of the Great Powers and in defiance of the League of Nations, the Japanese had established control over the whole of Manchuria (q.v.). In Japanese internal history, the Mukden Incident marked the beginning of a militaristic reaction that was to end party government (May 1932) and follow an aggressive policy until the defeat of 1945.

Münchengrätz, Agreements of (18–19 September 1833). A meeting between Metternich and Tsar Nicholas I at Münchengrätz (now Mnichovo Hradiště in Czechoslovakia) resulted in two agreements: by the first, the Austrians and Russians affirmed support for maintenance of the Turkish Empire and agreed to act together if partition of the Empire appeared imminent; by the second, the two powers guaranteed their Polish possessions and promised assistance to each other if faced by rebellion in Poland. A third agreement was signed a month later in Berlin by which Austria, Russia, and Prussia declared their willingness to assist any sovereign who appealed for help against insurgent liberalism. The terms of these agreements are not so important as the fact that Metternich had succeeded in re-establishing the close diplomatic contact of the three East European autocracies normally associated in the minds of Western liberals with the 'Holy Alliance' (q.v.).

Munich Agreement (29 September 1938). A settlement of the crisis over Czechoslovakia, reached in conference at Munich by the British, French, and Italian prime ministers (Chamberlain, Daladier, and Mussolini) and Hitler, by which the Sudetenland (q.v.) was to be ceded to Germany, and Polish and Hungarian demands for frontier adjustments were to be made at the expense of Czechoslovakia. When these changes had been carried out, all four of the Powers represented at Munich would guarantee the rump of Czechoslovakia against unprovoked aggression. One third of the population of Czechoslovakia was thus transferred. At the time, the Munich Agreement was warmly received by many people in Britain, France, and Germany, since it was believed that it had saved Europe from war. When, in March 1939, the Czech Government was induced to ask Hitler for German military protection, even Chamberlain began to see that the Agreement had opened the way for German domina-tion of Central Europe. Neither Czechoslovakia herself, nor Russia (who, with France, was Czechoslovakia's ally) were invited to the Munich Conference or consulted about the Agreement. Defenders of the Munich policy maintain that even if it did not give 'peace in our time' (as Chamberlain prophesied), it gave the West a vital year to improve its armaments; critics reply that Germany was better prepared for war in 1939 than in 1938 and that the Czech defences, which were surrendered with the Sudetenland, would have kept out the German Army for several months at least.

Munich Putsch. An abortive attempt by Hitler to overthrow the State Government of Bavaria on 8–9 November 1923, as a prelude to a march on Berlin and the establishment of a Nazi régime in Germany. Although Hitler was supported by General Ludendorff (q.v.), the putsch was ill planned and disintegrated when Bavarian police opened fire on a Nazi demonstration some two thousand strong, killing sixteen of Hitler's supporters. Hitler was subsequently tried for treason and sentenced to five years' imprisonment; Ludendorff was acquitted. The sixteen victims became the leading martyrs of the Nazi movement.

Municipal Corporations Act (September 1835). Carried by the Second Melbourne Ministry, provided a uniform pattern of government for 178 boroughs and cities; town councils were to consist of a mayor (to hold office for a year), aldermen (elected by councillors), and councillors (elected for three years by ratepayers). Many of the corporations had been self-elected and corrupt; the Act thus formed a basic charter for the development of local government, in accordance with the spirit of the Parliamentary Reform Act of 1832. The Act did not apply to the City of London (which still retains its old constitution) or to some sixty small towns, which were, however, brought into line by consolidating Acts in 1882–3.

Murat, Joachim (1767–1815). Son of an innkeeper, was an early associate of Bonaparte, helping to suppress the Vendémiaire Rising of 1795 (see *French Revolution*). After serving in the first Italian campaign, he acquired a reputation as the finest cavalry commander of his day during the Egyptian expedition. He led the troops which carried out Napoleon's *coup d'état* of Brumaire. He married Napoleon's youngest sister in 1800, and was made a Marshal in 1804. In 1808 he savagely repulsed the insurgent people of Madrid and was soon after made King of Naples. He continued to serve in the French Army, leading the cavalry in Russia and fighting at Leipzig (q.v.). He sought in vain to preserve his Neapolitan throne by negotiating with the Allies in 1813–14. In April 1815 he tried to raise the Italian people to support Napoleon's return from Elba but was decisively defeated and forced to flee to France. After Waterloo, he again sought to lead a revolt in Calabria, but within a week was arrested, court-martialled, and executed (13 October).

Mussolini, Benito (1883–1945). Born near Forlì in the Romagna, the son of a blacksmith and a schoolmistress; was himself a schoolteacher for a year, but fled to Switzerland (1902) to evade military service and, while working as a manual labourer, picked up socialist ideas, particularly the syndicalism (q.v.) of Sorel. Mussolini went back to Italy in 1904 and was a socialist agitator and journalist for eleven years before resigning from the Socialist Party because it criticized him for favouring war against Austria in 1915. He was wounded on the Isonzo Front and returned to Milan as editor of *Il Popolo d'Italia*. He formed at this time groups (*fasci*) of working men to agitate for social revolutionary changes; these groups were merged into a Fascist Party in March 1919. The Fascists broke up Communist meetings and demanded full implementation of Italy's demands at the Paris Peace Conference. They vigorously supported the poet Gabriele d'Annunzio (1863–1938), who had seized Fiume (q.v.) and from whom Mussolini borrowed much of the political ritual of Fascism. From February 1921 Italy was in a state of incipient civil war, with serious riots in Bologna, Florence, and Milan. Terrified by the threat of a Communist revolution, King Victor Emmanuel III appointed Mussolini Prime Minister in October 1922 (see *March on Rome*) and as *Duce* (leader) he headed a coalition of Fascists and nationalists. He assumed dictatorial powers in November, but allowed muted parliamentary opposition until after the murder of Matteotti (q.v.) in 1924. Full Fascist government was established in 1928–9; Italy was made one constituency, in which the electorate voted for or against 400 candidates nominated by the Fascist Grand Council; disputes between workers and employers were settled by a National Council of Corporations. Mussolini carried out an extensive programme of public works, ended the quarrel between Church and State by the Lateran Treaties (q.v.) of 1929, and, from the Corfu Incident (q.v.) of 1924 to the attack on Abyssinia (q.v.) of 1935, indulged in an aggressive foreign policy. Although at first hostile to Hitler's Germany because of its ambitions in Austria (Italy's neighbour), the similarity between the Fascist and Nazi systems and the international ostracism imposed on Italy because of the Abyssinian War led Mussolini to bring the two countries together in what he called the 'Axis' (q.v.) of 1936. At Easter 1939 he annexed Albania (q.v.). He declared war on Britain and France on 10 June 1940, when France was already defeated. On the following 28 October his troops invaded Greece, but were repulsed and, soon after, suffered reverses in Libya and East Africa. These defeats weakened Mussolini's prestige, especially as the Fascists had always sought to inculcate admiration for the glories of war. By the summer of 1941 Mussolini had become virtually a German pensionary, but it was not until 25 July 1943 that a *coup* by King Victor Emmanuel and Marshal Badoglio forced him to resign. He was imprisoned, but was rescued from the Appennines by German parachutists (12 September 1943) and set up a Republican Fascist Government, which administered German-occupied northern Italy. On 28 April 1945 he was captured by Italian partisans and shot on the shore of Lake Como while attempting to escape into Switzerland. His corpse was taken to Milan and hung in the Piazzale Loreto amid demonstrations of public execration.

Nanking, Treaty of (1842). Between Britain and China. Concluded the so-called 'Opium War' (q.v.). The treaty ceded Hong Kong to

Britain and opened the ports of Canton, Amoy, Foochow, Nangpo, and Shanghai (subsequently known as the 'Treaty Ports') to foreign trade. With a commercial treaty, signed in the following year, these conditions enabled the British to secure a predominant position in the China trade.

Nansen, Fridtjof (1861–1930). Norwegian Arctic explorer and internationalist. Born near Oslo. Nansen was leader of the first expedition to cross Greenland (1888), and in 1893 sought to drift across the polar basin in a ship locked in the ice, the *Fram*. After spending eighteen months in the vessel, Nansen and a companion travelled by sledge and skis across the ice to a point further north than any earlier explorer (86° 14′). Nansen's reputation as an explorer made him a national hero and facilitated his entry into politics at the turn of the century. He was able to assist Norway (q.v.) acquire independence from Sweden in 1905 and became the first Norwegian Minister in London. He became an early champion of the League of Nations idea and organized relief work in Russia during the famine that followed the Revolution and Civil War. For these services he was awarded the Nobel Prize in 1922.

Napoleon I, Bonaparte (1769–1821. Emperor of the French 1804–15). Born at Ajaccio in Corsica, entered the French Army in 1785, specializing as an artillery officer. He was given command of the secondary Army in a pincer offensive against Austria in 1796, but, through his victories in the north of Italy (especially Lodi and Rivoli, q.v.), established his reputation as the first great General of the Republican Armies, and himself dictated peace terms to the Austrians at Campo-Formio (q.v.). After an abortive campaign in Egypt, he returned in 1799 to overthrow the Directory ('Brumaire', q.v.), and was appointed First Consul, being made Consul for life in 1802. From 1799 to 1814 he was thus the autocrat of France and the dependent territories his conquests secured for her. It was during the Consulate that he accomplished his greatest reforms (the *Code Napoléon*, q.v., and the Concordat, q.v.) as well as winning the War of the Second Coalition (q.v.). By crowning himself Emperor in the presence of the Pope in Paris, he ensured recognition of his right to authority while assuming a title that would enable him to rule over a greater unit than the old Kingdom of France. (See *Empire of France*.) In the War of the Third Coalition (q.v.) of 1805–7 he won the remarkable victories of Austerlitz (q.v.) and Jena (q.v.) and forced the Russians to accept a reversal of alliances at Tilsit (q.v.). From 1808 his power began to wane; he was faced with the failure of the Continental System (q.v.), and the Peninsular War (q.v.) began to drain away his reserves. He was able to win his fourth campaign against the Austrians by the victory of Wagram (July 1809). He invaded Russia in June 1812 and, although victorious at Borodino. (q.v.), never redeemed the retreat from Moscow (q.v.), and with weary troops was left to fight the War of the Fourth Coalition (q.v.), with the inevitable defeat at Leipzig (q.v.). He abdicated on 11 April 1814, and was granted the right by the Allies to rule the sovereign principality of Elba (retaining the title of Emperor). He escaped from Elba in February 1815, landing near Cannes, and advanced on Paris. From 20 March to 22 June 1815, he again ruled as Emperor from Paris, in the episode known as the 'Hundred Days', which ended at Waterloo (q.v.). He was conveyed to St Helena as a prisoner of war, where he died. He had married Josephine Beauharnais in 1796 but divorced her in January 1810, as she had not borne him any children. He then married the Austrian Archduchess Marie Louise, daughter of Emperor Francis I, who bore him a son in March 1811. The boy was known as the King of Rome during the Empire, was brought up in Vienna as the Duke of Reichstadt, and was accepted by loyal Bonapartists as Napoleon II from 1821 until his death in 1832, although he never used the title. (See also *Bonaparte Family*.)

Napoleon III (Charles Louis Napoleon Bonaparte, 1808–73), Emperor of the French 1852–70. Nephew of Napoleon I, being the son of Louis Bonaparte, King of Holland, and Hortense Beauharnais, the Emperor's step-daughter. As a young man, brought up mainly by his mother, he travelled extensively, living in Italy, Bavaria, Switzerland, and London. He twice (1836 and 1840) made abortive attempts to lead a Bonapartist rising against the July Monarchy; after the second occasion he was imprisoned at Ham in the Somme Marshes, but escaped in 1845 and returned to London, where in April 1848 he enlisted as a special constable during the Chartist demonstrations. The power of his name and the nostalgic appeal of the 'Napoleonic Legend' led to his being elected President of the Second Republic (q.v.) in December 1848. He offered France security against social unrest and was always warmly supported in the provinces, although distrusted in Paris. On 2 December 1851, he extended his presidential authority by a *coup d'état* and, exactly a year later, accepted the imperial title, thereby inaugurating the Second Empire (q.v.). By allying with Britain in the Crimean War, he secured the Peace Congress for Paris (1856) and for ten years

231

was regarded as the arbiter of Europe. He retained many of the habits of a conspirator, secretly meeting Cavour at Plombières (q.v,) in 1858 to plan a joint war for the Italian cause, while retaining a garrison at Rome to safeguard Pius IX (q.v.) and making a separate peace in 1859 without informing his ally. He had a fertile mind, but his ideas were not always in the realm of the practical; when in 1861 he allowed corrupt speculators to encourage him to establish a French-dominated Empire in Mexico (q.v.) he was committing France to an enterprise which fatally weakened his system. By 1865 Napoleon was a sick man unable to make quick decisions. He was outmanoeuvred by Bismarck during the Austro-Prussian Seven Weeks War of 1866, from which Napoleon had hoped to gain compensation for France, and remained isolated when Bismarck provoked the Franco-Prussian War of 1870. He was captured at Sedan (q.v.), imprisoned in Germany, and spent the last two years of his life in exile at Chislehurst, Kent. In 1853 he married Eugénie de Montijo (1826–1920); their son, the Prince Imperial (1856–79), was killed fighting in the British Army against the Zulus.

Narodniki. Supporters of a secret Russian revolutionary movement in 1873–4 and in 1876, deriving its name from the *hozhdenie v narod* ('going to the people') activity of its first student supporters, who went out from the universities, clad as peasants, to try to convert villagers to socialism. Most of their ideas were too complicated for the peasantry, and the movement was a failure. The Russian Government took savage action against the Narodniki in 1877. The Narodniki formed one phase of the more general 'Populist' movement (q.v.).

Navarino, Battle of (20 October 1827). Incident in the Greek War of Independence. Since the Turkish Government had failed to accept a recommendation of the Great Powers to make an armistice with the Greeks, a squadron of British, French, and Russian ships commanded by Vice-Admiral Codrington hunted out the combined Turkish and Egyptian Fleets in the bay of Navarino (in the Morea) and, when fired on, replied with such effect that over fifty ships were sunk. The action was much criticized in Britain, where opinion was sharply divided between Philhellenes and Russophobes; it was felt that in destroying the Turkish fleet Codrington had removed the most effective obstacle to a Russian descent on Constantinople. Navarino was the last occasion upon which the three powers co-operated in a military operation until the Dardanelles campaign of 1915.

Nazi-Soviet Pact. The name given to the Russo-German Treaty of Non-Aggression signed by Molotov and Ribbentrop (q.v.) in Moscow on 23 August 1939. The published terms of the Treaty, which was supposed to last for ten years, included pledges to refrain from aggression against each other and an undertaking of neutrality in case either country were involved in war. Secret clauses assigned spheres of influence in Eastern Europe; the Russians were to have a free hand in Finland, Latvia, Estonia, Eastern Poland, and Bessarabia, while Germany was to have Lithuania and the rest of Poland. Subsequently, a further secret accord (28 September 1939) transferred Lithuania to the Soviet sphere in return for extension of the German area in Poland. The treaty represented a major change in the policy of both countries and confirmed the feeling in the West that a German attack on Poland was imminent. The Russians seem to have been reacting to a sense of humiliation and suspicion of the West after the Munich Agreement (q.v.) and the failure of Britain and France to accept Russian terms for an alliance. The Russians may, too, have wished to precipitate war between 'the two imperialist camps'. For Germany, the change of policy ensured the isolation of Poland. After the German victories of 1940 there were signs of friction between the two states, particularly over Russian tendencies to enlarge her sphere in south-eastern Europe. The Pact was broken when the Germans invaded the U.S.S.R. on 22 June 1941.

Nelson, Horatio (1758–1805, created a Baron 1798, Viscount 1801). The son of a Norfolk rector, entered the Navy in 1770, participated in the occupation of Corsica (1774), losing an eye during the fighting. In 1797 he was promoted Rear-Admiral because of his distinguished service at the battle of St Vincent, and lost an arm in attacking the Canary Islands. In the following year he failed to prevent the French from transporting Bonaparte's expedition to Egypt but subsequently trapped the French fleet at the Nile (q.v.) and destroyed it. After serving in the Baltic and raiding the Danish fleet at Copenhagen (q.v.), he became commander in the Mediterranean (1803) and for two years blockaded Toulon. From January to October 1805 he pursued Villeneuve's fleet across the Atlantic and back finally defeating it at Trafalgar (q.v.), where he was shot by a French sniper as he stood, resplendent in all his four orders of knighthood, on the quarterdeck of *Victory*. Nelson's supreme confidence in his mission enabled him to impart enthusiasm and give free rein to a courageous initiative which, with lesser leaders, would have led to disaster.

Nesselrode, Count Karl Robert (1780–1862). Russian statesman. A member of a German family that had entered Russian service. Nesselrode was quickly promoted to responsible posts, and, at the age of thirty-four, was chief adviser to (and Minister in attendance on) Tsar Alexander I in Paris. In the following year he held a similar position at the Congress of Vienna. From 1822 to 1856 he was Russian Foreign Minister, the longest tenure of that office. Nesselrode was himself cautious and conservative. He believed that Russia would best secure influence in Turkey by a policy of support rather than of intimidation; hence his greatest success (on paper) was the Treaty of Unkiar Skelessi (q.v.) of 1833. He maintained that the Crimean War was contrary to his policy and was forced upon Russia by the intrigues of Britain and France; it was upon his recommendation that Alexander II accepted peace in 1856. He was fundamentally opposed both to encouragement of Slav unrest in the Balkans and to imperial expansion in Asia. Nesselrode was regarded as a reactionary by European liberals because of his hostility to Polish national rights and his willingness to assist the Austrians to suppress the Hungarian Revolt of 1849. (See *Revolutions of 1848*.)

Netherlands, Kingdom of the. Created in 1814 by the union of Holland, Belgium (q.v.), and Luxemburg (q.v.) under William of Orange-Nassau, whose family had made the Stadtholdership of the former Dutch Republic hereditary. The United Netherlands had little in common; religious differences and a conflict between the agrarian interests of Holland and the industrial interests of Belgium helped to intensify the national discord that led to the Belgian proclamation of independence in 1830, finally recognized by the Dutch in 1839. The Duchy of Luxemburg became independent with the accession of Queen Wilhelmina in 1890. The Netherlands remained neutral in the First World War, but in the Second World War were invaded by the Germans and occupied from May 1940 until May 1945.

Much of the commercial prosperity of the Netherlands depended on the resources of the Dutch East Indies, which were fully exploited by the end of the nineteenth century. The Dutch were faced by frequent colonial revolts, the most serious being in Java in 1825–30 and 1894–6. In August 1945 the Dutch East Indies proclaimed their independence as the Republic of Indonesia, but remained in conflict with the Netherlands Government for another four years.

Neuilly, Treaty of (27 November 1919). The peace treaty with Bulgaria after the First World War. The terms imposed on Bulgaria were less severe than on the other ex-enemy states, partly because Bulgaria had influential British sympathizers and partly because it was felt that hard terms in the Balkans would only lead to fresh wars. Nevertheless, Bulgaria lost Western Thrace to Greece (thereby being cut off from the Aegean Sea) and ceded two small areas to Serbia. Rumania was confirmed in possession of the Dobrudja which she had taken from Bulgaria in 1913 after the Balkan Wars (q.v.). The Bulgarian Army was limited to 20,000 men. Bulgaria was made liable for Reparations (q.v.).

New Deal. The social and economic reforms of F. D. Roosevelt (q.v.) between 1933 and 1939. The First New Deal (1933–5) aimed at relief and recovery from financial depression and unemployment: financial measures included an Emergency Banking Relief Act, an Economy Act, and the creation of a Federal Emergency Relief Administration. A Civilian Conservation Corps (1933–41) found work for two million in reforestation projects; the Civil Works Administration (C.W.A.) found jobs on public works projects for four million; the creation of the Tennessee Valley Authority (T.V.A.) as an independent public corporation to construct dams and power-plants increased the economic potentialities of a region including parts of seven states; industrial competition was regulated under government supervision by the National Industrial Recovery Act. The Second New Deal (1935–9) was especially concerned with social security for the working population and guarantees for the small farmer. At the same time, it saw the creation of the Works Progress Administration (W.P.A.) to supervise and coordinate many of the earlier projects. The New Deal aroused the opposition of many industrialists; in 1936–7 there was a notable conflict between the administration and the Supreme Court caused by the judiciary's attempt to block social legislation.

New Economic Policy (N.E.P.). A modification in communist practice instituted in Russia by Lenin in March 1921, following peasant disturbances and riots in Petrograd and Kronstadt. The N.E.P. allowed some freedom of internal trade, re-introducing limited private commerce and re-establishing state banks. It was formally abolished by the Bolshevik Party Congress of January 1929, which gave full support to the first of Stalin's Five-Year Plans (q.v.).

Newfoundland. Became England's first colony at the end of the sixteenth century but was neglected, except by the fishing trade, until after the Napoleonic Wars. A representative assembly was set up in 1832, and responsible government followed in 1855. The Newfoundland Parliament ran into grave financial difficulties on several occasions, notably between 1924 and 1933, when Newfoundland reverted to the status of Crown Colony and the United Kingdom accepted responsibility for its finances. In July 1948 a referendum narrowly decided in favour of confederation with Canada, and Newfoundland became a Canadian province on 1 April 1949.

New Zealand, Dominion of. With the dissolution of the New Zealand Company in 1851, the colony was granted a constitution (1852), and four years later received the right of responsible government. In 1891 New Zealand representatives participated in an Australasian Federal Convention at Sydney, where a draft constitution was prepared for a confederation. Subsequently, fear of being dominated by the Australian States (and especially by New South Wales) led the New Zealanders to reject the idea of joining the Australian Commonwealth, which was proclaimed in January 1901. New Zealand continued as a self-governing colony until 1907, when use was made of the title of 'Dominion' both in the Colonial Conference of April and in the Governor-General's 'Speech from the Throne' in Wellington on 21 June. The New Zealanders celebrated the privilege of Dominion Status on the following 26 September.

Ney, Michel (1769–1815). Born in the Saar, the son of a cooper. Ney played a prominent part in the victory of Ulm (q.v.), was created a Marshal in 1806, and given the special honour of being gazetted 'Bravest of the Brave' by Napoleon after the Battle of Friedland. His valour at Borodino (q.v.) led Napoleon to create him Prince of the Moskowa. After the Retreat from Moscow he never again showed the same verve, and his movements in the Leipzig Campaign tended to be dilatory. In 1814 he was retained in the Army by Louis XVIII, but when Napoleon returned from Elba, Ney preferred to desert to his cause rather than obey orders to arrest him. Ney fought at Waterloo, but was subsequently captured, court-martialled, and shot in the Luxemburg Gardens in Paris on 7 December 1815. The execution, to which Louis XVIII personally was opposed, aroused resentment throughout France.

Nicholas I, Tsar of Russia (born 1796, Tsar 1825–55). Succeeded his brother Alexander I (q.v.) and was required almost immediately to suppress the Decembrist Conspiracy (q.v.). In home affairs, Nicholas was more reactionary than Alexander. Although he completed codification of the laws (1833) and granted personal freedom to serfs on state lands (1838), he was mainly concerned with strengthening the autocracy. In 1826 he established the 'Third Section', a form of secret police with informers throughout the empire. His Education Minister, Uvarov, publicly based his policy on the famous fundamental trinity of 'Autocracy, Orthodoxy, and Nationalism', and discouraged the growth of schools and universities. The Tsar's repressive tendencies may also be seen in his suppression of the Polish Revolt of 1830–1 and intervention in Hungary in 1849. His Turkish policy was misunderstood in Britain, particular suspicion being aroused by his partition proposals. He coined the phrase 'the Sick Man of Europe' to describe Turkey. He died while the essential weaknesses of his system were being demonstrated by the Russian defeats in the Crimean War (q.v.).

Nicholas II, Tsar of Russia (1868–1918, Tsar 1894–1917). The son of Alexander III. As Tsarevich he went on a world tour, opening the terminus of the Trans-Siberian Railway at Vladivostock and exhibiting an interest in the Far East that was to continue into his reign. Shortly after his accession he married Princess Alexandra of Hesse-Darmstadt (a granddaughter of Queen Victoria), who became a fanatical believer in the Russian autocratic tradition and urged Nicholas to be a strong ruler, despite the pathetic weakness of his character. Nicholas had no sympathy with the liberal aspirations of his subjects; early in his reign, he dismissed the political reforms petitioned by the *zemstvo* of Tver as 'senseless dreams'. Industrial unrest, bad harvests, and the disastrous Russo-Japanese War (q.v.) led to a state of revolution in 1905. The Tsar was forced to summon a Duma (q.v.), but he continued to distrust representative government and, being a bad judge of men, tended to select second-rate careerists as his advisers. From 1906 both Nicholas and the Tsarina were unduly influenced by the charlatan Rasputin (q.v.). Although singularly unsuited for high military office, Nicholas assumed Supreme Command of the Russian Armies in September 1915, and it was at his headquarters at Pskov that he was forced to abdicate, 15 March 1917. (See *Russian Revolution*.) He was kept in seclusion in various parts of Russia until 16 July 1918, when he was murdered, along with his family, at Ekaterinburg (now Sverdlovsk), on the orders of a local Bolshevik commander who feared that the royal family would be rescued by counter-revolutionary troops.

Nietzsche, Friedrich Wilhelm (1844–1900). German philosopher. Born in Saxony, studied at Bonn and Leipzig, died in Weimar.

Between 1878 and 1889 (when he went out of his mind) Nietzsche wrote a number of works stressing the importance to society of the creation of a vigorous élite of ruthless realists under a superman who would enjoy the exercise of power unrestrained by moral considerations, since the natural leader is 'beyond good and evil'. For many years, Nietzsche was regarded as an essentially destructive writer, contemptuous of humanitarianism, Christianity, and liberalism. He was himself basically an individualist, with no pronounced nationalistic sentiments, but his posthumous works were edited by his sister Frau Elisabeth Förster, a fanatical Pan-German, who appears to have amended them so as to assert her own views. It was thus possible in the 1920s and 1930s for Nietzsche to be hailed by Mussolini and Hitler as the master prophet of right-wing authoritarianism.

Nightingale, Florence (1820–1910). A member of a cultured upperclass family, she was determined to improve hospital conditions in Britain and pursued the (then unconventional) course of training as a nurse in Paris and Prussia. At the end of October 1854 she induced the War Secretary, Sidney Herbert, to send her to Scutari (opposite Constantinople) with a body of thirty nurses, to assist in caring for the wounded in the Crimean War. She was able to improve medical services, and as 'The Lady with the Lamp' became a symbol of comfort to the sick. She returned home in 1856 broken in health, but spent the rest of her life pressing for public health reform and organizing the training of nurses. She received the Order of Merit in 1907.

Nile, Battle of the (1 August 1798; also known as the Battle of Aboukir Bay). Fought between a British fleet commanded by Nelson and the French force that had brought Napoleon to Egypt. Nelson succeeded in placing the French fleet between two lines of British vessels and thereby achieved a striking victory. Only two of Napoleon's thirteen vessels escaped. Nelson thus effctively cut off the Egyptian expedition from its base.

Nore Mutiny (May 1797). Bad food, poor medical services, lack of shore leave, and erratic pay led the Channel Fleet in April 1797 to refuse to leave their moorings at Spithead and put to sea. The Government, after a few days, increased their pay and issued a royal pardon. This indulgence encouraged dissidents in the North Sea Fleet at the Nore, who mutinied in the following month. The Nore mutineers demanded not only improved service conditions, but radical political changes as well, although these remained ill defined. Differences between the men with social grievances and those with political ambitions enabled the Government to suppress the mutiny and hang the leader, Richard Parker. Only four months after the mutiny, the same fleet under Admiral Duncan (1711–1804) won a decisive battle against the Dutch at Camperdown.

Normandy Landings. On 6 June 1944 (D-Day), Allied forces under the command of General Eisenhower began the liberation of Western Europe from the Germans by landing on the Normandy coast between the Orne River and St Marcouf. Artificial harbours were constructed along a strip of beach, so that armoured vehicles and heavy guns could be landed. Heavy fighting continued in Normandy for a month, the Allies taking Cherbourg on 27 June and the British and Canadians capturing Caen on 9 July, thus enabling tanks to break through the German defences and penetrate the interior of France. Paris was liberated on 25 August and Brussels on 2 September. The German frontier was first crossed on 12 September.

North America Act (1867). See *British North America Act*.

Northcliffe, Lord (Alfred Charles William Harmsworth, 1865–1922; created a Baron 1905, Viscount 1917). British newspaper magnate and propagandist. Born in Dublin, the son of a barrister, entered a newspaper office in 1880. In 1888 he founded a weekly paper, *Answers*, in which he used for the first time techniques of sensational (and commercially sound) journalism. With his younger brother, Harold (who became Lord Rothermere in 1913), he built up a successful business in periodicals, extending their scope into daily journalism in 1894 when he purchased the *Evening News*. In May 1896 the *Daily Mail* was founded, selling for a halfpenny, whereas most of the dailies cost a penny. By 1899 it had twice the circulation of any other paper. The *Daily Mirror* was founded in 1903, the *Observer* purchased in 1905 (but sold in 1911), and in 1908 Northcliffe became chief proprietor of *The Times*. He financed new ventures in motoring, aviation, and polar exploration, chiefly for publicity purposes. He pressed for vigorous direction of the First World War, was sent on a diplomatic mission to the U.S.A. in 1917 and on his return was made Director of Propaganda to Enemy Countries, a position which he used to encourage the subject nationalities to demand independence. Northcliffe enjoyed the exercise of power, and suffered in his later years from megalomania. He achieved a newspaper revolution, introducing the tendentious headline and the bright story that would appeal to a huge reading public.

North German Confederation (1867 to 1871). A union of Prussia and the other German states north of the River Main, established by Bismarck after the Prussian victory over Austria and the German states in the 'Seven Weeks War' of 1866. The component states retained their own administrations, but placed their military forces and foreign policy under the Federal Government. A Federal Council (Bundesrat), dominated by the Prussian representatives, shared legislative powers with an elected house (Reichstag). When the German Empire was proclaimed at Versailles on 18 January 1871, the North German Federal Constitution was modified to admit the three states south of the Main (Bavaria, Württemberg, and Baden). The institutions established in 1867 continued throughout the German Empire.

Norway. United to Denmark from the fourteenth century until the Napoleonic Wars. In 1807 the Norwegians secured from the Danes a national assembly and a university of their own. In November 1814 the Norwegian Assembly, under Swedish pressure, was induced to declare the country a free and independent kingdom, united to the crown of Sweden. Norway retained its parliament (*Storting*). Norwegian nationalism developed in the 1840s and 1850s, but it was not until the adoption of universal suffrage in 1898 that the Norwegians began to demand complete independence. The *Storting* declared the union with Sweden dissolved in June 1905, a decision confirmed by a plebiscite and accepted by Sweden a few months later. Prince Charles of Denmark ascended the throne as King Haakon VII, ruling until his death in 1957. Norway remained neutral in the First World War, but in the Second World War became the victim of a surprise German attack on 9 April 1940. Resistance continued until 10 June, especially in Narvik, which had been recaptured by Anglo-French forces on 13 April and held out for eight weeks. A German-dominated administration was set up in Oslo under Vidkun Quisling (q.v.). Norway was not liberated until the collapse of Germany in May 1945.

Novibazar, Sanjak of. A corridor of territory separating Serbia and Montenegro, which remained in the Turkish Empire after the Congress of Berlin (q.v.). The Sanjak was traditionally a centre of Serbian national feeling and, to prevent unification of the Serbs and Montenegrins, it was occupied by the Austrian Army in 1878. At one time the Austrians hoped to find a route through it for a railway line opening up trade with Salonica but they abandoned the project because of natural obstacles. They evacuated the Sanjak in 1908 as a conciliatory move following the annexation of Bosnia-Herzegovina (q.v.). In 1912, during the Balkan Wars (q.v.), the Serbs and Montenegrins overran the Sanjak, partitioning it between them. After 1918 the Sanjak was incorporated in Yugoslavia.

O'Connell, Daniel (1775–1847). Called to the Irish Bar in 1798. In 1800 he began the campaign against the Act of Union (q.v.) which made him known as 'The Liberator'. He founded the Catholic Association in 1823 and was elected M.P. for County Clare in 1828, but as a Roman Catholic could not sit in the Commons until the Catholic Emancipation Act (q.v.) of 1829. The Irish people could not understand his motives in supporting the Whigs in the 1830s, and he lost much of his influence. His attempts to organize a mass Irish movement for repeal of the Union in 1843 failed because he appeared too cautious for the more revolutionary 'Young Ireland' Party (q.v.).

O'Connor, Feargus (1794–1855). A fiery Irish barrister, who became a Radical M.P. for Cork in 1832, being unseated in 1835 for lacking the necessary property qualification and thereafter becoming a leading Chartist (see *Chartism*). He owned and edited the Chartist periodical *Northern Star*, and dominated the militant northern group of the movement. He was elected M.P. for Nottingham in 1847 and organized the Chartist demonstration of 1848, presenting the much ridiculed third petition to the Commons. In 1852 he became insane, but his influence was so great that, when he died after three years in an asylum, 50,000 people attended the funeral.

Old Catholics. The name given to small national groups of dissident Catholic churches which broke away at some time in the eighteenth or nineteenth centuries and which linked themselves loosely by the Declaration of Utrecht of 1889. The most important group was from Germany, Austria, and Switzerland and was formed in 1874–5 by German-speaking Catholics who rejected the Dogma of Papal Infallibility decreed by the Vatican Council of 1870 (q.v.). The distinguished ecclesiastical historian von Döllinger (1799–1890), who was an influential supporter of a more liberal form of Catholicism, presided over the first conferences of Old Catholics, although he never formally joined the sect. There are Old Catholic communities in Holland (dating from a dispute in 1724) and among Slav immigrants in the U.S.A., as well as in the countries mentioned above.

Omdurman. Town facing Khartoum across the Nile and used as capital of the Sudan (q.v.) by the Khalifa from 1885. The site of the battle fought on 2 September 1898 in which Kitchener (q.v.) defeated the Dervishes and thereby destroyed the Khalifa's power and established Anglo-Egyptian control of the Upper Nile.

'Opium War'. The name given to the fighting between the British and the Chinese, 1839–42. The name is derived from the *casus belli*. In 1839 the Chinese confiscated a quantity of opium at Canton that belonged to British merchants. The British Government maintained that Chinese courts had no jurisdiction over British subjects and could not authorize the seizure of their property. The Chinese refused demands for reparation, fired on British warships, and forbade trade with Britain. The British retaliated by bombarding Canton and occupying Hong Kong. The fighting was ended by the Treaty of Nanking (q.v.). Compensation was duly paid for the confiscated opium.

Oregon Question. A dispute over the western boundary between the U.S.A. and Canada, which had been left undetermined in 1818 because the mountain chain of the area had not been explored. The British were interested in the region between the Columbia River and the 49th Parallel because of its value to the fur trade. The Americans claimed the land because their explorers had opened it up and had been followed by settlers who were farming the valleys. Acute tension developed in the early 1840s, when the Americans were indulging in a fever of territorial expansion (see *'Manifest Destiny'*). The two chief planks in the platform of the successful Democrat candidate in the 1844 Election (James K. Polk) were the annexation of Texas (q.v.) and recognition of American rights in Oregon. An Agreement was signed between Britain and the U.S.A. on 15 June 1846, by which the Americans acquired the territory now comprising the states of Oregon, Washington, and Idaho (all south of the 49th Parallel) while Britain obtained Vancouver Island.

Orlando, Vittorio Emmanuele (1860–1952). Italian statesman. Born in Sicily, became Professor of Constitutional Law at Palermo. In 1916 he was appointed Minister of Justice and was made Prime Minister at the height of the Caporetto disaster (q.v.). His Government (October 1917 to June 1919) saw a strengthening of Italian morale, culminating in the victory of General Diaz at Vittorio Veneto (October 1918). He attended the Paris Peace Conference as one of the 'Big Four' but was soon on bad terms with President

Wilson who regarded Orlando's territorial ambitions as inconsistent with the principle of national self-determination. Orlando's failure at Paris, and his inability to find a remedy for the growing social unrest led to his political eclipse. He withdrew from politics when Mussolini came to power in 1922.

Orsini Plot. On 14 January 1858 an Italian patriot, Felice Orsini, attempted to assassinate the Emperor Napoleon III (q.v.) and the Empress Eugénie on their way to the Paris Opera. Both were unhurt, but two people were killed and a hundred wounded. Orsini regarded Napoleon as a traitor to the Italian cause, which he had supported as a young man and a private citizen. Although Orsini was duly executed, the French official press published his last letter, an appeal to Napoleon to help liberate Italy. The plot had the incongruous effect of awakening Napoleon's dormant interest in the Italian problem and led him six months later to invite Cavour (q.v.) to meet him secretly at Plombières (q.v.) to plan a joint Italian policy.

Ottawa Conference (21 July–20 August 1932). An economic conference of the Dominions and the mother country held in Canada during the world depression. The Conference adopted a series of agreements for a limited amount of Imperial Preference (q.v.), following the adoption in the previous February of new protective tariffs by the British Government. The idea of Imperial Preference had been revived in Canada in 1930, when it had been hoped to secure some protection for wheat prices, but the British Government failed to take any action until faced by the severe financial crisis of 1931 with its consequent re-thinking of economic policies.

Ottoman Empire. The name generally given to the Turkish Empire. The Ottoman dynasty ruled over lands in Anatolia from the late thirteenth century, and rapidly spread into Europe, capturing Constantinople in 1453, and remaining as the reigning house in the Turkish Empire until the abolition of the Sultanate by Mustapha Kemal (q.v.) in 1922. The Ottoman Empire reached its zenith in the sixteenth century, stretching from the Persian Gulf to Morocco in the south and from the Crimea to the eastern approaches to Vienna in the north. The empire began to decline with the failure to capture Vienna in 1683; the apparently imminent dissolution of the Ottoman Empire gave rise in the late eighteenth century to the diplomatic problem known as the 'Eastern Question' (q.v.), but the Empire was bolstered up by one or other of the Great Powers until the end of the First World War.

Owen, Robert (1771–1858). Born in Montgomeryshire. At ten Owen was apprenticed to a draper in Stamford. After working in London, he borrowed capital to establish a workshop in Manchester, and in 1800 became a partner in a Scottish mill. He was able to set up a factory at New Lanark, which he worked on model lines, refusing to employ young children, giving older ones further education, limiting working hours for adults, and establishing a cooperative store. Although Owen was the first person in Britain to use (in 1817) the term 'socialist' to describe his experiment, he had no sympathy with attacks on the rich or attempts to foster class hatred. His *New View of Society* (1813) emphasized the value of the cooperative ideal and maintained that a planned economy could cure the evils of poverty. He spent the years 1825–9 in the U.S.A. vainly striving to establish a socialistic community at New Harmony, Indiana. On his return he concentrated on extending the cooperative movement (q.v.) and helped found the Grand National Consolidated Trades Union (q.v.) in 1834. His son, Robert D. Owen (1801–77), was a socialist leader in New York State.

Oxford Movement. The group within the Church of England which sought between 1833 and 1845 to restore the High Church traditions of the seventeenth century. The movement was led by John Keble (1792–1866), John Henry Newman (1801–90), and Edward Pusey (1800–82), all of whom were Fellows of Oriel College, Oxford. Although it reflected the major political and social uncertainties of the time – and, in particular, anxiety over the implications of Catholic Emancipation (q.v.) and the Parliamentary Reform Act of 1832 (q.v.) – the movement is normally dated from Keble's sermon on 'National Apostasy' delivered at St Mary's, Oxford, on 14 July 1833, criticizing the proposed suppression of ten Irish bishoprics. Subsequently, it won influential support through Newman's series of *Tracts for the Times*, intended to spread Anglican principles 'against Popery and Dissent'. Tractarianism (as the movement is sometimes called) revived liturgical ceremonial, which had fallen into abeyance, emphasized the social obligations of the Church (especially through 'settlements' in the slum areas of the big cities), and led to the introduction of religious communities within the Church of England. It aroused opposition both in Oxford and the whole country, and in the face of this hostility many Tractarians felt obliged to leave the Church of England and become Roman Catholics. Newman's *Tract 90* (February 1841) provoked such a storm by its interpretation of some of the Thirty-Nine Articles that the series ended. Newman himself was received into the Church of Rome in October 1845 and became a

Cardinal in 1879. Keble and Pusey remained, however, within the Church of England, shaping the Anglo-Catholic tradition by their scholarship and advice.

Paine, Thomas (1737–1809). Born in Norfolk, became an excise officer until dismissed for seeking increased pay. In 1774 he emigrated to Pennsylvania. Two years later he published *Common Sense*, a forthright demand for the complete independence of the American colonies. He was secretary to the first American committee on foreign affairs and served with Washington's armies. He returned to England by way of France in 1787 and published *The Rights of Man* (1790–2) as a reply to Burke's criticisms of the French Revolution. Fearing prosecution, he fled to France in 1792, was made a French citizen, and became a member of the Convention. He was imprisoned in 1794, completing his *Age of Reason* while under threat of execution. In 1802 he was able to return to America, but his extreme religious views and political radicalism made him a social outcast. His bones were brought back to England in 1819 by his former antagonist, Cobbett (q.v.).

Palestine. Became part of the Ottoman Empire in 1517. It was conquered by British troops under Allenby (q.v.) in 1917–18, and became a British mandate in 1920. The Balfour Declaration (q.v.) promising the Jews a national home was incorporated in the mandatory statement. British administration was hampered by the contradictions between its obligations to the Jews and the claims of the Arabs. Serious anti-Jewish rioting occurred in 1921 and 1929. Attempts to restrict immigration led to Jewish-sponsored riots in December 1933. Persecution of the Jews in Europe intensified unrest in Palestine. The Peel Report of 1937, a proposal to establish Jewish and Arab states while retaining a British-mandated area, was accepted by most of the Zionists (q.v.) but rejected by the Arabs and open warfare developed between Jews and Arabs at the end of 1937, continuing throughout 1938. A British offer of eventual independence made in May 1939 led to further incidents and was postponed because of the Second World War. Terrorism broke out again in 1946, the British Headquarters in the King David Hotel at Jerusalem being blown up by Zionist extremists on 22 July, with 91 deaths. In November 1947 the United Nations voted for partition of Palestine into a Jewish State (Israel) and an Arab State (later united to Jordan). The British mandate ended in May 1948; war followed between Israel and the Arab States, ending in an uneasy truce in July 1949.

Palmerston, Lord (Henry John Temple, 1784–1865, succeeded to an Irish viscountcy in 1802). Became a Tory M.P. in 1807, remaining in the Commons for 58 years, holding office for more than 48, 38 of them with Cabinet rank. He was Secretary of War from 1809 to 1828 but, under Canning's influence, his conservatism weakened and in 1829 he became a Whig. He was Foreign Secretary from 1830 to 1841, except for the four months of Peel's First Ministry. During these eleven years Palmerston worked for 'the independence of constitutional states', seeking the settlement of disputes (Belgium, the Eastern Question, etc.) by international conference in London. It was during his second spell at the Foreign Office (1846–51) that he developed the high-handed blustering diplomacy, filled with patriotic prejudice, with which his name is generally associated and which was typified by his insistence on blockading Greece in 1850 to obtain compensation for Don Pacifico, a Gibraltar-born Portuguese moneylender whose house in Athens had been ransacked by an angry crowd. Palmerston was Home Secretary from 1852 to 1855, succeeding Aberdeen as Prime Minister when it was clear that the country needed a war leader to secure victory in the Crimea. In his later years, Palmerston's judgement was unsound; he overrated the danger of a French invasion in the early 1860s, sympathized with the Confederates in the American Civil War, and thought he could bluff Bismarck over the Schleswig-Holstein Question (q.v.) of 1864. He became less interested in domestic affairs, rejecting proposals for an extended franchise from his more liberal supporters. His easy-going temperament and cavalier attitude to foreigners made him popular with the British people, but he was frequently the despair of the Queen, and sometimes of his colleagues. He died in office.

Panama Canal. The canal, 40 miles long, links the Atlantic and Pacific Oceans, saving a voyage of over 6,000 miles around South America. Plans to construct a canal were first considered in the sixteenth century, but it was not until 1879 that a start was made by a French company, employing Ferdinand de Lesseps (q.v.) as chief engineer. De Lesseps worked for eight years on the canal, but was hampered by malaria and yellow fever, which killed 22,000 workers. The company was grossly mismanaged and failed in 1889 (see *Panama Scandal*). Improved medical knowledge induced President Theodore Roosevelt (q.v.) to encourage Americans to construct the canal. The U.S. Government made payments to both the Republic of Colombia and the new Republic of Panama (which, with American support, seceded from Colombia in 1903). The Canal Zone, an area of over 500 square miles, was placed under American military government, and American Army engineers, headed by Colonel Goethals, completed the canal, which was opened for traffic on 15 August 1914.

Panama Scandal. The reputation of de Lesseps (q.v.) was so great in France after the construction of the Suez Canal that, when it was known that he had become president of a Panama Canal Company, thousands of small investors hastened to pour their savings into the venture. Financial control of the Company was exercised by Baron de Reinach, Cornelius Herz, and a group of international figures of doubtful probity, many of whom were Jewish. Mismanagement and corruption led the company into bankruptcy (February 1889). Although the Government tried to hush up the scandal, de Lesseps and his associates were put on trial and sentenced to imprisonment in February 1893, although, in fact, none of the leading figures served their terms. The scandal greatly discredited the Radicals (especially Clemenceau, whose newspaper had been financed by Herz) and led to violent anti-semitism in France, the Jews becoming convenient whipping-boys for those who had lost their savings.

Pankhurst, Emmeline (1858–1928). Leader of the British suffragettes (q.v.). Mrs Pankhurst (maiden name, Goulden) was born in Manchester and married Richard Pankhurst, a barrister and advocate of women's rights. In 1889 she formed the Women's Franchise League, but it was not until 1903 (five years after her husband's death) that she was persuaded by her daughter, Christabel, to found the more militant Women's Social and Political Union. After a meeting with the Prime Minister in May 1906, Mrs Pankhurst despaired of securing the vote from a Liberal Government, and began to resort to violent tactics. She was arrested twice in 1908 and 1909. In 1911 she resorted to window-breaking and was again arrested. In prison in 1912, she went on hunger strike and was released, but a campaign of arson in 1913 led her to be sentenced to three years' penal servitude, from which she was released within a year. During the War she helped persuade women to go into industry and the armed services. When women secured the vote in 1918 she left the I.L.P., to which she had belonged since 1892. At the time of her death she was a Conservative candidate for Parliament.

Panslavism. A movement emphasizing Russia's historic mission to liberate the Slav peoples of South-Eastern Europe from the Ottoman and Habsburg Empires and to secure their union under Russian control and protection; at the same time, Constantinople and the

Straits were to be in Russian hands. Panslavism developed out of the older and more definitely religious idea of Slavophilism; it may be dated from the Moscow Slavonic Ethnographic Exhibition of 1867. It was frowned upon by Tsar Alexander II and his foreign ministers, but enthusiastically supported by the ruling class. The principal publicist of the movement was the newspaper-owner Katkov, while its most successful champion was General Paul Ignatiev, ambassador at Constantinople from 1864 to 1877 and chief architect of the abortive Treaty of San Stefano (q.v.), which sought to realize Panslav ambitions. Panslavism died down after the Russian failure to dominate Bulgaria (q.v.) in 1885–6 but it was deliberately revived in a modified form in 1914–15. The movement was always primarily an instrument of Russian nationalism and never stood for union of *all* the Slavs; significantly, it offered nothing to the Poles.

Paris Commune. See *Commune of Paris (1871)*.

Paris, Congress of. An international conference held in Paris in February–March 1856 under the presidency of the French Foreign Minister, Walewski (1810–68, an illegitimate son of Napoleon I), to settle the Eastern Question after the Crimean War. An attempt by Napoleon III to use the Congress for a general revision of European frontiers was frustrated by the British and the Austrians, although Cavour (q.v.) was allowed to make a powerful plea for Italian national rights. The Treaty of Paris was, however, primarily concerned with the Black Sea area; Russia surrendered the mouths of the Danube and part of Bessarabia to the future Rumania (q.v.) and Kars to Turkey; Russia also renounced claims for a religious protectorate over Christians in Turkey; warships and fortifications were prohibited on the Black Sea; the Danubian Principalities (q.v.) were placed under guarantee of the Great Powers, and an international commission was to regulate traffic on the Danube. At the same time, the Congress defined disputed points of international law on the rights of neutrals in war. The most important section of the Treaty, the neutralization of the Black Sea, remained valid only until 1870, when the Russians announced that they no longer considered themselves bound by these clauses and proposed to construct a Black Sea Fleet. (See *Straits Question*.)

Paris Exhibitions. The Second Empire twice used the idea of a major exhibition as a shop window for new industries and a symbol of national prestige. The Paris Exhibition of 1855 proved that the city had recovered from the turbulent unrest of seven years before and was claiming the leadership of European fashion, while the Exhibition of 1867 showed off the rebuilding schemes of Haussmann (q.v.). The Third Republic held three international exhibitions in Paris; in 1878, when the Trocadero was built; in 1889, the Eiffel Tower; and in 1937, the Palais de Chaillot.

Paris Peace Conference. A congress of the 'Allied and Associated Powers' meeting in Paris from 18 January 1919 to 20 January 1920, to determine the Peace Settlement which was embodied in the Treaties (q.v.) of Versailles, St Germain, Neuilly, Trianon, and Sèvres. Until July the Conference was dominated by the 'Big Four' – Wilson (U.S.A.), Clemenceau (France), Lloyd George (Britain), and Orlando (Italy). Decisions were later taken by the 'Council of Heads of Delegations', generally Foreign Ministers; the settlement of the Hungarian and Turkish frontiers was finally left to a Council of Ambassadors. International commissions of experts were despatched from Paris to report on disputed areas.

The work of the Conference was hampered by five main factors: (i) conflict between the objectives of the Big Four (thus Wilson and Clemenceau differed over the League of Nations, Wilson and Orlando over the Adriatic, Lloyd George and Clemenceau over Poland, etc.); (ii) pressure-groups at home urging harsher peace terms (e.g. 370 M.P.s telegraphed Lloyd George to raise the sum of German Reparations; French military circles wished Clemenceau to detach the Rhineland from Germany); (iii) isolationism in the U.S.A. (which eventually led Congress to reject Wilson's undertakings); (iv) impatient nationalist groups which secured regions still under discussion by force of arms (see *Fiume, Teschen, Vilna*); (v) uncertainty over Russia's frontiers because of the Civil War. The Conference, nevertheless, achieved a higher degree of ethnic self-determination than had existed before; it was hoped that weaknesses would be rectified by the League of Nations (q.v.).

Parliament Act, 1911. A measure passed by Asquith's Liberal Government depriving the House of Lords of all power over 'money bills' and restricting it to a suspensive veto on other legislation of two successive sessions. At the same time, the Act altered the duration of a Parliament from the seven years laid down in 1716 to five. A reduction in the power of the Lords had been rendered necessary by the Opposition tactics of using the considerable Conservative majority in the Lords to prevent reforms passed by the elected Liberal majority in the Commons, a device that reached a climax with the rejection of the 1909 'People's Budget' of Lloyd George (q.v.). The Parliament Bill was introduced in May 1910, after a general election had confirmed the Liberals in office. The Lords sought to amend the Bill out of all recognition, Parliament was again dissolved and a second general election won two more seats for the Liberals. The Bill was ultimately passed by the Lords in August 1911, after George V had guaranteed that he would, if necessary, create 250 Liberal peers to ensure its passage.

Parliamentary Reform. In the early nineteenth century the British system of parliamentary representation was full of anomalies. Migration of the population to new industrial regions had created urban areas that were unrepresented, while leaving old constituencies with a mere handful of electors. Besides these 'Rotten Boroughs' there were still 'Pocket Boroughs' where patrons could secure the return of their own nominees. There was no uniform basis for the franchise in the towns, although in the counties most forty-shilling freeholders had the vote. In Scotland and Ireland conditions were even worse than in England and Wales.

When the Whigs came into office in November 1830, their leader, Earl Grey (q.v.), determined to satisfy the growing demand for parliamentary reform. In March 1831 a Reform Bill was unsuccessfully introduced into the Commons by Lord John Russell (q.v.). After a general election, a second Bill passed the Commons (September) but was thrown out by the Lords. Unrest grew in the country, and King William IV offered to create new peers if the Lords continued to reject the measure. The First Reform Act (1832) was accordingly passed by the Lords on 4 June. The Pocket and Rotten Boroughs were abolished; seats were redistributed so as to form constituencies in the new towns; the franchise was extended in the boroughs to all householders rated at £10 or over, and in the counties to £10 copyholders and £50 leaseholders (the forty-shilling freehold qualification being retained as well). Separate Acts were subsequently carried for Scotland and Ireland. The effect of the reform was to enfranchise the upper middle classes.

Further extension of the franchise was delayed until after Russell had succeeded Palmerston as Prime Minister (1865). Russell's proposals were, however, rejected by a group of his own Liberals and it was left to the Conservatives, under Lord Derby and Disraeli, to carry through the Second Reform Act (1867): seats were again redistributed, and a million town labourers were added to the electorate. Gladstone passed the Third Reform Act (1884), extending the franchise to some two million agricultural labourers; a major Redistribution Act (1885) merged the smaller boroughs with the counties and gave additional members to the big cities. After the First World War the Representation of the People Act (1918) gave the vote to all men over the age of twenty-one and all women over the age of thirty; women between the ages of twenty-one and thirty secured the vote in 1928.

Other parliamentary reforms have included the abolition of the necessity for M.P.s to have a property qualification (1858), the Ballot Act (q.v.) of 1872, the Parliament Act of 1911 (q.v.) and the Commons resolution to establish payment of Members (10 August 1911).

Parnell, Charles Stewart (1846–91). Born in County Wicklow, a member of an Anglo-Irish Protestant family, although his mother was the daughter of an American naval officer. Parnell, who was educated at Cambridge, became an M.P. in 1875 and succeeded Isaac Butt as leader of the Home Rule (q.v.) movement two years later. Parnell, a gifted orator, used two methods to focus attention on Irish grievances: the obstruction of the business of the House of Commons; and the organization of defiance among the Irish peasantry, 'boycotting' unpopular landlords. Parnell was arrested in October 1881 for inciting the Irish, but while he was in prison, disorders grew worse, and Gladstone released him. He denounced the Phoenix Park murders (q.v.) and later won a libel action against *The Times* which had maintained, on the evidence of forged letters, that Parnell had secretly connived at the murders. Parnell supported Gladstone's Home Rule Bill and remained a powerful political figure until 1890, when he was named as co-respondent in a divorce suit brought by one of his closest colleagues, Captain O'Shea. Public opinion swung so violently against Parnell that he lost his hold on the Irish Party. In seeking to recover it his health broke down.

Pašić, Nikola (1845–1926). Chief minister of Serbia 1891, 1904–8, 1910–18, and of Yugoslavia 1921–6. He was also head of the delegation of Serbs, Croats, and Slovenes to the Paris Peace Conference of 1919. Pašić was largely responsible for the establishment of the Karadjordjević dynasty on the throne of Serbia (q.v.) in 1903 and for Serbia's political success in the Balkan Wars (q.v.). He was, however, too moderate for the Serbian militarists who formed a secret society, the so-called 'Black Hand' (q.v.), which he was forced to dissolve in 1917. Pašić was always at heart a Serb rather than a Yugoslav, and although he had concluded the Pact of Corfu (q.v.), with the South Slav exiles on an equal footing, he tended to treat the Yugoslav State created in 1918 as a mere territorial extension of Serbia, an attitude that was to prove disastrous for the well-being of the new Kingdom.

Pasteur, Louis (1822–95). French chemist and biologist. Born in a small town in the Jura and educated at the École Normale in Paris. He became Professor of Chemistry at Strasbourg in 1849 and Director of Studies at the École Normale in 1857, retaining the post for the rest of his active life. Pasteur's most dramatic scientific discovery was the virus of rabies (1881), which enabled him to introduce inoculation against hydrophobia (1885). His researches were concerned not only with the use of inoculation as a cure and a safeguard against many diseases, but also with the introduction of antiseptic methods into surgery. In 1888 the Institut Pasteur was established in his honour, as a Paris centre of medical research. His name is commemorated in the process, on which he concentrated much of his later research, by which bacterial action in liquids is countered by heat treatment. Unlike most of the French scientists of his generation, he was a pious Catholic, with reactionary political leanings.

Paul, Tsar of Russia (born 1754, Tsar 1796–1801). Son and successor of Catherine the Great, was mentally unstable. In foreign affairs, Russia entered the War of the Second Coalition (1798–9), but the Tsar insisted on changing to the side of France in 1800. In home affairs, he was responsible for the first clear law of succession to the Russian throne (through the male line) and in 1797 issued a decree limiting the serf to three days' work for his master each week, provided the work was agricultural. Paul was murdered on 24 March 1801 in a palace revolution. He was succeeded by Alexander I (q.v.).

Pearl Harbor. Main U.S. naval base in Hawaii. Although there had been no declaration of war, Japanese carrier-borne aircraft attacked Pearl Harbor early on Sunday 7 December 1941. Within less than two hours, the Japanese had sunk or disabled 19 ships (including 5 battleships), destroyed 120 aircraft, and killed 2,400 people. The Japanese force had gathered in the Kurile Islands and had put to sea on 26 November. Diplomatic negotiations between the U.S.A. and Japan were still going on when news of the Japanese attack reached Washington. Congress declared war on Japan on 8 December; Germany and Italy, Japan's allies, declared war on the U.S.A. on 11 December. The American naval losses at Pearl Harbor gave an initial advantage to Japanese sea-power.

Peel, Robert (1788–1850, succeeded to baronetcy 1830). Born near Bury, the son of a Lancashire cotton manufacturer with enlightened ideas, had a brilliant academic record at Harrow and Christ Church, and became a Tory M.P. at the age of twenty-one. He held junior office under Lord Liverpool in 1812 and entered Liverpool's Cabinet as Home Secretary in 1822, achieving a number of reforms in the prisons. He was again Home Secretary from 1828 to 1830 and it was in this period that he founded the Metropolitan Police. In 1829 he piloted the Catholic Emancipation Act (q.v.) through the Commons, although it represented for him a major change in principles. He established a new conservatism among the Tories by his 'Tamworth Manifesto' of 1834, an address to his constituents in which he accepted the fundamental reforms carried out by the Whigs under Grey and Melbourne. He was Prime Minister for four months in 1834–5 and from 1841 to 1846 headed a Conservative Government, originally pledged to maintain the Corn Laws (q.v.) but marked from the first by a series of Free-Trade budgets. The Irish Famine finally won Peel's support for abolition of the Corn Laws, a change of heart which split his party. The rebels, led by Disraeli (q.v.), secured the fall of the Government over an Irish Coercion Bill in June 1846, three weeks after the Corn Laws had been repealed. The Peel Government had carried through some enduring financial reforms, including the Bank Charter Act of 1844, which checked the growth of small banking houses and secured the note-issuing monopoly of the Bank of England.

Peninsular War (1809–14). In 1808 the British Government decided to send an army to the Iberian Peninsula in order to encourage Portuguese and Spanish resistance to Napoleon. Sir Arthur Wellesley (later Duke of Wellington, q.v.) landed at Lisbon in July 1808 and defeated Junot at Vimeiro but was subsequently induced to conclude the Convention of Cintra, by which French troops were able to evacuate Portugal unmolested. Sir John Moore replaced Wellesley in command and, although outnumbered ten to one, harried Napoleon's communications until killed in evacuating his men from Corunna (January 1809). Three months later Wellesley led the force back to Lisbon, defeated the French at Talavera in July, and then fell back to the lines of Torres Vedras, behind which he remained entrenched for two years, emerging to besiege the fortresses on the Spanish-Portuguese frontier (1811) and advance into Spain, heading for the Pyrenees. The French, under Soult, were defeated at Salamanca (July 1812) and Vittoria (June 1813) and entirely driven out of Spain, being finally broken at Toulouse (April

1814). Many European writers consider that British historians have overrated the importance of the Peninsular War among the causes of Napoleon's downfall. It should, however, be remembered that Wellington's Army kept a quarter of a million Frenchmen tied down in the Peninsula.

Perceval, Spencer (1762–1812). British Prime Minister. Perceval was educated at Harrow and Trinity, Cambridge, and became a Tory M.P. in 1796. After holding legal office in the Addington Government (1803–4), he became Chancellor of the Exchequer under Portland (1807), whom he succeeded as Prime Minister in 1809. He remained Chancellor in his own administration, which continued the war against Napoleon without conspicuous success or failure. Perceval was shot dead in the lobby of the Commons (11 May 1812) by John Bellingham, a bankrupt with a grievance against the Government.

Persia. Throughout the nineteenth century Persia remained a backward country exploited by the two rivals, Britain and Russia. There was a temporary improvement in conditions early in the twentieth century: a Revolution in December 1905 secured the first liberal constitution; and the Anglo-Russian Entente (q.v.) of 1907 eased friction between the two countries. During the First World War Persia's neutrality was violated by British, Russian, and Turkish troops, while a German agent, Wassmuss, organized raids by Persian irregulars on the British. The modernization of Persia dates from the *coup d'état* in February 1921 of an army officer Reza Khan (1878–1944), who reigned as Reza Shah Pahlavi from 1925 to 1941. He built up the Army and developed roads and railways. From the autumn of 1941 until 1946 Persia was occupied by British and Russian troops, which had moved in to expel German intriguers (and induced the Shah's abdication). His son, Mohammed Shah Pahlavi (born 1919), was forced to leave the country during anti-British demonstrations in 1951 (caused by the attempt of Dr Mossadeq to nationalize the Anglo-Iranian Oil Company), but returned to arrest Mossadeq and settle disputes with the British in a new agreement, 1954.

Pétain, Henri Philippe (1856–1951, Marshal of France 1918–45). A member of a peasant family from the Pas-de-Calais. He entered the military college of St Cyr in 1876 and followed an orthodox military career, teaching at the École de Guerre from 1906, becoming a Colonel in 1912 and being in command of an Army Corps in 1914.

His indomitable tenacity in defending Verdun throughout 1916 won him universal esteem and when mutinies broke out in the French Army in May 1917 he was made Commander-in-Chief with the immediate task of raising morale. He held this appointment until the end of the war, although from April 1918 he was subordinated to Foch (q.v), who had been made supreme Allied Generalissimo. In 1925–6 he commanded a Franco-Spanish force which defeated the Riffs in Morocco (q.v.), and in 1929 he became Inspector-General of the Army. He was Minister of War in the Doumergue Government of 1934. Pétain was sent as Ambassador to Spain in 1939 and brought back as Prime Minister on 16 June 1940, concluding an armistice with Germany six days later. On 10 July at Vichy (q.v.) he secured from the National Assembly the right to govern France by authoritarian methods, which he hoped would purge the country of 'moral decadence'. For two years he sought to put his ideas into practice as 'Head of State' in unoccupied France, but, after German troops overran the whole of France in November 1942, he became little more than a German puppet. In 1944 he was forced to accompany the Germans back across the Rhine. He was tried for treason by the French High Court of Justice in July 1945. He was sentenced to death, but this was commuted to life imprisonment.

'Peterloo'. Name given in derision to the action of local magistrates in using the yeomanry to arrest a radical speaker, Henry Hunt (1773–1835), when he was addressing an orderly crowd of some 80,000 people at a political reform meeting in St Peter's Fields, Manchester, on 16 August 1819. The yeomanry subsequently attempted to seize 'revolutionary' banners carried by the crowd. Cavalry were sent into the ensuing mêlée; eleven people were killed and four hundred injured. Peterloo was the worst incident of repression by the authorities during the period of unrest following the Napoleonic Wars. Hunt was sentenced to two years' imprisonment; the Manchester magistrates received a letter of congratulation from the Home Secretary, Viscount Sidmouth.

Philippines. A group of islands in the Far East. Ceded to the U.S.A. by Spain after the Spanish-American War of 1898 (q.v.). The Filipinos, led by Emilio Aguinaldo, conducted a guerilla war against the Americans and in favour of independence from February 1899 to April 1902. In July 1902 the Philippines were given a representative assembly. Demands for full independence were continued by the Filipinos, and the U.S. administrations prepared several plans for the gradual devolution of authority. In 1935 a Philippine Commonwealth was established, the islands enjoying a considerable measure of home rule, with an elected president. Further progress was impeded by the Second World War. The Japanese invaded the Philippines in December 1941, capturing the capital, Manila, on 2 January. United States and Filipino troops, under General MacArthur, held out at Corregidor in Manila Bay until May 1942. In 1943 Roosevelt announced that the U.S.A. would grant the Philippines independence as soon as the Japanese were ejected. The Republic of the Philippines was accordingly officially established on 4 July 1946, the U.S. authorities retaining certain naval and military bases.

Phoenix Park Murders (6 May 1882). An attack on Thomas Burke, the permanent under-secretary for Ireland, and Lord Frederick Cavendish, the newly appointed chief secretary, by a gang of Irish extremists, the 'Invincibles'. Both men were hacked to pieces with surgical knives. Eleven months later nine of the 'Invincibles' were brought to trial, five of them being hanged. The murders occurred during a period of collaboration between Gladstone and Parnell (q.v.), and, although Parnell denounced the assassins, the crime hardened English opinion against the Irish. The Government passed a severe Prevention of Crimes Act (valid for three years) which abolished trial by jury and gave the police exceptional powers of arrest.

Piedmont-Sardinia, Kingdom of. United under the House of Savoy by the Treaty of Aix-la-Chapelle in 1748. Although overthrown by Bonaparte in 1798, it was reconstituted in 1814. In 1821 Piedmontese liberals tried in vain to secure constitutional government; this was at last granted by King Charles Albert (reigned 1831–49) in March 1848. His attempt to free Lombardy from Austrian rule ended disastrously in the defeats of Custozza and Novara and he was forced to abdicate. His son, Victor Emmanuel III (q.v.) appointed Cavour (q.v.) as Prime Minister in 1852 and, although forced to cede Savoy itself and Nice, as territorial compensation to Napoleon III, was able to merge Piedmont in a united Kingdom of Italy (March 1861), retaining his capital at Turin until 1865.

Pilsudski, Jozef (1867–1935). Polish soldier and statesman. Born near Vilna, which was then in Russian Poland. At the University of Kharkov he began to read subversive literature, and in 1887 was arrested for socialist agitation and sent to Siberia for five years. In 1894 he became editor of the clandestine Polish socialist newspaper, *Robotnik*, in which he put forward strongly nationalistic views. In 1904 he went to Tokio to try and enlist Japanese help for the Polish revolt during the Russo-Japanese War. In 1914 the Austrian Government authorized him to lead a Polish Legion against the Russians, and he recruited a force of 10,000 men. In 1917 Pilsudski was interned by the Germans, who distrusted Austrian patronage of the Polish cause. On his release he went straight to Warsaw, where the acting government gave him command of all Polish Armies and made him provisional Head of State. He led the Polish Army against the Bolsheviks in 1919–20, and remained the dominant figure in Poland until the end of 1921, continuing as head of the Army until May 1923. He retired from political life for three years, but, exasperated by the instability of the democratic governments, he staged a military *coup* in May 1926 and from that date until his death nine years later was dictator of Poland in all but name, acting as Prime Minister from 1926 to 1928 and for a brief period in 1930, and remaining Minister of War throughout the period. He was one of the first statesmen to perceive the danger to Europe of a Nazi Germany. After vainly seeking to arouse his French ally, he authorized the conclusion of a Non-Aggression Pact with Germany (1934).

Pitt, William (1759–1806). Younger son of the Earl of Chatham (1708–1778). Called to the bar in 1780, became an M.P. in 1781, and Chancellor of the Exchequer in 1782, under Shelburne. With the fall of the Fox–North Coalition in the following year, Pitt became Prime Minister of a minority government, but gained a substantial majority at the election of 1784 and held office until 1801, eventually resigning because of George III's unwillingness to grant Catholic Emancipation. Pitt carried through basic changes in the tariff and financial systems; he was a strong believer in the *laissez-faire* doctrines of Adam Smith. He also repealed a number of penal laws against Roman Catholics, improved criminal administration, supported Wilberforce (q.v.) in his measures against slavery, remodelled the administrative machinery of government in India (1784) and Canada (1791), and prepared a measure of parliamentary reform. After the outbreak of war with revolutionary France in 1793, he tended to concentrate on overseas expeditions, to the neglect of the European theatre of war. He also introduced a number of repressive measures at home – a Traitorous Correspondence Act in 1783, the suspension of Habeas Corpus in 1794, the Seditious Meetings Act of 1799. Fearing Irish unrest after the rebellion of 1798, he persuaded the Irish Parliament to vote its own dissolution (see *Act of Union*, 1800). In his Second Ministry, from 1804 to 1806, Pitt negotiated the alliance with Russia and Austria that made possible the War of the Third Coalition. His health was already broken; he lived long enough to see the menace of a French invasion removed and to learn of the victory of Trafalgar, but the news of Napoleon's success at Austerlitz and the consequent collapse of the Alliance destroyed his will to live. He died on 23 January 1806, just four weeks after Austria (by the Treaty of Pressburg) had left the war.

Pius IX, Pope ('Pio Nono'; born Giovanni Mastai-Ferretti, 1792; pontiff, 1846–78). As a Cardinal he acquired an exaggerated reputation as a 'Progressive' and was believed, on his election, to be the 'Liberal Pope' for whom some Italian patriots, notably Gioberti (q.v.), had hoped. In 1848, rather than compromise the universal position of the papacy, Pius refused to participate in any war against Austria. On 25 November 1848, alarmed by 'Jacobin' clubs in Rome, he fled to Gaeta in the Kingdom of Naples and did not return until restored with French military help in April 1850. For twenty years his position was safeguarded by a French garrison. Although early in 1848 Pius had granted a constitution, this was not restored in the 1850s, and a reactionary policy was pursued by his Secretary of State, Cardinal Antonelli (1806–76). Pius re-established a Catholic hierarchy in Britain (1850) and Holland (1853) and made advantageous concordats with Spain (1851) and Austria (1855). Seeing his territorial possessions menaced by Italian nationalism, he tried to strengthen his spiritual position and in 1854 promulgated the first new dogma since the Counter Reformation (the 'Immaculate Conception'). In 1864 he published the *Syllabus Errorum*, criticizing contemporary liberal-radical beliefs. From December 1869 to October 1870, a Vatican Council (the first general assembly of the Roman Church for three hundred years) met in Rome and published the Vatican Decrees (q.v.). These included the Declaration of Papal Infallibility, a dogma that aroused the opposition of some governments, especially in Germany (the Kulturkampf, q.v.) and Austria, which denounced the Concordat of 1855. In September 1870 Italian troops entered Rome; for the last eight years of his pontificate the Pope regarded himself as a prisoner in his own palace of the Vatican.

Place, Francis (1771–1854). English radical. Place was born in London and became a journeyman but was unable to get work because as early as 1793 he had organized a strike. He then became a tailor but, beneath his shop in the Charing Cross Road, he kept a radical library, and this centre became a meeting-place for reformers in the period following the Napoleonic Wars. He led campaigns against the Sinking Fund and the Combination Laws (q.v.), securing their repeal in 1824 with the parliamentary help of Joseph Hume (1777–1855).

Although Place never entered Parliament, he played a considerable part in formulating the demands of the 'Political Unions' for parliamentary reform in 1832. He also helped draft the 'People's Charter' (see *Chartism*).

Plate, Battle of the River (13 December 1939). The first major naval engagement of the Second World War. The German pocket battleship *Graf Spee* encountered a cruiser squadron under Commodore Harwood (H.M.S. *Exeter*, H.M.S. *Ajax,* H.M.N.Z.S. *Achilles*) while commerce-raiding in the South Atlantic. Although inflicting heavy damage on *Exeter*, the *Graf Spee* was forced into Montevideo for repairs. While she was there, a considerable force gathered in the Plate Estuary but, rather than risk renewal of the battle, the *Graf Spee* was scuttled on Hitler's orders (17 December).

Plombières Agreement (July 1858). At a secret meeting at Plombières in the Vosges between Napoleon III (q.v.) and Cavour (q.v.), it was agreed that France would assist Piedmont in a war against Austria, provided the Austrians could be provoked to appear the aggressor. The terms of the agreement (which was not formally put on paper until later in the year) provided for Piedmont to expand into a 'Kingdom of Upper Italy', including Lombardy-Venetia and the northern duchies; there were to be separate kingdoms of Central Italy and of Naples; the territorial power of the papacy was to be limited to Rome. France was to be compensated by cession of Savoy and Nice, and by a marriage link between the Bonapartes and the Piedmontese Royal House. The resultant war lasted from April to July 1859. After the heavy casualties of the battles of Magenta (q.v.) and Solferino (q.v.), Napoleon prematurely made peace, and the settlement planned at Plombières was not fully carried out.

Pobedonostsev, Konstantin Petrovich (1827–1907). Professor of Constitutional Law at Moscow University 1860–5, where he tutored the sons of Alexander II. In 1880 he was appointed Procurator of the Holy Synod (the lay director of the Russian Orthodox Church), a post which gave him considerable influence until his resignation in 1905. He firmly believed that western institutions could not be grafted on to the traditions of Russian life. Autocracy was the only possible basis of government for Russia; parliaments, he said, are 'the great lie of our time'. Pobedonostsev's views profoundly affected the political outlook of Alexander III (q.v.) and Nicholas II (q.v.); he was responsible for encouraging Russian ill-treatment of other nationalities in the empire. By his policy, he convinced the growing revolutionary movement that Tsarist autocracy and religious Orthodoxy were inseparably linked and must fall together.

Poincaré, Raymond (1860–1934). French statesman; a member of an upper middle-class family from Lorraine, called to the Paris Bar in 1880 and elected a Deputy in 1887. A moderate anti-clerical, he became Education Minister in 1893, but returned to the back benches two years later and concentrated on his work as a commercial lawyer. He was appointed a Senator in 1903 and served as Finance Minister for a few months in 1906. In 1912 he headed a right-wing Coalition Government which was preoccupied with electoral reform and raising France's international prestige. Poincaré himself visited Russia so as to strengthen the Dual Alliance. He rapidly became so popular in France that he was elected President in February 1913. During his seven years' office he intervened in politics more than any of his predecessors since Macmahon (q.v.). His State Visit to St Petersburg in July 1914 facilitated the subsequent military cooperation of the two allies. In January 1922 he was again Prime Minister, the first ex-president to lead a Government; taking charge of foreign affairs himself, he pursued an ardently nationalistic policy, including the occupation of the Ruhr (q.v.). His Cabinet broke up in January 1924, but from July 1926 to July 1929 he headed a 'Government of National Union' which carried through stringent financial economies and secured the stabilization of the franc.

Polish Partitions. In the eighteenth century Poland was a weak kingdom with an elective monarchy. In 1772 Frederick the Great of Prussia proposed the acquisition of some of the Polish lands by her three powerful neighbours. The First Partition (August 1772) accordingly divided one third of Poland between Russia, Prussia, and Austria. The Second Partition (January 1793) was mostly to the advantage of Russia, the Austrians on this occasion not acquiring any lands. In 1794 a Polish Rising under Kosciuszko (q.v.) led to the occupation of the rest of Poland, which was divided between the three autocracies in the Third Partition (October 1795). After the defeat of Napoleon and the collapse of his puppet state the Grand Duchy of Warsaw (1807–14), there was a Fourth Partition (1815) by which the Russians extended their region westwards, thereby including Warsaw (which had been in Prussian Poland from 1795 to 1807). Hostility to Polish nationalism formed a common bond between the Russian, Prussian, and Austrian Governments throughout the nineteenth century, especially effective during the two great Polish Revolts against Russia (1830 and 1863). An independent Poland was reconstituted in 1918. In September 1939 the Polish Army was defeated by the Germans, who, by permitting the Russians to advance as far as Brest-Litovsk, carried through a Fifth Partition.

Poor Law. Legislation governing the public relief of poverty and destitution. The Elizabethan Poor Law of 1601 had imposed the obligation of providing assistance on the parish; this method was retained by the Speenhamland System (q.v.) of 1785. In 1834 the Poor Law Report (which is always associated with Edwin Chadwick, q.v.) proposed to transfer the burden of relief to boards of guardians representing a 'union' of parishes and elected by the ratepayers. No able-bodied man would receive assistance unless he entered a workhouse; the workhouses themselves were to be, in Chadwick's words, 'uninviting places of wholesome restraint'. These proposals were embodied in the Poor Law Amendment Act of 1834, which also established a Central Poor Law Department to ensure uniformity. The Act, a reflection of the current belief in the virtues of hard work, aroused considerable resentment, notably in the northern counties. The workhouses proved a social disgrace, especially for the aged and the young. Conditions began to improve when a Minister assumed responsibility for the Poor Law Board in 1847, an obligation passed on to the Local Government Board in 1871. The system of elected guardians persisted until 1929, despite an adverse report by a Royal Commission in 1909. In 1929 a Local Government Act made county or borough councils establish public assistance committees to supervise relief.

Popular Front. A coalition of left-wing and centre parties in opposition to fascism. The best-known Popular Front Governments were in France under Léon Blum (q.v.) from June 1936 to June 1937, continuing under Chautemps until January 1938, revived by Blum in March and April 1938, and led by Daladier until October 1938. The Popular Front Governments sought to carry out an extensive programme of social reform, while suppressing fascist groups. They were opposed by the conservatively minded Senate and eventually broke up because the socialists and communists distrusted Daladier after the Munich Agreement (q.v.). There was also a Popular Front Government in Spain under Manuel Azana, Largo Caballero, and Juan Negrin from February 1936 to March 1939. It was against this Government that Franco waged the Spanish Civil War (q.v.).

Populists. A general name given to groups of revolutionaries in Russia in the period 1870–81. The first group, Narodniki (q.v.), tried in vain to spread revolutionary socialist ideas among the peasantry, who formed the largest social class in European Russia. In 1877, when many Narodniki were arrested, the Populists organized a terroristic society, 'Land and Liberty', which carried out a number of assassinations. In 1880 this was replaced by two secret organizations, 'Black Partition' (which favoured peaceful propaganda in the earlier Populist tradition) and 'The People's Will', which was responsible for the murder of Alexander II in 1881. The Populists revived among the exiles of the 1890s and organized themselves as a distinctive political party, the Social Revolutionaries, in 1902; they continued to emphasize the prime importance to Russia of the peasant problem and, on this point, disagreed with Lenin (q.v.) and the Bolsheviks (q.v.), who looked for the revolutionary élite among the industrial workers.

Port Arthur (Lushunkow). Chinese seaport on the Liaotung Peninsula. In an important strategic position, commanding the Gulf of Pechili and the approaches to Peking. The Japanese captured Port Arthur from the Chinese in November 1894, but were forced by the European Great Powers to return it to China in the following spring. In December 1897 the Russians secured Chinese permission to winter their Far Eastern Fleet in Port Arthur, which in contrast to the fleet base of Vladivostok remained ice-free. In March 1898 the Chinese gave Russia a 25-year lease of the Liaotung Peninsula, including the harbours of Port Arthur and Talienwan. The Japanese made a surprise attack on Russian warships in Port Arthur (February 1904), and proceeded to occupy the neck of the peninsula, forcing the town to surrender in January 1905 after a gruelling siege. The lease of Port Arthur was transferred to Japan by the Treaty of Portsmouth (q.v.) of September 1905, and in 1915 the Japanese secured a further 99-year lease from China. The Russians returned with the Japanese surrender of 1945, and it was not until 1955 that Port Arthur was handed back to China.

Porte, The Sublime. An accepted title for the Government of the Ottoman Empire in Constantinople (i.e. as 'The Court of St James' for London). The Sublime Porte appears to have been a high gate in the wall of the main governmental building.

Portsmouth (New Hampshire), Treaty of (September 1905). Ended the Russo-Japanese War (q.v.). The Russians acknowledged Japanese predominance in Korea, transferred to Japan the lease of Port Arthur (q.v.) and the Liaotung Peninsula with its railway, and ceded the southern half of Sakhalin. Both countries agreed to evacuate Man-churia (q.v.) and restore it to China. The Treaty marked the end of Tsarist Russian expansion in the Far East. It was unpopular in Japan because it did not include a war indemnity. The signing of the Treaty in America confirmed the emergence of the U.S.A. as a world power, and was a tribute to Theodore Roosevelt's (q.v.) attempts at arbitra-tion.

Portuguese Republic. Proclaimed on 5 October 1910, after a three-day insurrection in Lisbon had forced King Manuel II to flee to Britain. Republican sentiment sprang from resentment at the ex-travagance shown by the monarchy in the previous half-century, from acute poverty among the workers, and from hostility to the reactionary policy of the Church. The new régime carried through a number of anti-clerical measures and adopted a liberal constitution, but it was not able to improve conditions among the workers and relied upon military rule to prevent violence. In the early 1920s the democratic government became notorious for its corruption and in-efficiency; Portugal remained a poor and backward country with a high rate of illiteracy. A military dictatorship was established in 1926. In April 1928 Antonio de Oliviera Salazar (born 1889) was ap-pointed Minister of Finance, becoming dictator of the country in 1932, a position confirmed by the adoption in 1933 of a fascist con-stitution, which, with amendments, has survived the Second World War.

Prairial. The period between 20 May and 18 June in the French revolutionary calendar. The Law of 22 Prairial (10 June 1794) was a decree giving arbitrary powers of arrest, condemnation, and execu-tion to the Revolutionary Tribunal of the Jacobin dictatorship. It remained valid only until the fall of Robespierre at Thermidor (q.v.) seven weeks later.

Prayer Book Revision. In the early twentieth century controversy over ritualistic details produced a demand in the Church of England for a revision of the Book of Common Prayer, the official service book which had been virtually unchanged since 1662. A Royal Com-mission on Ecclesiastical Discipline was appointed in 1904, with Sir Michael Hicks Beach as Chairman, and two years later issued a report in favour of Prayer Book revision. For more than twenty years revision was discussed by a group of bishops appointed by the Con-vocations of Canterbury and York, the Provincial Assemblies of the Anglican Church. In 1927 the final form of the Prayer Book, a compromise between medieval practice and modern sentiments, was passed by large majorities in the Convocations and in the Church Assembly, but was rejected by the House of Commons (238 votes to 205). In 1928 a modified book, which met some of the objections, was again passed by the Convocations and the Church Assembly, but still failed to get through the Commons, this time by 46 votes. The rejection of the Revised Prayer Book, by men who were for the most part not practising members of the Church of England, raised doubts in the minds of many Anglicans on the wisdom of maintaining an Established Church under modern conditions. No subsequent attempt was made by the Church to gain parliamentary sanction for the Revised Prayer Book; it is in use in many parishes without formal authority apart from the consent of the diocesan bishop.

Pretoria, Convention of (1881). Concluded by the Gladstone Government after the first of the Boer Wars (q.v.). The Transvaal was accorded self-government under British suzerainty, a restriction removed by a subsequent convention, signed in London in 1884.

Primo de Rivera, Miguel (1870–1930). Spanish dictator. The son of a Governor-General of the Philippines, was commissioned into the Army (1888) and fought in Morocco and in defence of the Philippines. He was made a Major General in 1910. The growth of anarchism and of a movement for Catalan autonomy weakened the position of the Spanish Monarchy, the prestige of which sank even lower with the killing of 12,000 Spanish troops by Riffs at Anual, Morocco, in 1921. With the approval of King Alfonso XIII Primo de Rivera seized power on 13 September 1923. The Spanish Parliament was dissolved, trial by jury suspended, the press censored, the leading democrats imprisoned, and the country placed under martial law. The dictatorship lasted until December 1925. Primo de Rivera endeavoured to set up a full fascist régime, urging the Spanish people to be loyal to 'Country, Religion, and Monarchy', but was faced with increasing discontent among the students and workers. He remained Prime Minister even after the end of the dictatorship, but was forced to resign in January 1930 and died two months later. His failure led to the downfall in April 1931 of the Spanish Monarchy, the republican politicians being able to accuse King Alfonso of having imposed a dictator on the country.

Prince Consort (Albert of Saxe-Coburg-Gotha, 1819–61). Married his first cousin, Queen Victoria, in 1840. He became her chief adviser, particularly on foreign politics, but the Queen was careful to preserve her constitutional rights. The Queen wished her husband to be known as the 'King Consort', but this idea provoked opposition, and it was not until 1857 that, as a compromise, he was given the title 'Prince Consort' by royal letters patent. The Prince's attempts to understand the British political and economic system were regarded by some of the Queen's Ministers as interference, and he was never a popular figure. He was genuinely interested in industry and agriculture as well as in music and art; the Great Exhibition (q.v.) of 1851 was largely his creation. He was extremely conscientious, and his work undermined his strength; he died from typhoid fever. The Queen remained fixed in the ways that he had determined.

Prohibition. The 'Prohibition Era' in the U.S.A. covers the period from January 1920 to December 1933, during which time the 18th Amendment to the Constitution (prohibiting the manufacture, sale, or carriage of alcoholic drinks) was valid. Temperance societies had urged Prohibition on state legislatures for over eighty years and had succeeded in securing restrictions in 19 states, the first of them, Maine, as early as 1845. A national agitation was started by the Anti-Saloon League in 1895, but did not receive wide backing until the war, when it declared the consumption of alcohol as unpatriotic because of the predominance of German-born citizens in the drink trade. During the 1920s there was considerable evasion of the Prohibition Law; the distilling and distribution of illicit drink ('bootlegging') fell under the control of criminal groups and led to a rapid rise in gang warfare, particularly in Chicago. Repeal of Prohibition accordingly became a plank in Roosevelt's Democratic Platform for the Presidential Election of 1932. National Prohibition was abolished by the 21st Amendment (proposed 20 February 1933, ratified 5 December); local Prohibition continued in certain states.

Provisional Government (of Russia). The liberal régime established on 12 March 1917, on the eve of the Tsar's abdication, and remaining in power until the Bolshevik rising of 6 November. The Provisional Government favoured the continued prosecution of the war against Germany and the establishment within Russia of republican democracy. It was hampered by conflict with the Bolshevik-controlled Petrograd Soviet. The Provisional Government was headed by Prince Lvov until 20 July, when he was succeeded by Kerensky (q.v.). (See also *Russian Revolution*.)

Quadrilateral. The Quadrilateral was the name given to the four Austrian fortresses of Peschiera, Verona, Mantua, and Legnago in

Lombardy-Venetia. The towns were converted into fortresses by Marshal Radetzky (q.v.), who successfully held all of them, except Peschiera, against the Piedmontese in 1848. Marshal Gyulai also used the Quadrilateral as his basic defence-line against the French and Piedmontese in 1859.

Quatre Bras, Battle of (16 June 1815). A fierce preliminary action to the battle of Waterloo (q.v.). Marshal Ney was ordered by Napoleon to halt Wellington's troops at Quatre Bras, while Napoleon himself disposed of the Prussians at Ligny, eight miles away. Although Napoleon defeated the Prussians, strong resistance from Wellington (and confusion over orders) prevented Ney from sending reinforcements that would have made the defeat decisive.

Quisling, Vidkun (1887–1945). Norwegian traitor. After serving as Norwegian Minister of War 1931–3, Quisling built up a Norwegian Nazi Party and established contact with Germany through the Naval Attaché in Oslo. In December 1939 Quisling went to Berlin and suggested to Hitler methods by which, with German aid, a Nazi Government might be established in Oslo. When in April 1940 the Germans occupied Norway, Quisling came forward as the administrator of a puppet pro-German 'government'. He continued to serve the Germans in this way until the liberation of Norway in 1945, when he was tried and executed. His name has become an eponym for any leader of an enemy-sponsored régime.

Radetzky, Josef (1766–1858). Austrian soldier. Radetzky first saw service against the Turks in 1788–9. He fought against the French in all the major campaigns of the Austrians during the Napoleonic wars, becoming Chief of Staff after the defeat of Wagram in 1809. He was ignored during the immediate post-war years but became Commander-in-Chief in Lombardy in 1831. In 1848 he was faced by the insurrection in Milan and was forced to withdraw his armies to the 'Quadrilateral' (q.v.). On 25 July 1848 he defeated the Piedmontese at Custozza, gaining a second victory at Novara on 23 March 1849, and recovering Venice (q.v.) in the following August. He remained as Governor-General of Lombardy-Venetia until 1857. Radetzky was a well-loved figure among his troops.

Radicals. In British politics a generic term for the members of various associations that desired thoroughgoing reform. There have been six main phases of British radical activity: (i) the agitation for political reform of 1790–4, carried out by such organizations as

The Friends of the People and The London Corresponding Society; (ii) a similar agitation, more militant in character, from 1815 to 1832, beginning with the middle-class Hampden Clubs (of which the first was formed in 1811 under the chairmanship of Sir Francis Burdett), being continued by popular orators such as Henry Hunt (see *Peterloo*) and Cobbett (q.v.), revived by Attwood (q.v.) in 1830 and gaining an illusory triumph with the First Reform Act; (iii) the decade of Chartism (q.v.); (iv) the 'advanced liberalism' of Cobden (q.v.) and Bright (q.v.) in the middle of the century; (v) the 'Birmingham radicalism' of Joseph Chamberlain (q.v.); (vi) the social reforms of Lloyd George (q.v.) between 1905 and 1912. Subsequently the radical tradition was grafted on to a wing of the Labour Party.

The term 'Radical' has also been used as a general term in the continental countries and the Americas. Unlike Britain, some states have a specific Radical Party, the most famous of which was the French Radical Party. It was organized in 1875 and dedicated to individualism. Much of its programme was fundamentally negative; it was hostile to the Church, to political authoritarianism, and to economic collectivization (whether through capitalist combines or socialist nationalization). This was the Party of, among others, Clemenceau, Combes, Herriot, and Caillaux; it was in power from 1898 to 1912 and from 1924 to 1926. The Party suffered from internal feuds and by the late 1930s had evolved, under Daladier, into a moderate middle-class centre group, a position it maintained throughout the Fourth Republic as well.

Railway Boom. When the Liverpool–Manchester Railway, which had been opened in 1830, began to make a large profit, Britain was swept by a fever of railway speculation. The most famous railway promoter was George Hudson of York, the 'Railway King', who made and lost a fortune in the north-east of England between 1836 and 1849. Investment in railways was at its highest between 1835 and 1837 and again from 1845 to 1847. Many of the lines were constructed between unsuitable places; others failed through unprofitable competition with rivals where one line on its own might have proved a financial success. The boom lasted until 1847; when it collapsed, it ruined thousands of small investors. A similar boom along the eastern seaboard of the U.S.A. in the mid-thirties was followed by a swift collapse. In France, too, several railway companies failed in 1847. As a result of this experience, many countries realized the necessity for constructing a railway system according to some general governmental plan. Such was the hold of *laissez-faire* principles on early Victorian society that this idea was rejected out of hand in Britain, although favoured by the report of a Royal Commission.

Ranke, Leopold von (1795–1886). German historian. Born in Thuringia and devoted his life to historical studies. In 1824 he published his *History of the Roman and German Peoples, 1494–1514,* in the preface to which he made the famous claim that the task of the historian was to 'narrate events as they had actually happened'. As Professor of History in Berlin from 1825 until 1872 Ranke sought to put his dictum into practice. He was virtually the founder of the science of historical evidence, a technique which imposed a discipline on the writing of history throughout Europe. In insisting that the historian must approach a subject free from presuppositions, Ranke was claiming for historical writing a new objectivity. His own output was prodigious his collected works fill 54 volumes – but his breadth of interest saved him from the besetting sin of some of his disciples, over-concentration on a narrow period of time. He had the advantage of access to archives never before opened for critical inspection, notably in the Italian states and in Rome. His greatest work was probably the study of the Popes of the sixteenth and seventeenth centuries, published between 1834 and 1837.

Rapallo, Treaties of. There were two treaties of Rapallo, signed within a short period of each other but between different states and entirely unconnected: (i) Italy and Yugoslavia, 12 November 1920, a temporary settlement of Adriatic disputes and a pledge of common action to maintain the peace treaties and prevent a Habsburg restoration; (ii) Germany and Soviet Russia, 16 April 1922, the re-establishment of diplomatic relations, a renunciation of financial claims on each side, and a pledge of economic cooperation. The Russo-German Treaty, unexpectedly concluded by delegates to the World Economic Conference at Genoa, was of great significance; it demonstrated the recovery of both states from the diplomatic isolation caused by revolution and defeat, and was both a challenge and a portent for the British and French.

Rasputin, Gregori (1871–1916). Russian peasant mystic monk who was an influential figure at the Tsar's court from 1905 until his death. Rasputin, who led a debauched private life, owed his position to his hypnotic healing power over the heir to the throne, the Tsarevich Alexei (1904–18), a haemophiliac. From 1911 Rasputin, confident in the protection of the Tsarina, interfered in politics, securing for his nominees the highest appointments in Church and State. At the same time, his alcoholic excesses and sexual orgies horrified many leading figures in St Petersburg society, and the press began to comment adversely on his influence. Once the First World War began, he was popularly believed to be a German agent – although the evidence is inconclusive. In December 1916 he was murdered by exasperated aristocrats. His activities discredited the monarchy (and, indirectly, the Church) in the eyes of the Russian people.

Rathenau, Walther (1867–1922). German statesman. Born in Berlin, the son of a German-Jewish industrialist. He studied engineering and became director of the great electrical trust A.E.G.S. which his father had founded. In 1916 the German Government gave him the task of organizing the country's war economy, so as to offset the effects of British blockade and maintain a supply of essential raw materials. Rathenau's drastic system of 'war socialism' effectively subordinated all production to state needs, with the Minister of War having the right to determine the work of all males between the ages of seventeen and sixty. When the Weimar Republic was established in 1918 his knowledge of economics was invaluable, and he entered politics as founder of a new 'Democratic Party', becoming Minister of Reconstruction in May 1921. Eight months later he became Minister of Foreign Affairs and secured financial agreements with the U.S.A. and France. He was also largely responsible for the Treaty of Rapallo (q.v.) with the Russians, whom he distrusted but was prepared to exploit. He was, however, more than a big-business man in politics; his intellectual interests gave him a rare understanding of Europe and a sense of international common dependence. In June 1922 he was assassinated by anti-semitic nationalists.

Reform Bills. See *Parliamentary Reform.*

Regency. The period in which the power of sovereignty was exercised by George, Prince of Wales (later George IV, q.v.), because of the madness of King George III. It extended from February 1811 until the King's death in January 1820. It was a time of achievement in literature and the arts, although sometimes censured for a prevailing spirit of ostentatious frivolity.

For the first twelve months the Regent's powers were limited by Act of Parliament in case the King should recover his reason and object to any of his son's actions. Since the Prince of Wales had cultivated the friendship of the Whig Opposition, it was thought that he would try and oust the Tory Government in their favour. The restrictions on his power allowed him to avoid committing himself for a year; he then used the critical situation of the Peninsular War as an excuse for avoiding a change in administration. His Whig friends felt betrayed; they remained out of office until after his death.

Reichstag Fire. On the night of 27 February 1933 the Reichstag (parliament building in Berlin) was destroyed by a fire which spread so quickly that arson was indicated. The police duly arrested a young Dutchman of low intelligence, van der Lubbe, who was tried, condemned, and beheaded. The Nazi Government claimed that the fire was the first move in a Communist conspiracy to unleash revolution in Germany. The Bulgarian Communist, Dimitrov, was arrested in Berlin and put on trial, but cleared himself through a brilliant defence in which he turned the tables on his accusers by maintaining that the fire was instigated by the Nazis to provide a pretext for taking emergency measures against left-wing parties. This explanation was also maintained by anti-Nazi German exiles, and has received general endorsement. Recent evidence suggests, however, that van der Lubbe set fire to the Reichstag on his own initiative, but that the Nazis exploited the incident, possibly hampering the fire services. At all events, the fire enabled Hitler to rush through decrees conferring totalitarian powers on the Nazi Party. The Reichstag has remained a burnt-out shell ever since.

Reinsurance Treaty (1887). A secret Russo-German Treaty to replace the Dreikaiserbund (q.v.). By the treaty, the two powers promised each other neutrality in war unless Germany attacked France or Russia attacked Austria-Hungary. The Germans also promised Russia support over Bulgaria and in case the Russians seized the entrance to the Black Sea (i.e. the Straits). The treaty remained valid only until 1890, and was not renewed. Bismarck, in revealing its terms in 1896, claimed it as a major diplomatic success but, in retrospect, it may be doubted whether it did more than delay the inevitable Franco-Russian Alliance (q.v.).

Religious Tests. See *Catholic Emancipation.*

Renan, Joseph-Ernest (1823–92). French theologian, philologist, historian, and man of letters. Renan was born into a poor Breton seafaring family. With financial aid from the famous Liberal Catholic, Dupanloup (1802–78), Renan was educated at theological seminaries in Paris until 1845, when, influenced by German biblical criticism, he developed profound doubts about the truth of Christianity. He devoted himself to studying the Semitic languages and the historical origins of the Christian faith. In 1863 he published the first of his eight volumes on Christian history; this was *La Vie de Jésus*, in which he sought to rationalize the life of Christ, denying the element of the supernatural and portraying Him as the last and greatest of the prophets. Renan also applied his analytical powers to problems of contemporary government. He thus became more than a prominent humanist; by suggesting that the discipline of intellectual study raises the individual above the common man, he offered a standard of detached political criticism which was to make his thought a dominant influence in Paris in the last quarter of the nineteenth century.

Reparations. After the First World War the peace treaties imposed indemnities on Germany and her allies; these indemnities were known as 'Reparations'. The wisdom of requiring large sums of money from defeated countries that had lost many markets was criticized at the time by a number of economists, especially Keynes (q.v.). Nevertheless, in April 1921, German Reparations were fixed at £6,600,000,000 (plus interest). Germany paid a first instalment of £50 million promptly but with inflation in 1922 suspended payments – an act that led to the occupation of the Ruhr (q.v.). In 1924 the Dawes Plan (q.v.) allowed Germany to secure a loan in order to pay Reparations. Further attempts by the Germans to secure revision of the final amount succeeded in 1929, when the Young Plan (q.v.) cut the figure by almost 75 per cent, and gave Germany until 1988 to make the payments. The general financial collapse of 1931 stopped all payment of Reparations. Germany paid, in all, about one eighth of the sum originally demanded but received in the years 1924–30 foreign loans to assist her financial recovery equivalent to one fifth of the original sum. Payment of Reparations imposed on Austria and Hungary was also considerably helped by loans, in this case backed by the League of Nations.

Republican Party. One of the two main political parties in the U.S.A. The first Republican Party was founded by Thomas Jefferson (q.v.) in 1792 to protect agrarian interests from the centralizing tendencies of Hamilton (q.v.) and the Federalists. It was also known as the Republican Democratic Party. This first party split over tariffs during the presidency of Andrew Jackson (q.v.); one section formed the 'National Republicans' or 'Whigs'; the other, supporting Jackson, continued as the 'Democratic Party' (q.v.). The second Republican Party was formed as an anti-slavery coalition of Whigs and northern Democrats in 1854 and drew up its basic programme at the so-called Wigwam Convention of 1859 in Chicago: a protective tariff, a law to foster the building of homesteads for western settlers, intra-continental railway development, safeguards for the immigrants, and, above all prevention of the spread of slavery to new territories ('Free Soil'). The Republicans came to power in 1861 with the victory of Lincoln (q.v.). After the Civil War they became the party of 'Big Business', believing in high tariffs, federal action, and economic imperialism. There have been four main periods of Republican Administration: 1861–93 (except for the Cleveland Presidency of 1885–9); 1897–1913; 1921–33; 1953–61. After the First World War the Republicans became isolationist in outlook and gave free rein to business interests, especially under Presidents Coolidge (q.v.) and Hoover (q.v.). The Republicans abandoned their isolationism after the Japanese attack on Pearl Harbor in 1941, but have continued to regard Asia as a more important centre of American activity than Europe.

Revolution of 1905. In Russia. Opposition to the government of Nicholas II (q.v.) had originally been caused by his refusal to establish constitutional government, and had been intensified by the suffering of both the peasantry (who carried a heavy burden of taxation) and the industrial workers. The defeats of the Russo-Japanese War (q.v.) brought discontent into the open. The disorders began on 22 January with the troops opening fire on a procession of workers ('Bloody Sunday', q.v.). The Tsar promised to summon a 'consultative assembly' in March, but this concession increased the agitation. There were strikes, agrarian outrages, and assassinations throughout the spring and early summer; a serious mutiny broke out in a battleship of the Black Sea Fleet, the *Potemkin*, in June, and other units of the Army and Navy were affected. From 20 to 30 October European Russia was paralysed by a general strike, directed in the capital by the first workers' Soviet. On 30 October the Tsar yielded and granted Russia a constitution; a legislative Duma (q.v.) was to be established and, for the first time, a Prime Minister was appointed (Witte, q.v.). This 'October Manifesto' split the revolutionaries; the majority of them were prepared to accept it, but the Soviet continued resistance and from 22 December to 1 January 1906, there was grim street-fighting in the working-class districts of Moscow. Order was restored by drastic methods in the countryside.

elected President, largely through the support of the provinces, because he appeared to be a guardian of order.

(ii) *Italy*. A movement for liberal constitutions, followed by a patriotic war to eject the Austrians from the peninsula. In February and March the rulers of Naples, Tuscany, and Piedmont, and the Pope, were induced to grant constitutions; of these only that of the Piedmontese survived the disappointments of the following months. Five days of street fighting in Milan (the *Cinque Giornali*, 18-22 March) forced Radetzky (q.v.) to withdraw the Austrian forces. The Piedmontese declared war on Austria on 23 March, but the other states, following the Pope's example, gave them little support. They were defeated at Custozza on 24 July and, after a seven-months armistice, at Novara on 23 March 1849. Unrest in Rome led to the flight of Pope Pius IX (q.v.) on 25 November and the establishment of the Roman Republic, eventually overthrown by the French in July 1849. In Venice the 'Republic of St Mark', which had been proclaimed on 22 March 1848, held out until 28 August 1849.

(iii) *The Austrian Lands*. Originally a movement for constitutional government. Rioting in Vienna led to Metternich's resignation and flight on 13 March. Further demands for a democratic government forced the Emperor to flee to Innsbruck on 17 May, but he consented to the convening of a Constituent Assembly, which met in Vienna from the end of July until early October; on 7 September it passed a law emancipating the peasantry from all remaining feudal dues. In June a Slav Congress in Prague led to Czech nationalist demonstrations, in which the wife of the Austrian military commander, Prince Windischgraetz, was accidentally killed; on 17 June Windischgraetz bombarded Prague, set up a military government and, after a further wave of radical unrest in Vienna during October, restored order there by similar methods. Schwarzenberg (q.v.) re-established Habsburg power, but induced the Emperor Ferdinand to abdicate on 2 December in favour of his nephew Francis Joseph (q.v.).

(iv) *Hungary*. A movement for Hungarian independence, led by Kossuth (q.v.). On 15 March the Hungarian Diet adopted the 'March Laws', a programme providing for responsible government from Budapest for all the Hungarian Lands, including Transylvania (q.v.) and Croatia (q.v.). The 'March Laws' were accepted by Emperor Ferdinand on 31 March. The Hungarian refusal to consider Croatian demands for independence enabled the Habsburgs to play off one racial group against another. With the backing of the Emperor, the Croats invaded Hungary on 17 September led by Baron Jellačić,

Revolutions of 1830. There were revolutions in several European states in the course of 1830–1. The generation which had reached political influence had become exasperated by the retrogressive measures taken by the various governments after the Napoleonic Wars. In France the restored Bourbons fell because of the reactionary policy of Charles X (q.v.) and his minister Polignac. The Revolt of July 1830 was an inspiration to other liberals. In Saxony, Brunswick, and Hesse-Cassel the rulers were forced to abdicate and constitutions were introduced; agitation in Hanover belatedly secured a constitution in 1833. More serious was the Polish Revolt in Warsaw, which drove out the Russian garrison, proclaimed a revolutionary government on 19 November, and was not finally suppressed by the Russians until September 1831. The revolt in Brussels of August–September 1830 secured the independence of Belgium (q.v.). In Italy there were risings in Modena, Parma, and the Papal States early in 1831; all these insurrections were put down by the Austrians. As a 'year of revolutions' 1830 was not so serious as 1848, partly because the main grievances were political and not economic and partly because the two key cities of Berlin and Vienna remained unaffected.

Revolutions of 1848. During 1848 there were revolutions in many European countries. Although they were not instigated by any one organization (and, indeed, differed considerably in objectives), they sprang from a common background: economic unrest, caused by bad harvests and famine in the countryside and unemployment and a recession of trade in the towns; a sense of frustration at the political sterility of the conservatism practised by Metternich (q.v.) or by Guizot (q.v.); and literary Romanticism, which had sown a crop of patriotic legends and reaped a harvest of intransigent nationalism. With few exceptions, the revolutions were the work of middle-class intellectuals whose ideas were mainly French in origin, and it was the February Revolution in Paris that served as the catalyst.

(i) *France.* Mainly a liberal movement, the work of the capital. Between 22 and 24 February the people of Paris, indignant at Louis Philippe's refusal to extend the franchise, overthrew the July Monarchy (q.v.) and established the Second Republic (q.v.). Conflict developed between the moderate middle-class reformers of Lamartine (q.v.), who regarded universal suffrage as the panacea, and the socialist minority, led by Louis Blanc (q.v.). In a second Parisian insurrection in June the left-wing movement was suppressed. At the end of the year Louis Napoleon (the future Napoleon III, q.v.) was their Governor. The Hungarian militia (*Honved*) under General Görgei successfully resisted both Jellačić and Windischgraetz. On 13 April, 1849, Kossuth declared that the Habsburgs had forfeited the Crown and appointed himself Regent. By July, however, the Hungarians were opposed not only by the Austro-Croatian army in the west but by a Russian army in the north (put at the disposal of Francis Joseph by Tsar Nicholas I) and by a Serbian insurrection in the south and a Rumanian insurrection in the east (Transylvania). The Hungarians were defeated by the Russians at Temesvar on 9 August and forced to surrender at Vilagos four days later. The Austrian General Haynau exacted a savage vengeance on the Hungarians; the 'March Laws' were withdrawn.

(v) *The German Lands.* A movement both for representative government in the various German states and for the creation of a united Germany. There were riots in Berlin from 15 to 21 March, when King Frederick William IV declared his willingness to 'merge Prussia into Germany' and agreed to summon a Constituent Assembly (which sat from 22 May until 5 December, and consistently showed a more radical attitude than any other German 'parliament'). The smaller German states followed Prussia's example, granting or withdrawing concessions according to the policy of Frederick William, who in his turn took heart from the successes of the Austrian counter-revolutionaries and, dissolving the Assembly, promulgated a constitution which maintained royal authority (5 December 1848). The idea of the united Germany was responsible for the Frankfurt Parliament (q.v.) which met from 18 May 1848 to 21 April 1849; it showed a narrowly nationalistic attitude to the other revolutions and, in the end, became dependent entirely upon the goodwill of Prussia. German national enthusiasm led to a brief military campaign to 'liberate' Schleswig-Holstein (q.v.) from the Danes, ended by an inconclusive armistice. The German nationalists also suppressed an incipient Polish revolt centred on Posen (Prussian Poland).

(vi) *Other regions.* (*a*) Britain; the news of the continental revolutions led to the final phase of Chartism (q.v.), the fiasco on Kennington Common of 10 April. (*b*) Ireland. An abortive insurrection was planned in Tipperary for 29 July; the 'Young Ireland' movement seeking to bring about a peasant revolt by an attack on a police post (which proved unsuccessful). (*c*) Switzerland. The German-speaking population showed considerable sympathy for the liberals across the frontier, and at Basle, fitted out a force that was intended to secure a more radical revolution in Baden. Switzerland was, however, still recovering from her civil war (the Sonderbund, q.v.) and Swiss political interests were concentrated on the new federal constitution promulgated on 12 September. (*d*) Denmark. An agitation to withdraw the rights of Schleswig-Holstein (q.v.) contributed to the war with the German states. In January 1849 the Danes secured a constitution from King Frederick VII. (*e*) Danubian Principalities (i.e. Rumania). The population of Wallachia forced liberal concessions from the Turkish Governor in June. With Turkish consent, the Russians marched into Wallachia in September, put down the liberal movement, and remained in occupation for three years.

Although the counter-revolutionaries successfully restored order, in one form or another, in each of the major centres of unrest there was a clear shift of authority away from absolute monarchy. The constitutional devices of Napoleon III, Schwarzenberg, and Frederick William IV may have been no more than crude imitations, but at least they tacitly assumed the power of the land-owning aristocracy to be on the decline. No one reimposed feudal obligations on the Austrian peasantry. It was left to Bismarck and Cavour to demonstrate that national unity could be achieved by other methods than 'speeches and majority-votes'.

Rhine Confederation. See *Confederation of the Rhine*.

Rhineland. An area in Germany bordering Belgium, Luxemburg, and France. It had formed a congeries of ecclesiastical states before the Napoleonic Wars, but was ceded to Prussia in 1815; the Prussians fully developed its rich mineral deposits. In 1918 many Frenchmen (including Marshal Foch) hoped to detach the Rhineland from Germany. The Treaty of Versailles stipulated that the Rhineland, although remaining German, was to be occupied by Allied troops for fifteen years and that a thirty-mile-wide demilitarized zone was to be created on the right bank of the river. When the French and Belgians occupied the Ruhr (q.v.) in 1923, they encouraged separatists to proclaim an independent Rhineland Republic at Aachen (21 October), which, however did not survive its 'President', Dr Heinz, who was assassinated the following January. The Locarno Treaties (q.v.) emphasized the permanence of the demilitarized zone; Stresemann (q.v.) secured agreements by which the British evacuated the Rhineland in November 1926 and the French by June 1930. After the advent of Hitler relations again became strained over the Rhineland Question. In March 1936, alleging that the French were planning the encirclement of Germany, he ordered German troops to take up positions in the demilitarized zone, thus violating the Versailles and Locarno treaties. The British and French, preoccupied with the crisis over Abyssinia, contented themselves with protests.

Rhodes, Cecil John (1853–1902). Foremost champion of the British imperial ideal in South Africa. Rhodes was born and educated at Bishop's Stortford. He went to Africa in 1870 for health reasons, and early acquired a fortune, returning to Oriel College, Oxford, to complete his education. He was a founder of the De Beers Company (diamonds) in 1880 at Kimberley, and in the following years acquired extensive interests in the Transvaal gold mines. In 1887 he founded the British South Africa Company (granted a Royal Charter in 1889) to develop the region north of the Transvaal now known as Rhodesia. He became a member of the Cape Colony legislature in 1880 and was Premier of the colony from 1890 to 1896, when he was forced to resign because of his connexion with the Jameson Raid (q.v.). Although Rhodes remained an influential figure, he never again held political office and died shortly before the end of the Boer War. He left over £6 million, much of it to Oxford University, including a large sum to endow scholarships tenable by men of high character from the British overseas empire, the U.S.A., or Germany.

Ribbentrop, Joachim von (1893–1946). Born in the Rhineland, travelled as a young man in Britain and Canada, served as a cavalry officer in the First World War, and subsequently became a salesman of wine. He joined the Nazi Party in the mid-1920s and was made an S.S. leader. Ribbentrop boasted of his foreign contacts and, both before and after 1933, ran a separate information service which provided Hitler with foreign intelligence independent of the German Foreign Office. Ribbentrop served as Ambassador in London from 1936 to January 1938, when he was recalled to become Foreign Minister, a post he held until 1945. He was responsible for giving German foreign policy a specifically Nazi bent, of which the climax was the Tripartite Pact (q.v.) of 1940. He himself regarded his greatest achievement as the Nazi-Soviet Pact (q.v.) of 1939. He was tried as a war criminal at Nuremberg and hanged in October 1946.

Ricardo, David (1772–1823). British economist. The son of a Dutch Jew who had made a fortune on the London Stock Exchange. Ricardo entered business in 1786 and began to write on economic matters in 1809, achieving fame in 1817 with his *Principles of Political Economy and Taxation*, a work that dominated British economic thought until the 1850s. Ricardo, following the theories of Malthus (q.v.), maintained that while wages tend to seek the lowest subsistence level, rents on land remained comparatively stable. Hence the landowning class would get rich by cultivating more land while the workers' wages remained low. Ricardo was M.P. for the Irish rotten borough of Portarlington from 1819 until his death.

Rights of Man, The Declaration of the. A formal pronouncement of the philosophy underlying the first phase of the French Revolution, debated by the Constituent Assembly throughout August 1789 and formally published as a preface to the Constitution of September 1791. The Declaration owed much to American precedent – it was privately discussed at the Paris home of Thomas Jefferson (q.v.) – and reflected the predominant ideas of the eighteenth-century enlightenment. 'Men are born free and equal in rights.' 'The aim of every political association is the preservation of the natural and undoubted rights of man. These rights are liberty, property, security, and resistance to oppression.' 'The principle of all sovereignty resides essentially in the nation.' Although later the Revolution denied many of these rights, the Declaration became the basic charter of European liberals for the next half-century. As Lord Acton said, it was 'stronger than all the armies of Napoleon'.

Risorgimento. An Italian word meaning 'resurrection'. Although used as a literary term in the eighteenth century, politically the word is specifically applied to the movement for Italian unification in the nineteenth century. The word gained general acceptance as the name of a newspaper founded by Cavour (q.v.) in 1847. There are generally considered to be four phases of the Risorgimento: (i) 1815–47, a period of moral and intellectual preparation, characterized by the Carbonari (q.v.) and the writings of Mazzini (q.v.) and Gioberti (q.v.); (ii) 1848–9, a period of abortive revolution, and disillusionment with the 'Liberal Pope' Pius IX (q.v.), but redeemed by the inspiring heroism of Garibaldi (q.v.); (iii) 1850–61, the period of Cavour and the primacy of Piedmont, with the successful liberation of Lombardy from Austria in the war of 1859, the union of the northern duchies with Piedmont in 1860, and the pincer-movement of Piedmontese troops and Garibaldi's 'Thousand' through the peninsula, culminating in the proclamation of a Kingdom of Italy in March 1861; (iv) 1861–70, a period of consolidation, marked by the acquisition of Venetia in 1866 (after a joint war with Prussia against Austria) and the occupation of Rome, 20 September 1870. The acquisition of *Italia Irredenta* (the Trentino, Istria, and the

South Tyrol) by the Treaty of St Germain of 1919 is sometimes regarded as completing the Risorgimento.

Rivoli, Battle of. Decisive battle of Bonaparte's first successful campaign on 14–15 January 1797 on the River Adige, some twenty miles north of Verona and ten miles east of Lake Garda. Napoleon (then aged twenty-seven!) was able to rout the Austrian army under Alvinzy by separating the infantry from the artillery. The victory led to the capture of Mantua and the retreat of the Austrians into the mountains.

Roberts, Earl (1832–1914; born Frederick Sleigh Roberts, knighted 1878, raised to peerage 1892, created an earl 1902). Born in India into an Anglo-Irish military family, and educated at Eton and Sandhurst. He gained the Victoria Cross in the Indian Mutiny, and became the idol of Victorian England during the Afghan War of 1879–80 by his march from Kabul to relieve Kandahar. Most of his military service was in India, but, after the initial Boer successes in 1899, he was sent to South Africa as Imperial Commander-in-Chief. His victorious advance in 1900 ended with the capture of Pretoria in June, and he returned to England at the end of the year, serving as Commander-in-Chief until the post was abolished in 1904. In the last ten years of his life, 'Bobs' became a passionate advocate of compulsory military service. He died while on a tour of inspection of Indian units serving in France.

Robespierre, Maximilien de (1758–94). Born at Arras, became a lawyer, and was elected as 'a representative of the Third Estate in Artois' in 1789, emerging as a leading radical in the National Assembly and becoming an early member of the Jacobin Club (q.v.). Robespierre derived his ideas from the doctrines of Rousseau, seeing himself as the 'Legislator' or incarnation of the 'General Will'. Austere in intellect, ruthless and incorruptible, Robespierre used the support of Paris to dominate the Committee of Public Safety and secure the elimination of his rivals (the Girondins and Hébert and Danton, all q.v.) between October 1793 and April 1794. With his friends Couthon (b. 1756) and Saint-Just (b. 1767), Robespierre established a dictatorship which lasted through the spring and early summer of 1794 and, by the Laws of Ventôse (q.v.) and Prairial (q.v.), began a social revolution which alienated the majority of the Convention. These measures, together with the religious cult of the 'Supreme Being', led to the arrest and execution of the Robespierrists in Thermidor (q.v.) 1794.

Rockefeller, John Davison (1839–1937). Foremost American oil magnate. Born in New York, became a book-keeper, but, following the discovery of oil in Pennsylvania, was able to form (with his younger brother, William) a company which could process oil cheaply. In 1867 Rockefeller organized the Standard Oil Company, incorporated in 1870. Within ten years, Rockefeller had secured a virtual monopoly of oil-refining throughout the U.S.A. Despite legislation aimed at breaking the all-embracing 'Trust' character of his concerns, the Rockefeller enterprises survived under different names as one unit. Like Carnegie (q.v.), Rockefeller devoted most of his fortune to philanthropic undertakings. It was, for example, the Rockefeller millions that enabled Chicago to have the best-endowed university in the world.

Roman Question. The problem of the relationship of the city of Rome, for fourteen hundred years the temporal possession of the Popes, to the movement for Italian unity. In November 1848 a popular insurrection forced Pius IX (q.v.) to flee, and a Roman Republic, led politically by Mazzini (q.v.) and militarily by Garibaldi (q.v.), was proclaimed in February 1849. Louis Napoleon (Napoleon III, q.v.), anxious to secure the Catholic vote at home, despatched a French force to Rome, which fought its way into the city (April–July 1849) and ejected the Republicans. A French garrison thereafter remained to guarantee the territorial rights of the restored Pope. When the Kingdom of Italy was proclaimed in 1861, Rome remained outside it and became a magnet for patriotic Italians. Garibaldi attempted to seize Rome in August 1862 but was captured by Italian troops at Aspromonte before making contact with the French. In December 1866 Napoleon III, believing that by moving the capital from Turin to Florence the Italians had renounced their Roman ambitions, withdrew his garrison. Garibaldi again organized raids on Rome and in October 1867 the French troops were sent back, defeating and capturing Garibaldi at Mentana (3 November). Despite attempts by Napoleon III to settle the Roman Question in international conference, the French remained in Rome until 19 August 1870, when the Franco-Prussian War necessitated their withdrawal. On 20 September 1870, the Italian Army broke through the walls of Rome at the Porta Pia and, after a plebiscite on 2 October, Rome was annexed to Italy and became the capital. Successive Popes refused to recognize the loss of their possessions and regarded themselves as prisoners in the Vatican, until the Lateran Treaty (q.v.) of 1929 settled the dispute by creating the Vatican City State.

Romanov Dynasty. The reigning family of Russia from 1613 to 1917. Strictly, after 1762 the dynasty was Holstein-Gottorp, for all subsequent Tsars were descended from Catherine the Great (both of whose parents were German) and her husband Tsar Peter III, who inherited the German duchy of Holstein-Gottorp from his father and whose claim to the Russian throne came from his mother, a Romanov princess and daughter of Peter the Great. The last Tsar, Nicholas II (q.v.), was murdered in July 1918 at Ekaterinburg (now Sverdlovsk) with his family.

Roosevelt, Franklin D. (1882–1945). President of the U.S.A. Born in New York, studied at Harvard and Columbia Law School. He became a Democratic Party Senator in 1911 and served as Assistant Secretary to the Navy in the Wilson Administration from 1913 to 1920. In August 1921 he was crippled by infantile paralysis; he regained partial use of his legs, and re-entered politics as a leading supporter of the unsuccessful Democratic candidate, Alfred E. Smith, in the presidential election of 1928. Roosevelt himself was at the same time elected Governor of New York State. In 1932 he stood as Democratic candidate for President against Hoover and secured an unprecedented majority of more than twelve million popular votes, winning forty-two states against Hoover's six. In his campaign, Roosevelt had announced that he would counter the great depression by a programme of public works, and, in his First Inaugural Address, he promised 'direct, vigorous action', maintaining 'that the only thing we have to fear is Fear itself'. His administration was therefore largely concerned with the 'New Deal' (q.v.) – vast schemes of public enterprise, support to the farmers, legislation to improve labour relations. In the 1936 election Roosevelt won every state except Maine and Vermont, the most outstanding success in any contested election. He shaped his own foreign policy, steering away from the Republican isolationism of the 1920s and forming closer ties with Britain and France. He was personally responsible for the decision to recognize Soviet Russia (November 1933), and, once war had come to Europe, carried formal neutrality to the point of co-belligerency in support of Britain. In June 1940 he authorized the transfer to the British of surplus stocks of arms, munitions, and aircraft, and in March 1941 he approved the Lease-Lend Act by which any country whose defence the President thought vital to the U.S.A. could obtain war supplies by sale, exchange, or lease. (The total Lease-Lend Aid during the war came to over 50¼ billion dollars.) With Churchill, on 14 August, 1941, he issued the 'Atlantic Charter' (q.v.). After the Japanese attack on Pearl Harbour (q.v.) and the entry of the U.S.A. into the war, his close connexions with Churchill contributed considerably to inter-Allied unity. He attended conferences with Allied leaders at Casablanca, Quebec (August 1943 and September 1944), and Cairo, and (with Stalin also present) at Teheran (q.v.) and Yalta. He has been criticized for placing too much reliance on personal contact with Stalin, for insisting at Casablanca (24 January 1943) on the 'unconditional surrender' of Germany, and for overrating the position of Chiang Kai-shek in China. His ideals inspired the foundation of the United Nations Organization, but, just a fortnight before the San Francisco Conference, he suffered a stroke and died (12 April 1945). In American constitutional history, he is remarkable as the first President to break the tradition that nobody should exercise authority for more than two terms; in 1940 he defeated Wendell Wilkie and in 1944 Thomas Dewey. He was succeeded by his Vice-President, Harry S. Truman.

Roosevelt, Theodore (1858–1919). President of the U.S.A. Born in New York, educated at Harvard, spent two tough years on a cattle ranch, assisted in New York City administration (1889–97), and as Assistant Secretary of the Navy (1897–8) prepared the fleet for the Spanish-American War (q.v.). He gained world fame as a Colonel commanding volunteer 'Rough Riders' in Cuba in this war. On his return he was elected Governor of New York, alarming some of his own Republican Party bosses by his energetic investigation of corruption. He became Vice-President to McKinley (q.v.) in 1901, succeeding to the Presidency on McKinley's assassination a few months later. As President (1901–9), Roosevelt favoured strong executive action, combating monopolistic 'Trusts' in the major industries. He preached what he described as 'the doctrine of the strenuous life', acting on his axiom that to 'go far' one must 'speak softly and carry a big stick'. This rare exuberance led him to pursue a forward policy in international affairs. It was Roosevelt who, in 1903, secured the right to construct the Panama Canal (q.v.), after sending American warships to Panama to ensure that Panama seceded from Colombia. Yet in 1906 Roosevelt was awarded the Nobel Peace Prize for his work as a mediator in the Russo-Japanese War of 1904–5. He supported his Secretary of State, Taft, in the presidential campaign of 1908 and withdrew from politics for a two-year world tour. On his return, he tried to re-enter politics, but, failing to secure Republican nomination in 1912, he stood as a Progressive ('Bull Moose') candidate for the Presidency, opposing both Taft and Woodrow Wilson (q.v.). Although Roosevelt polled more votes than Taft, his intervention enabled Wilson to win for the Democrats. The indefatigable Roosevelt spent 1914 exploring the so-called 'River of Doubt' in Brazil (now known as 'Rio Teodoro' after him). He was a forceful critic of Wilson's policy of neutrality (1914–17), all his sympathies being on the side of the British, with whose Foreign Secretary, Grey, he was on terms of personal friendship.

Rosebery, Earl of (1847–1929, born Archibald Philip Primrose, succeeded his grandfather as fifth earl in 1868). As a representative of the Scottish peerage supported the Liberal Party in the House of Lords from 1872 and held junior posts in Gladstone's Second Ministry, entering the Cabinet in March 1885 as Lord Privy Seal. He was Foreign Secretary for the six months of Gladstone's Third Ministry (1886) and, again under Gladstone, from August 1892 to March 1894. When, in that month, Gladstone retired, Queen Victoria sent for Rosebery to form a government without consulting the outgoing Prime Minister. Rosebery was popular in the country (his horses won the Derby in both the years of his premiership), but was distrusted by the Liberal rank and file, partly because he was a staunch Imperialist and partly because his tastes offended the nonconformists. The only innovation of the Rosebery Ministry was the inclusion of death duties in Sir William Harcourt's Budget of 1894; even this measure was privately resisted by Rosebery in the Cabinet. His Ministry fell in June 1895, when an unexpected vote in the Commons censured the Government for not having purchased a larger stock of the new cordite explosive for the Army. During the following ten years of Conservative rule, Rosebery moved to the right of the Liberal Party, becoming in 1902 President of the Liberal League, an organization of Liberal Imperialists which was strongly opposed to the allegedly 'pro-Boer' Lloyd George (q.v.). Rosebery never again held office; he denounced his party's 'People's Budget' of 1909 as 'inquisitorial, tyrannical and Socialistic', and opposed the Parliament Act of 1911 (q.v.). He was the author of a number of historical studies, notably of the younger Pitt and Napoleon. In 1888 he had served as first Chairman of the London County Council.

Royal Titles Act (April 1876). The Act of Parliament declaring Queen Victoria to be Empress of India. This additional title was received with indifference or even hostility in Britain (where it was felt to be essentially 'un-English') but it had a good effect in India as emphasizing the distinction between British and Indian historical traditions. Within ten years the Queen-Empress's interest in her Indian territories aroused general enthusiasm among the British.

Victoria was proclaimed Empress of India on 1 January, 1877. The idea of the Royal Titles Act sprang from the imaginative foresight of Disraeli, who was raised to the peerage four months after passage of the Act.

Ruhr, The. A leading mining and manufacturing region in Germany, on the right bank of the Rhine. In January 1923 French and Belgian troops were moved into the Ruhr Basin when the Germans failed to pay their quota of Reparations (q.v.). The Occupation was condemned by the British and Americans and aroused passive resistance among the Ruhr workers. The French received little benefit from their occupation but, rather than lose face, kept their troops there for two and a half years, withdrawing only on the eve of the Locarno Conference (q.v.) with its promise of better relations with Germany.

Rumania. Recognized as an autonomous principality within Turkey in 1862 when the Danubian Principalities (q.v.) declared their union under Alexander Cuza. Full independence followed in 1877, Prince Charles of Hohenzollern-Sigmaringen, who had ruled as Prince since 1866, reigning as King Carol I from 1881 until his death in October 1914. Rumania entered the Second Balkan War (q.v.) in time to secure Southern Dobrudja in the resultant peace treaty. Despite links maintained by Carol with the Triple Alliance since 1883, Rumania proclaimed neutrality in 1914 but was induced to enter the war on the Allied side in August 1916 by the promise of considerable territorial gains. By January 1917 most of the country was in Austro-German occupation, and Rumania made a separate peace on 5 March 1918, re-declaring war on Germany on 9 November and so gaining all her promised territory at the Peace Conference. Rumania thus more than doubled her size, receiving Transylvania (q.v.), Bessarabia, and much of the Hungarian plain. Internal politics between the wars were notoriously corrupt. In foreign policy Rumania was a member of the Little Entente (q.v.), but, when Germany became her best customer for oil, links with the Nazis were strengthened and a strong fascist party ('Iron Guard') emerged. Although the Rumanians surrendered some of their territorial gains to the U.S.S.R., Hungary, and Bulgaria in 1940, they remained bound to the Axis Powers by the Tripartite Pact (q.v.) and, under General Antonescu (1882–1946), readily participated in the invasion of Russia, subsequently suffering heavy casualties. When the Russians reached Rumania in the spring of 1944, the Rumanians changed sides and declared war on Germany (25 August). A predominantly Communist Government was imposed by the Russians in November

1945, and the country was declared a 'People's Republic' at the end of 1947.

Russell, Lord John (1792–1878, created Earl Russell 1861). Third son of the Duke of Bedford. Educated privately and at Edinburgh University and was elected Whig M.P. for Tavistock in 1813. In the 1820s he emerged as a champion of parliamentary reform and of the removal of religious disabilities. He was largely responsible for preparing the first Reform Bill and introduced it in the Commons in March 1831, although he did not become a member of the Cabinet until three months later. As Home Secretary from 1835 to 1839, he piloted the Municipal Reform Act (1835) through the Commons and lessened the number of crimes punishable by death. He was Secretary for War and the Colonies (1839–41) and became Prime Minister on the fall of Peel in 1846, for six years heading a Government that was dominated by Palmerston at the Foreign Office (until December 1851). Russell was Foreign Secretary for a few months in the Aberdeen Coalition (1852–3), continuing in the Cabinet without a portfolio until January 1855. He served for five months as Colonial Secretary in the first Palmerston Ministry later that year but relations between the two Whig leaders were frequently strained and he remained out of office for four years, consenting to return to the Foreign Office in the second Palmerston Ministry of 1859–65 and succeeding to the premiership in October 1865. He resigned in the following year, when his party split over the proposed Second Reform Bill. He never again held office.

Russian Revolution and Civil War. The Russian Revolution of 1917 was an intensification of the process which had weakened the autocracy after defeat in the Crimea (1856) and in the Far East (see *Revolution of 1905*). Although its origins lie in the incompatibility of the mystic authority of Tsardom with an increasingly industrialized society, the immediate cause of the revolt was the inability of the existing order to manage a world war. In two and a half years the Russians suffered five and a half million casualties; the troops were short of ammunition, the civilian population of food; the transport system was in chaos; and the Government was so divided by petty feuds that, in the last twelve months of Tsarism, there were four different Prime Ministers, three different War Ministers, and three different Foreign Ministers. There were two main groups of revolutionaries: the liberal intelligentsia, who believed that Russia could still win the war and be transformed into a democratic republic; and the Bolsheviks (and Social Revolutionaries), who thought the 'imperialist' war already lost and wanted to transform the whole economy. The first group carried out the February Revolution, the second group the October Revolution. (N.B. (i) Russia was still using the Julian Calendar in 1917 and was therefore 13 days behind the West, hence, according to western reckoning, each of the revolutions began in the succeeding month; (ii) the Russian capital, St Petersburg, had been renamed Petrograd in 1914.)

(i) *The February Revolution.* Strikes and riots broke out in Petrograd on 8 March, the troops siding with the rioters two days later. On 12 March the Duma (q.v.), refusing the Tsar's order to disperse, chose a Provisional Government (q.v.) under Prince Lvov. The Tsar, Nicholas II (q.v.), was induced to abdicate on the following day. Meanwhile, on 11 March the socialists had revived the Soviet (a Council of Workers', Peasants', and Soldiers' Deputies, first established in 1905). The Soviet challenged every action of the Provisional Government, especially after the return to Petrograd of Lenin (q.v.) on 16 April. An abortive attempt by the Bolsheviks to seize power on 16 July considerably weakened their influence and forced Lenin to seek refuge in Finland for three months. The Provisional Government, too, was weakened by a split between the new Prime Minister, Kerensky (q.v.), and the Commander-in-Chief, General Kornilov, who unsuccessfully attempted a *coup d'état* in September.

(ii) *The October Revolution.* Perceiving that the mass of the Russian people were apathetic, dreading another winter of war, and short of food, Lenin ordered his Red Guards to seize the Winter Palace, the home of the Provisional Government, on 6 November. On the following day an 'All-Russian Congress of Soviets' entrusted authority to the Bolsheviks, who organized a 'Council of People's Commissars' as the executive body. In the other key cities local Bolshevik representatives established administrations. Lenin promised 'Peace, Land, and Bread'. The workers were given control of factories, private trade was prohibited, and the property of the Church and counter-revolutionaries confiscated. An armistice was arranged on 5 December, followed by the Treaty of Brest-Litovsk (q.v.) on 3 March 1918. The first Soviet Constitution was promulgated in the following July.

(iii) *The Civil War.* Counter-revolutionary armies ('Whites') first organized resistance in December 1917; they were opposed by the 'Red Army', a force hastily improvised by Trotsky (q.v.). Several separate 'governments' were established, and civil war continued for nearly three years in five main regions, the lack of cohesion between the various movements contributing to the Bolshevik success.

(*a*) The Caucasus and Southern Russia. In December 1917 the

Don Cossacks rose in revolt under Kornilov. When he was killed, the command passed to General Denikin (May 1918–March 1920), who penetrated deep into Russia but was gradually ejected. General Wrangel held out in the Crimea until November 1920.

(*b*) The Ukraine. Resistance was offered by General Skoropadsky, whom the Germans had appointed as *Hetman*, or head of a puppet Ukrainian state. His authority collapsed with the withdrawal of German forces in November 1918. There followed some months of unparalleled confusion; Denikin's forces occupied the Ukraine from August to December 1919; the Poles, under Pilsudski (q.v.), held Kiev briefly in May 1920. Resistance ended in the summer of 1920.

(*c*) The Baltic. In October 1919 an army under General Yudenich advanced to the outskirts of Petrograd, but was thrown back by the Bolsheviks. The Russians also had to wage war against the armies of Latvia, Lithuania, Estonia, and Finland (all q.v.). All these campaigns ended in 1920; the Estonian in February, the Latvian and Lithuanian in July, and the Finnish in October.

(*d*) Northern Russia. In June 1918 the British and French landed troops at Murmansk, and seized Archangel in the following month, establishing a puppet government and conducting sporadic operations against the Bolsheviks until October 1919.

(*e*) Siberia. With the help of a Czech Legion (released prisoners of war) and of Japanese forces that had landed at Vladivostok in December 1917, Admiral Kolchak set up a 'White' Government at Omsk. For over a year his forces exercised some authority over the central section of the Trans-Siberian Railway. He was captured and executed by the Bolsheviks in February 1920. The Japanese continued to hold Vladivostok until November 1922.

Apart from the resistance of the 'Whites', there were peasant risings during 1920, caused in part by the severe famine, and a mutiny of the sailors at Kronstadt from 21 February to 17 March 1921. This was suppressed with considerable loss of life.

A number of Governments continued to withold recognition of the Soviet for some years after the end of the civil war; recognition was accorded by Britain in January 1924, but by the U.S.A. only in 1933 and by Yugoslavia not until 1940.

Russo-Japanese War (1904–5). Caused by rival attempts to penetrate into Manchuria (q.v.) and Korea (q.v.). The Japanese attacked the Russian fleet at Port Arthur (q.v.) on 8 February 1904, without a declaration of war. They proceeded to inflict a series of defeats on the Russian armies along the Yalu River and in Manchuria itself. A Russian attempt to recover the lost sea power by transferring the

Baltic Fleet to the Far East ended in the disastrous defeat of Tsushima (q.v.) in May 1905. The two Powers accepted American mediation, and peace was signed at Portsmouth (q.v.), New Hampshire, in September 1906. The loss of prestige by the Russians contributed to the outbreak of the Revolution of 1905 (q.v.).

Rutherford, Ernest (1871–1937, created a Baron 1931). British scientist, born in New Zealand. While a Professor at McGill University, Montreal, he was one of the first scientists to explain radioactivity by a disintegration theory. At Manchester University in 1911 he was able to bombard the atom with particles discharged by radioactive substances. From 1919, he supervised the experiments at Cambridge which led in May 1932 to the splitting of the atom.

Saar. A German district, rich in coal deposits, covering an area of over 800 square miles along the basin of the River Saar. It was administered by the League of Nations from 1919 to 1935, with its mines under French control as compensation for the damage done to French coalfields by German troops during the First World War. A plebiscite conducted by the League in 1935 declared overwhelmingly for restoration of the Saar to Germany, and the transfer was made on 1 March 1935. In 1945 the French again occupied the Saar and administered the district until 1 January 1957, when, after a further plebiscite, it once again became German territory.

Sadowa, Battle of (3 July 1866). Also known as Königgrätz. The chief battle of the Austro-Prussian War, fought in Bohemia some 65 miles east of Prague. The Austrians, under Benedekt, were decisively defeated by a Prussian force nominally led by King William but, in effect, by Moltke (q.v.). The Prussian victory was made possible only by the arrival of reinforcements under Crown Prince Frederick. After the battle, the Austrians offered little resistance, and an armistice was concluded on 26 July. Sadowa represents the end of Austrian dominance in the German lands and the beginning of Prussian hegemony in Europe. In one day the Austrians lost 24,000 men killed or wounded and 13,000 taken prisoner.

St Germain, Treaty of (10 September 1919). The peace treaty with the Austrian Republic after the First World War. The settlement confirmed the loss to Austria of all non-German parts of the former Empire and also deprived her of about one-third of the German-speaking population. The South Tyrol and the Julian March went to Italy; Slovenia, Bosnia-Herzegovina, and Dalmatia to Yugoslavia; Bohemia and Moravia to Czechoslovakia; Galicia to Poland; and the Bukovina to Rumania. The union of Germany and Austria (the Anschluss, q.v.) was forbidden. The Austrian Army was limited to 30,000 men, and the Republic was made liable for Reparations (q.v.). In 1914 the population of the 'Austrian' part of the Habsburg Empire had been 28 millions; the population of the rump of Austria left by the Treaty was less than 8 millions.

St Jean de Maurienne, Treaty of. An abortive secret agreement signed by the British, French, Russians, and Italians in April 1917, promising Italy the Turkish provinces around Smyrna (q.v.) as compensation for the redistribution of other parts of the Ottoman Empire, among the Great Powers after the war. Since the Greeks also subsequently claimed Smyrna, and since the Turks under Kemal offered strong resistance to the occupation of Asia Minor, the arrangement was allowed to lapse.

Salisbury, Marquess of (Robert Gascoyne-Cecil, 1830–1903; succeeded as third Marquess 1868). Educated at Eton and Christ Church, became Tory M.P. for Stamford in 1853. He was appointed Indian Secretary in 1866, but resigned because of his disapproval of the Second Reform Act. He returned to the India Office in 1874 and became Foreign Secretary early in 1878, attending the Congress of Berlin. He succeeded Beaconsfield as leader of the Conservative Party in 1881, and subsequently headed three governments (1885–6; 1886–92; 1895–1902). Although his second Ministry was responsible for the Local Government Act (q.v.) of 1888, his greatest interests were in foreign and imperial affairs. Except for a few months in 1886 and from October 1900 to his retirement in July 1902, he was always his own Foreign Secretary. He was responsible for British participation in the Mediterranean Agreements (q.v.) and for the diplomatic victory over the French at Fashoda (q.v.). His policy is often, misleadingly, described as one of 'Splendid Isolation' (q.v.). African affairs – and in particular the problem of the second Boer War (q.v.) – dominated his third Ministry. He was a Conservative of the old school who continued all his life to fear the rising tide of democracy.

Salonica (Thessaloniki). An ancient city on the Aegean, the chief port of Macedonia. In the late nineteenth century, the Austrians planned to construct a railway through the Balkans to Salonica, and develop the port, as they had already developed Trieste. The plan was abandoned because of the natural obstacles. Salonica was cap-

tured by the Greeks from the Turks on 9 November 1912 during the
Balkan Wars (q.v.), but was coveted by the Bulgarians, whose troops
had been only one day behind the Greeks. In October 1915, when
it was clear that the Central Powers and Bulgaria were about to
mount an offensive against Serbia, the British and France landed
troops at Salonica. The Greek King refused to support this force,
although the Allies received the backing of the leading Greek statesman Venizelos (q.v.). The Allies were unable to save Serbia but retained Salonica as a base for operations against Bulgaria, and it
was in Salonica that Marshal Franchet d'Espérey signed the armistice with Bulgaria, 30 September 1918. Between the wars, Yugoslavia was given a 'Free Zone' in the port. There was a major
transfer of populations in 1923, with Greek families (driven out of
Anatolia by Kemal, forcing the Turkish inhabitants to settle in the
Turkish Republic. In the Second World War Salonica fell to the
Germans in April 1941; before it was liberated the Nazis had virtually exterminated the large population of Jews, of Spanish origin,
who had settled in Salonica in the fifteenth century.

Sanctions. An economic boycott of a country resorting to war contrary to undertakings given to the League of Nations (q.v.). Sanctions formed the chief coercive power of the League and were
authorized under Article XVI of the Covenant. In October 1935
sanctions were imposed on Italy after Mussolini's attack on Abyssinia (q.v.). Oil, iron, and steel were, however, excluded from the
boycott as a compromise gesture; but since these commodities were
essential for war, the whole concept of sanctions was made ridiculous. By July 1936 sanctions had been raised by all the members
of the League, which never again resorted to the device.

Sand River Convention (1852). An agreement between the British
and the Boers giving the latter the right to manage their own affairs
in the Transvaal (q.v.). Two years later, the Bloemfontein Convention gave similar autonomous rights to the Boers in the Orange Free
State.

San Martin, José de (1778–1856). South American General. Born in
what is now Argentina, where his father was governor of a province
under Spanish administration. After serving with the Spanish Army
in Africa, Portugal, and Spain itself, he returned home in 1814, when
the Argentinians were revolting against Spanish rule. San Martin
was ordered to lead an army against Spanish power in Peru, but he
decided on a strategy that took him first across the Andes into Chile,

where he defeated the Spaniards and so facilitated the proclamation of Chilean independence in February 1818. In 1820 after a vigorous propaganda campaign, he succeeded in inducing the Spanish Viceroy in Lima to evacuate the city without fight, and, on 28 July 1821, he proclaimed the independence of Peru, although the Spaniards continued to resist in many parts of the country. San Martin favoured an independent monarchy for the states he had liberated, and in July 1822 visited Bolivar (q.v.) at Guayaquil to discuss the establishment of a unified monarchical government in liberated South America. He found himself in disagreement with Bolivar; moreover, in his absence, a hostile faction revolted in Lima. Disillusioned, he resigned his titles and returned to Europe, dying in voluntary exile in Boulogne thirty-four years later.

San Stefano, Treaty of (3 March 1878). Ended the Russo-Turkish War of 1877–8, which had been prompted by Panslavism (q.v.). The Treaty created a large autonomous state of Bulgaria (q.v.) that included Macedonia and had an outlet to the Aegean. It also gave Russia considerable gains in the Caucasus; enlarged Serbia and Montenegro; confirmed the independence of Serbia, Montenegro, and Rumania; and provided for payment by Turkey of a large indemnity. The Treaty aroused the opposition of the Austrians (who were alarmed by Bulgaria's gains in the western Balkans) and Britain (who thought that Bulgaria would become a satellite state giving Russia an overland route to the Mediterranean). The Congress of Berlin (q.v.) of June–July 1878 replaced San Stefano by another settlement less favourable to the Slavs. San Stefano left a legacy of Balkan discord; successive Bulgarian governments tried until 1941 to achieve the frontiers promised by the Treaty.

Sarajevo. Since 1850 the capital of the Yugoslav (formerly Turkish or Austrian) province of Bosnia (q.v.). On 28 June 1914 the Austrian Archduke Francis Ferdinand (q.v.) and his wife were shot in Sarajevo by a Serbian student, Gavrilo Princip, a member of a secret nationalist movement, Mlada Bosna ('Young Bosnia'), using weapons supplied by the Serbian terrorist organization known as the 'Black Hand' (q.v.). The Austrians, insisting that the Serbian Government had instigated the plot, delivered an unacceptable ultimatum to Serbia on 23 July, and when this was refused declared war on 28 July, thus precipitating the First World War. The complicity of the Serbian Government has never been proved and, given Serbian internal conditions at that time, is most improbable, but the plot was certainly encouraged by influential Serbian officers (who were on bad terms with the Government). The assassination led to serious riots in Sarajevo and to the trial and execution of many Serbs living in Bosnia; Princip was too young for the death penalty but he died in an Austrian fortress in April 1918, aged twenty-three. Princip was regarded as a national hero by both the inter-war and the Communist rulers of Yugoslavia.

Scharnhorst, Gerhard Johann von (1776–1813). Prussian soldier. Born near Hanover and served in the Hanoverian Army of 1793–5 before transferring to Prussian service in 1801. He was immediately chosen to train new troops, although he fought (and was wounded) in the campaigns of 1806–7. After the Peace of Tilsit (q.v.) in July 1807 he was left to reorganize the Prussian Army, which was limited to 42,000 men. He established a new relationship between officers and men and, by introducing short-service enlistment, improved training methods. It was his army that Blücher (q.v.) led to victory in 1813–15. Scharnhorst himself died of wounds received in Silesia in May 1813.

Schleswig-Holstein. The region comprising the southern part of the Jutland Peninsula, linking Denmark and Prussia. The Duchies had been united ever since the Middle Ages, with the King of Denmark as Duke. Holstein, however, was almost wholly German and Schleswig partly so. Holstein had become a member of the German Confederation in 1815. In 1848 a Danish nationalist movement sought to annex the Duchies to Denmark proper. The people of the Duchies resisted, and were supported by Prussian troops. A compromise settlement was reached in 1852, but the Danes continued to try to secure the Duchies. In 1863 King Frederick VII of Denmark died; he was succeeded by a collateral member of the family, Christian IX, whose claim as Duke of the Duchies was disputed in Schleswig-Holstein (which had always accepted the Salic Law, denying claims through females). The German states maintained that the rightful ruler of the Duchies was the Duke of Augustenburg, and Prussia (under Bismarck, q.v.) and Austria championed the German cause. In a brief war in the summer of 1864, the Danes were defeated and Schleswig-Holstein ceded to the German states. By the Convention of Gastein of 1865, Holstein was administered by Austria and Schleswig by Prussia. Complaints of anti-Prussian agitation in Holstein were used by Bismarck to justify his war against Austria in 1866. By the Treaty of Prague of August 1866 Schleswig-Holstein was placed under Prussian rule. The Treaty of Versailles of 1919 provided for the holding of plebiscites in Northern

Schleswig, where there was a large Danish population, and, in consequence, the region north of Flensburg Fjord was incorporated in Denmark in July 1920; the rest of Schleswig-Holstein remained in Germany.

Schlieffen Plan. In December 1905 General Count von Schlieffen (1833–1913), Chief of the German General Staff since 1891, retired. As a final testament, he completed an operational plan for war with France. With modifications, this plan formed the basis of the German attack in 1914. Schlieffen believed: (i) that the coming war would have to be fought against France and Russia, probably supported by Britain; (ii) that the decisive theatre would be in France and that Germany should remain on the defensive against Russia; (iii) that provided France were swiftly defeated, her allies would offer little resistance; (iv) that the French fortifications facing Germany were impregnable and should be outflanked by a scythe-like attack through Holland and through Belgium and Luxemburg, even though Germany was bound by treaty to observe their neutrality. In retirement, Schlieffen revised the plan each Christmas with the help of his son-in-law. His successor as Chief of the General Staff, the younger Moltke, decided to limit the sweeping movement to Belgium and Luxemburg. Subsequently German military critics held that Moltke failed to capture Paris in 1914, because he had departed from the plan of the 'masterly strategic genius'. This view was challenged by Dr Gerhard Ritter, who published in 1956, for the first time, the text of the full plan with its author's emendations and Moltke's comments. It is clear that there was not such a difference between the strategy of Schlieffen and Moltke as earlier historians had maintained. It may however be doubted whether the Schlieffen Plan deserves its high reputation, for its author had underestimated the strength of the Russians and the near-panic that their advance would cause in Berlin, the power of Belgian resistance, the effectiveness of the British Expeditionary Force, and the importance of the French railway system for bringing up reserves.

Schwarzenberg, Prince Felix (1800–52). Austrian statesman. A member of one of the great aristocratic families. He served as a diplomat in the lesser Italian states during the last part of the Metternich period, and was attached as political adviser to Radetzky's staff in Lombardy in the spring of 1848. Radetzky (q.v.) sent Schwarzenberg to Vienna, and it was mainly through the influence of the Army commanders that he was made chief minister on 21 November 1848. He engineered the abdication of the Emperor

Ferdinand and the succession of his eighteen-year-old nephew, Francis Joseph (q.v.). Schwarzenberg followed a vigorous policy, refusing any compromise with the Hungarian rebels and, in March 1849, introducing a constitution providing for a highly centralized state and promising representative government and a responsible ministry, although 'provisionally' the Emperor would rule through decrees. These institutions never came into existence, for once Schwarzenberg had reasserted control from Vienna, the 'concessions' were withdrawn (31 December 1851). Schwarzenberg himself concentrated on foreign affairs, and in November 1850 secured formal recognition by the Prussians of Austrian leadership in Germany. He died suddenly, still in office, in April 1852.

Sebastopol. City in the Crimean peninsula, main naval base for the Russian Black Sea Fleet, originally strongly fortified in the 1840s. The capture of Sebastopol became the prime military objective of the Crimean War, since it was believed that its destruction would secure the continued independence of Turkey. Sebastopol was accordingly besieged for twelve months from September 1854 by an Anglo-French force of some 50,000 men, subsequently supported by 15,000 Piedmontese. By the Treaty of Paris of 1856, Sebastopol was demilitarized, but the Russians began refortifying the base in 1871, and it recovered its importance within a few years. Sebastopol was again besieged during the Second World War, falling to the Germans in June 1942 after four weeks of heavy fighting.

Second Empire. The official style of the government of France from 2 December 1852 to 3 September 1870, the reign of Napoleon III (q.v.). The régime remained autocratic until January 1870, when political reforms transformed the government into a constitutional monarchy, sometimes termed the 'Liberal Empire'.

Second International. The second attempt at the organization of International Socialism (q.v.), set up in Paris in 1889. Although shattered by the outbreak of war in 1914, it reformed as 'The Labour and Socialist International' after the war and continues in that form today.

Second Reich. The German Empire from the proclamation of King William of Prussia as Emperor at Versailles in January 1871 to the abdication of William II (q.v.) in November 1918. Retrospectively, the Holy Roman Empire (q.v.) was styled 'the First Reich'. Hitler claimed the title 'Third Reich' for his régime.

Second Republic of France. Proclaimed on 25 February 1848, and lasted in name until the proclamation of the Second Empire on 2 December 1852. The movement that had overthrown Louis Philippe (q.v.) and established the Republic was essentially Parisian, and as the provinces adjusted themselves to the change of régime the government rapidly lost its radical characteristics. In June 1848 the failure of the 'National Workshops' of Louis Blanc (q.v.) led to serious street fighting in Paris, which left the propertied classes in control of government. In the Presidential election later in the year, Louis Napoleon Bonaparte (the future Napoleon III, q.v.) secured four million more votes than his nearest rival and assumed office in December, being styled the 'Prince-President'. The Constitution of the Republic limited the President to one four-year term of office; after narrowly failing to gain a constitutional amendment allowing him a further term, Louis Napoleon carried out a *coup d'état* on 2 December 1851, subsequently securing a new constitution allowing the President a ten-year period of office. This arrangement was short-lived; at the end of 1852 a proposal that the Prince-President should become hereditary Emperor was submitted to plebiscite and received nearly eight million affirmative votes, with only a quarter of a million against.

Sedan. French frontier fortress. Scene of the German victory of 1–2 September 1870. A French army, under Marshal Macmahon (q.v.), and accompanied by the Emperor Napoleon III, was trapped in Sedan while on the way to relieve another French army besieged in Metz. In the ensuing battle 20,000 Frenchmen were killed, a figure three times as large as the German casualties. Napoleon III himself surrendered to the Prussian King, and over 80,000 Frenchmen were taken prisoner. The news of Sedan precipitated the fall of the Second Empire and the proclamation of the Third Republic (q.v.) in Paris. Sedan was also the point where the Germans broke through the French defences in May 1940.

Seeckt, Hans von (1866–1936). One of a brilliant group of young German staff-officers at the beginning of the twentieth century, with more political perception and wider interests than the majority of his colleagues. As Chief of Staff to Mackensen on the Eastern Front, he achieved the break-through at Gorlice (May 1915). He served subsequently in the Balkans and, at the end of the war, was in Turkey. From 1919 to 1926 he was responsible for the secret building-up of the German Army, and circumnavigated the disarmament clauses of the Treaty of Versailles by cooperating over training and supplies with Soviet Russia. At home, he was prepared to use the Army dispassionately against either Communist or Nazi trouble-makers. During these years as Commander-in-Chief of the Army (Reichswehr) he was the most powerful person in Germany, but the jealous hostility of President Hindenburg forced his resignation in October 1926. Once Hitler had come to power, it was Seeckt's long-term planning that made possible the rapid transformation from an army of (nominally) 100,000 men to the conscript forces that won the victories of 1940.

Seize Mai (1877). French political crisis. Caused by the attempt of President Macmahon (q.v.) to secure a royalist government.

Serbia. A Balkan state, capital Belgrade. Although there was a large medieval Serbian Empire, it was overthrown by the Turks at the battle of Kossovo (1389), and Serbian nationalism remained quiescent until the revolt of Karadjordje Petrović ('Black George'), 1804–13. Karadjordje was forced into exile and eventually murdered by a rival Serbian leader Miloš Obrenović (Prince of Serbia, 1817–39 and 1859–60). The Turks recognized Serbian autonomy in 1830 and conceded full independence in 1878. The feud between the Obrenović and Karadjordjević families dominated Serbian politics and culminated in the murder of the last Obrenović, King Alexander, in June 1903. Peter Karadjordjević (the grandson of 'Black George') was thereupon elected King and reigned until 1921, although he appointed his son Alexander (q.v.) Regent in 1914. Serbian policy between 1903 and 1914 sought the 'liberation' of the Serb peoples still within Austria-Hungary and Turkey. Serbia more than doubled her size during the Balkan Wars (q.v.), but the conflict with Austria precipitated the Sarajevo Crisis (q.v.) and so led to war and occupation. In December 1918 Serbia joined Croatia and Slovenia in a triune kingdom which was later (1929) called Yugoslavia (q.v.). From 1941 to 1945 there was a German puppet state of Serbia, and in 1946 Serbia was reconstituted as one of the 'People's Republics' of the Yugoslav Federation.

Sèvres, Treaty of (10 August 1920). The abortive peace settlement accepted by Ottoman Turkey after the First World War, but never ratified. The main terms were: Greece to acquire Thrace and the Turkish islands in the Aegean with a five-year administration of Smyrna (q.v.) and its hinterland, pending a plebiscite; Syria, Mesopotamia, Arabia, and Armenia to be recognized as independent, the first two as mandated territories; the Dardanelles and Bosphorus to be demilitarized and administered by the League of Nations; Italy to retain possession of the Dodecanese and Rhodes; all claims to lands inhabited by non-Turkish peoples were renounced. Turkey was thus limited to a small area around Constantinople and extending 25 miles into Europe, and Anatolia (excluding Smyrna). The terms of the Treaty caused great resentment in Turkey (especially the concessions to Greece), and the republican movement of Mustapha Kemal (q.v.) refused to accept its terms, expelled the Greeks from Asia Minor and insisted on a new and milder settlement, the Treaty of Lausanne (q.v.) of 1923.

Shaftesbury, Lord (Anthony Ashley Cooper, 1801–85; succeeded as seventh Earl in 1861). Educated at Harrow and Christ Church. As Lord Ashley he was elected Tory M.P. for Woodstock in 1826 and held minor offices in 1828 and 1834. Although an opponent of parliamentary reform and an old-fashioned Tory, he became champion of all measures to improve factory conditions, promoting, among other Bills, the Factory Acts (q.v.) of 1833, 1844, and 1850 and the Mines Act of 1842. He also participated in much extra-parliamentary philanthropic work. He was an evangelical churchman, interested in bible societies at home and overseas.

Sherman, William T. (1820–91). American soldier. Born in Ohio, served in the Army from 1840 to 1855. Recalled to the Army with the outbreak of the Civil War, Sherman gained rapid promotion, becoming virtually a deputy to Grant (q.v.). His most famous campaign was the invasion of Georgia in the summer of 1864, followed in November and December by a 'march to the sea' of three hundred miles, which drove a wedge through the South. Sherman's troops were encouraged to pillage and destroy; they left a trail of devastation. Sherman accepted surrender of the last Confederate troops, 26 April 1865. From 1869 to 1884 he was Commander-in-Chief of the U.S. Army.

Shimonoseki, Treaty of (17 April 1895). Ended the war between China and Japan that had begun over Korea (q.v.) in the previous August. The Treaty confirmed the independence of Korea. China undertook to pay a considerable indemnity to Japan and to grant her a favourable commercial agreement. Formosa, the Pescadores, and the Liaotung Peninsula (including Port Arthur, q.v.) were ceded to Japan. Strong diplomatic intervention by the Russians, French, and Germans forced the Japanese to withdraw their claim to the Liaotung Peninsula within a fortnight of the signing of the Treaty, and

Port Arthur was returned to China. Nevertheless, the Treaty represented a major step towards Japanese domination of the Chinese mainland.

Sieyès, Emmanuel Joseph ('Abbé Sieyès'; 1748–1836). Born in Fréjus. Sieyès was a natural intellectual who became a priest without a real vocation; his conscience never allowed him to preach a sermon or hear confessions. As secretary to the Bishop of Tréguier, he came to sympathize with the poverty-stricken peasantry of Brittany. Settling in Paris in the winter of 1788–9, he gained a following among the young reformers by his *Essai sur les privilèges* and, even more, by his *Qu'est-ce que le Tiers État?* – a 20,000-word manifesto demanding that the Third Estate be recognized as a parliament empowered to prepare a constitution defining the rights of government. Sieyès more than anyone else was 'the Man of 1789', and it was on his proposal that the Third Estate assumed the title of National Assembly on 17 June. Although he sat on the committee that divided France into Departments, he gradually withdrew from public life, declining the Archbishopric of Paris in March 1791. Asked in old age what he had done during the Terror, he replied, '*J'ai survécu*' ('I stayed alive'). After serving on a diplomatic mission in Berlin, he joined the Directory in 1798 and, the following year, helped Bonaparte seize power (*Brumaire,* q.v.). It was Sieyès who planned the system of the Consulate, although Bonaparte so modified his ideas that he would not serve him. He was created a Count under the Empire, spent the years 1814–30 in exile in Belgium, and returned to die in Paris under the July Monarchy.

Simon, John (1873–1954, knighted 1910, Viscount 1940). Born in Manchester, the son of a Congregational minister. He was called to the Bar in 1899 and gained distinction in the Courts independent of his political career. He became Liberal M.P. for Walthamstow in 1906, Solicitor-General 1910, and Attorney-General 1913. He served as Home Secretary in 1915 and 1916, but resigned because his conscience was opposed to the idea of conscription. He was chairman of the Indian Statutory Commission of 1927–30 which produced the 'Simon Report' (q.v.). He headed the 'National Liberals' in the Mac-Donald Government and was Foreign Secretary from 1931 to 1935, favouring a policy of disarmament and conciliation and becoming the first British Cabinet Minister to visit Hitler (March 1935). He returned to the Home Office from 1935 to 1937, was Chancellor of the Exchequer under Chamberlain (1937–40) and Lord Chancellor from 1940 to 1945.

Simon Report, 1930. The report of a commission on India headed by Sir John Simon (q.v.). The report recommended an increase in responsible government in the provinces and indirect election for the central legislature. Subsequently the Round Table Conferences on India (meeting in London in 1931–2), and a 'White Paper' issued by the Government in 1933, went further than the Report and proposed an Indian Federation; the resultant India Act of 1935 (q.v.) was based on the Conferences and the 'White Paper' rather than on the Simon Report.

Singapore. An island to the south of the Malay Peninsula. Acquired by Sir Stamford Raffles (1781–1826) from the Rajah of Johore in 1819 for the East India Company. Singapore was controlled and developed by Raffles until 1823, becoming an important trading port within four years. From 1826 to 1867 Singapore, with other British settlements in Malaya, was administered by the Governor-General of India, but in 1867 the 'Straits Settlements' were constituted a separate colony. Singapore became a naval port and a commercial centre for south-east Asia. Japanese troops crossing from the mainland of Malaya on 8–9 February 1942, overwhelmed the island's defences and captured the city on 15 February, over 70,000 British and Australian soldiers being forced to surrender – in Churchill's words, 'the worst disaster and largest capitulation in British history'. Singapore was not liberated until the Japanese surrender of August 1945. The British Government thereupon began a period of successive constitutional reforms. The island became independent in 1958 and part of the Malaysian Federation in 1963.

Sinn Féin ('Ourselves Alone'). Irish republican party. Founded in 1902 by Arthur Griffith (1872–1922) to achieve a new status for Ireland (originally on the model of Deák in Hungary). The movement did not become influential until the Irish disorders of 1914 when there was an influx of fiery Dublin workers, headed by James Connolly, who ousted Griffith from leadership. The abortive 'Easter Rising' (q.v.) of 1916 gave Sinn Féin its martyrology. From October 1917 it was headed by de Valera (q.v.), and was at war with the British authorities in 1919–20. In 1922 a split in the movement led to its virtual disintegration, Griffith accepting the settlement establishing the Irish Free State, de Valera seeking to organize a new Republican Army and eventually claiming to continue the old tradition in his party, the *Fianna Fáil*.

Sino-Japanese Wars (i) 1894–5. This campaign, which was principally concerned with control of Korea (q.v.), showed the supremacy of the new Japanese Army and Navy, based on European models. The Chinese offered little effective resistance. Peace was made at Shimonoseki (q.v.) in April 1895.

(ii) 1937–45. The Japanese had been manoeuvring for war ever since the Mukden Incident (q.v.) of 1931. A clash between Japanese and Chinese forces on the night of 7 July 1937 began full-scale hostilities, no formal declaration of war being made by either side. The Japanese overran northern China in the autumn of 1937, capturing Shanghai and penetrating up the Yangtse in November. The Japanese tended to advance along the main railways, capturing the chief cities: Nanking fell in December 1937, Canton and Hankow in October 1938. The Chinese offered resistance in two forms; the Nationalist (Kuomintang, q.v.) Army of Chiang Kai-shek, based on the temporary capital of Chungking and receiving arms from Britain and the U.S.A.; and the Communist guerillas ('8th Route Army') under Mao Tse-tung, who inflicted several reverses on the Japanese in the course of 1938. The China campaign became engulfed in the Second World War after the Japanese attack on Pearl Harbor (q.v.) in December 1941. The Chinese kept a Japanese Army of over a million tied up on the mainland; in July 1942 they inflicted a serious defeat on the Japanese in Kiangsi. The Japanese eventually signed an act of capitulation to Chiang Kai-shek in Nanking on 9 September 1945.

Slave Trade, Abolition of the. In the later eighteenth century, humanitarian sentiment turned against the institution of slavery, and particularly the slave trade, first in Britain and later in the northern American states. In the 1770s British seamen still transported the greatest number of slaves from Africa to the Americas. The Anti-Slavery Committee was established in London in 1787, with the sympathetic approval of the Prime Minister, Pitt. Wilberforce (q.v.) introduced motions against the slave trade in 1789, 1791, 1795, and 1804; but it was not until 1807 that an Act abolishing the slave trade, so far as Britain was concerned, passed through Parliament, becoming law in May 1808. The U.S.A. forbade American participation from 1 January 1809. Among continental countries, the lead had been taken by the Danes, who were forbidden to trade in slaves after the end of 1802. Under Castlereagh's influence, a formal condemnation of the slave trade was made by the delegates to the Congress of Vienna in February 1815. The French forbade participation in the trade in the same year, the Spanish and Portuguese in 1820.

Slaves, Emancipation of. Slavery persisted for several decades after the formal condemnation of the slave trade, largely for economic reasons. Wilberforce continued to press for the abolition of slavery within the British Empire and, shortly before his death, an Act emancipating all slaves in British possessions passed through Parliament (August 1833); slave-owners were awarded £20 million compensation. Feeling was running high, at the same time, in the U.S.A., where William Lloyd Garrison began an emancipation campaign from Boston in 1831 and the Anti-Slavery Society was founded in 1833. The publication of Harriet Beecher Stowe's *Uncle Tom's Cabin* in 1852 provided the movement with a powerful weapon of propaganda. The decision in the Dred Scott Case (q.v.) of 1857 and the activities of John Brown (q.v.) helped to make slavery the chief issue in the Presidential campaign of 1860 and so precipitated secession and the American Civil War (q.v.). Lincoln proclaimed the emancipation of American slaves on 1 January 1863, Congress ratifying the decision in the 13th Amendment to the Constitution of December 1865.

Many Central American states ended slavery in the third quarter of the century; Venezuela in 1854, Puerto Rico not until 1873, and Brazil in a series of edicts between 1870 and 1888. The greatest difficulties facing the emancipators were in Africa itself, particularly the Congo (q.v.). It was easier to suppress slavery in coastal areas; thus the slave markets were closed in Zanzibar in 1873 and in Madagascar in 1877. In 1822 Liberia was founded as an African community for freed slaves returning from America; it was created an independent republic in 1847.

Slivnitza, Battle of (16–19 November 1885). Following the unification of Bulgaria (q.v.) the Serbian King, Milan Obrenović (who was under Austrian dominance), demanded territorial compensation and, when this was refused, went to war against Bulgaria (November 1885). To the general surprise, the Bulgarians routed the Serbs at Slivnitza. Serbia was only saved from complete disaster by an ultimatum from Austria-Hungary to Bulgaria demanding withdrawal of her forces. Although the peace settlement of March 1886 merely restored the pre-war situation, the political effects of the battle were considerable, as it secured recognition of the strength of Bulgarian national feeling while marking the nadir of Serbia's fortunes. (The battle formed the background for Bernard Shaw's *Arms and the Man*.)

Smuts, Jan Christiaan (1870–1950). Born in Cape Colony and educated at Stellenbosch and Christ's College, Cambridge. He became a lawyer in the Transvaal, and in August 1899 was the intermediary between Kruger and the British in a belated attempt to improve Anglo-Boer relations. During the Boer War he served as a divisional commander with the rank of General. He cooperated with Botha (q.v.) in negotiating the peace of Vereeniging and in his later political career. As Colonial Secretary under Botha, Smuts negotiated an agreement with Gandhi (q.v.) assuring the Asiatics in South Africa just treatment (1913). Smuts fought in the 1914–15 campaign in German South-west Africa and commanded the Allied troops that penetrated into German East Africa in 1916, capturing Dar-es-Salaam in September. In March 1917 he was sent to London on a political mission, became a member of the Imperial War Cabinet, and, in the following winter, carried out secret negotiations with Austrian representatives in Switzerland in the hope of securing a separate peace with Austria-Hungary. Smuts attended the Paris Peace Conference and assisted in the preparation of the League of Nations Covenant. He succeeded Botha as Prime Minister in August 1919, and remained in office for five years. When a National Coalition was formed under General Hertzog in March 1933, he joined the Government and, in the following year, founded the 'United Party' by linking his own supporters to the moderate nationalists of Hertzog; the republican and racialist group of Nationalists remained in opposition under Dr Malan. Smuts became Prime Minister again in September 1939, and continued in office until defeated by Malan's Nationalists in the election of May 1948. During the war, Smuts was regarded as the Elder Statesman of the Commonwealth; he participated in the Cairo Conference of 1942, conducted delicate negotiations with Eisenhower in Algiers in 1943, and assisted in the preparatory work for the United Nations Organization in 1944–5. He was made a Field-Marshal in 1941. Apart from his political activities, he was a botanist and a philosopher, the creator of the theory of holism.

Smyrna (Izmir). An ancient commercial port and religious centre on the west coast of Asia Minor. Captured by the Turks in 1424. The city had a large Greek community (nearly half a million in 1914), and with its hinterland was awarded to Greece for a trial period of five years by the Treaty of Sèvres of 1920. The Turkish Nationalists under Kemal (q.v.) refused to accept the loss of Smyrna and began military operations against the Greeks in June 1920. The Greeks succeeded in throwing the Turks back until August 1922, when, in a desperate counter-offensive, the Turks broke the Greek Army, which fled to the coast in confusion. The Turks occupied Smyrna in September, ruthlessly expelling the Greeks and setting fire to the city.

The Smyrna area was restored to Turkey by the Treaty of Lausanne of 1923. War, massacre, and forced emigration reduced the population of Smyrna from over a million in 1914 to under two hundred thousand in 1939.

Social Democrats. The name taken by the Marxist parties of a number of Central and Eastern European states before the First World War. The earliest appears to have been the German Sozial-demokratische Arbeiterpartei, founded at a Congress of all the German socialist groups at Eisenach in 1869 by Wilhelm Liebknecht (1826–1900) and August Bebel (1840–1913). Despite attempts by Bismarck to hamper the Party, it grew rapidly: in 1877 it polled 493,000 votes, in 1890 1,427,000, in 1912 4,239,000. It was kept out of office by coalitions of the 'bourgeois' parties.

Social-democrat parties, on the German model, were founded in Belgium (1885); Austria (1889, founded by Viktor Adler, 1852–1918); Hungary (1890); Bulgaria (1891); Poland (1892); Rumania (1893, disintegrated 1900 and refounded 1910); Holland (1894); Russia (1898); Finland (1903); Serbia (1903). The socialist parties of Britain (Labour Party, q.v.) and France (see *Jaurès*) developed along different lines.

Social democracy became a powerful force in the Scandinavian states. The Danish party was founded in 1878, the Norwegian in 1887, and the Swedish in 1889. All three were closely linked to the trade union movements in their countries and followed the British, rather than the German, pattern of development. The Swedish party achieved a virtual social revolution in the period 1924–36, and the Norwegian party carried through a programme for social security between 1935 and 1938.

Representatives of the national parties met in the congresses of the Second International (q.v.).

After the Russian Revolution, the orthodox Marxists seceded from most of the social-democrat parties, who were prepared to work for the gradual dissolution of capitalism and not for the violent revolution expected by the communist parties (q.v.).

Solferino, Battle of (20 June 1859). An indecisive battle, with very heavy casualties, fought in Lombardy in the Franco-Piedmontese War against Austria. Although it was technically a defeat for the Austrians, the casualty figures so alarmed Napoleon III (q.v.) that he offered the Austrians an armistice (without consulting his Piedmontese allies), which was concluded on 8 July. The carnage of Magenta (q.v.) and Solferino increased the demand for international medical services and so helped establish, in 1864, the International Red Cross.

Somme, Battle of (1 July–15 November 1916). A costly offensive mounted by the British and French along a twenty-mile stretch of the River Somme in north-western France. During the twenty weeks of fighting the Allies advanced, at the most, ten miles and lost 600,000 men, two thirds of whom were British. The Somme was the first battle in which tanks were employed (by the British, in September). The Germans were eventually forced into new positions, but rain and mud stopped the offensive. After the war, German Generals maintained that their losses had been so great on the Somme that they could never again raise a fully trained and efficient fighting force and that accordingly the Somme, for all its apparent futile costliness, was the real turning-point of the war.

Sonderbund. A league formed by the seven predominantly Catholic Swiss cantons in December 1845, to protect their interests against an attempt to strengthen the Federal Government by the Liberals (most of whom were non-Catholics). When the Federal Diet condemned the Sonderbund as a secessionist movement contrary to the Swiss Constitution, the seven cantons (which were mainly around Lake Lucerne) organized resistance, and there was a brief civil war in November 1847 before the Federal forces secured the dissolution of the Sonderbund and the expulsion from Switzerland of the Jesuits, who were alleged to have organized the league. The Federal action aroused the hostility of the Austrians and French, both of whom had planned intervention on behalf of the Sonderbund, but received the sympathetic support of Palmerston.

South Africa Act. An Act carried through the British Parliament in September 1909 giving approval to a constitution devised at a convention of representatives from Cape Colony, Natal, the Transvaal, and the Orange River Colony, held in Durban and Capetown between October 1908 and February 1909, and proposing the creation of a Union of South Africa, a dominion under the British Crown, with equal status for people of British or Dutch descent. The Union officially came into being on 31 May 1910; the first elections were held in the following September and gave victory to the party of General Botha (q.v.), who became the first Prime Minister. In June 1934 the 'Status of the Union Act' (passed in the South African Parliament) defined the Union as 'a sovereign independent state' with an eventual right of secession from the Commonwealth. A referendum in 1960 voted in favour of the Union becoming a Republic. In the following year, after persistent condemnation of the Nationalist Party's policy towards the coloured peoples of the Union, South Africa left the Commonwealth.

South African War. See *Boer Wars*.

Spanish-American War of 1898. Caused by the expansionist policy of the younger Republican politicians and by the repressive attitude of the Spanish colonial administration in Cuba (q.v.). The destruction of the U.S. battleship *Maine* in Havana on 15 February 1898, with the loss of 260 of her crew, outraged American public opinion, which assumed (without waiting for evidence) that Spaniards had blown up the vessel. Despite conciliatory messages from Spain, President McKinley asked Congress for a declaration of war (April). U.S. naval forces concentrated on the Philippines (where Dewey destroyed a Spanish squadron in Manila Bay without any loss of American lives); on Cuba (where Theodore Roosevelt, q.v., played a leading role in the expeditionary force and where another Spanish squadron was destroyed, with the loss of one American life); and in Puerto Rico. Peace was signed in Paris in December 1898; the U.S.A. gained the Philippines, Guam, and Puerto Rico; Spain also ceded Cuba, which was occupied by American troops pending proclamation of an independent republic.

Spanish Civil War (1936–9). Arose from the resentment of the Army leaders at the growing socialist and anti-clerical tendencies of the Popular Front Republican Government of President Azana. The Civil War began by a revolt of military commanders in Spanish Morocco on 18 July 1936. The insurgents were led by General Sanjurjo (killed two months later) and General Franco, who was proclaimed 'Chief of the Spanish State' in October 1936. The Government remained in control of Madrid, Barcelona, Bilbao, and Valencia; Cadiz, Saragossa, Seville, and Burgos declared for the insurgent nationalists. Spain became an ideological battleground for fascists and socialists from all countries. Russia sent advisers and technicians to the Government, and opponents of fascism organized an International Brigade which was involved in heavy fighting along the River Ebro throughout 1938. German air power contributed considerably to Franco's victory, the pilots perfecting techniques of dive-bombing which they were to use in the Second World War. Franco also had the assistance of more than 50,000 Italian 'volunteers'.

The military campaigns of the Civil War fall into four main phases. (i) In the first six months the advantages of surprise and superior military strength enabled the rebel nationalists to carry all before them in the west and the south. The determination of urban workers and miners, and the desire of the Basques and Catalonians for autonomy (which they would clearly not obtain from the nationalists) enabled the Government to rally resistance in the east and extreme north. By the end of 1936 Franco held rather more than half of Spain, including the length of the Portuguese frontier, a vital supply link. (ii) In 1937 the nationalists sought to cut off Madrid and drive a wedge through 'Government' territory by advancing from Teruel on Valencia. In both instances the nationalists failed: the International Brigade, based on Madrid, defeated a largely Italian force at Guadalajara; the 'Government' troops recaptured Teruel. The nationalists were, however, successful in the north, capturing the Basque port of Bilbao in June. (iii) In 1938 even greater assistance reached Franco from Germany and Italy (despite attempts by the British and French to impose a policy of 'non-intervention'). The nationalists were thus able to resume the offensive throughout Spain. In August they at last severed 'Government' territory, after a six-month thrust towards the sea. Throughout the year Madrid withstood a siege and it was not until Christmas that the nationalists broke through on the Catalan Front. (iv) Intrigues between rival factions and a change of Russian policy (which cut off aid) led to the rapid collapse of the 'Government' forces in 1939. Barcelona was taken on 26 January and Valencia and Madrid surrendered on 28 March. Some three quarters of a million lives were lost in the course of the Civil War.

Speenhamland System. A method of out-door relief for the poor. Originally devised by Berkshire Justices of the Peace meeting at Speenhamland, near Newbury, in May 1795. It provided a sliding scale of allowances, varying with the price of bread and size of the family concerned, to be paid from the rates to supplement the wages of labourers. The Speenhamland system was never specifically authorized by legislation, but it was soon adopted in every English country except the far north and west. The system was an honest attempt to deal humanely with the rising problem of pauperism, but the Speenhamland justices had made a fundamental mistake in rejecting the idea of a fixed minimum wage in favour of a subsidy from the rates. The disadvantages of the system did not become clear until the rise in unemployment after the Napoleonic Wars and the consequent increased claims on relief. Magistrates complained that the system subsidized laziness: farmers paid low wages, throwing an unfair burden on the general ratepayers; the labourers themselves suffered, because relief depended on the price of bread, and the price of other necessities rose so alarmingly that the Speenhamland system did not even guarantee a survival wage. The weaknesses of the system were shown by the serious agrarian disturbances in the southern counties in 1830, and the system was abandoned by the Poor Law of 1834 (q.v.).

Speransky, Michael (1772–1839). Russian reformer and jurist. The son of a country priest, became the chief adviser to Tsar Alexander I on constitutional reform, and was responsible for the creation in 1810 of the Council of State and the first regular system of state budgets in Russia. His attempts to secure representative central and local assemblies aroused the opposition of conservative groups, and he was temporarily exiled in 1812. He returned to favour under Nicholas I and set himself to codify the Russian legal system, a task completed in 1832.

'Splendid Isolation'. British foreign policy during the Salisbury Governments of 1895–1902 has frequently been described as being based upon the principle of 'splendid isolation'. While the other European Great Powers tended to line up in two rival camps, Britain was able, because of her naval strength, to remain without an ally until 1902 – when a treaty limited to Far Eastern waters was made with Japan. It is, however, a mistake to assume that Salisbury favoured isolation under all circumstances. He disliked indefinite undertakings for possible action in hypothetical circumstances at some future date, but he was always prepared to make limited agreements for particular objectives; thus he made the Mediterranean Agreements (q.v.) with Italy and Austria-Hungary, and cooperated with France and Russia during disturbances in Crete in 1896. The phrase 'splendid isolation' was used in the Canadian Parliament (16 January 1896), appeared as a heading in *The Times* six days later (reporting a speech by Joseph Chamberlain), and was first used by Salisbury in the Guildhall speech of 9 November 1896, as a mildly sardonic rebuke to the complacent self-righteousness of some of his critics. It is ironical that Salisbury, who always regarded complete isolation as a disaster, should have had the phrase posthumously attached to his policy.

Stalin, Josef Visarionovitch (1879–1953, family name Djugashvili). Born in Georgia, the son of a cobbler. Educated in a seminary, from which he was expelled for holding revolutionary views in 1899. He was twice exiled to Siberia, escaping each time. In 1902–3 he was in

Paris, in 1906 at the Stockholm Conference of Russian Social Democrat exiles, in 1907 at the London Conference. When the Bolshevik Central Committee was established in 1912 he was recognized as its expert on racial minorities and in 1913 completed, in Vienna, his study *Marxism and the Nationalities Problem*. He became editor of *Pravda* in 1917, assisted Lenin in Petrograd during the October Revolution, and was made Commissar for Nationalities in the government that Lenin established, holding the post until 1922 when he became Secretary of the Communist Party. In the Civil War he helped organize the defence of Petrograd against the 'Whites' of General Yudenich, and distinguished himself in defending Tsaritsyn (renamed Stalingrad in his honour) against General Denikin. When at the end of 1923 it was clear that Lenin was dying, Stalin allied himself to Zinoviev (q.v.) and Kamenev to keep Trotsky (q.v.) out of office. The dispute with Trotsky continued until January 1929, when he was exiled to Turkey, Stalin meanwhile having broken with his former allies and used his position as Party Secretary to impose his will on the party at the 15th Congress (December 1927). From 1928 Stalin began his policy of achieving 'Socialism in One Country' through the Five-Year Plans (q.v.). In 1933 and again from 1936 to 1938 he enforced his views through trials in which his opponents, many of them veteran Bolsheviks or Army leaders, were charged with treason and condemned (see *Yezhovshchina*). On 7 May 1941 Stalin, who had hitherto relied upon indirect political control, became Prime Minister (Chairman of the Council of Ministers), a post he retained until his death in March 1953. As Commissar of Defence and a Marshal of the Soviet Union he assumed supreme direction of the Russian war effort and attended the conferences of the Allied statesmen at Teheran, Yalta, and Potsdam. After the war he sought to retain as rigid a grip on the policies of the newly communist states as he had on the Russian political machine. He failed only in the case of Yugoslavia, where Marshal Tito successfully defied him in June 1948. Since Stalin's death, his successors have accused him of encouraging a 'personality cult'. In October 1961 the 22nd Party Congress, after attacks on his persecution in the 1930s, ordered the removal of his embalmed body from the mausoleum in Red Square to a plain grave beside the Kremlin wall.

Stalingrad (now Volgograd). A city on the lower Volga (formerly Tsaritsyn). Had its name changed to Stalingrad in 1928 to commemorate its defence by Stalin in the Russian Civil War. On 5 September 1942, German units under General von Paulus advanced on

Stalingrad from the Don Basin. The Russians resisted street by street, until in November a relief force under General Zhukov cut off the German communications and besieged the besiegers. Despite stubborn German resistance, the Russians gradually closed in on the city, capturing Paulus and his staff on 31 January 1943. Twenty-one German divisions fought at Stalingrad; the Russians took 90,000 prisoners. It was the farthest point that the Germans penetrated into Russia. In November 1961 Stalingrad was renamed Volgograd.

Stamboliisky, Alexander (1879–1923). Bulgarian peasant leader. Stamboliisky, the son of a peasant, became an active agrarian agitator in 1897 on returning to Bulgaria from Germany, where he had studied agriculture. From 1908 to 1915 he was notorious as a brilliant demagogue, and was then imprisoned for opposing Bulgaria's entry into the war. He helped to force King Ferdinand's abdication in 1918, and was Prime Minister from October 1919 until June 1923. During this period Stamboliisky was virtually a peasant dictator, instituting a régime which imposed considerable burdens not only on the bourgeoisie but on the urban proletariat as well, and left the peasantry almost free from taxes. He was overthrown by a right-wing *coup d'état* in which he was murdered, the occasion of his fall being an attempt to cooperate with the Yugoslavs in suppressing I.M.R.O. (q.v.), rather than resentment at his one-sided agrarian policy.

Stambulov, Stefan (1854–95). Bulgarian statesman. Stambulov was educated at a seminary in Odessa but, fearing exile to Siberia, left in 1871, retiring to Rumania. A year later, at eighteen, he became a teacher at Trnovo and was thus able to take a prominent part in the revolutionary agitation in Bulgaria of 1875. In 1886 he was accepted as natural leader of Bulgaria when that country defied the Great Powers and secured the union of Eastern Roumelia. He was officially created Regent in September 1886, and lent his support to the newly elected Prince, Ferdinand of Saxe-Coburg. For seven years Stambulov was Bulgaria's 'strong man', seeking reconciliation with the old enemy, Turkey, and being prepared to forget 'unredeemed Macedonia'. Stambulov's strength of character made him many enemies, including Ferdinand, who dismissed him in January 1894 and connived at his brutal murder in July 1895.

States-General. The traditional political representative system of the French Monarchy, first summoned in the thirteenth century, falling in abeyance after 1614 and revived only on the eve of the

French Revolution (q.v.). The States-General consisted of representatives of the First Estate (the clergy), the Second Estate (the nobility), and the Third Estate (the commonalty). The King issued the decree summoning the States-General on 8 August 1778, but the meeting did not actually open until 5 May 1789. Throughout May there was a dispute whether the three Estates should sit together or apart. On 10 June, the Third Estate forced the hand of the two privileged orders by calling for a common assembly. The States-General as an institution may be said to have disappeared on 17 June, when the Deputies declared themselves to be a 'National Assembly', but it was not until 5 November that all distinctions between the three Estates were formally abolished.

Stavisky Case (1934). A discreditable episode that brought France to the verge of civil war. Serge Stavisky, a company promotor of Russian Jewish origin, was accused of issuing fraudulent bonds on the security of the municipal pawnshop of Bayonne but, before the charges could be pressed, committed suicide (3 January 1934). Investigations showed that Stavisky had dabbled in other dubious speculations and appeared to have been protected from legal action by well-disposed Ministers and Deputies. Subsequently a high official in the 'Public Prosecutor's' Department in Paris was found murdered, allegedly to safeguard some well-known figures. The scandal was exploited both by the Communists and by the right-wing Fascist and Royalist groups, who maintained that the incident proved the corruption and inefficiency of the whole system of democratic rule in France. Serious rioting occurred in Paris on 6, 7, and 9 February, followed by a general strike. The Republic was saved only by the establishment of a broad coalition government whose members had not had their reputation besmirched by the scandal. The Stavisky Riots had a lasting effect on French politics; the ideology of the right-wing demonstrators became the official doctrine of the Vichy régime (q.v.).

Stein, Baron Heinrich Friedrich Karl vom und zum (1757–1831). Prussian statesman. Born near Nassau and educated at Göttingen. He became a Prussian civil servant in 1780 and was responsible for improving communications, especially in the western territories. His zeal for reform led him to be made chief minister in October 1807, at a time of Prussian humiliation after Tilsit (q.v.). In the fourteen months that he was in office he accomplished a social and political revolution by issuing an edict to emancipate the serfs (promulgated 1807, effective 1810), by encouraging land reform, and by making changes in the administration of central and municipal government. French intrigues forced him to flee to Austria in December 1808. In 1812 he went to St Petersburg and served Alexander I until the fall of Napoleon, acting as administrator of the liberated German territories 1813–14. His plan for a genuine political union of the German states was rejected by Metternich at the Congress of Vienna.

Stephenson, George (1781–1848). British engineer. Stephenson was born at Newcastle, the son of a colliery engineer. He carried further experiments undertaken by Richard Trevithick (1771–1833) who had built a locomotive to run on rails as early as 1804. Stephenson began by constructing locomotives for colliery tram-loads, building successful engines at Killingworth (1814–17). He supervised the engineering work on the Stockton–Darlington Railway (1822–5). In 1829 his locomotive, the *Rocket*, won the Rainhill trials for the new Liverpool–Manchester Railway (opened in 1830). By reaching a speed of 35 m.p.h., the *Rocket* demonstrated that railways could be fast conveyors of passengers as well as an economical way of moving coal from a pit-head. Stephenson's son, Robert (1803–59), was also a famous engineer, and constructed bridges across the Menai Straits, the St Lawrence, and the Nile.

Stolypin, Peter (1862–1911). Russian statesman. Stolypin first attracted the attention of Nicholas II by the energy with which he suppressed the 1905 agrarian disturbances in Saratov Province, of which he was Governor. The Tsar appointed him Minister of the Interior in May 1906, making him Prime Minister two months later, a post he held until assassinated in a Kiev theatre in September 1911. Stolypin followed a policy of moderate reform, seeking to balance the liberal elements in the Duma (q.v.) by creating a new class of medium farmers (the Kulaks, q.v.) who would be essentially conservative. At the same time he narrowed the franchise for election to the Duma by introducing a property qualification. His period of office was also marked by harsh treatment of rioters in the countryside through a system of 'field courts martial' and by a revival of persecution of the Jewish population. Stolypin, however, began a scheme for social insurance, improved education, and sought to extend the system of zemstva (q.v.).

Straits Question. An international dispute concerning rights of passage through the Dardanelles (q.v.) and the Bosphorus (q.v.). In 1833 a secret clause to the Treaty of Unkiar Skelessi (q.v.) assured the Russians that the Turks would close the Dardanelles to foreign warships while imposing no restrictions on Russian vessels coming out of the Black Sea. This remained the ideal solution for Russia but was invalidated by a series of later agreements. The Straits Convention of July 1841 (signed by Britain, Russia, France, Austria, and Prussia) closed the Straits to all foreign warships while Turkey was at peace, a stipulation reaffirmed by the Treaty of Paris (q.v.) of 1856. A conference in London in 1871 (accepting the Russian re-militarization of the Black Sea) also re-stated the principle of 1841 but contained clauses allowing warships to pass the Straits even in peace if the Sultan considered the independence of Turkey menaced by the action of another Power. The 1871 decision formed the basis of the statements on the Straits made at the Congress of Berlin in 1878, although Salisbury (q.v.) on that occasion made it clear that the British regarded themselves as free to send warships up the Dardanelles, even without an invitation, should the Sultan appear to have lost his freedom of action.

In 1885 and 1895 the Turks, with the backing of the other powers, refused to allow British vessels up the Straits. British policy changed in 1896, Salisbury declaring in favour of free passage of the Straits for all vessels. This idea was now unacceptable to the Russians but, after finding the Straits closed to them in the Russo-Japanese War, they too adopted the policy that Salisbury had urged. In 1908 and again in 1912 the Russians tried to revise the Straits Convention but still had to face the opposition of Germany and Austria-Hungary. After the First World War the Treaty of Lausanne (q.v.) imposed a new settlement; the Straits were demilitarized but warships were allowed full right of passage so long as Turkey was at peace and so long as no *one* state sent a fleet larger than the Russian force in the Black Sea. The Montreux Convention (q.v.) of 1936 not only allowed the Turks to refortify the Straits but allowed the Russians to send through warships of any class, except aircraft-carriers and submarines, while limiting non-Black-Sea Powers to light warships.

Stratford de Redcliffe, Viscount (1786–1880). Born Stratford Canning. The son of a London merchant, taking the title by which he is better known on being made a peer, 1852. While a Cambridge undergraduate he was given a minor Foreign Office post by his cousin, the Foreign Secretary, George Canning (q.v.). He spent most of his public life in Constantinople, where he was in charge of British interests for 24 years in all – 1810–14, 1824–9, 1841–5, 1847–58. He also served as British Minister in Washington from 1820 to 1824. Stratford's commanding presence, sympathetic insight, and patience won him the support of the Turks, who never doubted his declared intention of postponing as long as possible the disintegration of the Ottoman Empire. His contemporaries believed that he instigated the Russo-Turkish War of 1853; this legend is not supported by the diplomatic archives. He worked throughout his period as Ambassador to secure internal reforms; he believed that a Russian attack would destroy not only these reforms but the Turkish Empire as well. He was, however, determined to prevent the Russians from setting up a virtual protectorate over Turkey, and used his position as unofficial adviser to the Sultan to induce the Turks to follow a firm course in their diplomatic negotiations. He became an easy scapegoat for the blunders and contradictions of the Aberdeen Ministry.

Stresa Conferences. There were two conferences held at Stresa in the 1930s. The first was a meeting of representatives of sixteen governments under the auspices of the League of Nations in September 1932 to discuss assistance to the states of eastern and central Europe in their economic difficulties. The second conference was in April 1935, and was between the Prime Ministers of Britain, France, and Italy (MacDonald, Flandin, and Mussolini) and their Foreign Secretaries to discuss the formation of a common front against Germany in view of Hitler's denunciation of the clauses in the Versailles Treaty limiting Germany's armaments. The conference, which issued a formal protest, was the last demonstration of unity by the three former Allies against the former enemy. Within six months Mussolini's invasion of Abyssinia had ranged him with the delinquent Hitler, and the so-called 'Stresa Front' had disintegrated.

Stresemann, Gustav (1878–1929). German statesman. Born in Berlin, and became a member of the Reichstag in 1906, succeeding in 1917 to the leadership of the National Liberals (re-named 'People's Party' in 1919). During the war Stresemann was an ardent nationalist and parliamentary mouthpiece of the High Command. Under the Weimar Republic he moderated his views. While still believing that Germany was destined to dominate Europe, he emerged as leader of the group that favoured 'Fulfilment', winning the confidence of the Western Powers by an attempt to carry out the Treaty of Versailles. Although Chancellor only from August to November 1923, he continued as Foreign Minister until his death (October 1929) and secured the reversal of Germany's diplomatic position. His greatest personal successes were the Pact of Locarno (q.v.) in 1925 and the entry of Germany into the League, with a permanent seat on the Council (1926). He reduced the figure of Reparations (q.v.) and, shortly before his death, negotiated an agreement for Allied evacuation of the Rhineland (q.v.). He was awarded a Nobel Peace Prize in 1926.

Strossmayer, Josef (1815–1905). Croatian cleric and champion of the Yugoslav ideal. He was Bishop of Djakovo from 1849 until his death, and took a prominent part in restraining the illiberal tendencies of the Hungarian authorities in Croatia in the second half of the century. He founded a South Slav Academy at Zagreb (then called Agram) in 1867 and established a university there in 1874. Strossmayer was a liberal Catholic and opposed the doctrines of papal infallibility at the Vatican Council of 1870. He corresponded extensively with Gladstone and did much to awaken the interest of western liberals in the idea of South Slav unity.

Succession States. The term applied to the states that were established after the First World War on territory that had belonged, in whole or in part, to the former Dual Monarchy of Austria-Hungary, i.e. Czechoslovakia, Rumania, Yugoslavia, Poland, Austria, and Hungary. Technically, Italy also was a 'Succession State', having acquired the South Tyrol, the Julian March, and Fiume, but she is not generally considered in this category.

Sudan. The Sudan was conquered by Egyptian forces under Hussein (fifth son of Mehemet Ali, q.v.) between 1820 and 1822 and the city of Khartoum founded in the following year. The region served as a reservoir for the Arabian slave trade (which was only partially suppressed during the governorship of General Gordon, 1874–9). The revolt of the Mahdi (q.v.) began in 1883. Resisting offers made by Gordon, who had been sent to withdraw Egyptian troops from the Sudan, the Mahdi besieged Khartoum, taking the city in January 1885 and killing its defenders, including Gordon. In 1896 Kitchener (q.v.) began the reconquest of the Sudan, avenging Gordon's death by his victory at Omdurman (q.v.) in September 1898. Four months later the Sudan was organized as an Anglo-Egyptian condominium. A constitution providing for Sudanese self-government was issued in 1953 and the British and Egyptian Governments accepted a Sudanese request for full independence in January 1956.

Sudetenland. An area in northern Bohemia adjoining Germany, inhabited in 1919 by some three million German-speaking people, who had previously belonged to Austria-Hungary and who, by the Treaty of St Germain, were assigned to Czechoslovakia. The Sudetenland lies east of the mountains which form the natural strategic frontier between Germany and Czechoslovakia; it contains rich mineral resources, and in Pilsen has the largest munitions factory in Central Europe. The majority of the political leaders of the Sudetenland were prepared to remain in Czechoslovakia until after the advent of the Nazis in 1933. In 1935 a Nazi-financed Sudetendeutsche Partei, led by Konrad Henlein, gained election successes and began an active campaign against the Czechoslovak State, increasing their demands after the union of Germany and Austria in March 1938. In September 1938 by the Munich Agreement (q.v.), the Sudetenland was assigned to Germany, its transfer implying the surrender by Czechoslovakia of her main line of defences. The Czechoslovaks regained control in 1945, expelled all German-speaking inhabitants, and organized the settlement of Czechs from other parts of Bohemia in the area.

Suez Canal. A concession to build a canal linking the Mediterranean and Red Seas was granted to Ferdinand de Lesseps (q.v.) in November 1854, and an international Suez Canal Company, originally dominated by Frenchmen, was formed in 1858. Work began on the canal, which is slightly more than 100 miles long, in April 1859, and it was officially opened by the Empress Eugénie in November 1869. The British had originally opposed the project, believing that it was a French attempt to secure a footing in the Levant and thus indirectly menace India. British policy was abruptly reversed in November 1875 by Disraeli who purchased for the Government from the Khedive 40 per cent of the shares in the Company, thus making Britain the largest single shareholder. In 1888 the Suez Canal Convention was signed at Constantinople by all the Great Powers; it provided for 'free and open' navigation 'in time of war as in time of peace' for all vessels. This right was denied to Spanish vessels in the Spanish-American War of 1898, to 'enemy' vessels in the two world wars, and to Israeli vessels by the Egyptians since 1948. British troops were responsible for the defence of the canal from 1883 to 1956, and repulsed Turkish raids in February and March 1915. In July 1956 the Egyptian Government nationalized the canal, although the Suez Canal Company's concession did not expire until 1968. Anglo-French military intervention against Egypt in November 1956 led to the temporary blocking of the canal.

Suffragettes. Women who were prepared to take active steps to secure voting rights. In Britain the word dates from the formation by Mrs Pankhurst (q.v.) of the Women's Social and Political Union in 1903 which, from 1906 to 1914, undertook increasingly militant action to further the suffragette cause, its members enduring imprisonment and forcible feeding. Women over the age of thirty were enfranchised in 1918; women between twenty-one and thirty in 1928. The term 'suffragette' seems to have been in use in the U.S.A. earlier than in England; the American Woman Suffrage Association was established in Cleveland, Ohio, as early as November 1869. In 1890 it fused with the more aggressive 'National Woman Suffrage Association', and, under the leadership of Susan Anthony, resorted to militant tactics that had already gained the vote for women in eleven states before the First World War and secured general female suffrage by the 19th Amendment to the Constitution, 28 August 1920.

The earliest country to give the vote to women was New Zealand (1893). In Europe women were first given the vote in July 1906 when the Tsar signed a decree establishing a new Diet for Finland. The women of Norway were given the vote in the following year.

Sun Yat-sen (1867–1925). Chinese revolutionary, was born near Macao, the son of a peasant. He was educated in Honolulu, was converted to Christianity, and for some years was an American citizen, training as a doctor in Hong Kong. He realized the need to unite the various anti-Manchu revolutionary movements and in 1894 set up his 'Save China League', an organization which depended to a large extent on the support of exiles. He was kidnapped by Chinese consular officials in London in 1897, but released on the intervention of the Foreign Office. In 1898 he proclaimed his 'Three Principles' – 'Nationalism, Democracy, and Socialism' – which remained the basic ideal of his 'League of Common Alliance' (1905) and later of the Kuomintang (q.v.). The Chinese Revolution (q.v.) of 1911 found him in the U.S.A. but he hastily returned to China and in January 1913 became 'President of the United Provinces of China', elected by a revolutionary assembly in Nanking, an office he resigned after a few months in the vain hope of giving the country genuine unity. He remained in opposition to Yuan Shih-kai and his clique, but retained a considerable following in southern China, particularly around Canton. In 1922 he began to accept Russian help and in 1924 modified his doctrines in a series of lectures so that communists might join the Kuomintang. Upon Sun's death in March 1925, both the nationalist wing of his followers (under Chiang Kai-shek) and the Communists claimed to be his rightful heirs, his widow later becoming a vice-president of Communist China.

Suvorov, Alexander (1729–1800). Russian soldier, born in Moscow. Fought against the Swedes, the Prussians, and the Turks in the wars of the eighteenth century. He was a favourite General of Catherine the Great, but he gained unenviable notoriety for the excesses committed by his troops in Bessarabia in 1790 and in putting down the Polish revolt in Warsaw (1795). From 1796 to 1799 he was out of favour, but was given command of the Russian Army that fought against the French in the north of Italy. Between April and August 1799 his troops, collaborating with an Austrian force, drove the French out of Milan and Turin and crossed the St Gotthard Pass to pursue them into Switzerland. At the end of September, the Russians were forced back into the Vorarlberg, and Suvorov was summoned to return to St Petersburg. Although he died in disgrace, his feats in Italy and Switzerland have become legendary.

Sweden. Formerly a dominant power in the Baltic, had lost much of its influence by the early nineteenth century. Finland (q.v.) was lost to Russia in 1809. The fall in Swedish prestige induced Generals Adlerkreuz and Klingspor to arrest King Gustavus IV, force him to abdicate (March 1809), and proclaim his uncle, Charles XIII (1809–18), establishing a new constitution which, with amendments in 1864, has formed the basis of Swedish government ever since. In 1810 the Swedish Estates elected Marshal Bernadotte (q.v.) as heir to the throne. In 1815 Sweden exchanged her last Germanic possession, Pomerania, for Norway (q.v.) which remained united to Sweden until 1905. Sweden has succeeded in remaining at peace since 1814 and has based her foreign policy on the principle of neutrality, although cooperating from time to time with her Scandinavian neighbours. In 1924 the Swedish Socialist Party (under Hjalmar Branting and Rickard Sandler) undertook pioneer work in social legislation, a reforming programme maintained by later Socialist governments in the 1930s.

Swiss Confederation. Although a loose union of Swiss cantons had been established in the fifteenth century, there was no effective central authority for another four hundred years. From 1798 to 1802 Switzerland constituted the Helvetic Republic, a French puppet state; Napoleon conceded a high degree of purely local independence to the cantons. During the Congress of Vienna (q.v.) of 1815, the Great Powers accepted the principle of the 'Perpetual Neutrality' of Switzerland. At the same time a Federal Pact provided for the establishment of a Diet containing representatives of the individual cantons. After the brief civil war caused by the Sonderbund (q.v.), the Swiss adopted a new constitution (September 1848). This was very democratic in character, but provided for effective central government while retaining the local administration of the cantons. With slight modifications, which have increased federal authority, this constitution has remained in being ever since 1848, and the Powers have respected Switzerland's neutrality.

Sykes-Picot Note. A secret agreement signed on 16 May 1916 by Sir Mark Sykes (for the British Government) and Georges Picot (for the French), providing for the partition of the Ottoman Empire after the war. France was to acquire directly or indirectly the whole of Syria, the Lebanon, Cilicia, and Mosul, while Britain was to be compensated in what was subsequently known as Transjordan, Iraq, and northern Palestine. The rest of Palestine was to be under an international régime. An undefined 'Arab State' was to be established. The agreement ran counter to some of the assurances given by T. E. Lawrence (q.v.) to the Arabs he had raised in revolt against the Turks. The terms of the agreement, along with other 'secret treaties', were published by the Bolsheviks in the spring of 1918 and provoked considerable controversy.

Syndicalism. A movement to secure ownership of industry by the workers through 'direct action' (i.e. strikes and, in particular, the general strike). The syndicalists would establish an administration based upon the control exercised by the workers in an industry. The most important syndicalist theorist was Georges Sorel (1847–1923), who published his *Reflections on Violence* in 1908; some of his views were later modified by Mussolini to provide a basis of industrial organization for Fascist Italy. Genuine syndicalism was powerful in France before the First World War and had some following in Britain between 1911 and 1914. The syndicalists in the U.S.A. organized themselves as the I.W.W. (Industrial Workers of the World), established in 1905 as 'one great industrial union ... founded on the class struggle', a violent movement that scared American public opinion and was suppressed in 1918. Syndicalism remained influential in Spain up to the end of the Civil War; elsewhere its power declined in the early 1920s.

Syria. Formed part of the Turkish Empire until the end of the First World War. The French had shown ambitions in Syria for many years, notably in 1798–9 under Bonaparte. From October 1918 to July 1920 there was a contest for control between the Arabs, led by Emir Feisal (later ruler of Iraq, q.v.), and the French, who maintained that Syria had been recognized as falling in their sphere of influence, by the Sykes-Picot Note (q.v.). Syria was created a

French mandated territory in April 1920, but the French had considerable difficulty in preserving order. From July 1925 to June 1927 there was a serious insurrection of the Druses, who twice forced the French to withdraw from the capital, Damascus, the scene of particularly heavy fighting. In 1936 the Popular Front Government (q.v.) reversed French policy over Syria, promising independence within three years, an undertaking that was not kept, partly because of the World War and partly because of the diehard attitude of some French military leaders. Supporters of Vichy (q.v.) remained in power in Syria after the French collapse of 1940. In July 1941 British and 'Free French' (q.v.) troops forced their way into Syria and took over the country, fearing the establishment there of German air bases. Syrian independence was proclaimed on 1 January 1944, but the French military authorities were still unwilling to concede the loss of their position, and in May and June 1945 fighting broke out once again in Damascus between the 'Free French' and the Syrians, the British actively sympathizing with the Syrians. French and British troops finally withdrew in April 1946. A period of political confusion culminated in the proclamation of the union of Syria and Egypt in the 'United Arab Republic' (1957), but Syria re-asserted her independence in September 1961.

Taff Vale Case. A legal action of great importance for the development of trade unions. It was brought in 1901 by the Taff Vale Railway Company (of South Wales) against the Amalgamated Society of Railway Servants for damage to railway property done by its members in a strike called by the union. The courts found the trade union legally responsible for the action of its members, and ordered it to pay £23,000 compensation. This decision caused much resentment among trade unionists, who regarded the judgement as a deliberate attempt to weaken the strike weapon. After the Liberal electoral victory of 1906, the Campbell-Bannerman Government passed a Trade Disputes Act giving trade unions immunity from such actions.

Tahiti Dispute (1843–4). The island of Tahiti in the Eastern Pacific had been a centre for British missionary activity since the beginning of the century. The natives had been induced to petition Britain to make the island a Protectorate in 1826, but Canning rejected the overture. In 1836 a French warship forced the Tahitians to accept French missionaries, and there began a period of Anglo-French rivalry in Tahiti in which the French Admiral, Dupetit-Thouars, and the British Consul and missionary, Pritchard, aroused strong reactions in the public at home, despite attempts by the respective governments to keep the absurd affair in proportion. The British again rejected a Tahitian request for formal protection in 1838. In 1843 Dupetit-Thouars formally proclaimed a French protectorate and in the following year imprisoned Pritchard. Tempers ran high in the French and British Parliaments, and there were threats of war by irresponsible groups. Eventually Pritchard was released with a thousand pounds in compensation, and the storm died down. Nevertheless, it considerably weakened Anglo-French relations, which had generally been friendly during the Orleanist Monarchy. Tahiti was formally annexed to France in 1888.

Taiping Rebellion. A movement of religious mysticism and agrarian unrest in China, 1850–64. The rebellion was strongest in Kwangsi; from 1853 to 1864 the rebels' capital was Nanking. It was led by Hung Hsiu-chuan and Yang Hsiu-ching. Although Hung, an intensely religious figure, declared that he was establishing 'The Heavenly Kingdom of Great Peace', he failed to give his territories protection or to work out any system of administration. The Taiping régime endured for so long only because of the anarchy in other parts of China, much of which was in the hands of bandit leaders who lacked the idealism of Hung. The Taiping movement seriously weakened the dynasty, and showed the urgent need of the Empire to achieve an orderly system of government and to reduce the fiscal burden on the poorer peasantry. The rebellion was eventually suppressed with the aid of foreign officers, notably General Gordon (q.v.). A number of basic reforms were subsequently carried through by Tseng Kuo-fan and Li Hung-chang, but they did little more than scratch the surface of the problem.

Taisho. The period of Japanese history covered by the reign of the Emperor Yoshihito, 1912–26. During these years Japan emerged as one of the Great Powers, partly because of her participation as an Allied state in the First World War and her penetration of Russia after the Revolution, and partly because of the application of modern techniques to her economic resources. The Emperor himself took no active part in politics. Imperialism abroad (see *Twenty-one Demands*) coincided with political liberalism at home; the electorate was doubled by a Reform Act in the spring of 1919 and universal male suffrage was granted in March 1925. At the same time, there was considerable industrial unrest (intensified by the suffering caused by the great Tokio earthquake of 1 September 1923), and open rebellion in Korea.

the Tsar of Russia. The legitimate dynasties were restored in Spain, Naples, Piedmont, Tuscany, and Modena. The Congress re-established the Swiss Confederation, giving a guarantee of Switzerland's permanent neutrality. Austria received not only Lombardy-Venetia but Dalmatia, Carniola, Salzburg, and Galicia. Prussia obtained Posen, Danzig, a large part of Saxony, considerable gains in Westphalia, and the former Swedish territories in Pomerania. The Norwegians were united to Sweden. Britain retained Malta, Heligoland, Cape of Good Hope, Ceylon, Tobago, Santa Lucia, and Mauritius; she was also given a protectorate over the Ionian Islands (effective until 1863).

Apart from the territorial changes of the Final Act, the Congress made several pronouncements of general importance: it established the principle of free navigation of the Rhine and the Meuse; it formally condemned the slave trade; it recommended an extension of the rights granted to the Jews, especially in Germany; and it settled questions of ambassadorial precedence, establishing the system of international diplomacy that lasted throughout the nineteenth century and beyond.

Vilna. Medieval capital of Lithuania (q.v.), the cause of a serious dispute between Lithuania and Poland between the wars. Vilna was seized by Polish irregulars in October 1920 and formally incorporated in Poland in 1922, being returned to Lithuania in October 1939.

Vimy Ridge. A defensive position held by the Germans in the battle of Arras, April 1917. It was captured after very bitter fighting by Canadian troops.

Volgograd. See *Stalingrad*.

Waitangi, Treaty of (1840). An agreement concluded by the first Governor of New Zealand (Captain William Hobson) with some 500 Maori chiefs, by which they surrendered their sovereignty to Britain in return for guarantees of their personal possessions and ownership of land. Disregard of these guarantees precipitated the first Maori War (q.v.) in 1843.

Wakefield, Edward Gibbon (1796–1862). British expert in colonial policy. In 1814 Wakefield entered the diplomatic service, but his unconventional behaviour led, in 1826, to a three-year prison sentence for eloping with an heiress under false pretences. While still in Newgate he published *A Letter from Sydney*, advocating the systematic colonization of Australia by the sale of land at a reasonable price in suitable areas. By this means, he hoped to ensure that new farms would have capital behind them and not be spread over vast territories that would prove impossible to control. Although a modified version of Wakefield's plan was tried in New South Wales, it had more success in New Zealand. He was a founder of the National Colonization Society (1830) and a member of the company that founded South Australia (1836). He accompanied Durham (q.v.) to Canada in 1838. From 1839–46 he was London agent of the New Zealand Land Company, although he disagreed with British policy towards the Maoris, whom he held to have been unduly favoured in the Treaty of Waitangi of 1840 (q.v.). He spent the last nine years of his life in New Zealand, working for the attainment of self-government.

Wallachia. See *Danubian Principalities.*

Wall Street Crash (1929). The most dramatic event in the inter-war Depression (q.v.). From 1927 the U.S.A. had experienced an artificial boom, fed by rash speculation in securities, lacking adequate coverage. On 24 October 1929, fear of the probity of certain concerns led to a panic on the stock market, thirteen million shares changing hands on one day. On 29 October sixteen million shares were sold. Banks subsequently failed, there were major business disasters and rising unemployment. The Crash led to a business Depression throughout America and had repercussions in Europe as well.

War of the First Coalition (1792–7). The first alliance against revolutionary France was made by Austria and Prussia in February 1792, the French declaring war in April. The original Allies were joined by Sardinia-Piedmont (1792), Britain, the Netherlands, Spain (1793), Naples, and the Papal States. In the autumn of 1792, Prussian troops penetrated deeply into France but were thrown back, and the Netherlands were occupied in 1794–5. In March 1795 Prussia made a separate peace, followed by Spain in June. Piedmont, Naples, and the Papal States were overrun in 1796. Bonaparte's Italian Campaign of 1796–7 forced the Austrians to accept the Treaty of Campo-Formio (q.v.) in October 1797, and only Britain remained at war.

War of the Second Coalition (1798–1801). The alliance was primarily the work of Pitt. Britain, Russia, Austria, Naples, Portugal, and Turkey agreed in December 1798 to combine their efforts against

France. With Bonaparte in Egypt, and the Directory disintegrating, the Allies gained rapid successes in Italy, but disputes between the Russians and Austrians led to a Russian withdrawal from the coalition in October 1799. Bonaparte took the field against the Austrians in May 1800, defeating them at Marengo and Hohenlinden and forcing them to conclude the Peace of Lunéville in February 1801. The Turks had already made peace in January 1800, and the Portuguese were defeated by Spain (France's ally) in September 1801. Britain remained at war until the Treaty of Amiens (q.v.) 1802.

War of the Third Coalition (1805–7). In April 1805 Pitt negotiated an alliance with Russia, extended to Austria in August. The Austrians were defeated at Austerlitz (q.v.) in December, and made peace at Pressburg. Prussia entered the coalition in the summer of 1806, but was defeated at Jena and Auerstadt and forced to make peace. The Russians continued resistance until July 1807, when they allied with Napoleon at Tilsit (q.v.). The British, having secured the victory of Trafalgar (q.v.), remained in the war.

War of the Fourth Coalition (1813–14). The French disaster in Russia in 1812 and the Prussian change of sides in February 1813 led Castlereagh (q.v.) to offer British financial aid for those resisting Napoleon. Castlereagh's policy led to the formal foundation of the Fourth Coalition in agreements signed with the Russians and Prussians in June 1813, to which Sweden (who had been in British pay since March) subscribed. The Austrians joined the coalition in August, Bavaria in October, and Wurtemburg and Saxony during the battle of Leipzig (q.v.). The Allies entered Paris on 31 March 1814, secured the abdication of Napoleon on 11 April and signed a preliminary peace treaty with the French in Paris on 30 May.

Washington, George (1732–99). First President of the U.S.A. Born in Virginia. After military service against the French, 1755–9, Washington became an early champion of American independence, and was chosen to command the Continental Army against the British in July 1775, his outstanding military achievement being the secret march from the Hudson to Chesapeake Bay in 1781 which led to the surrender of Cornwallis at Yorktown, thereby ending the war. In the first years of the Republic, Washington was forced into political life by disputes between the various states over federal powers. He presided over the Federal Convention of 1787, which adopted the Constitution, and was unanimously elected President of the U.S.A., assuming office at an inaugural ceremony in New York on 30 April

1789 and retiring at the beginning of 1797. Washington followed an increasingly Federalist policy, favouring the fiscal policy of Hamilton (q.v.) and finding himself at variance with the decentralizing tendencies of Jefferson (q.v.), who was his Secretary of State from September 1789 until December 1793. In foreign policy Washington favoured neutrality. His farewell address of 17 September 1796 forms his political testament; it cautioned America against a party system organized on geographical lines and urged the avoidance of permanent alliances with foreign nations.

Washington Conference (21 November 1921–6 February 1922). Summoned on American initiative to discuss naval disarmament and the question of the Far East. It was attended by representatives of Britain, France, Italy, Portugal, Belgium, Holland, Japan, China, and the U.S.A. The Conference resulted in a series of treaties: (a) an American-British-French-Japanese guarantee of each other's Pacific territories; (b) a collective guarantee of China's independence; (c) an undertaking by Japan to restore Kiaochow (q.v.) to China; (d) a Naval Convention pledging the powers not to build any capital ships for ten years and establishing between Britain, the U.S.A. and Japan a ratio of 5:5:3 for capital ships.

Waterloo, Battle of (18 June 1815). The final defeat of Napoleon after his return from Elba. With an advantage in numbers and artillery, the French attacked the British under Wellington and tried to force their way through to Brussels, eleven miles to the north. The British infantry, in squares, repulsed the attacks and advanced on the French in the evening, linking up with the Prussians under Blücher (q.v.). The French Army disintegrated, and Napoleon was forced to abdicate four days later.

Watt, James (1736–1819). British inventor. Born at Greenock, Watt became a maker of mathematical instruments to Glasgow University, before undertaking the experiments which enabled him to develop the first rotary steam engine (1782). Watt was financed by Matthew Boulton; their joint work made possible the application of steam power to machinery, and so facilitated the development of large-scale industry in Britain, centred on towns near coalfields.

Weimar Republic. The name by which the German Federal Republic of 1918 to 1933 is generally known. In February 1919 the National Constituent Assembly was convened at Weimar, a town on the river Elbe with a tradition of liberalism, so as to eliminate the danger of intimidation in Berlin by either militarists or communists. A constitution providing for a seven-year presidential office, bicameral government, and proportional representation, and guaranteeing federal rights, was adopted on 31 July 1919. The National Assembly remained at Weimar until the spring of 1920, when it returned to Berlin.

The first President of the Republic, Friedrich Ebert, who was in office from February 1919 until his death in February 1925, was a moderate socialist and sought to organize the Republic in the democratic spirit of the Constitution. His successor, Field-Marshal von Hindenburg (q.v.), was a nationalist and, at heart, a devoted monarchist.

The Republic suffered economic difficulties from the outset, since the privations of the wartime Allied blockade were followed by the burden of Reparations (q.v.). A financial collapse in 1922–3 was followed by a period of recovery, resulting partly from governmental economies but even more from foreign loans and the 'Dawes Plan' (q.v.). The American financial depression of 1929, which was followed eighteen months later by the failure of a major central European bank (the Austrian *Credit Anstalt*), led to an even more severe economic crisis and to mass unemployment (5 million in December 1931). The economic disaster destroyed the political balance that had lasted from 1924 to 1929, the so-called 'Era of Stresemann' (q.v.). Elections held in September 1930 marked the emergence of a National Socialist (Nazi) Party, led by Hitler, which secured 109 parliamentary seats against its previous 12. This political trend was maintained in the following two years, until in the election of July 1932 the Nazis became the largest single party, with 230 seats. The Nazi programme of a strong national centralism as opposed to the federalism of Weimar, of anti-semitism (q.v.), and of a vigorous foreign policy appealed to an electorate that had become disillusioned with the democratic parties and terrified by the alternative of communism. The Nazi hostility towards socialism secured for the party the backing of powerful capitalist interests, while Nazi denunciation of the Treaty of Versailles (q.v.) appealed to nationalistic groups who had never forgiven the original Weimar Assembly for accepting the Treaty. Yet, despite the verdict of the electorate, Hindenburg sought to keep out of office a party that was so clearly opposed to the Weimar system. Attempts to administer Germany by delicately balanced coalitions failed, and in January 1933 Hitler was appointed Chancellor. Less than two months later (23 March) he carried through an Enabling Act which suspended the Weimar Constitution.

Weizmann, Chaim (1874–1952). Born near Pinsk in Russian Poland, but emigrated to Britain. As a biochemist he held an influential position in the explosives department of the Admiralty from 1916 to 1919. He was recognized at this time as the leader of British Zionism (q.v.), and was consulted by the Foreign Office during the preparation of the Balfour Declaration (q.v.) of 1917. He became head of the World Zionist movement in 1920 and of the Jewish Agency for Palestine in 1929. He was elected first President of Israel in 1948.

Wellesley, Richard Colley (1760–1842; succeeded his father as Earl Mornington in 1781, created Marquess Wellesley in 1799). The elder brother of the Duke of Wellington (q.v.). Wellesley was appointed Governor-General of India in 1798 and was responsible for frustrating Napoleon's plans to subvert the Indians. He defeated Tipu Sahib in Mysore in 1799, and, in the Maratha War of 1802–5, overthrew Sindhia and Holkar. His conquests thus more than doubled the size of the territories under the control of the East India Company, but his arrogant independence alienated his superiors in London and he was recalled in 1805. From 1809 to 1812 he served as Foreign Secretary and from 1821 to 1828 he was Lord Lieutenant of Ireland. His junior officers in India maintained that Wellesley wore his decorations on his nightshirt; while this seems improbable, the story illustrates the unsympathetic sense of superiority which prevented him reaching the heights attained by his brother.

Wellington, Duke of (Arthur Wellesley, 1769–1852; knighted 1805, Earl of Wellington February 1812, Marquess October 1812, Duke 1814). Educated at Eton, commissioned in the army 1785. From 1796 to 1805 he served in India, both as administrator and soldier. He saw little military service between 1805 and 1808, sitting in the Commons as M.P. for Rye. In 1808 he took the first British force to Portugal, but was recalled after a few months for allowing the French to evacuate the country after inflicting a defeat on them. He was exonerated by court-martial and returned to the Peninsular War (q.v.) in February 1809, remaining in Portugal and Spain until he. victoriously crossed the Pyrenees in 1814. He attended the Congress of Vienna (q.v.) and commanded British troops at Waterloo (q.v.). In January 1819 he entered Lord Liverpool's Cabinet as 'Master-General of the Ordnance' – an office which, despite its military description, allowed him to undertake diplomatic missions, notably to the Congresses of Aix-la-Chapelle (q.v.) and Verona (q.v.). He left the Cabinet in April 1827 but nine months later agreed to form a government and was Prime Minister until November 1830. Although under Peel's pressure he accepted Catholic Emancipation (q.v.), he continued to be a strong opponent of parliamentary reform, incurring some unpopularity. In old age, the 'Iron Duke' became the idol of early Victorian England.

Westminster, Statute of (1931). An Act affirming that dominions are 'autonomous communities within the British Empire, equal in status ... united by a common allegiance to the Crown and freely associated as members of the British Commonwealth of Nations'. The statute, which is the basic charter of the modern Commonwealth, confirmed resolutions carried at the Imperial Conferences of 1926 and 1930.

Wilberforce, William (1759–1833). The most forceful advocate of the abolition of the Slave Trade (q.v.). He was elected M.P. for Hull in 1780 and sat for Yorkshire 1784–1812 and Bramber (Sussex) 1812–25. He was a close friend and supporter of the younger Pitt. He became a fervent believer in evangelical Christianity, and contemplated taking Holy Orders, but was persuaded instead to remain in the Commons, where he could use his considerable power of oratory in denouncing the Slave Trade. He first introduced a Bill for abolishing the Slave Trade in 1791 but it was not passed by the Commons until 1804 and was, even then, twice rejected by the Lords. It eventually became law in 1807. In his later years, he supported the movement for the total abolition of slavery (q.v.), which was accomplished in 1833, shortly before his death. His son, Samuel Wilberforce (1805–73), was Bishop of Oxford from 1845 to 1869, where the efficiency of his administration served as a model for other dioceses.

William II (1859–1941; German Emperor and King of Prussia 1888–1918). Son of Emperor Frederick (who died after only three months on the throne) and of the eldest daughter of Queen Victoria. He received a strict military education, in which he showed much strength of character, triumphing over the physical disability of a withered arm. Two years after his accession, he dismissed Bismarck and sought to follow a 'new course', in which he asserted Germany's claim to world leadership by such actions as the Kruger Telegram (q.v.) and his visit to the ostracized Sultan of Turkey. His personal vanities – a pride in sea power, a desire to ape Frederick the Great, a genuine conviction that he was the adjutant of Providence – led him to strike attitudes of arrogance that made foreign contemporaries regard him as a warmonger. The evidence suggests that he was, in reality, the captive of the German Officer Corps, bound by them to declare war on two fronts in 1914 (although he had wished to limit it to one) and forced by them to abdicate in November 1918, when it was clear that the Allies would not grant Germany peace terms so long as the Kaiser remained on the throne. For more than twenty years he lived the life of a country gentleman at Doorn in Holland, eventually dying with the German invaders on guard at his gates, having refused an offer of asylum in Britain and a proposal by Hitler that he should return to one of his former estates.

William IV (1765–1837. King from 1830). Third son of George III, succeeded his brother, George IV. William served in the Navy as a young man and was a friend of Nelson; he always remained interested in naval affairs. Despite a twenty-year liaison with the actress Mrs Jordan, he settled down to a simple family life with his Queen, Adelaide, whom he married in 1818. He showed more political wisdom than his elder brother, particularly in 1832 when he used his influence to secure passage of the Reform Bill through the House of Lords at a time when public opinion was hardening against the upper classes. As William's two daughters died in infancy, he was succeeded by his niece Victoria.

Wilson, Woodrow (1856–1924). President of the U.S.A. Born in Virginia. After graduating from Harvard, he followed an academic career, specializing in constitutional law and history. He was a Professor at Princeton from 1890 to 1902 and President of the University 1902–10. His educational reforms made him enemies at the University, and he abandoned teaching for politics, serving as Democratic Governor of New Jersey 1911–12. He secured Democratic nomination for President in 1912 and was elected with the unprecedented majority of over two million, much of his success resulting from the split between the Republican President, Taft, and Theodore Roosevelt (q.v.). In home affairs Wilson concentrated on anti-trust measures and, by the Federal Reserve Act of 1913, reorganized the national banking system. Mexican raids over the U.S. frontier forced him to send a punitive expedition in 1916. He followed strict neutrality in the First World War, seeking statements of war aims from the rival belligerents and being prepared to mediate. He won the 1916 Election on the slogan 'He Kept Us Out of War', but the resumption by the Germans of unrestricted U-boat attacks (1 February 1917) and intrigues shown by the Zimmermann Telegram (q.v.) forced him on 6 April 1917 to enter the war as a co-belligerent 'associated power', free, if he wished, to make a separate peace. On 8 January 1918, Wilson issued his Fourteen Points (q.v.) as a basis for peace, stressing the need for a League of Nations. Wilson attended the Paris Peace Conference of 1919, his rapturous reception in Europe blinding him to political realities not only among the Allied politicians, who were less high-minded than he, but also in the U.S. Senate, which had already passed under Republican control. He was forced in Paris to accept compromises, trusting that the League would right the wrongs of the treaties in due course. On returning to America, Wilson found that the Senate would not ratify the Treaty of Versailles (which contained the League Covenant). Three weeks after beginning a nationwide campaign to win public support for his ideas, Wilson collapsed (26 September 1919). He was an invalid for the last three and a half years of his life.

Witte, Serge (1849–1915). Russian statesman. Although born in Tiflis, Witte was a member of a family of Baltic Germans long in Russian service. He was educated at Odessa University, and became an administrator of provincial railways. His ideas were formed by the economic theories of List (q.v.), and he was determined to do for Russia what List's followers had done for Prussia. In the late 1880s he was made Minister of Communications, a post he combined with the Ministry of Finance from 1892 to 1903 (at the same time controlling commerce, industry, and labour relations). His greatest achievement was the construction of the Trans-Siberian Railway (q.v.) and the Chinese Eastern Railway through northern Manchuria. He also secured loans from France which assisted the increasing industrialization of European Russia. His policy of gradual economic penetration of Manchuria was too cautious for an influential group of militarists, who secured his dismissal in 1903 and whose expansionist policy led, in the following year, to the Russo-Japanese War. Witte was recalled by Tsar Nicholas II to negotiate peace at Portsmouth (q.v.), New Hampshire; and when the Revolution of 1905 (q.v.) forced the Tsar to establish a constitutional government, it was Witte whom he made first Prime Minister. He managed to float a loan for £80 million in Britain and France (which freed the Russian Government from financial dependence on the Duma) and was then dismissed, after only six months in office. He was unpopular with Nicholas II and his entourage and was never again in power. He strongly opposed the war of 1914 and spent his last months as a Russian Cassandra.

World War, First. The immediate cause of the War was the spread of nationalism in the Balkans, as shown by the assassination at Sarajevo (q.v.) and the determination of the Austrians to destroy the

Serbian 'hornets' nest'. The reasons why this conflict could not be localized lie further back. Among them was the division of Europe into rival camps by a system of alliances, originally defensive in character but made dangerous through a lessening of international trust by successive crises – Morocco in 1905, Bosnia in 1908–9, Agadir in 1911 (all q.v.). Anglo-German relations had worsened because of naval rivalry and, to a much lesser extent, trade competition.

Austria-Hungary declared war on Serbia on 28 July 1914; Russia mobilized along the German and Austrian frontiers on 29 July; Germany declared war on Russia on 1 August and on France on 3 August, invading Belgium on the same day; Britain declared war on Germany on 4 August. Germany and Austria-Hungary were joined by Turkey (November 1914) and Bulgaria (October 1915). The original Allies were supported by eighteen other states, the most important being Japan (August 1914), Italy (May 1915), and the U.S.A. (April 1917).

The main area of fighting against Germany was along the Western Front, where, after the repulse of the initial German advance to the Marne, both sides constructed defence-works, so that a line of trenches extended from Nieuport on the Belgian coast, through Ypres, Arras, Albert, Soissons, and Rheims to Verdun. For three and a half years neither side advanced more than a few miles along this line, despite new weapons such as poison gas (first used by the Germans at Ypres in April 1915) and tanks (first used by the British on the Somme in September 1916). In the early spring of 1918 the Germans again broke through to the Marne, but a few weeks later were thrown back into Belgium.

Apart from initial Russian advances to the Carpathians and to Tannenberg, and an offensive under Brussilov against the Austrians in the summer of 1916, all the fighting on the Eastern Front consisted of an exhausting defence by the Russians. Attempts were made by the Allies to assist them by opening the Straits through a campaign at Gallipoli (April 1915–January 1916) but without success. The Bolsheviks secured an armistice in December 1917.

In the Balkans the Serbs threw back the Austrians' original offensive, but were defeated by a combined force of Germans, Austrians, and Bulgarians in the winter of 1915–16. The Allied Expeditionary force at Salonica eventually broke through the Bulgarian lines in September 1918.

The Italian Front was stabilized along the River Isonzo for two and a half years, before the Italians were forced back from Caporetto to the River Piave in October 1917, avenging their defeat by the victory of Vittorio Veneto a year later.

Outside Europe there was a campaign against the Turks in Palestine, with British forces based on Cairo gaining the decisive victory in October 1918. The Turks were also forced on to the defensive by the Russians in the Caucasus and by British Imperial troops in Mesopotamia. In Africa there was a protracted campaign, mostly by South Africans, against the German colonies. The Japanese mopped up German possessions in Asia.

There were naval actions against isolated cruisers in the Pacific and South Atlantic, and against the Austro-Hungarian fleet in the Adriatic, but the main battle between the British and German fleets was fought at Jutland (31 May–1 June 1916). The German naval staff concentrated on defeating the British by the use of the submarine (U-boat). In the spring of 1917 the U-boats had brought Britain close to starvation. Submarine attack was countered by the adoption of a convoy system and the development of such new weapons as the depth charge. Aircraft (and airships) were used at first to support military and naval operations; later they brought total war to cities behind the lines, including London.

The German Armistice was signed on 11 November 1918. A Peace Conference to settle the form of the new Europe opened in Paris ten weeks later.

(*See also under individual battles, etc.*)

World War, Second. Had its origins in German unwillingness to accept the Versailles frontiers, and the Anglo-French pledge to support Poland of April 1939. German forces invaded Poland on 1 September 1939 and overran the country in four weeks. Britain and France declared war on Germany on 3 September but avoided major operations. In April 1940 the Germans occupied Denmark and Norway (where Allied troops resisted for two months). The invasion of Belgium and Holland on 10 May 1940 opened the period of 'lightning war' (*Blitzkrieg*), in which penetration by German tanks and use of air power encompassed the fall of the Netherlands within four days, Belgium within three weeks, and France within seven weeks. Failure to secure air superiority over Britain frustrated Hitler's plans of invasion and, while continuing submarine attacks on British supply routes, the Germans moved eastwards, invading Yugoslavia and Greece in April 1941 and attacking Russia on a 2,000-mile front on 22 June (in alliance with Finland, Hungary, and Rumania). British military efforts concentrated on the Italians, who had joined the Germans on 10 June 1940 but who were so badly defeated within fifteen months that they became a liability to their allies. Relentless German advances in Russia brought them to the outskirts of Leningrad and Moscow and to the Volga, but from November 1942 they were gradually thrown back, the last invading forces being expelled from prewar Russia in August 1944. Japan's desire for Asiatic expansion induced her to attack British and American bases on 7 December 1941 (Germany and Italy declaring war on the U.S.A. three days later). Within four months the Japanese were masters of south-east Asia and Burma, and it was not until June 1942 that naval victories in the Pacific stemmed their advance. In the war against Germany, the second battle of Alamein at the end of October 1942 marked the turn of the tide for the British. Allied troops ejected the Germans and Italians from North Africa (October 1942–May 1943), invaded Sicily and Italy, and forced the Italians to make a separate peace (3 September 1943). The German hold on Europe was weakened by guerilla risings, notably by Tito's Partisans in Yugoslavia and the Maquis in France. A 'Second Front' was launched against the Germans by the invasion of Normandy on 6 June 1944, Paris being liberated on 25 August. Despite the German use of flying bombs and rockets against British bases, the Allies advanced across the pre-war German frontier early in February 1945 and linked up with the Russians on 28 April on the Elbe. The Germans accepted unconditional surrender at Rheims on 7 May. Meanwhile the British mounted a land offensive against the Japanese in Burma, while the Americans undertook heavy air attacks, culminating in the dropping of two atomic bombs on Japan itself. The Japanese surrendered on 14 August 1945.

(*See also under individual battles, etc.*)

Wright Brothers (Wilbur, 1867–1912, and Orville, 1871–1948). Pioneers of aeroplane construction, sons of a bishop in one of the smaller American sects. Received only formal schooling, but developed an interest in aeronautics and constructed gliders at Kitty Hawk, North Carolina. In the course of 1903 they built an aeroplane powered by a twelve horse-power petrol engine. On 7 December 1903, Orville Wright made the first flight in a powered aircraft – 40 yards. They spent two more years improving the machine and were able, by the end of 1905, to fly a distance of 24 miles. Three years later, they brought their aircraft to Europe, pioneering powered flight in Britain, France, and Italy.

Yezhovshchina. A Russian term describing the Great Purge in the U.S.S.R. between 1936 and the end of 1938. The word is derived from N. I. Yezhov, who was made head of the Russian secret police (the N.K.V.D.) early in 1936 and who supervised the liquidation of dissident groups within the Bolshevik Party and the Red Army. The purge appears to have sprung from a desire by Stalin to rid the Party of possible rivals to his leadership. Although, at the time, attempts were made to associate some of the accused with treasonable contacts 'with a foreign Power' (presumably Germany), no evidence has been discovered in documents captured since 1945 that would substantiate the charges. The Yezhovshchina numbered among its victims ten close associates of Lenin, three Marshals of the Soviet Union (including the Chief of the General Staff, Tukachevsky), six members of the executive organ of the Party (Politburo), and 400 out of the 700 Generals (Army Commanders to Brigadiers) in the Red Army. Many leading foreign communists living in the Soviet Union at this time were shot, imprisoned, or disappeared. No reliable figures exist for the extent of the Purge in the lower levels of Soviet administration. It certainly fell heavily on non-Russian peoples and suspect minority groups (i.e. the Germans who had settled around Saratov on the Volga in the eighteenth century). Mass arrests during the Yezhovshchina normally led to forced labour rather than execution. Hundreds of thousands of Soviet citizens were sent to open up regions of the Arctic or build new centres in Siberia. Towards the end of 1938 Yezhov himself disappeared, and so too did many N.K.V.D. officials; their precise fate is uncertain. Many forced labourers were allowed to return to their homes in the course of 1939. Persecution of the German minority was renewed after the outbreak of war in 1941.

Young England. The name given to a romantic Tory movement in the period 1839–45. 'Young England' sought to preserve a paternal feudalism and to check the challenge of Peel and the middle-class conservatives to the traditional structure of society. It was led by two members of aristocratic families, then in their early twenties, George Smythe (1818–57) and John Manners (1818–1906), the son of the Duke of Rutland. The movement would have been of little importance had it not attracted the enthusiastic support of Disraeli (q.v.), who developed its ideal of a benevolent aristocracy in his novels. 'Young England' broke up in 1845 over the Maynooth grant (q.v.), which Manners supported and Disraeli opposed.

Young Ireland. An Irish revolutionary movement in the 1840s. The name was taken from Mazzini's 'Young Italy' movement (q.v.). It was led by Protestants, Smith O'Brien, and John Mitchel. In 1843 the movement was largely responsible for the political eclipse of Daniel O'Connell (q.v.). The 'Young Ireland' leaders quarrelled among themselves and lacked constructive ideas. In 1848 they sought to promote revolution in Ireland; Mitchel was arrested and sentenced to fourteen years' transportation before his plans had matured, but O'Brien incited a peasant rising in Tipperary. This was quelled within a few days and O'Brien, too, was transported to Australia.

Young Italy. A revolutionary society established in March 1831 by Mazzini (q.v.).

Young Plan. A committee presided over by an American, Owen D. Young, meeting in Paris in 1929, worked out a plan by which German reparations (q.v.) would be paid over a period of $58\frac{1}{2}$ years through a special Bank of International Settlement at Basle. At the same time, the cost of reparations was reduced to about a quarter of the figure originally asked in 1921. Because of the world financial crisis Germany was unable to make any payments in 1931–2 and, as Hitler on coming to power in 1933 refused to pay reparations, the Young Plan was, in effect, stillborn.

Young Turks. Name applied to an abortive movement of reform in the Ottoman Empire, 1908. Originally the 'Young Turks' were exiles living in Western Europe who, around the turn of the century, wished to mitigate the repressive policy of Abdul Hamid (q.v.) by liberal reforms, including implementation of the Constitution of 1876. From 1903 onwards the movement had links with dissident national minorities, especially in Macedonia and Armenia. In December 1907 exiles in Paris established contact with Army officers, led by Niazi Bey, who rebelled in Macedonia in July 1908. The movement spread rapidly and was taken over by a 'Committee of Union and Progress' consisting of young officers led by a triumvirate – Enver, Talaat, and Jemal. On 24 July Abdul Hamid gave way to the officers and restored the Constitution. A Turkish Parliament met in December 1908 but revealed serious splits between the originally liberal exiles and the 'Young Turk' officers, who rapidly adopted a narrowly nationalistic policy. The influence of the triumvirate increased during the Balkan Wars and led to a strengthening of links between Turkey and Germany, although the 'Young Turk' exiles had favoured Britain and France. Enver and Talaat continued to dominate Turkish politics until their dismissal in October 1918.

Ypres. Medieval Flemish city. Destroyed in the First World War by the fighting that raged around it continuously for four years. It was never captured by the Germans. The first battle of Ypres (12 October –11 November 1914) was an offensive by the Germans against the British; the Germans only succeeded in capturing the Messines Ridge. In the second battle (22 April–24 May 1915) the Germans again failed to break the British front, even though they used poison gas for the first time in warfare. The third battle (June–November 1917) was a British offensive, first against the Messines Ridge and later Passchendaele (where there were 300,000 casualties). Finally, in the fourth battle (September 1918) the British joined the general offensive which rolled the Germans back along the Western Front until the Armistice.

Yugoslavia. A movement for the union of the South Slav peoples, known originally as 'Illyrianism', began early in the nineteenth century, but it was not until the First World War that a South Slav State (a 'Yugoslavia') became possible, with the prospect of detaching Croatia (q.v.), Slovenia, and Bosnia-Herzegovina (q.v.) from Austria-Hungary and uniting them with Serbia (q.v.) and Montenegro (q.v.). The Pact of Corfu (q.v.), an agreement on the formation of a unitary kingdom under the Serbian dynasty, was signed on 20 July 1917, and the 'Kingdom of Serbs, Croats, and Slovenes' came into being officially on 4 December 1918. King Alexander (q.v.) formally changed the name of the Kingdom to 'Yugoslavia' on 3 October 1929. The governments established by Prince Paul (Regent 1934–41) followed an increasingly pro-German policy until on 27 March, 1941, a *coup* in Belgrade by Air Force officers under General Mirković abolished the Regency and set up a pro-Allied government under General Simović. The Germans invaded Yugoslavia ten days later, destroyed Belgrade by dive-bombing, overran the country within a fortnight, and forced the Simović Government into exile. Resistance was maintained in Yugoslavia by rival guerilla groups, the Serbian Chetniks (under General Mihailović) and the communist-led Partisans (under Marshal Tito). Allied help, originally given to Mihailović, was shifted to Tito because of the collaboration of Chetnik units with the Germans. On 29 November 1943, Tito established a 'government' at liberated Jajce in Bosnia. British attempts to reconcile the Tito régime and the exiled government failed; Yugoslavia became a republic in November 1945, with Ivan Ribar as President. Mihailović was captured by Tito's troops in 1946, tried for collaboration and war crimes, and shot. In 1948 Tito's independent tendencies led to a breach between Yugoslavia and Russia. Tito himself became President early in 1953.

Zeebrugge Raid (23 April 1918). The outstanding example in the First World War of what would later have been known as a 'commando operation'. Zeebrugge, the Belgian port at the mouth of a canal to Bruges, was used by the Germans as an advance base for U-boats and destroyers. A naval and marine force, commanded by Admiral Sir Roger Keyes in *Vindictive*, landed on Zeebrugge Mole to destroy gun positions, while blockships were sunk in the canal entrance to prevent U-boats from getting out. Although the Germans subsequently cleared a channel for U-boats, the operation served as a boost to morale at a time when the Allied cause was under considerable strain. A similar attack on Ostend was less successful.

Zemstvo (plural *zemstva*). A provincial or district council in Tsarist Russia. The zemstva were established in January 1864 as part of the reforming policy of Tsar Alexander II (q.v.) and were a great advance in the system of local government. Each zemstvo was elected indirectly in three separate 'Curiae' (electoral colleges) for nobility, townsmen, and peasantry, but inevitably the gentry had a predominant influence. Zemstva functioned in the twenty-seven provinces of European Russia from 1865–6 until 1917. Seven other provinces had zemstva by the late 1860s, but the system did not apply to frontier regions inhabited by non-Russian racial groups or to the greater cities (which had their own municipal councils from 1870). The zemstva carried out valuable work in public health organization, agricultural development, road-construction, and primary education. Since there was no central representative parliament in Russia before the Revolution of 1905 (q.v.), the zemstva played an important role in the formation of a political intelligentsia. Many of the elected deputies and even more of the officials and teachers held radical views and caused the zemstva to be regarded with some suspicion. In 1890 the right of peasant election was virtually abolished, but the zemstva remained as the outstanding political force of moderate liberalism until swept aside by the extremists in the Revolution of 1917.

Zeppelin. The name given to a type of rigid airship invented by a German Count, Ferdinand von Zeppelin (1838–1917). The first zeppelin was constructed in 1900, but it was not until 1908 that a twelve-hour flight over Switzerland stirred German national enthusiasm. In 1909 Zeppelin formed the first passenger air-travel company in the world (which in five years flew 100,000 miles without a casualty). Zeppelins were used in the First World War by both the German Army and Navy and played an important reconnaissance role in the battle of Jutland (q.v.). In February 1915 zeppelins crossed the North Sea and bombed Yarmouth, extending their raids to London in the following summer. Although they had a greater range and larger bomb-load than aircraft, improved defences made them vulnerable, and their raids ceased after a disastrous mass attack on London in November 1917. Between the wars German zeppelins were commercially more successful than the airships of other countries and from 1928 to 1937 maintained the first transatlantic airline service, which was suspended when the zeppelin *Hindenburg* was burnt out on arriving in New York, 6 May 1937. The last zeppelins were broken up early in 1940.

Zimmermann Telegram. A coded message of 19 January 1917 from the German Foreign Secretary, Arthur Zimmermann (1864–1940), to the German Minister in Mexico. The telegram urged the conclusion of a German-Mexican alliance so that, if the U.S.A. entered the war against Germany when the Germans resumed unrestricted submarine warfare against neutrals and belligerents on 1 February, the Mexicans would cross the American frontier. In the peace settlement the Mexicans would thereby recover 'lost territory in New Mexico, Texas, and Arizona'. The telegram also indicated that Germany was trying to induce Japan (an Allied state) to change sides and attack the U.S.A. in the Pacific. The message was intercepted by British naval intelligence (which possessed the German code), forwarded to Washington, and released to the press on 1 March, at a time when feeling was already running high against Germany because of the activities of her submarines. The telegram accordingly aroused a storm of protest throughout the U.S.A. Additional resentment was caused by the fact that one version of the telegram was discovered to have been sent to the German Ambassador in Washington over the private wire of the State Department, which the Germans had been given permission to use to facilitate the transmission of peace overtures. The telegram played a considerable part in inducing Congress to accept the idea of war with Germany (which was declared on 6 April 1917).

Zinoviev, Gregori (1883–1936). Russian Bolshevik leader. Born Gregori Radomyslsky, adopting 'Zinoviev' as a *nom-de-guerre* while in secret opposition to Tsarism. He returned from Swiss exile with Lenin in April 1917, and held high position in the Third International (q.v.) from 1920 to 1926. In this position it is alleged that he sent the so-called Zinoviev Letter to British Communists, urging them to promote revolution. This 'Letter' was published in the British press on 25 October 1924, four days before a General Election, and played a considerable part in the defeat of the Labour Government. Zinoviev broke with Stalin in 1926, was branded as a supporter of Trotsky (q.v.), and expelled from the political bureau of the Communist Party in the same year. In January 1935 he was tried and condemned to imprisonment for treason. He was brought from prison to stand trial a second time, charged with plotting with enemy powers, and was executed in August 1936.

Zionism. A movement for the return of the Jews to Palestine. It stems from reactions to the anti-semitism (q.v.) of the 1880s. The movement was really launched by Theodor Herzl (1860–1904), a Hungarian-born Jewish journalist, under whose inspiration the First Zionist Congress was held at Basle in 1897 'to secure for the Jewish people a home in Palestine guaranteed by public law'. Until Herzl's death the movement was led from Vienna, shifting its headquarters to Cologne in 1904 and Berlin in 1911. During the First World War, Chaim Weizmann (q.v.) won British support for some of the movement's aims and secured the Balfour Declaration (q.v.) of 1917 and the League of Nations mandate for Palestine (q.v.). Some assimilated Jews at first opposed the Zionist movement, believing that it would undermine their position in the countries they lived in, but, between the wars, the movement won support from almost every section of the Jewish community and culminated on 14 May 1948 in the proclamation of the state of Israel.

Zollverein. A customs union creating a Free Trade area in Germany under Prussian auspices. The Prussian territories as agreed by the Treaty of Vienna sprawled across northern Germany, but their economic development was hampered by antiquarian tariff barriers. Within Prussia there were sixty-seven different tariffs and thirteen non-Prussian enclaves, each with a different fiscal system. Internal customs duties in Prussia were abolished in 1818. One of the enclaves was induced by the Prussian Finance Minister, Motz, to hand over its customs administration in 1819; six other small states followed suit in 1822. Other German states, perceiving the economic strength that was accruing to Prussia, formed unions of their own in 1828, but, as the resources of the Prussian union were greater, they too were forced into the Zollverein by the end of 1833. More states joined in the following eleven years, although the great seaports such as Hamburg and Bremen were strong enough to remain outside. The Zollverein is often held to have prepared the way for German unification under Prussia; this is not strictly accurate. Under the influence of the Protectionist theories of List (q.v.), the Prussians erected new tariff barriers aiming at the creation of a small Germany, which was really an expansion of Prussia and an exclusion of Austria, but this policy was resented by Prussia's partners, nearly all of whom seized the opportunity of fighting against Prussia in 1866. The creation of the Zollverein meant, however, that Germany's railway system was centred upon Berlin – with obvious political and military consequences.

Zulu War (1879). The Zulu people had, in the early nineteenth century, acquired a formidable military organization under successive warrior kings, one of whom, Cetewayo (who became King in 1873) menaced the Boer republic of the Transvaal (q.v.), thereby inducing the Boers to seek British military protection. The British High Commissioner, Sir Bartle Frere, determined to destroy the Zulu forces and, acting on his own initiative and against the wishes of the Beaconsfield Government in London, ordered Lord Chelmsford to march into Zululand in January 1879. The Zulus made a surprise attack upon a camp at Isandhlwana (22 January) and slaughtered sixteen hundred men, half of them British. There were other serious military blunders, through one of which the Prince Imperial (only son of Napoleon III), who had volunteered for the British Army, was killed. Eventually ten thousand reinforcements arrived from England under Sir Garnet Wolseley, who, with Chelmsford, destroyed the Zulu Army and captured Cetewayo at Ulundi (4 July). The Zulu War was exploited by Gladstone in his Midlothian Campaign (q.v.) to show the folly of Beaconsfield's imperialism, although, in fact, the slowness of communications between London and South Africa had allowed Frere to push the Government into an impossible situation.

*Two other Penguin Reference Books
are described on the
following pages*

A DICTIONARY OF POLITICS

REVISED EDITION

Florence Elliott and Michael Summerskill

This guide to modern politics has been fully revised and contains
entries on such recent developments as the latest independent
states of Africa. It provides a comprehensive and informative
background to current events and includes life histories of those of
the world's leading politicians who are alive at the time of going to
press. The political institutions, recent histories, and economies of
almost every independent state in the world are discussed. There
are entries on important overseas possessions. Places which fall
into neither of these categories, but which are centres of dispute, are
treated separately. The aims of some of the leading political parties
of the world are explained. International organizations are described. Political beliefs and dates of many important declarations,
pacts, and treaties are clearly set out. Cross-references have been
included in any entry where further explanation might help the
reader to a better understanding of the subject under discussion.

The authors, who are married, studied law and history at Oxford.
Mr Summerskill is a barrister and works in the City, and his wife
has had experience in adult and technical education.

A DICTIONARY OF SCIENCE

E. B. Uvarov and D. R. Chapman

In this new edition of the *Dictionary of Science* its value to students
and laymen alike has been extended by the addition of explanations
of many new words which have come into use during the last ten
years. This is particularly true in physics, where recent advances
have given rise to large numbers of new ideas and terms such as
atomic energy, radar, and radioactive isotopes. Many new terms
relating to modern advances in chemistry have also been added.
Together with this new material, the student will find in this book
reliable definitions and clear explanations of the simpler terms
used in astronomy, chemistry, mathematics and physics, as well as
short notes on all the chemical elements and their most important
compounds conveniently arranged in alphabetical order. The
intelligent layman will find this dictionary helpful when faced with
the numerous scientific and technical terms which are increasingly
becoming an important part of our daily lives.

*For a complete list of books available please write to Penguin Books
whose address can be found on the back of the title page*